Hammer of the Left

Hammer of the Left

DEFEATING TONY BENN, ERIC HEFFER AND MILITANT
IN THE BATTLE FOR THE LABOUR PARTY

John Golding

Edited by Paul Farrelly

POLITICO'S

First published in Great Britain 2003 by
Politico's Publishing, an imprint of
Methuen Publishing Limited
215 Vauxhall Bridge Road
London SW1V 1EJ

1 3 5 7 9 10 8 6 4 2

A CIP catalogue record for this book is available from the British Library

ISBN 1 84275 079 8

Printed and bound in Great Britain by
Creative Print and Design

CONTENTS

ACKNOWLEDGMENTS

Firstly my thanks to Lewis Minkin for his book *Contentious Alliance*. Had my good trades union brothers not been so upset by his lack of balance, they would not have pressed for this book to be written. My wife Llin also wanted it done for the better reason that she believed strongly that honour was due to Roger Godsiff and John Spellar and our team of union loyalists for saving the Labour Party in the early 1980s.

It is a book I did not want to write, but sadly no book so far has done justice to this fight. Most accounts by 'experts', indeed, have been written without even talking to us! Many biographies, too, are full of inaccuracies and 'economy with the truth'.

Of course, I have been helped by many people. Without the research by Paul Richards-Mole, it would never have got off the ground and without the restructuring and criticism of Paul Farrelly, it would never have been finished.

For help with the computer, my thanks go too to Steve Lewis and, for their archives, to the TUC Library and the National Museum of Labour History. Most of this book has been written from the minutes of Labour's NEC. If the style has suffered as a result, these have at least given me the accuracy (and unfairness!) I have worked hard to bring.

I should also acknowledge the journalists and their newspapers, for use of whose material I am very grateful. I always enjoyed greatly the contributions of the *Guardian* – Labour Party members' favourite newspaper – in particular Simon Hoggart, Julia Langdon, Keith Harper and Ian Aitken. Mention is also due to Adam Raphael, then at the *Observer*.

I owe a great debt to Tony Bevins, whose integrity and cynical wit I came to appreciate greatly. At *The Times*, Donald Macintyre, Julian Haviland and Philip Webster were also very sound. And Paul Routledge also made a contribution!

For me always the most important newspaper was the *Daily Mirror*. The political team headed by Terry Lancaster wrote in a style and tone I enjoyed and they helped me in the fight for moderation in the Labour Party more than most.

My thanks go, too, to the many individuals who have given me the benefit of their memories and, very importantly, to the Benn Diaries, which – conducted in the privacy of his own mind – are not always accurate, to say the least.

My thanks most of all go to all those who stood and fought to save the Labour Party.

John Golding
Winter 1998

My thanks go particularly to Iain Dale and John Berry for their work in publishing John's book, to Roger Godsiff and John Spellar for their comments and to Neil Kinnock for writing the foreword.

Thanks, too, to the Guardian for its kind permission to include the obituary of John, which I wrote for the newspaper.

The words in this account are John's. Where I have edited, I have done my utmost to stay true to John in style, tone and his trademark, mischievous sense of humour.

From talking to John as he compiled this memoir, I know that too he would have been among the first to congratulate Michael Foot, who at the time of publishing is celebrating his 90th birthday. And to acknowledge him for finally losing patience and allowing the Labour loyalists to sweep out the Bennite hard left and their fellow travellers, including Militant.

As for Tony Benn, he retired at the 2001 election at the same time as Llin, now the Baroness Golding of Newcastle-under-Lyme. The difference, though, speaks for itself. After 40 years of hard, attentive work, Llin left a seat which has remained solidly Labour. Benn's former constituency Chesterfield, however, holds the unhappy distinction as the only coalfield seat to fall to the Liberal Democrats!

This book belongs most of all to Llin and to the memory of John Golding.

Paul Farrelly
July 2003

FOREWORD

Neil Kinnock

John Golding wanted Labour to be elected and re-elected to government as the Party of justice, jobs, security and opportunity. Those purposes were and are shared by many. What made him different was his ruthless diligence in organising for them.

In Labour's years of near self-destruction in the late 1970s and 1980s, he was merciless in his treatment of anyone or anything that he considered to be standing in the way of achievement of those objectives. His relentless organisation, his plotting to beat plotters, his use of sectarian methods to beat sectarians are without precedent or copy.

This book is a dipped-in-vitriol documentary of those efforts. It tells the story without deference to the Marquis of Queensbury or anyone else, but with gallows humour, pace and fish-hook frankness.

Because of that it provides a chronicle for students, a cracking read for anyone with a taste for raw politics, and an object lesson for any political party that allows itself to drift away from electoral reality and into the wilderness of illusion and self-obsession.

Neil Kinnock
July 2003

INTRODUCTION

Today the Labour Party is seen as a strong, modern party which is largely efficient and effective. Its Leader, Tony Blair, elected by the entire membership, enjoys great authority and the Party has been reformed at every level. Great effort is put into the way in which the Party both reflects and helps to form public opinion. But it was not always so and, if the Party is not careful, it will not always be so in the future.

This book describes how the Party between 1978 and 1983 not only suffered two electoral defeats, but nearly disintegrated due to the activities of the left.

The 1979 defeat came mainly from the public's reaction to the onslaught unleashed on the Labour government by irresponsible left wing trade unionists in the Winter of Discontent. The defeat of 1983 came down to the adoption of unacceptable left wing policies, particularly on defence, and deep divisions in the Party. In neither election was most of the electorate in any mood to support the extremism of militant unions, nor of left wing politicians determined to impose an extremist, dogmatic, intolerant socialism on the British people.

Because I understood this so clearly, I fought the left fiercely on Labour's governing National Executive Committee (NEC) from 1978 to 1983 and it is principally of these years that I write.

These years chart the rise and fall of the hard left in British politics and of their standard bearers, the aristocratic Anthony Wedgwood Benn, his Liverpudlian sidekick Eric Heffer and the vile Trotskyist Militant Tendency. This is the story, blow for blow from inside the ring, of the blood, sweat and certainly no tears in their defeat.

In the early part of this period, it was very hard going indeed. The left wing majority on the Party's National Executive Committee in 1978 was hell-bent on destroying the Labour government and made life intolerable for the Prime Minister, Jim Callaghan. Things were so bad in that year that I brought together a group of trade unionists on the NEC to give Jim some co-ordinated support.

While this 'Loyalist Group' made some impact – removing the impression that the Prime Minister was totally friendless – it could not by its very nature save the Labour Party. The Loyalist Group was always in a minority on the NEC and for real change to take place, needless to say, it had to command a majority. And to forge that we needed the combined support of our General Secretaries and Presidents, who generally sat on the General Council of the Trades Union Congress (TUC), the pinnacle of the country's organised labour movement.

While the left marched on, after a long period of inaction at this highest level, the job of saving the Party was finally undertaken by a small group of moderate trade union General Secretaries and Presidents and their political officers, who came together in 1981 to organise a serious, effective fight against extremism. There was a great need to do so, as it was not only the electorate that had deserted the Labour Party. So, too, had many Labour Members of Parliament and other activists, unable to cope with fighting the fanaticism of the left. And those leading right wingers, who refused to join the lemmings of the new Social Democratic Party (SDP), were incapable of saving Labour from the inevitable destruction of a long period of left wing control.

These changes could not be achieved just by speeches or 'normal political means'. What was needed was to emulate the tactics of the left and set to work organizing. 'Fixers' were needed of the kind which abounded on the left – people who would put in a vast amount of time and effort, secretly bringing about alliances to win votes and elections in the Party.

This is the story of those 'fixers', who – while only having rudimentary success in the constituencies – built an effective machine in the unions to dismantle the forces of darkness. It is a tale of intense manipulation and intrigue by both the left and their moderate opponents for control of the Labour Party. And it is unusual, I might say, because it is written this time from the point of view of the moderates.

I was persuaded to write this book by brothers in the trades unions who were irate at the 'imperfections', to put it politely, of Lewis Minkin's

Contentious Alliance. This 'history' they rightly saw as not only unfairly biased towards the soft left, but also incorrect in great respects as far as they were concerned.

This book aims to improve on that: my aim is to be accurate but unfair. Although I was reluctant to squander time which otherwise would be spent fishing, on race courses or in the garden, my wife Llin – a good 'brother' throughout – believed strongly that the true story of the moderate fight-back should finally be told. Not all my brothers agreed. My great friend John Spellar, now a senior government minister, wrote to me saying that 'my instinct tells me that these things are better not written down'. John was one of the prime movers in this story who like Roger Godsiff, now the MP for Birmingham Sparkbrook and Small Heath, and others made an enormous contribution by being prepared to stay in the shadows in order to organise victory for the forces of sanity.

They are, however, not the only heroes of this story. Full honour also has to go to those trade union General Secretaries who had to deliver the vote for moderation despite being vilified and threatened in public and private by left wing fanatics – men such as Frank Chapple, Terry Duffy, Bill Sirs, Bryan Stanley and Sid Weighell – and to those on the NEC such as Sam McCluskie, who were subject to intense pressure within their organisations for the support they gave to this fight-back.

If the heroes are of interest, perhaps more so are many of the villains. Some of those we fought now hold high office in a New Labour government. Others, such as Neil Kinnock (whom I later came to advise) and Tom (now Lord) Sawyer, have since been given the credit for the fight-back. Perhaps Llin is right and it is time for the record to be put straight.

To help the reader a footnote with trade union names and abbreviations is included at the back of this book. The glossary was necessary not only because it helps the general reader, but also because the unions and, indeed, the Labour Party have changed so much. Old trade union Labour, which I am, and the Party I have written about are things of the past.[1]

I must now add a warning. This story, although it has a happy ending, is not for the squeamish. It is definitely not for those who believe that reason always prevails in politics and that for success all you need is people to design appealing policies.

Nor is it for those who believe that nice guys always win in the end. It is a book about the vanity and ambition of individuals, of smoke-filled rooms and shoddy deals.

In other words it is about politics proper, not political idealism. For those looking for grand designs and theories, it is about both cock-ups and conspiracies, about how in politics events are not only settled by good luck or foul fortune, but also by how much effort those struggling to survive and win are prepared to put in.

Above all, this book is about the importance of personalities and the clash of personalities. And for me personally, it is the story of five years' hard labour inflicted on an innocent bystander.

PROLOGUE

A New Look at an 'Old Labour' Government

We didn't lose – we threw it away! Four years after gifting power to Margaret Thatcher, that's how I summed up the 1983 general election for Labour. What we in the Labour Party have to ensure is that we never throw it away again. And to do that, we have to make certain that the Party never again comes under the control of the left.

The Labour government of 1974 to 1979, although it worked hard for working people, was destroyed by the greed and malice of left wing controlled unions. Throughout its lifetime, in their drive to become ever more powerful, the left exploited each of the government's many difficulties. In the Party itself, they used their control of the NEC and strong influence at the Annual Conference not to support the Labour government but to oppose and harass it. And when they had driven Jim Callaghan out of office, they spent their time not fighting Thatcher, but scheming and conspiring among themselves to change the very nature of the Party in order to give themselves even greater power and take it away from the path of moderation.

To understand the background to the civil war in the Party between 1978 and 1983 we should first briefly look at certain aspects of the Labour governments under Harold Wilson and Jim Callaghan. It need only be 'briefly', because both Bernard Donoughue in his book *Prime Minister* and Kenneth Morgan in his biography of Callaghan have already written so authoritatively about this period.

For many of us, winning the February general election in 1974 was a shock, to say the least. Indeed, exhausted by the campaign it took a long time to sink in that – Ted Heath having failed to entice the Liberals into a coalition – Wilson was going to form a minority Labour government.

We had never expected to win; not once had Labour led in the opinion polls. Heath had called the general election after the energy crisis caused by the miners' strike had forced industry on to a three-day week. The natural public reaction was to support the government against strikers who were seen to be holding the country to ransom.

Just a week before polling day, I had even written off my own Newcastle-under-Lyme seat, in a traditional coal mining area in north Staffordshire which has been Labour-held since 1919. We were saved, however, by Derek Robinson, a young Pay Board official who supported Labour and who announced that false figures had been used by the government against the miners; and by Enoch Powell, by then an Ulster Unionist, advising Tories to vote Labour because of Heath's support for the Common Market. Although we got 230,000 fewer votes than the Tories, we won 301 seats to their 297.

As ever, the expectations of many Labour supporters were sky high, but those in the know were far less optimistic. We knew the difficulties we faced: inflation and the world economic crisis meant we could not make the expected improvements in the welfare state and individual living standards. These difficulties were hardly eased after Wilson only managed an overall majority of three at the year's second general election, which he called in October 1974, expecting to win easily. With our razor-edge majority, we already feared it might all end in tears.

Except for a very short period, the Labour governments of Wilson and Callaghan never had an easy ride. The atmosphere of optimism – in business as well as politics – that had been around on Wilson's first election victory in 1964 had disappeared by the early 1970s. In the 1960s we believed in a future of continual progress. We fervently thought we could use much of the 4 per cent annual growth in wealth assumed in the National Plan to extend the welfare state and so tackle the problems of poverty and ill health. We felt as if the nation had won some great universal lottery.

The feel good factor was truly at its height. We did not have to bother our heads about unemployment. For us the problems being created were from so-called over-employment. All our talk revolved around introducing labour-saving measures and using labour more efficiently. And, of course, tackling the problems that the great bargaining powers of the unions had posed for the government.

We were troubled by full employment not unemployment. In 1967, I had written with Ken Jones a Fabian tract on 'Productivity Bargaining' arguing that we trade unionists should get rid of all our restrictive practices in return for hard cash. We just could not envisage that we would face the scourge of unemployment again. We had all been taught about John Maynard Keynes' ready-made solution, should it rear its ugly head again: spend, spend and spend again on public works.

Labour's new Chancellor of the Exchequer, Denis Healey, never noted for being fair to opponents, put all the blame on his Tory predecessor, Anthony Barber for making a shambles out of the sound economy which Labour had handed over in 1970. Both Barber and Heath had cut taxes and increased public spending. Wages had been linked monthly to the cost of living.

These policies – which, I must say, seemed to many of us in the unions as beneficial and wholly in line with Keynes – had produced a nightmare scenario for the incoming Chancellor. Our balance of payments was in trouble and public borrowing far too high. Prices were rising by 13 per cent and the money supply by double that. Output was down because of the miners' strike and the 'Three Day Week'. We were in a dreadful state!

Healey's pessimism reflected an enormous change in political and economic thinking from that of the 1960s. Our whole world picture, indeed, was changed by the consequences of the massive increase in oil prices in 1973. In his autobiography, Denis points out that this huge hike had added £2.5 billion to Britain's current account deficit, had lifted the cost of living by nearly 10 per cent and reduced our gross domestic product by 5 per cent. Eventually this harm would be offset in Britain by the development of our own oil industry, but not yet. For the 1970s, it meant that Labour could not bring about many of the social changes its members and supporters expected.

While Healey pasted Barber for all this, the government was plagued by rising unemployment and escalating inflation. Following advice from the International Monetary Fund (IMF) of the traditional Keynesian school, Healey tried to offset rising unemployment by increased spending in his first Budget, but this caused difficulties when other countries did not follow suit. Additionally, the Treasury miscalculated the increase in our Public Sector Borrowing Requirement (PSBR) and we were soon faced with massive problems of overspending.

We were also faced with escalating wage settlements. In his book, Donoughue writes about the Cabinet refusing to tackle these problems and giving priority instead to the referendum on the Common Market. Healey meanwhile, in the best tradition of the middle classes, laid the blame squarely on the unions.

Having attempted to control prices, he said he expected the unions to give something in return. In his third Budget in April 1975, Healey complained bitterly that the unions had not kept their side of the bargain. Wages were going up faster than prices, even though the government had carried out its side of the 'Social Contract' by repealing Heath's anti-union legislation, starting to redistribute wealth through tax changes, increasing pensions and other benefits and by increasing the social wage to £1,000.

Those of us working with the unions took the belting he gave us, but there was little that we could do. Our members were frightened. Given the rapid increase in prices, the wage settlements we might negotiate might prove inadequate to maintain living standards. They also had the bad habit of looking over their shoulders believing, generally correctly, that even if they showed restraint other workers would not.

And so increased prices led to higher wage demands and increased wages led to higher inflation – the classic vicious circle. The problem Wilson had inherited in 1974 had got so far out of hand by August 1975 that inflation had risen to 26.9 per cent. We were being compared abroad with 'banana republics' – except we couldn't afford the bananas.

It did not need a genius to point out the obvious – that both inflation and public spending had to be brought under control. However, this was not easy for a Prime Minister and Cabinet elected on a policy of high growth, high expenditure and the rejection of incomes policy. But promises or no promises, the government had no choice. It was forced to impose public expenditure cuts and in July 1975 implemented a non-statutory pay policy, under which pay rises were restricted to £6 all round.

Both came as manna from heaven to the left in the Party and the trade unions. These were real sticks with which to beat the government.

Up to this time, the left had spent their time jumping up and down about issues of little interest to the working-class – like atom bomb tests, the switch of Benn from Industry to Energy (no transfer fee being paid by either department) and ditching the nationalization of 25 major companies promised in Labour's 1973 programme.

Likewise, while the left were bitterly upset by the deportation of the CIA whistleblower Philip Agee and the journalist Mark Hosenball, at the alleged behest of CIA, and what they claimed was the use of systematic torture in Northern Ireland, they must surely have known that these were not the subjects being discussed in pubs and clubs up and down the land. In any case, had they been, the working class would not only have approved, but demanded stronger action!

These issues were important to party activists, but to few others. Public expenditure cuts and wage controls were a different kettle of fish. These were issues which working people knew would make life more difficult. In consequence the left could, and would, exploit them to the full.

In the first year, despite opposition, the pay policy was very successful – supported strongly and loyally even by Jack Jones and Hugh Scanlon, the left wing leaders of the Transport and General Workers Union (TGWU) and the Amalgamated Engineering Union (AEU).

The next year was more difficult. Not only had the left mobilized opposition, but flat pay deals had caused real resentment through the erosion of differentials between skilled workers and the others. The class system in Britain was at its most intolerant within the working class itself: the artisans regarded themselves as vastly superior to the semi-skilled below them and so on down the ladder.

So, on becoming Prime Minister in April 1976 after Wilson's resignation, Callaghan faced enormous problems. Although he personally wanted a 3 per cent wage limit with tax concessions, an agreement was reached from July 1976 for one year of increases of £2.50, with £4 for skilled workers and a general ceiling of 5 per cent. This went down like a bomb, particularly when the Treasury made matters worse by bungling a revaluation which led to the collapse of the pound. Humiliatingly, the international bankers of the IMF were brought in to bale us out and imposed a financial discipline which led to further job losses and uproar within the Labour movement.

There was great excitement at the Annual Labour Party Conference when Healey – who days before had turned back from the airport rather than go abroad during the crisis – was then flown to Blackpool, where he was allowed only five minutes to speak.

When Healey entered, moderates throughout the hall – including even those from the National Union Mineworkers (NUM) – actually rose to cheer him. Denis had been given a standing ovation under the most trying of circumstances. But, while speaking for his meagre five minutes, he was roundly booed by the left.

Times were certainly tough for Denis. But it was a tragedy that the policies he pursued, the brutal manner particularly in which he defended them and the intense dislike of trade unions he developed were later to cost him the leadership of the Party and the possibility of becoming Prime Minister.

Unfortunately Denis never grasped the dictum, given to me once by a counter clerk in the Small Heath Unemployment Benefit Office that: 'Honey always caught more bees than vinegar.' Indeed, vinegar was never strong enough for Denis, who chose to pour vitriol wholesale on trade union leaders faithfully representing their members.

He was right to insist that we could no longer go on destroying our economy as we were. But he would have been more effective had he used persuasion on his natural allies in the wider Labour movement, rather than abuse. In this way he might not only have modified trade union attitudes, but had more success in the fight against the left.

Having said that, his brutality when addressing the loonies inside the NEC was completely understandable. In February 1977, at a joint meeting of the Cabinet and NEC, he pointed out that 'after the cuts we will still be borrowing £8.7 billion on the PSBR next year.....the rules of arithmetic are inexorable and they cannot be compromised. Don't bleat to the government about things we can't control...the alternative strategy would be to abandon the international approach in favour of a siege economy.'

Incidentally, on this occasion, Benn very untypically defended the government: 'It is hard for the government. We haven't a parliamentary majority. There is the slump and international pressures and difficult nego-tiations with the TUC'.

He was right – there certainly was a slump. Between 1974 and 1976 unemployment had risen from 528,000 to 1.25 million and would rise again in subsequent years. Likewise, we lost even our slender parliamentary majority following a string of by-election defeats in Greenwich, Woolwich, Walsall, Workington, Birmingham Stetchford, Ashfield, Ilford North and Liverpool Edgehill and the desertion of Reg Prentice in October 1977. Not only did we lose our tiny majority, the defeats were so massive as to be totally humiliating and demoralising.

In November, 1976 Callaghan sent Fred Peart to the Lords and then we lost his safe Workington seat, despite having an outstanding candidate. And there was worse to come. March, April and May of 1977 were terrible months for Labour. At Birmingham Stetchford there was a 17 per cent swing against us. Benn blamed the result on a right wing candidate, a right wing Budget and a right wing Lib–Lab deal – 'a test of the Callaghan approach, an approach which is fatal' – but that was far from the whole truth.

I canvassed hard in that election and know first hand that an important reason the Brummies switched was to punish us because Roy Jenkins had gone to Europe on a huge salary.

The same was true on 29 April, 1977 when, as a result of David Marquand following Roy Jenkins, we lost a 22,000 majority at Ashfield. We did badly, too, in the May local elections.

The by-election defeats, however, arose not only from the resentment electors feel when their MP leaves between elections for a well-paid job in pastures new. There was also a widespread feeling that, despite its impressive social record, the Labour government had let the people down. And, in truth, how could they think otherwise when they were told this day in, day out by leading lights on the left of the Party?

Indeed, the 1974–79 Labour governments were so maligned by black propaganda put out by Benn and others for their own purposes, it is worth taking a fresh look at how much, despite the difficulties, they actually achieved and how working people, in particular, had been well looked after.

Not only had the industrial relations laws and incomes control measures of Ted Heath been reversed, but the status of workers raised, too, by the Employment Protection Acts, the Trade Union and Labour Relations Acts and equal pay and sexual discrimination legislation.

We had taken positive steps to reduce youth and long-term unemployment and to save industries at risk. The Manpower Services Commission

(MSC) and the Health and Safety Executive came to play an important role and the Advisory, Conciliation and Arbitration Service (ACAS) was created. The Labour government introduced an Industry Act, the nationalisation of shipbuilding and aircraft and started to regulate dock work.

It was not only at work that working people benefited. The introduction of the 'Family Allowance', though the subject of much criticism, was a boon to millions of mothers. Yet despite this good work, which would seem radical today, the government was plagued by continual harassment from the left.

On the doorstep, too, people told us that they were fed up with what they saw to be signs of economic failure, inflation, unemployment and balance of payments problems. The new Tory leader, Margaret Thatcher, was the prime beneficiary of the dissatisfaction. But it was encouraged, too, by the Labour left led by Benn and Eric Heffer, Militant and other organisations who encouraged Party members and supporters in the belief that the only reason the Labour government could not satisfy their inflated, unrealistic expectations was because they had 'sold out.'

Some years later at Conference, Jim Mortimer, the Party's General Secretary, said of Militant: 'They are wrong to attack Labour governments. When I was at ACAS, I had the opportunity of following very closely the work of the Department of Employment and its Labour ministers with Michael Foot, Albert Booth, Harold Walker and John Golding. In all those years I never found a single issue on which our colleagues betrayed the Labour movement. Of course from time to time we made some mistakes.. . . but I have no doubt whatever that the Labour ministers with whom I was dealing from day to day were consciously and with purpose acting in the interests of the working people of Britain.'

He was right. We worked our socks off to try and alleviate the problems created by the increase in oil prices. We created a Temporary Employment Subsidy Scheme, until it was stopped by the European Commission, as well as a Short Time Working Compensation Scheme to help ordinary working people. To my door came deputation after deputation of trade unionists and workers asking us to save their jobs – and we did everything we could to help.

My pride and joy was a Job Release Scheme, suggested to me by a constituent in a working men's club, which gave retirement to older workers and jobs to the young.

We worked, too, with the Manpower Services Commission, on which the TUC played a crucial part, on temporary employment programmes particularly for youngsters.

My preoccupation was to find opportunities for those I called the 'rough and tumble': people with no qualifications and little ability to look after themselves. This led me to clash with one organisation Youth Aid which, in the person of Clare Short, wanted me to provide high quality programmes for the more able.

I knew, however, that Labour's job was to look after those who cannot look after themselves and was grateful for our Employment Secretary Albert Booth's commitment that every youngster still unemployed a year after leaving school would be given the opportunity of some form of work.

I was delighted, too, to hear Callaghan use a speech at the Labour Party Annual Conference to bounce the MSC into agreeing to special provision for the long-term unemployed – something both the TUC and the Confederation of British Industry (CBI) had resisted strongly.

In all the work that we in the Department of Employment did to alleviate the jobs crisis, we had the total support of Healey and Callaghan. Both, in my everyday personal experience, were always deeply concerned about unemployment, especially youngsters and the long-term jobless.

Callaghan personally arranged for me to go to Hamburg to study what the Germans had already done to help youngsters compete more successfully for jobs. We worked hard and managed to alleviate some of the hardships. I travelled the country week by week talking to unemployed youngsters and careers officers, meeting local authorities, unions and employers.

Occasionally I would have to argue with shop stewards about taking youngsters on government schemes but generally the only rough meetings were with local Trades Councils – little local TUCs, if you like – which were all too often hotbeds of left wing extremists without a tap of responsibility.

How bad these 'tinpot TUCs' were in general can be seen from an incident that occurred in the 1970s. When the Newcastle-under-Lyme Trades Council – unusual in its moderation – congratulated the TUC General Council proper on its support for the Social Contract, its secretary (Llin) received a reply putting the case for the Labour government and chastising the trades council for sending such a letter!

When I raised this with Len Murray, the then TUC General Secretary, he explained after investigation that the only 'standard reply' for letters headed 'Social Contract' had been prepared on the basis that only abusive letters would be received from Trades Councils. To receive a letter of congratulation was more than they could cope with!

Most of the Trades Councils, as well as left wing Constituency Labour Parties (CLPs), attacked not only the handling of the recession and unemployment but also the government's pay policy, which Harold Walker was tackling with great courage.

In 1977/78 the guidelines had been set so that pay settlements should not rise by more than a single figure and earnings should not rise by more than 10 per cent. One of my treasured memories is of Walker's sermon to Methodist ministers, who were demanding a settlement outside the guidelines, on the nature and importance of morality!

The growing opposition to the policy among trade unionists was highlighted, however, when TGWU delegates howled down Jack Jones at their Biennial Conference. We were now plunging headlong into the disastrous Winter of Discontent, which we will look at in more detail later.

The loss of parliamentary seats forced Callaghan and Foot to create a Lib–Lab pact in March 1977 as an alternative to fighting an election which we certain to lose – despite Benn's blinkered view that, if there were an election, we wouldn't do badly. Union leaders, in particular, wanted the government to survive and said so strongly at the time at the Labour Party – Trades Union Liaison Committee on 21 March. They were highly critical of the left, because they would only bring the government down.

As it turned out, in Cabinet only Benn, Peter Shore, Stan Orme and surprisingly the future European commissioner Bruce Millan voted against doing a deal with the Liberals. Showing his true ambivalence about our election prospects, Benn wrote: 'It might be better to have it now rather than later. If we lost it would be the end of the government, but by God at least things would be clarified a bit.' But some of us were not particularly interested in 'getting things clarified'. For those of us who wanted to bring tangible improvements to the working class, the loss of a Labour government would be an unmitigated disaster.

Staying in office, however, meant a very bumpy ride. The left were constantly disloyal, as when, for example, the 1977 Budget was partly scuppered by Jeff Rooker and Audrey Wise joining forces with the Tories to carry a provision – the infamous Rooker-Wise amendment – raising tax thresholds, which cost £440 million

Despite such local difficulties, however, we soldiered on and indeed for some time the economy improved. Of course, life in parliament itself remained difficult. We went from crisis vote to crisis vote. The disloyalty of the left stood out in stark contrast with the sacrifices that some MPs made to keep a Labour government in office.

One of these was Sir Alfred 'Doc' Broughton, MP for Batley, who, despite suffering from a dreadful chest disease which meant that he could hardly move, came down by car with his wife Lady Broughton whenever there was an important vote and sat in my room so that he could be nodded through the lobbies by the whips. My main duty was to fetch his Horlicks from the Members' Tea Room. It was like being back in an air raid shelter.

While Doc Broughton spent his last days suffering to save the Labour government, however, Benn, Heffer and others were doing their best to destroy it. It is with them that we will continue our story.

ONE

The Toads

The world has held great Heroes,
As history books have showed;
But never a name to go down to fame
Compared with Mr Toad.

From *Wind in the Willows* by Kenneth Graham.

No modern Prime Minister has an easy, tranquil life. Few, however, have faced as many difficulties as Jim Callaghan did between 1976 and 1979 or have become as tired and exhausted. Without a parliamentary majority, not only did he have to contend with the massive economic problems from the oil crisis but also the enormous trouble created by two characters straight out of the world of make-believe: Anthony Wedgwood Benn and Eric Heffer.

Both, while being modelled in their own ways on Toad of Toad Hall, called themselves Labour Members of Parliament. They made life hell for Callaghan because, even though they had no strength in the Cabinet or the Parliamentary Labour Party (PLP), they did control the Party's NEC and were close to dominating the policy-making Annual Conference.

By their misuse of power, they and their left wing allies helped destroy Callaghan's government and almost brought about the destruction of the Labour Party – as, by fair means and to my mind foul, they tightened their stranglehold, adopting aims and policies which were totally unacceptable to the British electorate.

To understand the reasons for their rise and fall and how they achieved frightening success – until, by the use of their own tactics against them, they were cut down to size – we need to know a little about their backgrounds and those of their 'co–conspirators'.

Anthony Wedgwood Benn

We begin with Anthony Wedgwood Benn, as his mother still insisted on calling him at that time. In a vain attempt to identify himself with the working class, however, he had adopted the name 'Tony Benn' and had started drinking tea from a mug and visiting fish and chip shops.

'Wedgie', as I generally called him (in a shoddy compromise between the rigid correctness of his mother and his self-adopted stage name) was the son of a Liberal MP turned Labour. This genetically determined characteristic to move from the centre to the left with age, which is quite at odds with human nature, should have been modified by his private education at Westminster School and at New College, Oxford. But obviously it was not.

After a spell as a BBC radio producer, he had brought the political career of the distinguished MP Arthur Creech-Jones to an end at a selection conference at Bristol caused by parliamentary boundary redistribution and in 1950 was duly elected to the House of Commons.

On the death of his father in 1960, Benn was elevated to the peerage and so, according to the rules of the time, forced to leave the Lower House. This was a terrible blow, because in those days it was thought to be impossible for a lord to become Prime Minister. Benn, however, was already desperate to make his name in the Commons and achieve the highest office in the land.

As we shall see later, when Benn needs to conduct a campaign to further his own career and interests, he does so with a single-minded determination. This occasion was no exception and he won the struggle to renounce his peerage and stay in the Commons. Even if he ultimately failed to become Prime Minister himself, he did help Sir Alec Douglas Home – a Tory peer also turned commoner – to get to Number 10 and was indirectly, therefore, of great assistance in making Harold Wilson Prime Minister!

Benn's subsequent career in the House of Commons was as brilliant as everyone expected. He was an exceedingly bright, attractive, hail-fellow-well-met-chap with remarkable charisma, who carried people along with him in all his many enthusiasms. Extremely plausible, he spoke clearly, movingly and persuasively. He had a magical talent with words. He went from strength to strength and everyone predicted great things.

And then somehow things went badly, sadly wrong. While he continued to enthuse the young and the idealistic, he became a pain in the neck to most people around him and completely lost their confidence. Those who got to know Benn at close quarters simply could no longer stand him.

I was a case in point. I first met Anthony Wedgwood Benn when he visited the University College of North Staffordshire Labour Club a couple of years after his election as an MP in November 1950. He played table tennis with verve and spoke with even greater enthusiasm. Benn was a great success with me and others.

I could not have imagined – and my imagination by then had become pretty well developed – that the time would come when by helping Labour's Chief Whip Michael Cocks to keep his seat as an MP in another boundary redistribution in Bristol, I would effectively stop this golden boy from becoming leader of the Labour Party and potentially Prime Minister.

In these early years, like so many others, I believed and proclaimed that Benn was God's gift to the Labour Party. And so while I was working for the Post Office Engineering Union (POEU), when Benn became Postmaster General I was delighted. I thought that this man would give us all the things we rightly wanted as trade unionists – including industrial democracy and the right of the Post Office to make its own telephone equipment.

Although Charles Smith, the union's then General Secretary, who had been MP for Colchester, warned me that I might well find the Right Honourable Gentleman a damp squib, I continued to have high hopes of him then and subsequently as Minister of Technology. Indeed my good friend John Starmer, who succeeded me as Political Officer of the POEU, reminded me constantly that it was I who 'sold Benn to him'.

It was I, indeed, who sang his praises to those under my charge as the union's education officer. To all this, I plead 'guilty as charged'. I hate to admit that I fell victim to a confidence trick, but many others far less gullible than I had fallen prey too. Indeed, who could resist the smile, the interest he appeared to show in you as an individual, the concern he showed for the whole world, but particularly yours? And so when Benn visited the POEU Annual Conference, I looked after him and was proud to do so. Indeed, my relations with him were so good that at one stage, very shortly after I entered parliament myself, he persuaded Eric Varley, his Minister of State in the Department of Technology, to take me on virtually sight unseen as his Parliamentary Private Secretary (PPS).

This act of kindness on Benn's part was to have fateful consequences for him. From being a disciple, I became such an implacable critic and opponent that I became infamous for it. The reason was that, on seeing Benn at work, my enthusiasm for him waned rapidly, while my respect for Varley grew and grew. I came to realise that there was all the difference in the world between sparkling promise and steady delivery.

Performance at the dispatch box, or in debate, gave no indication of the ability of a minister to get things done in his department. Indeed, I came to believe that the ability to carry the House of Commons led individuals to think that they needed to put less effort into running their departments.

It was, I think, while working as a PPS that Benn told me that instead of agreeing to the POEU proposal for full industrial democracy, he had simply given us a member on the Post Office board. He also told me he had rejected the POEU proposal to allow the Post Office, a nationalised industry, to manufacture its own equipment in competition with private industry, because this was opposed by the General and Municipal Workers' Union (GMWU) and the AEU. When it came to action rather than words, Benn was completely wishy-washy.

In consequence, I soon came to the conclusion that the Secretary of State's backbone had gone missing. This view was reinforced strongly when, in January 1972, while driving with Benn from Silverdale Colliery in my constituency to visit pickets at the nearby Meaford power station, he suddenly asked: 'John, what shall I tell them that will please them?'. This question upset me greatly, as I had been brought up in union life to believe that when the chips were down, you owed your members the truth. I gently suggested he might discuss the dispute seriously with them, but he didn't take the advice. As ever he just stuffed them up with what he believed, rightly, they wanted to hear. While the men thought he was wonderful, my respect for him tumbled even further. Indeed, it had gone forever.

This incident made such a mark on me that I once discussed it with Frank McElhone, MP for Glasgow Gorbals, who was elected on the same day as me and was also one of Benn's PPSs. Frank said that he had experienced the same feelings on watching Benn bewitch the Clyde Shipyard workers. Frank believed that Benn – in opposition at least – craved to be loved by what he thought to be the authentic voice of working class revolt and would go to any lengths to attract and hold that devotion.

That overarching ambition, and desire to be loved, eventually destroyed Benn and it was not as though he was unaware of the problem. He once told Tom Jackson, the postmen's leader: 'Well, I am thought to be ambitious and I would like to be Leader of the Labour Party. I stood last year in order to get my policy across but I am sufficiently old hand at this not to wreck my life by ambition. I have seen too many people, like Herbert Morrison, ruined for life.'

Unfortunately Benn's ambition not only led him into a life which left him so often completely exhausted and depressed – which didn't really matter – but it also destroyed the chance of having a Labour government for so many years – which mattered a lot.

Benn's famous Diaries are a fascinating tale of ambition, intrigue and ruthless determination.

He once remarked, after seeing a second rate film on the Borgias, that it was interesting to see that Italian politics in the late fifteenth century and Labour politics then were identical. The lust for power and the loyalties needed are the same, though one was in the name of God and the other in the name of the working class.

I heard Denis Healey, obviously gone soft in his old age, say not too long ago that he does not believe that Benn was driven by ambition. I do not agree. In the Benn Diaries this streak comes across again and again as he constantly quotes people saying that he will be leader one day: Michael Foot, Labour Party Conference delegates, Clive Jenkins, Joe Gormley and the Americans (all of them?), to name but a few.

It was this ambition he certainly pondered when Tony Crosland, then Foreign Secretary, died and David Owen, MP for Plymouth Devonport, then a rising star, took his place as a potential future Prime Minister.

During 1977, he got it into his head that one day Margaret Thatcher would come to power, upset the people with her reactionary policies and provide the scenario whereby he would emerge as the great left leader that the people were looking for.

What a disastrous conviction this turned out to be. It gave him a desire to see the end of Callaghan's Labour government and to continue to plot for years for the day when he would become Leader. And this zealot did not expect quick results.

At the end of 1977, he wrote that:

> the country is moving sharply to the right . . . the real battle is within the Labour movement now and it is a struggle for the soul of the movement. Jim Callaghan is riding high . . . It may be that one has to lengthen one's timescale – the whole of the 1980s may pass before we see a change . . . the major issues of the 1980s will be the battle against federalism in the Common Market, the struggle to get back to full employment and sustain the welfare state, and the question of civil liberties and the role of the security forces.

When Arthur Scargill, the extreme left miners' leader, also suggested that Benn would become Leader if Labour lost the 1979 election, Benn replied: 'I'm not so sure because a lot of left wing MPs would be defeated and the PLP could drift back to the right. Also the trade union leaders would have to work with the new government and wouldn't want a critical left wing Labour Party, which might embarrass them in front of their own rank and file.'

Whatever reservations he had about his own chances at any particular moment, Benn nevertheless always did what he could to keep his name in the frame. Thus, when it was thought in 1978 that Jim was about to retire, Benn prepared for the leadership. For other reasons, too, he was already making contact with influential trade union General Secretaries.

Then, during a 'leadership planning meeting' with his office team, he was encouraged by the ever-devoted and willing MP Michael Meacher, who offered to draw up a list of people from the PLP who might be prepared to vote for him as Leader in the event of Jim leaving. Meacher then was one of the closest of his clan, which included Tony Banks, a flashy young trade union researcher, Jo Richardson, Ian Mikardo's secretary, and Chris Mullin, egghead, journalist and author.

He was not so encouraged the following April when two other advisers in his office team, Frances Morrell and Francis Cripps, advised him not to

21

stand against Callaghan because it would upset both the PLP and the unions. Worse still, they told him that he wouldn't win even if Jim did go.

This put Wedgie in a terrible dilemma. While he recognised realistically that his own chances were nil – 'because he hadn't worked at it and because the views he held were unacceptable to the majority of the PLP' – he thought that Jim was ready to go and that Healey, the pugnacious Chancellor of the Exchequer, was set to take over.

He didn't want Denis, whom he believed to be neither a socialist, nor sympathetic or indulgent of him, to become Leader. However, if he went along with the faithful Frances Morrell and supported Environment Secretary Peter Shore to keep Denis out, Shore would then be the Leader for a very long time. Benn was truly between a rock and a hard place.

We will never know whether his ambition would have overcome his distrust of Healey because, after the general election defeat in 1979, Jim went to the PLP and announced that there was no vacancy for his job.

Benn's scheming had at least alerted him to the fact that he could not possibly win under the existing rules then, whereby MPs alone elected the Leader, because that system had one fatal drawback. In the intimacy of the PLP, the electors knew first hand the strengths and weaknesses of the people they were voting for. That is why Meacher would not have needed a book to record Benn's support – the back of an envelope would have done.

Benn's chances, of course, might have been very different if the rules were changed to extend – in an 'Electoral College' – the franchise to include activists in the Party and the unions. In September, 1979, Scargill summed it up for him: 'If there was an election in July and Denis was elected, there would be an opportunity to dislodge him after an electoral college had been established. That may be the best strategy.'

By Christmas, Benn had evidently made the most elementary preparations in case there was a Leadership election in 1980. He had already photocopied the *Times Guide to the House of Commons*, cut out all the Labour MPs' names and photos and stuck them on a sheet of paper with their biographical details – all 278 of them. Benn had also marked the photocopies 'for' or 'against' and then sorted them into piles. One can imagine his huge disappointment as he gazed down at the tiny pile of 'fors' and the huge piles of 'againsts'. Is it any wonder, then, that what he wanted most from Santa Claus was an electoral college![1]

'I don't think I have a chance of being elected by the PLP if the election takes place before the establishment of an electoral college' he wrote, in a revealing piece in his Diaries, speculating that Jim would be pressed to withdraw by those who could win in the PLP but not otherwise.[2]

'I think the strategy is this: get a body of opinion organised so that if Jim retires in the summer it should be left to the Deputy Leader to carry on till Conference has endorsed an electoral college; then have a leadership election after that. If there is a leadership contest before the Conference, despite that advice, I should get the NEC to ask all constituency Party General Management Committees (GMCs) to vote on their preferences and publish them, so that MPs will at least know the views of CLPs; also to get MPs to publish who they voted for so that reselection could influence the leadership elections to a small degree.'

'Next year I have to turn my mind more to PLP support. I don't want to be knocked out in the first ballot, and I would do much better in a final contest against Healey than against Silkin or whoever.'

This passage makes it quite clear why he fought so hard for a change in the rules for the election of the leader and the reselection of MPs. Forget Benn's later clarion call of 'greater accountability' – put simply, the changes were needed to make him leader.

Was this to be Benn's great chance? He had certainly dreamed of the day and drawn up tentative plans. At the same time, he will have recalled a slanging match in the tea room of the House of Commons after which he had written of the crowd of angry MPs who had surrounded and hurled abuse at him: 'They are having a collective nervous breakdown. They are in a state of panic, and the hatred was so strong that I became absolutely persuaded that this was not a Party I would ever be invited to lead and nor could I lead it.' And he was right. While some of his cronies thought he should stand in 1981 and Scargill urged Benn to stand against Foot in 1982, Benn knew that he wouldn't have stood a cat in hell's chance. He would have been humiliated. After Foot had become Leader, Benn could only dream of the day that Michael would retire. Until then, he would satisfy himself fighting for the deputy leadership.

From the account so far, which relies heavily on Benn's own Diaries, it can be seen that Benn was a party to continual conspiracies. His diaries are littered with references to private meetings called to ensure that nothing he wanted was left to chance.

The people who were involved in these meetings included Tony Banks, Frances Morrell, Francis Cripps, ex-mandarin and serious leftie Brian Sedgemore, Norman Atkinson, Labour Party Research Secretary Geoff Bish, Audrey Wise, Joan Maynard, Dennis Skinner, tiny Trot Tony Saunois, Frank Allaun and also Neil Kinnock.

One way, incidentally, in which he kept in touch during the Labour government with others in the Cabinet 'of a like mind', as Thatcher would have put it, was at Sunday evening dinner parties where issues relating to government policy could be raised and discussed away from the ears of Callaghan and Healey.

A group which included Foot and his wife Jill, Shore and his better half, Albert Booth and his wife Joan, the economist Thomas Balogh and his wife and Judith Hart with her husband Tony would meet for dinner and discuss affairs of state.

From Benn's point of view, they do not appear to have been very happy occasions. He appears to have often left them quite depressed. At one time, the others seem to have dropped him because he remarks that he had not seen the usual crowd for two months although 'they obviously have been meeting.'

It is not surprising that he was cast into outer darkness. He constantly created disputes and tension, rowing particularly with Foot. In the long run this, particularly, was to prove his undoing.

Eric Heffer

One of the surprising features of the Benn Diaries is the relative scarcity of references to Eric Heffer. Loud Eric has faded in the consciousness of today's New Labour elite, but he was very much joined in people's minds then as a leader of the loony left with Benn in the 1970s and 1980s. The reason for the omission is that Benn may have seen Heffer – who shortly after the 1979 general election declared that he would stand as Leader – as a rival always prepared to undermine his position among the left.

Eric, who died in 1991, was certainly quite a different kettle of fish from Benn. I never went through any honeymoon period with Eric. Only Doris, his lovely, long-suffering wife, could claim that. And yet to many people Eric was a loveable character. He certainly lacked the hypocrisy I associate with Benn.

Although he had succumbed somewhat to the life at Dolphin Square, the plush apartment complex a stone's throw from the House of Commons, and revelled in his role as a *Times* columnist and instant TV pundit, Eric still had his roots firmly based in Liverpool. And, as he said on one occasion, 'he did have a working class mother-in-law to account to'.

Eric, who had led a strike of choirboys at the age of eight, had been a carpenter and shop steward in the shipyards and had experienced a stormy relationship with the 'Commissars' as a young member of the Communist Party. During the war, he served in the RAF and at the end of the conflict the Communist Party opposed the unofficial strikes led by Eric as they were undermining the new Labour government.

Eric, as we will see, never had any such qualms about undermining any Labour government nor attacking any Labour Leader, though he never liked being attacked himself. Nor did he ever forgive the Communist Party for virtually inviting Doris, as it did, to leave such an undisciplined comrade.

When John Torode, the *Guardian* journalist, asked him whether he was still a Marxist, he replied that he didn't think so but the Labour Theory of Value had a lot in it. Torode summed him up as a Libertarian Christian Socialist with just a tinge of philosophical Trotskyism. Others like myself preferred the term 'big-headed bully'.

In a revealing article in 1979, the writer Sharon Churcher set out Eric's own criteria for a future Leader in the Nye Bevan mould: 'working-class, a good left-wing socialist who also had an intellectual background and who was not afraid of mixing with the aristocratic elements because he'd still got his roots.'

As she wryly observed, 'this description does seem to fit one Eric Heffer', while reporting that 'he is also tactfully but firmly putting the word about that he is neither a clone nor a lieutenant of the party's greatest pseudo proletarian, Anthony Wedgwood Benn'.

Heffer believed, indeed, that Benn was disbarred from identifying with the people by his aristocratic origins. Additionally Eric was usually one of the first to denounce Benn's crackpot ideas, such as his 1980 idea for the creation of a thousand peers. Heffer was not only Benn's reluctant ally and companion at arms (some unkindly said 'stooge'), but at the same time his rival.

In July 1983, as Heffer stood for the Party Leadership, the *Sunday Express*'s 'Crossbencher' column gave an incisive insight into their relationship:

> For years Mr Heffer has lived in Mr Benn's shadow at Westminster. Linked to him inseparably by their shared extremism. But growing increasingly to dislike the cold aristocrat for his bloodless theorising and his sycophantic entourage of power-mad social workers and polytechnic lecturers. So much in contrast to Eric's fervent working class socialism deeply rooted in the dockyards and steelworks of Britain. For years he has endured the indignity of playing the hind legs of the Benn-Heffer pantomine horse. But now at last he has the chance to show the world that he is his own man.

He had, indeed, tried to show much earlier that he was his own man. While Benn so often left his dirty work to others, at least Heffer usually did it for himself. Come to think of it, I suppose he had to because no one else would do it for him. Certainly, as far back as 1980, Eric didn't mess around organising a clarion call for him to stand – he just put it out himself that he would challenge Callaghan. It is much to Eric's credit that, while he put forward his own claims, he also did his level best to undermine Benn's.

Heffer, like so many active combatants in Labour's civil war, was often to be seen briefing journalists in the Members' Lobby. He was also much in evidence in Annie's Bar, a House of Commons drinking hole, open all hours, where journalists bought MPs drinks on expenses and gained useful gossip and information in return. A great advantage of Annie's from Eric's point of view was that Benn would never be present and, of an evening, the *Guardian* columnist Ian Aitken was rarely missing.

But Eric, unlike Benn, never had a realistic chance of becoming Leader. Despite all his efforts, he made little progress because, except to a very few, he just didn't seem leadership material. He had none of Benn's charisma nor ability to excite those on the left, whom he needed to impress to be able to fulfil his ambition.

And, unlike Benn, he was simply unable to shrug off defeats. In 1980, the Shadow Cabinet election results were a big shock to Eric. As the *Sun* said at the time: 'His image yesterday of a bad loser contrasted sharply with left-wing champion Tony Benn who said nothing.' While seen by some as a 'kindly complex character', others weighed him up as a shambling hulk whose ambition outstripped his ability.

True, Eric did his best to change their view. He adopted the comic habit of trying to appear statesmanlike and dressed to match. When the *Guardian* reported that he had a taste for expensive upper class shirts and good classical suits, Heffer protested: 'they're very ordinary suits. I buy them at C&A... and how can a shirt be upper class'.

For many MPs on the left, Heffer was a figure merely of derision. He was all over the place and, even in his relations with his natural allies, consistency was never a charge you could level at Eric. He was, indeed, forever stirring up the PLP and defending himself in the tea room from angry attacks launched by irate colleagues following yet another of his infamous gaffes. Meanwhile, moderate MPs simply detested him.

Eric was always shooting his mouth off, not least when it came to laying into the unions too. Ironically, his proposals for the brothers were very much those of New Labour, although his motivation was so very different. When he wrote that 1980 could be a 'make or break year in the sense that the Party can continue to grow and develop as a socialist party or can allow itself to be sidetracked into becoming a mildly reformist social democratic party', he was well aware that the trade union leadership could still prove to be the stumbling block to the socialism of Eric's own mind.

In an important speech to the Institute of Workers Control in January 1980, he delivered a scathing attack on union leaders, all of whom he said should be elected, and on their use of political funds. I particularly remember this because I was the political officer of the POEU. Like others, I did not hesitate to return the fire.

Heffer advocated a campaign within the unions not only against Thatcher, but also to consolidate the left's reform of the Labour constitution. He wanted to see reform of the trade union block vote system at Conference to make it 'fairer'. In reality, splitting the block vote by allowing union delegates to vote individually would have undermined the voice of each union.

Eric's desire to interfere in trade unions' internal affairs knew no bounds. He proposed that the Party dictate, effectively, how unions should dispose of their political funds, notwithstanding that affiliation to Labour was just one way a union might achieve its political objectives. For good measure, he also tried to lay down which budding MPs the unions might or might not sponsor.

As the *Guardian* wrote: 'the Heffer package would significantly weaken the centralised union domination of Labour Conferences as well as undermining the patronage powers of senior union leaders. No wonder that a number of leading general secretaries, much interested in the way that the Labour Party runs its affairs, are muttering angrily that he should not involve himself in their private business.'

That certainly was my point of view. Each union had its own methods of taking decisions and it was not for the Labour Party to decide how it should conduct its business. I once went to an AEU selection meeting, where Hugh Scanlon's comment on one candidate who had scored only three out of ten was that while he was not good enough to be a union officer, he would certainly make an MP!

When he was not emulating Thatcher by attempting to put the unions in a straitjacket, Heffer was grandiosely setting out the goals for a Labour government: including wholesale nationalisation, democratic workers' management, withdrawal from the EEC and a nuclear-free Europe and Soviet Union.

Eric's policies were all very vague – but the left pretended to know what they actually meant – and his burning desire to produce them an appealing platform was fulfilled. Like most of his thinking, it certainly appealed to no-one else – not least Callaghan and moderate union leaders, whom Eric famously once attacked at the 1980 Conference as 'tame pussycats'.

When it came to standing up to Militant, the Trotskyite revolutionary organisation, however, Heffer himself was certainly a tame pussy cat of the well-neutered variety.

Eric claimed that his opposition to action against Militant was based on tolerance and a dislike of purges and that the Militant papers collected by Labour's well-respected National Agent Reg Underhill, which we will deal with later, were forgeries.

An alternative view, which I endorse, is that Eric was well and truly under the thumb of Militant on Merseyside and would sacrifice anything to keep his parliamentary seat. While he was anti-Stalinist and stood up to the biggest of the union barons, Eric was simply too scared to move against Militant.

The Rise of the Left

Both Benn and Heffer owed their advance to the rapid rise of the left in the Labour Party and trade unions in the 1970s and early 1980s. During this time, the left gained sway over the bulk of the Constituency Labour Parties, certain unions, Conference and the NEC, which had traditionally been right of centre.

The Labour Party at its foundation had been created as an alliance between trade unionists and socialist groups. The two – Labour and Socialist – were not identical. Many of the trade unionists were and still are simply 'Labour' and so are our electors.

I remember going with Roger Stott MP, then the candidate for Westhoughton, in a by-election into the lounge of an old people's home where an old lady asked me if Roger was Labour. When I replied 'Yes', the lady smiled and said: 'I'm so pleased. My father told me always to vote Labour and never Socialist'. He was a man after my own heart.

While Socialists were very rare among the electorate, there were many thousands of them to be found in the Party. Until the late 1960s and early 1970s, when the old order started to change, these Socialists had been kept in order by the Labour right who were entrenched on local councils and in the unions.

This changed radically from the late 1960s, when for a number of reasons there was a big swing to the left. The success of the 1945 Labour government in extending education to the masses had produced a new generation of Party members educated in the universities and polytechnics, who were more radical than their parents.

This generation persuaded themselves that their book learning was of far greater value than the experience and judgement of their working class parents and that they knew all the answers. Many rejected the simple Labour approach and became, in the words of Bryan Stanley, my General Secretary at the POEU, 'theory mongers' who accepted and preached the wisdom of Marx, Engels and their ilk.

This ideology, and a general tendency to wear blinkers, led them to attack the aspirations and performance of Labour governments. When in the 1970s it became quite clear that neither the Wilson nor the Callaghan government would establish a utopian socialist society in Britain, the attacks intensified and the attraction of the left's platform grew. Wilson, elected by the left, had aroused expectations which he would not or could not satisfy. In turn, the left never acknowledged Labour's many real achievements nor the difficulties of the day. They were only concerned to criticise.

Their disenchantment with Labour's economic policies was accompanied by a strong growth in support of the Campaign for Nuclear Disarmament (CND) and unilateralism together with a growing opposition to the Common Market. Following Wilson's support for the Americans in Vietnam, the religious pacifists left the Party and others became increasingly discontented with Labour's foreign policy.

In addition, quite legitimate discontent also festered over the behaviour of particular individuals – over Dick (now Lord) Taverne, for instance, who resigned his parliamentary seat and then defeated Labour in a by-election in 1973 after his Lincoln constituency party, in a running dispute, had carried two votes of no confidence in him because of his support for the Common Market.

Reg Prentice, the MP for Newham North East in London, was also a great embarrassment to the right. Although at one time on the left, he had become more and more reactionary and upset many by supporting the Tory government's prosecution of the Shrewsbury pickets in 1972.

Consequently, he became a target for the left in Newham, which led to 150 MPs, including Cabinet members, sending a letter of support for him to his CLP (I refused to sign because I thought he had brought the problem on himself by neglecting his constituency party).

Subsequently, he behaved so badly that by 1977 – before Prentice made his supporters look silly by joining the Conservative opposition – Healey was refusing to use parliamentary convention and call him my Right Honourable Friend. Indeed, Benn records that he was told that Prentice had discussed the possibility of his joining the Tories with Michael Heseltine, even while he was still in the Labour Cabinet.

The disenchantment created by right wing defectors was increasingly fostered and channelled by organisations on the left. This large and growing army of malcontents provided willing recruits for Benn's crusades. They gave enthusiastic support to his and Heffer's ambitions and their demands for both internal party constitutional reform and the implementation of 'socialist policies' by a Labour government.

For them, as for Benn himself, belonging to the Labour Party at large was not enough. This new breed of member organised into one faction after another. The importance of these groups in recruiting left wing supporters and giving them a sense of belonging, purpose and direction at the time must never be underestimated.

Through these groups the message was sold and guidance given on action. While the organisers were involved in cynical manoeuvring, many of the supporters believed passionately that the only way forward was to work hard for the left wing causes against the hated right. They were recruited for crusades and fought with all the zeal of religious fanatics. And there – when he realised that he could use these organisations for his own purpose – constantly calling them to prayer and battle was Benn himself.

Heffer's power base, meanwhile, was the left wing Tribune Group formed in 1966 by a group of MPs: Ian Mikardo, Stan Orme, Russell Kerr, Norman Atkinson, Stan Newens and Heffer himself. Benn did not join until 1981, when he was persuaded that he needed its support for the Deputy Leadership election and he left shortly afterwards.

Tribune was very diverse and had a great deal of credibility amongst the non–extreme, soft left in the constituency parties. Between 1974 and 1979 it gave shelter to many of those who attacked the Labour government and was far more instrumental in creating the chaos that existed between 1977 and 1983 than David and Maurice Kogan's 1982 book *The Battle for the Labour Party* gives it discredit for.

It was from Tribune that the proposal to change the method of electing the Leader came. Indeed, Ian Mikardo's Tribune pamphlet – which dealt with 1) controlling the elections to the NEC; 2) changing the constitution (i.e. election of the Leader) for their own ends; and 3) putting more Tribune MPs in place – was very influential.

While Benn tried to use Tribune for a short time to further his personal ambition, he was more heavily involved in the multiplicity of left wing groups specifically set up to influence elections and policies within the

Party. He actively encouraged them, indeed, whenever it was in his interest to do so. The only group that he was cool towards was the Communists, who themselves were at war with Militant.

While there were signs of this type of left wing caucus group in the student protest days of 1967–8 – the Socialist Charter Organisation, for example – it was the creation by Vladimir Derer of the very important Campaign for Labour Party Democracy (CLPD) in 1973 which marked the beginning of Labour's civil war.

Established as a reaction to Wilson's refusal to honour the Party's pledge to nationalise the top 25 companies, CLPD issued a clarion call for the left, demanding that the NEC ultimately wrested control of the manifesto from the Leadership and put through every mad, half-baked or self-contradictory policy passed by the barmies (and for that matter the misguided, but well-meaning) at Annual Conference.

Ironically none of its founding aims was achieved in the way CLPD intended. Indeed, the left always voted down any proposal I made for proper consultation to take place with constituency parties. While control by the NEC of the manifesto never came to pass, as we shall see, they were more successful with other issues later including mandatory reselection of sitting MPs.

CLPD's first President, Frank Allaun was a very ineffective man. But it was run on the ground by three very skilful organisers: John Lansman, a Cambridge graduate, Victor Schonfield, the jazz critic, and Vladimir Derer. All three were superb 'fixers' and wore the badge, like we fellow organisers on the right, with pride.

Schonfield, their fixer-in-chief – despite being beaten at the time – deserved the compliments bestowed upon him by Benn for having organised the reselection debate at the 1978 Labour Party Conference so beautifully. In these years, many flattering references were made to my deviousness, but I freely acknowledge that these people made me look a novice as far as political infighting was concerned.

They made alliances with anyone who would help them including Benn and pernicious Trotskyite and other hard left groups which, in turn, were only too willing to use CLPD for their own purposes.

Like so many of these left wing groups, CLPD was very much London-based and the very memory of some of its leading supporters gives me the shudders – oh, the thought of Joan Maynard, Bernard Dix (a National Union of Public Employees (NUPE) researcher who wore leather jackets), Jo Richardson and Audrey Wise all in one room together! Added to this political house of horrors were the trade union officials: Ernie Roberts MP, Alan Sapper of the TV technicians, and Bob Wright of the engineers union.

I can well understand why, in 1978, Neil Kinnock and Stan Orme sent in their apologies for not attending CLPD's annual general meeting. It was too much to expect anyone to suffer for the cause by being together with this lot!

Kinnock did not remain one of their favourite sons. Almost certainly prodded by Michael Foot, in 1979 he helped prevent an early decision being taken on the control of the manifesto. Some fixers such as Lansman came to be very critical of Tribune, the parliamentary group to which both Foot and Kinnock belonged. They believed that Mikardo, as well as Kinnock later, had let them down badly.

At a very early stage, therefore, Tribune was at odds with the CLPD. Many of its members were opposed to automatic re-selection of MPs and wanted to concentrate on the election of the Leader. The CLPD, not led by MPs, however, was insistent that re-selection be tackled first.

We will look at CLPD's tactics in more detail later, including the way they instilled supporters with confidence, effectively drafted model resolutions and – rather like New Labour's Millbank machine nowadays – provided newsletters with arguments for them to use.

For the moment it is sufficient to note that they chose carefully limited objectives for each Conference, carefully planned how to achieve them and then organised to ensure that they could command sufficient votes to be successful. Their effort was put into planning the 'fixing' at Conferences, rather than discussing policy.

Very early on in 1975, the leaders of CLPD realised that to be successful they had to mobilise union support and created a trade union sub-committee. Francis Prideaux, a hospital worker, and Schonfield worked hard on contacts, including Bernard Dix, one of NUPE's many wild men, and Bob Wright. Ron Todd, later to become General Secretary of the TGWU, and Eric Clarke of the Scottish Mineworkers also helped.

Among the unions, CLPD received national support from Alan Sapper's ACCT, Clive Jenkins's ASTMS, the construction and technical (TASS) sections of the Amalgamated Union of Engineering Workers (AUEW), the Fire Brigades Union (FBU), the print union NATSOPA (often known as 'not sober'), NUPE and from many left wing branches not only in left wing unions but also in moderate controlled ones. You could, indeed, never take anything for granted in any trade union. When, for example, my fight against the left was at its height, my strongest supporters in Newcastle-under-Lyme included the TGWU, NUPE and the Bakers – all left-controlled at a national level – and the most antagonistic was a branch of the more moderate GMWU.

On the NEC, CLPD used the most fanatical group it could find – Richardson, Skinner, Maynard and, of course, Benn. I sometimes thought that its potential recruits were subjected to a stringent psychological test, to be rejected if the slightest sense of compassion was detected.

All their hard work, of course, did immense damage to the Party. Apart from the disputes CLPD fostered over constitutional changes, its stance on public ownership, opposition to the Common Market and unilateralism were to play a major role in Labour's defeat at the 1983 general election.

Militant

We moderates had to battle with many left wing groups, but the most dangerous and pernicious of all was Militant.

Alone amongst the elite revolutionary Trotskyite groups, Militant came to realise the blindingly obvious – that they would neither come to power by calling on the working class to rise up in arms nor win elections if they stood as socialists outside the Labour Party. They decided instead on 'entryism' – by getting Militant members to join the Labour Party, gain control and use its electoral appeal to win seats.

To achieve this they became skilled at targeting constituency parties – particularly in Liverpool, Bradford, London and Bristol – and trade unions such as my own, the POEU, and far more importantly NUPE. Once in, they worked incessantly at taking control – in conjunction with other left wing groups, if necessary.

In their book, the Kogans give a good definition of Militant's aims: Trotskyites believe in the overthrow of the state by force. They insist that a socialist society cannot be achieved through parliament and that parliament must be superseded by the rule of the working class through the party: the dictatorship of the proletariat. This will then be replaced by rule by the masses through workers' councils.

Whereas I had been taught about the evils of the Communist Party in the 1940s, my first encounter with a disciple of Leon Trotsky was in the 1950s at Keele University in my future constituency Newcastle-under-Lyme. There I listened, bemused, to him arguing bitterly over interpretations of the history of the Soviet revolution with Henry Collins, an extramural lecturer and strong supporter of the Communist Party. Everything seemed to revolve around a missing volume from the Kremlin Library shelves. Watching them argue the point with greater and greater passion, I gained the immediate impression that they were mad and that impression has never faded.

It was reinforced by the discovery that in the 1950s there were Trotskyites who truly believed that the revolution was at hand. Ray Challinor was a fat, jovial but pugnacious Trotskyite from the mining village of Silverdale studying at Keele. He incidentally was one of those several pacifists who tried to persuade me of the errors of my thinking by punching me in the face. Fortunately, this was not in his mind on that beautiful spring day when he told me that he had been into the back of a bookshop in London the previous week and had been given the date of the revolution.

Seeing that I did not immediately take out my diary, he went on to whisper that we must prepare ourselves for a date in October the following year. I shook my head and told him that if he popped into the local pub, the Sneyd Arms – used in those days not by academics but by miners, farm workers and other working people – he would see immediately that the Trotskyist leadership had picked the wrong date.

The one they had given clashed with both cribbage and darts matches throughout North Staffordshire. Obviously this message was conveyed back to the comrades because, as far as I can remember, the revolution never came.

The Trotskyites of the Revolutionary Socialist League – otherwise known as the Militant Tendency – were, however, increasingly persuasive and pervasive.

On 13 January, 1980 the *Sunday Times* announced that 'conclusive evidence that a Trotskyite faction has infiltrated the Labour Party and successfully set up a national network aimed at turning the party into a revolutionary Marxist body has been acquired by the *Sunday Times*.'

'It strongly supports the view,' the newspaper wrote:

based on estimates made after last year's Labour Party Conference, that the Militant faction of Trotskyites is a powerful and sometimes controlling force in more than 60 constituency parties. It also reinforces anxiety about the faction's plans to replace moderate Labour MPs by its own supporters and to influence party policy at the next general election.

An internal 'bulletin', issued to Militant activists, has been obtained by the *Sunday Times*. Dated October 1978, it shows how the activists' strength has grown since Labour's National Executive decided to take no action against them in 1977. It confirms the growth of their wider activities inside the Party as a separate organisation with its own aims – something specifically forbidden by Labour's constitution. In 15 detailed pages, it discloses the inroads made by the faction under the direction of the editorial board of the Trotskyite paper, *Militant*.

'The responsibility is on each and every comrade to build the revolutionary party,' it says. After referring to much support from members of public service unions, it added that the faction was also concerned to build a solid industrial base and approvingly noted support by shop stewards in eleven major West Midlands factories. They disclose that local cells recruit from public meetings of *Militant* readers and that every supporter was expected to take along at least one sympathiser. They had been particularly successful in the Young Socialists: 'Our growth in strength and influence augurs well for the future. The basis has been laid, in the trade unions, youth and immigrant community, for a rapid growth in the number of supporters.'

In a long justification for its infiltration activities, the Militant report implicitly concedes that it could not get mass support outside the Labour Party; the Militant faction, it says, understands 'the loyalty, that British workers instinctively have towards the Labour Party.'

Despite the fact that *Militant* by then had 60 full-time workers, even as late as 14 December, 1981, however *Guardian* journalist Martin Linton (now the Labour MP for Battersea) was able to write dismissively:

For years the left felt it could afford to ignore Militant . . . True, they had two or three supporters in every constituency, sometimes up to a dozen, but they were so sectarian that they seemed unlikely to gather more support. Their motions were always defeated by a huge majority at Labour Party conferences, their candidates were always well beaten in the national executive elections and they never had a single MP in Parliament. Their only success was in gaining control of the Labour Party Young Socialists. They were in Michael Foot's phrase more of a 'pestilential nuisance' than a threat.

By then, however, I had long known the very serious threat Militant entryism posed for the Labour Party. Ironically, it was Les Huckfield – the MP for Nuneaton, later a fervent supporter of Militant, but still a right wing minister at the time – who had drawn my attention while I was employment minister to the way in which a Militant organiser in the Midlands was financing himself by exploiting the rules to draw unemployment benefit.

My experience was not that the soft left ignored Militant but that, at the beginning, they positively supported it and worked with Militant's Young Socialist representative on the NEC. They took no action until Foot realised that Militant was more than a 'pestilential nuisance' and persuaded Kinnock and Joan Lestor much later that they had effectively helped to create a monster.

I knew more than most about the extent of Militant's pernicious web of influence because early in 1979 I was involved in a legal dispute with the group. Unfortunately now, part of the legal settlement was not to make further reference to the dispute. While sticking to my agreement, I can say that this experience taught me the extent to which Militant had infiltrated the Party and was tolerated by left wing MPs, including such present day paragons as Kinnock and Clive Soley.

Later, after Neil had become the best known Trot basher of us all, when asked about his earlier support by *The Times*, his spokeswoman Patricia Hewitt responded: 'It sounded too unlikely even to bother about asking him about it. I guess it's about as accurate as the rest of that paper (*Militant*),' she said.

While I became personally committed to a war against Militant, it is not too difficult to understand why these lefties tolerated it. Some, such as Heffer, were acutely conscious of the importance of Militant in their own area and danced to their tune in order to remain as MPs. Others, such as Kinnock, put up with them as natural allies within the left in the fight against traditional right wing Labour.

The bravest opponent of Militant was Reg Underhill, the Party's National Agent. In 1975, he had undertaken an enquiry into Militant which had been ignored by the NEC. His report was only taken out of the cupboard when, at the beginning of 1977, the newspapers highlighted the Trotskyist infiltration of the Labour Party and Tom Bradley – the MP for Leicester East and aide to Roy Jenkins – revived the issue on the NEC.

Brushing resistance from Benn, Heffer and Joan Lestor to one side, by the narrow margin of 11 votes to 9, Foot successfully moved that there be a sub-committee of five to look at the Underhill Report.

Although presented with clear evidence of Militant's objectives by Reg (on 25 May, 1977), however, the NEC's report was a damp squib. Rather than throw Militant out, it decided instead that they should be combated by recruiting more members, by education, ensuring that Constituency GMCs were properly constituted and by paying more attention to the Young Socialists. It was a cop-out!

Equally controversially, the NEC report, moved by Foot, re-iterated that they were against witch hunts and recommended that the evidence against Militant should not be published. It was said that the documents, all incidentally authentic, 'had come in plain envelopes'. Interestingly, Benn, far from peddling the standard line that the evidence was fake, believed that it had been obtained from the offices of Militant by the Security Services.

While both John Cartwright MP, who represented the Co-ops on the NEC, and Bryan Stanley of the POEU accepted the conclusions of the report, they wanted publication and circulation to the full NEC. Neither were successful, however, because Foot stood out against both.

Then all went quiet on this front except for an argument at the start of 1979 about the appointment of Militant's Andy Bevan as the Party's youth officer and later his activities in the general election, regular lamentations from Jim Callaghan and Shirley Williams and my own legal battle against Militant.

Bryan Stanley, who chaired the NEC's Appointments Committee, described how astonished he was to hear Ron Hayward – who had the deciding vote – announce that he was going to support Bevan. After the 'left-wing NEC had rubber-stamped the recommendation, a tremendous boost was given to Militant activities inside the Labour Party,' he said. Militant was allowed to grow and undermine the traditional Labour Party by Benn and Heffer and, indeed, everyone on the NEC.

They vacillated when what was needed was a swift wooden stake straight to the heart.

TWO

Dire Straits in 1978

To understand the psychology of the Labour Party at this time, it is important to remember that the Party was created initially as an alliance between trade unions and socialist societies and only later were individual members admitted. Labour, therefore, was naturally a trade union party.

The constitution recognised these roots with an Annual Conference, the party's supreme policy-making body, in which unions and socialist societies had by far the majority vote over Constituency Labour Parties, into which the individual members were organised.

History, too, was embodied in the NEC – the body charged with running the Party's affairs – which consisted of the Leader and Deputy Leader elected by the PLP; the Treasurer, elected by Conference as a whole but effectively, because of their voting strength, by the trade unions; five women elected on the same basis; nine constituency representatives, elected at conference by constituency delegates; twelve trade union representatives, elected by the trade union delegates at the conference; a representative of the co-ops and socialist societies and one for the Young Socialists.

Traditionally the NEC had been right wing and loyal to the parliamentary Leadership because both the constituencies and the unions at Conference had been overwhelmingly moderate in character.

The NEC had provided a leadership to Conference, which had then given support to the Leader and the PLP. The Leader would call also in all the main union officials to let them know what was needed, so the vote could be duly collected. With the big swing to the left, this changed. Neither constituency nor union representatives were willing to play ball with a right wing Leader.

The NEC had effectively come under the control of the left in 1975. By then, through sheer hard work and meticulous attention to detail, various factions of the left controlled a substantial number of constituencies, union national executives and Labour Party and TUC Conference delegations.

This posed great difficulties for Callaghan when he became Prime Minister in 1976. At a typically tense joint Cabinet and NEC meeting held on 16 February, 1977, for example, Callaghan upbraided the NEC for being too negative and urged that they tell the country more about Labour's achievements. When asked to retract by Barbara Castle, who hated Jim, he refused, stating that he would never forget that the NEC had organised a public demonstration against the government. On this occasion, Heffer countered that 'the NEC is not made up of left wing crackpots' and simply continued with Frank Allaun to attack the government.

To understand the ludicrous situation, whereby a Labour government in office was not supported but aggressively undermined by the Party's highest representatives, we need to look at the left's tactics in the unions and Party at large.

Constituency Labour Parties

Constituency parties fell like dominoes to the left as a result of hard work, scheming, deceit and thuggery. I came to know first hand of their methods because from time to time they tried to take over my constituency in Newcastle-under-Lyme. Unfortunately for them in Newcastle, and in neighbouring Stoke-on-Trent whence they went afterwards, my agent Llin and I beat them at their own game with the loyal support of Party members.

I also learned much about them from other MPs. Known in the tea room of the House of Commons as someone who not only detested but fought left wing bully boys, I would be asked to advise fellow Labour MPs. The Irishman Michael O'Halloran would in his distinctive whisper relate all the horrors that he and other moderates faced in Islington. The voice of Robert Kilroy-Silk would be somewhat smoother but even louder on the question of Militant on Merseyside.[1]

To begin with, committed left-wingers – the 'bed-sit brigade' – were drafted into local parties in areas of great Labour strength with the job of taking them over.

Constituency parties were run by Executive Committees elected at the Annual General Meeting by members of the General Management Committee (GMC). This turn was made up of delegates from ward branches, the Women's Section, Young Socialists, trade unions and other affiliated organisations such as the Co-op, the Fabians and the Socialist Educational Association (SEA).

For the left to get control of the GMC, which at that time chose the MP, meant gaining control of ward parties, ensuring that sympathetic union branches and socialist societies were affiliated and sent delegates and also ensuring the existence and control of a Young Socialist branch.

In many areas it was fairly easy for young professional, middle-class people to take over wards and GMCs. During the 1950s, I was a member of the West Ham North constituency and remember how badly it was run. Membership was small because it wasn't easy to join and I had to make quite an effort to transfer mine from elsewhere. Although part of the reason was apathy, it is also true that many old-timers did not want to see an increase because they were frightened that newcomers might be a threat.

They were, of course, quite wrong: the larger the membership of 'ordinary people', the safer the local leadership would have been. When left wingers persisted and joined, they often found it easy to take control when membership was small and attendance at meetings even smaller. Indeed, only four or five people were needed to to take control of some wards and ensure that their delegates to the GMC supported a particular faction. It was, of course, these wards which the left picked off first.

Many became Branch Secretaries very quickly, this being a hard-working job which few wanted. While the Secretary's job today can be a chore, it was even harder before the arrival of all our new technology, word processors, photocopiers and the like. Under the rules, becoming a Branch Secretary automatically put the newcomers onto the GMC, too, and this proved a bonus to the left.

The left played what we call the 'numbers game' i.e. they set about getting control of as many wards as possible to get a majority of the delegates at the GMC. Placing members was possible because cheaper accommodation was easier in working class areas than in middle class districts. Once they had control in a particular ward, they would move to another – always placing just enough members to make the most of the troops under their command. The exact same tactics Lenin and Trotsky used to such effect in revolutionary Russia were being played out in Britain in the 1970s.

Not that the numbers were always necessary. A small group of strongly committed newcomers, plotting before meetings and then pushing hard at the meeting itself, would often get its own way even though older members might have doubts.

If the old-timers refused to be bulldozed, the newcomers would claim they were brighter, better educated and therefore knew better. Other techniques would be brought into play, including bullying and blatant twisting.

Intimidation initially helped Militant in the 1970s and early 1980s to make great progress, but was ultimately – as we will see – a major factor in its downfall.

Foot, for instance, was told by his fellow Aldermaston peace marchers that at meetings Militant supporters would sneer at and abuse the ordinary members, many of whom quickly gave up. Others, who did not, had rougher treatment – including being mobbed after meetings, receiving nasty telephone calls and being threatened with physical violence.

Meetings, too, would be kept going often until after midnight, with the left knowing that older members would leave. After taking control of the party officerships, the left kept going on until moderates gave up, allowing non-agenda items to be taken as 'emergency business', of which nobody except the left caucus had any warning.

In this way, when the left did not get what they wanted by fair means, they got it by foul. They cheated their way into positions of power and justified it to themselves in terms of acting in the interests of the working class. In the name of the 'dictatorship of the proletariat', they did all they could to remove control of the Party from the working class in solidly working class areas.

To prevent parties being taken over needed great vigilance. Just before one AGM of the Newcastle-under-Lyme GMC, I discovered that Mike Tappin – a university lecturer, who later became an MEP – had organised an attempted takeover using a 'list' or 'slate' of supporters.

He justified himself to me later by saying that the working class weren't fit to control the Labour Party!

Discovering his plan in time, those of us who had been in the Party rather longer and were proud of our working class origins, copied his technique and issued our own list. The many trade unionists on the GMC made sure that we fought off this challenge.

In other constituency parties, from time to time, the left would cheat by telling only their own supporters when meetings were taking place, by putting in false inflated figures of membership to get more delegates and by stating the rules incorrectly.

While it was harder to influence the local union branches, the left did have some success. They would first secure the affiliation of branches where the leadership was sympathetic to the left and then find delegates. They would also do this with bodies such as the SEA, Fabians and the Co-op, which had the right to affiliate to the constituency. They also formed Young Socialist branches to which they applied an iron discipline.

As well as hijacking GMCs, they were also able to deselect local councillors and put in their own people to give themselves control of councils. But control of GMCs was all important. It enabled them also to control the selection and deselection of the MP and gave them the right to be represented at Conference, take part in the election of the NEC and help formulate policy.

The ability to send delegates to Conference gave Militant, in particular, a national platform.

The Life of Conference.

The left put their control and influence in the constituencies to great use at Annual Conference. Their organisations met secretly to draw up an agreed list of people to support in elections, together with priority policy proposals, and then 'sold' them strongly through their supporters. This uniformity of purpose was bound to achieve results against a right wing which, until it woke up, failed to do likewise.

The left, by concentrating their votes on a limited, agreed number of candidates obtained many more successes than the right who spread their votes more widely.

The carrying of left wing propositions at Conference created huge difficulties for Callaghan and Healey. Effective organisers, particularly Vladimir Derer in CLPD, circulated constituencies with many copies of model resolutions, that were passed, placed on the Conference agenda, composited for debate with other resolutions and, wherever possible, supported by left wing constituency and union delegates.

Over many years I approached Annual Conference with varying attitudes. In the early 1960s I would go full of excitement, wonder and awe. In the early 1970s, I would go with the union delegation for laughs. In the nineties, I went just to the social activities and treated them as a reminder of 'all our yesterdays'. In the late 1970s and early 1980s, however, I went to each Conference totally psyched up, knowing that the adrenaline would flow for a whole week of struggle in a mainly hostile environment.

Many delegates – 1,200 in all, half of them from constituencies – went to Conference chosen by the left, armed by the left and ready to fight for the left. Leaving nothing to chance, the left tried to make it impossible for the union-dominated Standing Orders Committee, responsible for determining the Conference agenda, to brush aside their chosen subjects.

The first fights took place in the compositing meetings held on the eve of Conference. Because it was impossible to debate all the hundreds of resolutions sent in, those on the same subject used to be brought together and 'composited'. Putting your resolution into a composite meant you also accepted other parts.

The Chairman of the Compositing Committee and its officer (a member of the Labour Party staff) would generally expect to produce at least two composites – one 'for' and one 'against', i.e. one satisfying the left and one the right.

To ensure that the left composite was not cobbled together on the spot – a hazardous business – the left organisers prepared one carefully in advance and planted it with someone they could trust, who was attending and would argue effectively for it.

The composite meetings, held on the Saturday, provided the first buzz of excitement. If a delegate failed to turn up, his union or constituency proposition fell. Of course, this rarely troubled the left. They made sure their delegates arrived and, playing safe, generally arranged for several constituencies to table roughly the same resolution.

There would also be great competition to see who would move and second the proposition on the Conference floor. When a large union was involved, often the official could overawe – some would say bully – constituency delegates into agreeing that the union do this. Very often, however, Militant members, confident speakers well-versed in the arts of manipulation, would stand up against right wing unionists.

The next stage was for the left organisers to talk to the left on the NEC, which endorsed the final Conference agenda. Dennis Skinner and others would need to ensure that the NEC recommended acceptance of left proposition. All needed to be 'fixed' and was. Benn, for example, records in his Diaries how he paid attention to Conference Arrangements Committee so that nothing could go wrong.[2]

As well as trying to fix compositing meetings, organisers on both sides would be following closely what was happening in the union delegations. These differed greatly, but each would have a meeting in a smoky hotel room at which decisions would be taken in advance of the Conference. In some unions these were over quickly; in others the process would take hours. Most unions, however, were riven by factions and torrents of blood would flow on the carpet

For delegates, Saturday afternoon and Sunday morning would be full of gossip and anticipation. Rumours would be rife over who was likely to go on the NEC and who ejected. Mikardo will be off, they might say, and Skinner on – 'and serves him right!'

Along the front, at Blackpool or Brighton, delegates and visitors would stop and swap information, some more reliable than others: 'The T&G have decided this . . . '; 'NUPE is definitely going to support that . . . '; 'We've got control of the AEU again this year'; the shopworkers are still meeting, it's touch and go.'

Delegates wanting to rub shoulders with the famous would call in at the Imperial or the Metropole, the headquarters hotels in Blackpool and Brighton. Here, there would be an even bigger buzz. Dozens of journalists would be quizzing Benn, Skinner and me on events at the NEC.

The relationship with journalists was very important. Throughout my time on the NEC, Frank Allaun as Chairman of Press and Publicity and Michael Foot repeatedly made attempts to discourage the holding of unofficial press conferences

One of my first discoveries on the NEC, however, was that the left briefed journalists regularly and in detail, particularly the *Morning Star* and the *Guardian*. I decided to follow their example. The *Guardian* – made up of a mixture of Tribunite, Trotskyite and later SDP journalists – could not be expected to support a right wing, union hatchet man and didn't. Other posh papers were more helpful to me – especially *The Times* – and also the tabloids and the TV. These we needed to get our message across: that the moderates within the Labour Party were still in there fighting.

At the Imperial and Metropole, the 'fixers' also came to meet, swap notes with their own side and decide what to do next – Alan Meale of the left always looking worried with a frown; Roger Godsiff, laid back, with a broad smile constantly breaking from his ever-serene look.

There was much drink, much gossip and endless speculation. And then Conference actually began. On the floor, delegates sat in blocks. MPs, Lords and prospective parliamentary candidates sat in one, where cynicism reigned supreme and parliamentary behaviour of the worst kind was evident at moments of crisis. In other blocks throughout the hall sat the union delegates, male, white, middle-aged and working class. They were mostly businesslike, well-used to conferences and relying heavily on one or two in the delegation to keep them abreast of what was happening. They needed to because they would spend more time in the bar than the constituency delegates. My own POEU delegation was always bitterly divided between right and left, although this did not prevent us from sharing a bag of sweets. We even fed Joel Barnett, the Treasury Chief Secretary, in the MPs' block.

Constituency delegates were younger, more left wing, more passionate, less obviously working class and the least well-behaved of all. In the constituency section of the hall, newer delegates delighted in identifying the personalities and then following the lead of left wing leaders in their treatment of them. The rules were simple: cheer the left and boo, barrack and slow handclap the right. It was like a football match, save that it was more sinister, brutal and menacing. The hatred was real.

When dinner time came, out you went through an army of pamphleteers and placards condemning the Labour leadership into the autumn air outside. For delegates still revelling in the wonderland of Conference, there was always a good demo to enjoy or worthy cause to support. In the afternoon – in those bad old days – ballots were taken for Treasurer, the NEC and the Standing Orders Committee, heightening the atmosphere of battle.

The left knew the constituency section of the NEC would be OK, as their slate would ensure that no right winger could possibly win. They could never be as certain about the Women's and Trades Union Section, nor about the position of Treasurer. The left's union organisers had been at work but the likes of Tony Banks and Alan Meale were simply not in the same league as Roger Godsiff, then the Political Officer of APEX – the Association of Professional, Executive, Clerical and Computer Staff – who conjured rabbits out of hats.

Conference debates themselves were pitched battles. In the evening, there were fringe meetings to attend, trade union and other receptions to be gate-crashed, where you could listen to the latest rumours about the ballot results and pass them on. To get into a trade union reception was a bonus. You not only got close to the high and the mighty, but drank for free as well.

Not long after I joined the POEU, the union held a cocktail party to celebrate re-affiliating to the Party. The object of this event, so we told each other, was to make contacts and important personalities were invited. Harold Wilson, the Prime Minister, had promised to come and we were all excited. Sadly, he was held up and Charles Smith – the POEU General Secretary at the time, a former MP himself and stickler for good manners – ordered that the reception carry on until Harold arrived.

Those there seemed only too eager to postpone their suppers and help by drinking on. The only worried person was me, completely sober, who as political officer had responsibility for the expense which was becoming excessive. When the expense was, indeed, challenged at the next union conference it was explained that the reception had to go on longer than planned because Wilson had arrived late. This was accepted – with the usual cynicism, of course.

The following year, the generosity of the POEU having become a byword in every boarding house, everyone in town decided to attend. Important Labour regional organisers – able to help the POEU get seats in parliament and to whom nothing could therefore be refused – organised whole coach outings to the reception. The hotel room was packed out and even more was drunk than the previous year.

At the next POEU conference, an explanation was demanded and the Treasurer Charlie Morgan was told: 'Don't tell us that Wilson arrived late again.' 'No,' said Charlie, 'I'm pleased to report that Harold Wilson arrived on time. The problem this year was that George Brown, his Deputy, arrived early!'.

At receptions – and indeed everywhere – new delegates were stuffed up with stories denigrating the right wing Leadership. In fact, I was continually amazed at the number of delegates who believed everything they were told about the Labour right.

One of the great myths concerned our presumed connection with the CIA. Benn, indeed, himself wrote: 'the right wing of the Labour Party is American-financed for that purpose' i.e. to keep the Communists out.'[3]

On one occasion Llin and I took Ken Perry – the union convener in the Rists Lucas factory in Newcastle – and one of his shop stewards into a small Blackpool cafe for dinner. As we went through the door, we heard a young Trot enquire of his elder companion: 'What's Golding doing in a place like this?'. His mentor, the old Trot, replied knowingly: 'He's come for his CIA money'. On hearing this, I went to the counter and said: 'Four double egg and chips please,' paused and then added: 'Do you take dollars?'. The look on the face of the young Trot was one of pure joy!

On another occasion, I picked up three hitch hikers from a service station near Birmingham. One of them, about 25 years old, sat in the front and two younger ones sat in the back. The older one opened up the conversation 'What job do you do?' he asked, after saying he was a Liverpool social worker. Knowing a thing or two about Liverpool social workers, I pondered and replied 'trade union official', thinking this would lead to less aggro than if I said 'MP'.

'Oh,' said the LSW, 'and where do you come from? 'Newcastle-under-Lyme,' I replied truthfully. 'Do you see John Golding?', asked the LSW looking me in the face. 'I see him from time to time,' I said, referring to those rare occasions when I resorted to a mirror. 'He's a terrible man,' said the hitch hiker. 'He is destroying the Labour movement'. I smiled knowingly to the LSW and returned often to the subject on the long journey to take advantage of my companion's insight into the evils of Golding. At the end of the journey I thanked him for opening my eyes in this way.

The Trades Unions

It was not only the Trots and social workers from the constituencies who swung Conference and the NEC for the left. That could not have been achieved without the help of the unions, who dominated the voting. Sadly, in the 1960s and 1970s, the situation within the unions had changed from those happy days when a handful of individual leaders – commanding almost half of the Conference votes – had carved things up simply to give support to the Leader.

Now they were as likely to use their muscle in support of the left, especially the public sector unions following their disputes with the Labour government over wages, conditions and cuts in public spending.

Not that the growth of the left in most unions arose from any great revolutionary fervour on the part of their members. While the left set out to control the unions for both industrial and political reasons, members voted not on political grounds but rather for officials whom they had been told would look after their wages and conditions.

Union members tolerated the unrepresentative political activity of officials so long as they delivered the goods.

The left was greatly strengthened by the election of Jack Jones in the TGWU and Hugh Scanlon in the AEU, which later became the AUEW. For different reasons, the right was also weakened by the replacement in the GMWU, which later became the GMB, of Lord Cooper by David Basnett in 1973.

That is not to say that union leaders in the early 1970s were totally unreliable and disloyal. In fact, Jones and Scanlon were extremely courageous in defence of Healey's economic policies, which were so unpopular with the left. They did not, however, give the same support to realistic defence or foreign policies. As a rule of thumb, the more remote policies were from their union responsibilities, the more left wing were those they supported.

Additionally, they made life more difficult for the Leadership by casting the bulk of their NEC votes for left wingers. As the union vote determined who was to be Treasurer, the five women's seats on the NEC and the 12 union seats, this was disastrous. Their sentimental left attachments put the NEC and its important sub-committees firmly under the control of Benn and the left between 1975 and 1982.

Unfortunately, they carried on voting for the comrades even when they realised they were dealing with people who were idiotic, dangerous or both. They were responsible, for example, for making Norman Atkinson Treasurer in 1976 – withholding their vote from Eric Varley – and replacing Eirene White, the MP for Flint, by the left winger Joan Maynard.

The new behaviour also came about not only because of the change of leaders, but also because the 'Barons' themselves became less powerful in their own delegations. Even where the leadership remained moderate, a new breed of activist was being elected to delegations, who was less likely to follow their lead.

One reason was the change in the left's composition in the unions. Traditionally, the Moscow-supporting Communists had been the main opposition to right wing union leaders. But by the early 1970s, with the discrediting of the Communist Party, their place had been taken by their opponents on the left – the Trotskyites.

This had bad consequences for the Labour Party, because the Communists – as a separate party – were denied attendance at Conference, whereas the Trots and Militant were allowed in. Their 'entryism' gave them the ability to destroy a party whose aims and aspirations they opposed.

Other left wing organisations also began to work within the unions, including the 'Rank and File Movements' in the late 1960s and 1970s – originally encouraged by Jack Jones himself – which were dedicated to bringing union leaderships to heel.

For a variety of reasons, then, the swing to the left in the Party was marked. The only place that the right was still powerful, despite losing some ground, was the PLP. The scene was set for violent clashes and Labour's left-dominated NEC made certain they came.

Labour's National Executive in 1978

I joined the National Executive Committee of the Labour Party at the Blackpool Conference in 1978, my election in the union section being a rare setback for the left. My success was partly due to my reputation as a minister willing to help the unions and the popularity of my union boss Bryan Stanley among the big union barons. Had Benn known what was to come, he would not have just described my election as 'unfortunate'- for him it was to be disastrous.

Then, however, he was safe in the knowledge that the only right wingers elected were Jim Callaghan; Tom Bradley MP representing the Transport and Salaried Staffs Association (TSSA); Neville Hough, the GMWU representative from the Black Country; Fred Mulley, the Secretary of State for Defence; Gerry Russell from the AUEW Executive; Shirley Williams, Secretary of State for Education; Russell Tuck, Assistant General Secretary of the National Union of Railwayment (NUR) and me – just 8 out of 31.

To these should be added, for a short while at least, the unreliable Les Huckfield who beat the right's John Cartwright in the Co-op and Club Section – as at that time Huckfield was more concerned about the threat from Militant than was Cartwright.

Apart from us few, the NEC election was a triumph for the left, of hard and soft varieties.

The left wing Norman Atkinson, MP for Tottenham, beat the moderate Eric Varley easily for the Treasurership. Four out of the five in the Women's Section were of the left: Judith Hart, Joan Maynard, Lena Jeger (MP for St Pancras & Holborn South) and Renee Short (MP for Wolverhampton).

In the union section, Alan Hadden of the Boilermakers, Doug Hoyle of the ASTMS, Alex Kitson of the TGWU, Sam McCluskie of the seamen, Syd Tierney of the shopworkers' union USDAW and Emlyn Williams of the National Union of Mineworkers (NUM) were all, at that time, identified with the left. In addition a Militant Young Socialist, Tony Saunois, was elected unopposed.

From the right's point of view, it was an utter disaster. The total dominance of the hard left in the constituencies was shown by how they were able not only to defeat the popular Jack Ashley, MP for Stoke South, but the one time hero of the Socialist left, Ian Mikardo, MP for Bethnal Green and Bow – replaced by Dennis Skinner, the Beast of Bolsover, as the barmies wreaked revenge after Mikardo had dared compromise on the compulsory reselection of MPs, a left wing totem.

The success of the left 'slate' was of greater significance than simply ensuring continued control of this particular NEC. It also gave those who organised 'the list' great political power. However popular you might have been, you did not readily upset the left 'fixers' who controlled the list. There was no point in following Mikardo into the wilderness. If he could not save himself, what hope was there, without kowtowing, for ambitious newcomers setting out on the path of fame and glory?

For several years, the constituency left on the NEC was kept in line by this ruthless Machiavellian machine. Only in 1982 was Kinnock able to beat the system, though Joan Lestor was not. Once elected on the left ticket, you were expected to vote according to the decisions of the left caucus, which came together before meetings to decide a 'line'. And this left caucus was controlled effectively by those who controlled the list. Time after time left-wingers taking sensible decisions in NEC sub-committees were forced by the left fixers to change their vote at the full NEC itself.

At this time, in late 1978, those who supported the Labour government had no effective organisation either at Conference or on the NEC. With the support of the slimey Labour General Secretary Ron Hayward and the Party's Research Secretary Geoff Bish, the left rode roughshod over all opposition. They treated Callaghan, Fred Mulley and Shirley Williams, in particular, with contempt.

Immediately after the 1978 Conference, I watched how Benn and his allies were keen to pick a quarrel over the Queen's Speech, which would set out the government's programme for what was to be the last session before the 1979 general election.

At the very first meeting of the new NEC on 4 October, it was decided that Bish would prepare a discussion document before we met the Cabinet. In other words, the 'Left Wing Socialist Government in Exile' would present its alternative programme.

In the event, Benn – then chairman of the NEC's powerful Home Policy Committee – and his fellow lefties were frustrated, because the meeting was put off until a fortnight before the Queen's speech was due. In Cabinet, Benn thought it wrong that the Speech should be considered with the NEC so late and claimed it had already gone to the palace. When the joint meeting was finally held, Skinner announced he had heard that the speech had gone to the printers already and didn't want to be involved in a pointless discussion. Instead of just ignoring all this huffing and puffing, however, Foot gave his word 'as a socialist' that no final decisions had been taken.

One result of the bust-up was that the Cabinet agreed to hold joint meetings on a monthly basis – and then subsequently used the meetings, badly attended by NEC members, to expose the shortcomings of that less than august body.

Inevitably, there was also an early punch-up on economic policy. At the 1978 Conference, a proposition drafted by Benn and his son Hilary (now MP for Leeds Central and a junior minister) – calling for selective import controls, the reversal of public spending cuts, early retirement and a shorter working week – had been carried with overwhelming NEC support, despite Callaghan's protests that it was an attack on the government's economic policy.

Benn and all his allies knew there was no way the government could either afford or accept it. The Queen's Speech, therefore, stuck to the anti-inflationary line because the government had no alternative. Nevertheless, the NEC attacked the government's economic and European policies throughout the winter. Healey, indeed, received more stick from Labour's NEC than from the Tories!

One particularly nasty meeting stuck long in my mind: a special meeting of the Home Policy and International Committees on 27 November, 1978 to discuss the European Monetary System (EMS).

This meeting typified the bullying tactics of the left. Skinner told Healey he was only where he was because the Labour movement had put him there, whereupon Denis replied that 'mouthing of ideological claptrap' got you nowhere and told Skinner that he didn't carry a certificate to speak on behalf of the working class. Later, as Healey was speaking, Heffer simply shouted 'rubbish, rubbish' before Benn brought heckling Eric to some sort of order.

We will look in detail at the catastrophic effect of disagreements on Europe later. Suffice it to say now that that this vitriolic meeting carried a strongly worded resolution against the EMS. And when Shirley Williams moved that the manifesto for the European elections be drawn up by the International Committee, the Home Policy Committee and the Back Benchers' Liaison Committee of the PLP, Heffer had plenty of backing to ensure that the PLP was simply brushed aside. Crucially at that dreadful meeting, too, Healey was also forced to defend his anti-inflation policy and the recent increase in the Minimum Lending Rate (MLR).

As ever, he put his arguments brutally. For anyone who knows *The Wind in the Willows*, it was Badger facing down the weasels in the Wild Wood – no place for the faint-hearted, but a joy for people who love to see a real pugilist at work. I enjoyed every minute of it, looking around at the distraught faces as Denis thundered on. 'MLR was now an administered rate,' he hectored, 'but it mustn't get too much out of line with the discount market, since that would benefit discount houses.'

Most of us had experience only of street markets, as Denis clearly realized. Norman Atkinson, who regarded himself as something of a financial expert, did his level best to make a good impression by nodding at points he clearly did not understand. Doug Hoyle, whose voting record against the Labour government was a matter of pride to the Tory Chief Whip, screwed his face up and scowled, as Denis ploughed with his *tour de force* to justify the two per cent rise taking the MLR up to 12 per cent.

Benn sat, with wild eyes popping out on their stalks, as Denis made the evidently outrageous point that we needed a period of quiet in financial markets in a politically difficult time over the winter and that the MLR increase had now made this possible.

Skinner and Allaun – taking the role of the Weasels – did their best to discomfort Badger, but they might as well have saved their breath. Skinner argued that the rise was unnecessary and would hit Labour mortgage payers. He looked sorely put out, though, when in a bout of one-upmanship Allaun jumped in to remind Healey about council house rents instead!

Then, with sarcasm that would have put down a rhino, Hoyle congratulated Healey for not having blamed the unions this time. Denis didn't even notice, remarking wearily that unemployment was down by 107,000 from the peak and inflation had been cut by half over the past 12 months.

'If we had not increased MLR, there could have been a sterling crisis over the winter,' he said. 'There will be a general election soon and we should be drawing more attention to the many points of agreement between the NEC and the government.' A rare burst of wishful thinking!

Following the meeting, of course, Hoyle and Skinner submitted a motion condemning the increase in the MLR and calling for the adoption of 'the

Alternative Economic Strategy (AES) passed by successive Labour Party Conferences'.[4]

Then the General Secretary held a press conference, announcing to the world this attack on a Labour government, which would shortly be facing a general election!

Under Benn, the Home Policy Committee kept up its attacks right to the end. On 12 February, 1979 it opposed cuts in public expenditure and decided that there should be a joint Cabinet-NEC meeting 'to discuss economic and industrial issues'. Resolutions from Allaun and the Militant Trot Saunois, too, spouted the usual claptrap.

For years, it was still beyond belief to me that only weeks away from a general election, the Labour government was threatened in this way by the National Executive Committee of its own party.

Jim did not suffer completely in silence. There was a great deal of tension at the meeting on the Queen's Speech on 23 October about where ministers' loyalty lay, to the NEC or the Cabinet.

At the Cabinet meeting which discussed the Queen's Speech, Callaghan reported Skinner's comments that he would make everything on the NEC public knowledge. The Prime Minister made it clear that, if this happened, ministers would be ordered to remain silent. Though Benn knew that this would be essential to maintain the Cabinet's collective responsibility, he would not accept this.

The issue arose again after Benn had spoken in favour of the government rejecting the Franco-German EMS proposal and advocating a pledge in the Queen's Speech that we would veto any European monetary scheme that was against British interests.

'Tony has advanced his own point of view,' Jim told the press. 'The Cabinet has not yet reached a decision but when it has, collective responsibility will then be operative and any member of the Cabinet coming out against the decision would face the consequences.' This put the cat right among the pigeons because Benn's position was clearly the majority view on the NEC.

This caused Heffer to write to the General Secretary about the position of ministers on the NEC and Jim's effective gag.[5] And at the Organisation Committee in December, despite opposition from Tom Bradley and me, Benn and Kinnock pushed through a resolution, by 8 votes to 4, that a delegation be sent on behalf of the NEC to the Prime Minister to discuss the relationship of ministers and the NEC – and that a sub-committee, of all things, be set up to consider the issue.[6]

In the event, however, Benn withdrew from of the delegation and kept his head down!

Callaghan was greatly upset by this particular episode. At the NEC on 21 December 1978, when certain members wished to defer the discussion on collective Cabinet responsibility, Jim insisted on making a statement.

It was the first time, he said, that a Prime Minister would have been prevented from addressing the NEC. He then laid down the line that he was not prepared to waive the rule of ministerial collective responsibility for NEC members, although he had always applied the rule 'liberally and with tolerance', unlike Wilson.

He pointed out that for years innumerable ministers had been members of the NEC without difficulty. If any ministers couldn't square their NEC position with that of Cabinet collective responsibility, then resignation or dismissal were possible. Jim made it clear that you couldn't have one rule for NEC members and different rules for others. If the NEC, Jim warned, tried to lay down new rules, then he might have to think again about his tolerant approach. 'Leave it as matter of good sense,' he asked. It must have been left, because I cannot remember going on any delegation.

And while all this was going on, the NEC were making a total shambles of running the Party – on which they should have been concentrating rather than fighting the Labour government.

A Party Paralysed

In 1978, the Party was in chaos and in the years following it managed to get even worse.

'It's a shambles.' Wherever MPs, regional organisers, agents or experienced local Party officers met, whether in the tea room of the House of Commons, at 10 Downing Street, or regional conferences – this was the verdict on the state of the Party. 'It's a shambles', one of us would say and everyone else would agree. Ron Hayward, the General Secretary, was fond of quoting words from Keir Hardie, one of the founders of the Party, dating back to 1888: 'Perfect your organisation, educate your fellows, look to your register, spread the light and the future is yours.'

The Party cards carried the exhortation: 'The victory of ideals must be organised.' But in 1978 'that lot at Transport House', as Labour's HQ was generally called, would have had Hardie turning in his grave.

Demoralisation was the order of the day. Our membership was falling, there were fewer and fewer agents and Head Office organisation was a joke. Our popular vote meanwhile was dropping and by-election results were disastrous. To pile on the misery, the Party was facing a cash crisis and was grinding to a halt.

Norman Atkinson, the Treasurer since 1976, was quite incapable of doing the job. By 1979, ringing his hands as ever, he announced that the Party had no reserves and faced a deficit of £1.4 million over the coming three years.

The lefties feigned shock and blamed the unions for not increasing affiliation fees. One day, when Atkinson asked the NEC 'What shall I do?', there was an uncharacteristic silence. In a constituency somebody, at least, would have piped up: 'Why don't we have a raffle or a jumble sale?'

But the NEC had long since lost any organisational initiative. They were capable of holding mass demonstrations, at which Militant collected thousands of pounds for themselves, but they were incapable of raising money for the Party.

The irony was that the NEC couldn't itself have run a chip shop without bankrupting it. The left leadership was totally incapable of running the Head Office of the Labour Party, never mind the country.

The situation came to a head when the TGWU, in desperate need of additional accommodation, gave the Party notice to quit from Transport House and it was decided to re-house in a derelict property in Walworth Road, miles away from the House of Commons.

To renovate the building was obviously going to be expensive and the Party was broke. The NEC launched a 'Buy a Brick' scheme but the response was pathetic. It was generally thought by members that the NEC itself dropped sufficient bricks in a year to build a dozen headquarters.

By 1978, only £145,477 had been raised. The Party now, however, had to pay £160,000 rent and £160,000 rates, a far cry from the £50 rent plus rates charged by the TGWU. When the unions stepped in with a lifeline, they were mortified to find that the 'brick money' had actually been spent on lavish carpets, furniture and trimmings. 'Nothing is too good for the workers', Ben Tillett had said. And the new Walworth Road staff took him at his word before the Party finally moved into the building in March, 1980.

Why were things so bad?

Much can be put down to the failings of the General Secretary, who was not only disloyal to Callaghan, but not up to his job. He was incapable of co-ordination and instilling any sense of direction. He presided over a divided, inefficient Head Office that was also becoming increasingly infiltrated by Militant and other lefties.

Andy Bevan, the Trot Youth Officer was one example. He and Nick Sigler, a left wing researcher, were able to push the real sense of grievance felt by many staff about the pay and the general conditions under which they worked. Benn and Heffer preached left idealism while the Party's employees fared badly. Captain Bligh would have been pushed to have caused such a state of anarchy.

In the unions, Joe Gormley of the Mineworkers and Terry Duffy of the Engineers took a stand: they simply would not dole out more to this bunch of incompetents.

Others of us said 'get rid'. Get rid of the General Secretary, get rid of Norman and his fellow left wing NEC members, get rid of the ever increasing number of left wing researchers, get rid of the waste and above all get rid of *Labour Weekly*, the official newspaper which, while costing us a fortune, was totally biased to the left.

And we would have 'got rid' at an earlier stage, had it not been for the fact that the right could no longer rely on support from the GMWU to sort out the Party in such a rough and ready fashion. Its new General Secretary, David Basnett, allied himself with left wing union general secretaries in an attempt starting in 1977 to reform the Party by the use of reason alone. It was far beyond reason already, however, and looking back, it was clear that Basnett was just the lapdog of Clive Jenkins, the high-living, left wing leader of the Association of Scientific, Technical and Managerial Staffs (ASTMS) – a pathetic enough fate for anyone.

Basnett had become General Secretary of the GMWU in 1972 and plays an important – albeit generally a self-important – role in this story. Had he given the union's traditional total loyalty to the Labour Leadership, events in the late 1970s and early 1980s would have been very different. Unfortunately, like so many of his kind, he failed to see the light in time.

He himself was inclined to the soft left but his failure to help us was motivated more by his bad relations with Terry Duffy and Frank Chapple, the right wing leaders of the Engineers and the Electricians, over the Isle of Grain industrial dispute and his resentment of what he thought was bad treatment from both Healey and Callaghan.

Although at an early stage Basnett professed to like Jim, his pride was deeply wounded when Callaghan announced there would be no election in October 1978. As ever at important moments, he had both press statements and champagne at the ready.

Like other union leaders, he had worked particularly hard to ensure that the TUC Congress had gone smoothly in the run up to the general election. After being asked for money for the general election at one meeting at Number 10 in 1978, Basnett had helped set up Trades Unions for Labour Victory (TULV) to mobilise support from trade unionists.

But his hurt by Jim was as nothing to his resentment of Healey. Basnett was one of the 'Neddy Six' trade union leaders the six members of the TUC's General Council who sat on the country's National Economic Development Council and who negotiated so unsuccessfully on pay before the Winter of Discontent. The bruising that Denis gave Basnett was to cost him the Leadership both in 1981, when Basnett helped to persuade Foot to stand, and in 1983 when he supported Roy Hattersley in order to stop Denis once and for all.

Basnett was egocentric and believed his role was to act as the kingmaker and then take advantage of this by being appointed to the Cabinet. In truth, many believed that Jenkins on so many occasions pulled his strings.

This was galling to those of us who wanted to fight the left and regretted that some first-class fighters in the GMWU, such as Derek Gladwin, Callaghan's campaign manager, and David Warburton, were not able to play a full part in stopping the rise of Benn and Heffer.

Gladwin and Warburton had already been responsible in 1977 for putting a proposition to the GMWU conference calling for reform of the Party. At a cosy chat over a meal with Benn, Basnett told him that they wanted a Commission of Enquiry into the Party which included trade union general secretaries and others not on the NEC.

Seeing how disastrous this might be for him, Benn rebuffed this, arguing that the NEC could hardly be expected to acknowledge its own incompetence. He argued that a Commission would open old wounds, look like a reprisal and would, in any case, open up the question of the union block vote.

Benn was so worried that the next day he warned Callaghan that it would be a disaster to have an enquiry which would be critical of the Party just before the general election. Callaghan's response was to refer to his own concern about the control of the Party by a small coterie of left-wingers.

Sadly the GMWU proposal did not even reach our Conference agenda in 1978, despite the fact that Gladwin was the Chairman of the Standing Orders Committee. The left on the NEC had organised stiff resistance.

Following this failure Basnett, in his self-appointed role as the man most likely to save the Labour Party, enrolled the help of about 10 unions to put pressure on the NEC. He himself wanted an all-embracing enquiry which would cover not only the financial and organisational weaknesses of the Party, but also its internal democracy.

Using trade union pressure, he secured an enquiry into organisation. The left, however, remained opposed and it was allowed to fizzle out and no final report was ever made. A proposal to form a joint committee of senior trade union officials and NEC members, with a co-ordinator to oversee organisation, was carried but never implemented.

Leaving aside his massive ego, Basnett meant well. But he set out thinking that by reason and logic alone he could persuade the left wing NEC to re-organise the Party. But they were never open to reason and logic. They were convinced that everything they did was right and that there was no need to make any concessions. It was put to Basnett over and over again that the only way to make progress was to fight the left, not to make alliances as he did with the TGWU, Jenkins, Bill Keys (the influential left wing leader of SOGAT, the print union), NUPE and so on, thus keeping the left in control of the NEC. If only he had listened.

After the 1979 election – when it was too late for a generation of Labour supporters – Basnett again picked up the candle of reform. Suffice it to say, however, that at this time he had never seen the left on the NEC actually at work, nor had any understanding of how bad these barmpots and bigots were.

Worse still, he failed to appreciate how their disloyalty to the government would contribute to its downfall.

THREE

The Winter of Our Discontent

I followed the terrrible story of the Winter of Discontent as a minister within the Department of Employment.

This bitter dispute over pay policy with the unions, fomented by the left, the terrible strikes and social disruption paved the way for 18 years of Conservative rule. People still remember the images of rubbish piling up in the streets, hospital patients left stranded by strikers and the refusal of local-authority staff to bury the dead. It was a horrific period which killed off forever the concept of a Labour movement founded on humanity and care for one's fellow man.

Labour's strong appeal to the electors in 1974 was that it could get on with the unions. By 1978 and 1979 that claim appeared absurd, laughable even.

Of course, it should never have happened. We had weathered the difficult times and then fell apart just when things were picking up. The government was making economic progress against all the odds.

The Chancellor, who had to deal with rampant inflation and massive increases in public spending, against a background of oil-induced recession, was able to report that unemployment was falling and price rises had been brought under control.

If only we could hold on, we would soon reap the benefits of North Sea oil. But sadly, we never saw the promised land.

Ironically, in 1977/78 pay settlements were not expected to rise above a single figure. Then for 1978/79, the Treasury calculated that there would be money available from economic growth in the coming year. Callaghan and Healey put a proposal to the 'Neddy Six' that tax thresholds be raised, giving a boost to the lower paid, on condition that the restrictions on pay continued.

Union leaders, however, simply would not wear this. They told 'the politicians' in no uncertain terms that they had borne the brunt of wages policy for several years, that their members were becoming more and more restless and that they simply could not hold the line any more. Jack Jones, they were only too aware, had been defeated at the TGWU's 1977 Conference, which had voted for neither pay restraint nor limitations on free collective bargaining. Quite simply, the unions wanted to grab the benefit of any upturn themselves and to hell with politicians and the general election.

The government had also incidentally already added to their problems by the introduction of Child Benefit. This, in union officials' minds, meant more for women and less for men – a most undesirable re-distribution! There was also great opposition to the government's decision in 1978 to back the full implementation of massive increases recommended by the Top Salaries Review Body. Indeed, even right wingers at the PLP told a peeved Callaghan that, on this, he was completely out of touch.

On 20 July 1978, the Cabinet discussed the White Paper on pay: 'Winning the Battle on Inflation'. At its heart was the infamous 5 per cent pay norm – which with the inevitability of some drift would help keep inflation in single figures and less than the 10 per cent inherited from Ted Heath, a key consideration for the forthcoming general election. The containment of inflation, too, was itself necessary to reduce unemployment.[1]

Unfortunately, Healey and Callaghan were blind to all the warnings. Healey has since said his biggest mistake was to support Callaghan, who at one time wanted a nil norm, and that they should instead have gone for a more flexible 'single figures formula'. At the time, however, Healey recommended the 5 per cent norm, saying that although the unions would not endorse it, that was what they were expecting.

The Cabinet, too, was bitterly divided. Environment Secretary Peter Shore had reservations about 5 per cent, while Stan Orme, the Secretary of State for Social Security, was opposed to any norm at all. Albert Booth put the strong Department of Employment point of view, to which I had contributed, that while a norm was required 5 per cent was too low, as was 7 per cent. Booth, the Secretary of State, would have direct responsibility for handling the forthcoming Winter of Discontent and was deeply affected by it. Harold Walker, the Minister of State who handled pay policy, also gave sound advice but his expertise was too little used.

Supported by Owen and Hattersley, however, Callaghan came down strongly in favour of the 5 per cent, knowing full well that the unions could destroy the policy and with it the government, if they so wished.

Strange negotiations took place with the 'Neddy Six'. While they suggested that increases be made, they never turned the 5 per cent down flat. In his influential book, *Prime Minister*, Bernard Donoughue said ministers came to the view that the union leaders were acquiescing, without their actually ever saying so. In truth, rather than face a brutal diatribe from Healey, they kept quiet and waited for the general election, which would let them off the hook. There was certainly no understanding between the two sides whatsoever during these negotiations.

Like many, the unions were totally confident that there would be an autumn general election in 1978 and, indeed, believed Callaghan had confirmed this to them privately during a visit to his farm immediately prior to the TUC Annual Congress.

At the TUC, however, Callaghan gave a bizarre rendering of 'Waiting at the Church', indicating that the event had been postponed, but no one took the hint. When Jim put an end to the possibility of an autumn election in his broadcast on 7 September, there was great bitterness among union leaders. They now faced a very difficult situation. They could no longer hide the fact that they could not deliver a 5 per cent deal.

I was one of those who advised strongly against an autumn election, believing that we would be beaten in the West Midlands which was crucial to victory. The reason was that many workers had come to resent our incomes policy, particularly the skilled and those in the profitable car industry.

Not only were the polls against us, but the workers would have voted against the 5 per cent wage restriction in any case. On top of this, other issues such as immigration and the sale of council houses would have sunk us. Those who believe that we could have won then in the autumn are the sort that make their judgements from reading the *Guardian*, rather than getting out on to the streets.

Had we gone before the Winter of Discontent, however, we would not have been so heavily thrashed as we were. Those of us who advocated waiting did not foresee the way in which the kamikaze left wing union leaderships would set out on their voyage of self-destruction. We would be beaten by left wing unions who, in setting out 'to give Callaghan and Healey a lesson', not only destroyed the wages policy, but also the Labour government and, indeed, the Labour movement.

In his Diaries, Benn records conversations in September with both Jack Jones, who had retired as TGWU General Secretary, and his successor Moss Evans. Jones thought they could get through on pay, using productivity and local bargaining as tools, although he foresaw that cash limits would be a problem for the public sector. Evans was less positive. Turning to the tough situation at Ford, he pointed out that the boss Terry Beckett had himself received an 80 per cent increase and the company had made a £264 million profit.

Evans, Alf Allan from USDAW and Len Murray from the TUC tried to persuade Healey, Booth and Hattersley that a fourth year of restraint wasn't on, something which they should have worked out for themselves from Jones' defeat at the TGWU Conference. Evans wanted flexibility and disagreed with Callaghan, who thought 'the people' were behind him. The reality is that people are always in support of wage restraint – for other people. They will happily support national wage policies, so long as they are the exceptions. Many of us did our best to support Jim, knowing we were bound to be defeated. The arguments that took place in smoked-filled rooms over beer and sandwiches were echoed in union branches, executives and conferences. They culminated in debates at the TUC and our own Conference, which led to decisions critical of the government.

At Conference, while Foot sought a 'fudge', the hard left including Militant and Skinner worked to ensure that the NEC itself would recommend rejection of 5 per cent. Barbara Castle, still smarting a decade on from her humiliation over 'In Place of Strife' at the hands of Callaghan and the unions, was also prepared to stir things up.

The issue facing the NEC was what recommendation to make to Conference on Composite Motion 37, which attacked the 5 per cent wage policy and called for a national campaign against wage restraint.

At the NEC, Heffer moved in support of the motion. Callaghan, however, laid down the gauntlet, saying 'we cannot govern if this is accepted'. Benn, who couldn't support the left without losing his Cabinet job, cleverly proposed remittance to a special meeting of the TUC–Labour Party Liaison Committee. Finally, the NEC decided to call for remittance of the proposition attacking the 5 per cent policy.

Not that Conference took any notice. After a call for loyalty from Foot, delegates chose disloyalty and the motion was carried massively. A loyalist motion, thanking the government and calling on the movement to support it, was narrowly defeated. Too many unions had already been mandated at their conferences where the issue had been exploited by the left.

The left, immediately after the general election and for many years to come, attacked Callaghan for ignoring these resolutions. This lie was given great credence by Frank Allaun and Ron Hayward at the 1979 Conference.

The truth, however, was very different – and this was put on the record by both Foot and Callaghan. After the defeat at Conference, the government did see the light and beat a retreat. Indeed, talks to recover the situation began the very next week.

By 15 October, 1978 Benn himself reveals in his Diaries;

The Neddy Six have come up with a scheme under which the TUC would use its influence to reduce inflationary pay schemes. In return, there would be a public sector pay freeze, perhaps for six months. Michael thinks that if a deal could be settled on Friday night then there might be a special meeting of trade union executives to endorse it and the TUC could then present it as an abandonment of the 5 per cent.[2]

An agreement was reached, which was approved at Cabinet on 9 November. Sadly, owing to a number of cock-ups, the TUC did not ratify the unanimous recommendation of its own Economic Committee. Two members were absent, including Moss Evans. And he did not brief his two other members, one of whom voted against.

As Callaghan said: 'It was a great blow to me personally and to the government, when the news reached us on 14 November – six weeks after

Conference – that opinion was equally divided in the TUC and so the agreement could not come into effect.'

Following the meeting Tom Jackson, the Chairman of the TUC General Council and a staunch government ally, was furious. 'How do you square socialism with the prize going to the strong and the weak to the wall?' he scorned. 'I do not believe that each trade union is an island, that each trade union has a God-given right to get 30, 40 or 50 per cent. Rapacious prosecution of self-interest is nothing to do with trade unionism. The British trade union movement, as expressed in the decision yesterday, has begun to forget where it came from and where it is going.'

Tom, a larger-than-life character with his great drooping moustache, went on to attack the alliance between the left, Keith Joseph and Margaret Thatcher. He slated NUPE in particular for scuppering an agreement which would have given so much to their members. Unfortunately, his comments were undermined when it was revealed that his own union, the Union of Communication Workers (UCW), had itself decided to submit a 25 per cent wage increase to the Post Office. This was entirely typical of the situation at the time.

Callaghan himself later claimed that he knew that, with the failure to reach agreement, the government could not survive and he was right. Before that time, however, the whole sorry, sordid tale had still to unfold.

It began on 3 November, when workers at Ford went on strike disregarding Beckett's leaflet pointing out that the 5 per cent was government policy! They were more interested in Ford's profits, better pay and Moss Evans' certainty that the union could afford a strike. From then on it was all downhill, with claims and settlements spiralling out of control.

The Cabinet in early December bowed to the inevitable and abandoned its 5 per cent limit, moving to 8 per cent without making any statement. But by now, this was irrelevant. In December, Ford settled for 17 per cent and British Oxygen for 10 per cent. To make matters worse, the oil tanker drivers wanted 30 per cent, road hauliers 25 per cent to 30 per cent, local authority manual workers 40 per cent and British Leyland production workers 37 per cent. It was impossible to settle at these figures and strikes became the order of the day.

The government had to act: it was time to use one of the sanctions set up to operate against private employers to enforce the incomes policy. Except suddenly there were no sanctions any more. The penalties had to be withdrawn after a left wing revolt led to a defeat in the House of Commons. Nine Labour members had abstained, including John Prescott. Although they voted the following night with the government on a motion of confidence, they had effectively destroyed it.

By Christmas, the going rate was 15 per cent and there seemed nothing the government could do, except take deep breaths. A new pay code was botched together during the parliamentary recess, which provided for the public abandonment of the 5 per cent limit, strong pay controls in the private sector and comparability in the public sector, together with low pay supplements and a TUC code against violent picketing.

Jim then headed off to an international conference in Guadeloupe and, worse still, extended his absence by popping off to Barbados for a few days where the press photographers had a field day. The comments of those suffering at home, while 'Sunny Jim' was basking abroad were barely repeatable. Callaghan's press conference on his return was a total disaster. Asked about the deteriorating situation, Jim dismissed the question as parochial. 'Crisis, What crisis?' ran the headlines and enormous damage was done.

The crisis was there for all to suffer and see. As Bernard Donoughue, Callaghan's adviser, summed it up so well: the country was virtually paralysed and the pickets were ensuring a future victory for Thatcher.[3]

While the oil tanker drivers settled for 12 to 15 per cent, by then an official strike of road hauliers led to another 100,000 workers being laid off. When Jim appealed to the TUC, they had to tell him they could not help.

The Cabinet was urged to introduce a State of Emergency and call in the troops. Callaghan, however, a trade unionist through and through, could not bring himself to go so far and we in the Department of Employment strongly supported him.

On 16 January, 1979 Callaghan – who was punch drunk by this time – surfaced to announce the introduction of exemptions for the low paid, comparability for public servants and on 29 January he met the full TUC General Council – all 40 of them – at 10 Downing Street. The bill for beer and sandwiches must have been enormous! At the end of January, the lorry drivers went back with wage increases of up to 20 per cent and the water workers finally settled for 14 per cent. It reminded Callaghan of Munich.

After the cave-in to the lorry drivers, all hell broke out in the public sector. A million and a half public service workers went on strike in pursuit of crazy wage demands, shutting schools, hospitals and vital public services across the country. In the grip of one of the worst winters in memory, those ambulances still operating were stopped at the gates by pickets. Members of NUPE and COHSE (the Confederation of Health Service Employees) decided which patients to admit to hospital. In Liverpool the dead remained unburied and the fire service went on strike.[4]

While Jim was asking how the Cabinet would was survive, Thatcher was taking full advantage. Union-bashing pushed her personal popularity ahead of Jim in the polls and by the beginning of February, the Tories enjoyed a whopping 19 per cent lead. Then, to pile on the agony, on the very same day as the poll, NUPE announced it was going to dump rubbish in the constituencies of members of the Cabinet.

At this time, I recall canvassing with Llin in Newcastle and the reaction was horrific. One man who had been a union branch secretary told us he would never vote Labour again because the wild men had taken over. The reaction was typical.

On 14 February, in a meeting at 10 Downing Street the government capitulated completely, shunting the 5 per cent inflation target off into the distant future. The TUC's love token on that Valentine's Day was a commitment to try and control strike tactics, which were being described as 'bully boy' methods even by life-long members appalled at what was being done in the name of trade unionism.

Is it any wonder that by 15 February, the Tories were 20 per cent ahead? What was surprising to many of us was that we had any support left at all? Our depression deepened even further that day when we learned that, to top it all, Len Murray, the TUC General Secretary, had told Jim that NUPE's union executive had flatly rejected a deal he had made with the public sector workers, giving them an 8.8 per cent increase plus productivity and comparability.

This outrageous decision, designed – I thought – to destroy the government rather than protect NUPE's members, completely demoralised Callaghan. He was also upset by the way that Cabinet ministers themselves did not hold the line. And, to the disgust of those of us in the Department of Employment, he now put Hattersley in general charge of pay.

Slowly, the pay storm of the Winter of Discontent blew itself out, but not until vast increases had been given to civil servants and the teachers had claimed an additional 36 per cent.

There was only one victor from the Winter of Discontent – Margaret Thatcher. Without the industrial disruption caused by militant trade unionism, despite the antics of Benn & Co we could have won the general election.

While the government had to share responsibility with the Neddy Six and the TUC General Council for the failure to reach satisfactory agreements, the responsibility for the traumatic TV images which led to terrible defeat in the general election of 1979 rests solely with unions such as NUPE and the TGWU.

While Moss Evans and the Ford workers have long since been forgotten, many of us will never forget the damage done by NUPE led by Alan Fisher, Bernard Dix, Reg Race and Tom (now Lord) Sawyer, which through its aggressive tactics destroyed the Labour government and ended, indeed, for ever more the substantial influence of the trade union movement in the Labour Party.

FOUR

Loyalist Group Formed

On all fronts we were battered, bruised and bloodied by the onslaught of the left. In government, in the Party and out there in the country, we were exhausted by the sheer war of attrition. But those of us temperamentally suited for a street fight were not going to simply roll over and die.

The damage done to the Labour government by the antics of the left led to the creation of a trade union-led 'Loyalist Group' on the NEC, in an attempt to shield Callaghan from some of the worst excesses of Benn, Heffer & Co.

I describe it as 'loyalist', rather than 'right wing' or 'moderate', because that is basically what it was at the outset. Combining a mix of politics and personalities, the group's basic philosophy was 'let us win the general election first and argue later'. It did not enjoy a majority on the NEC for several years, nor did it extend beyond the NEC. The group's prospects of success, therefore, were strictly limited. But it did lay the foundations for a determined fight back later by the moderates against the left.

The inspiration was Bryan Stanley, my General Secretary at the POEU. In 1978, after chairing NEC's powerful Organisation Committee, he decided to step down from the NEC to concentrate on union work. It was decided that I – still the POEU's Political Officer, MP for Newcastle-under-Lyme and a junior Employment Minister, to boot – had more time to spare! Thus I came to be nominated in his place and duly elected, as we have seen, at the 1978 Conference.

At first sight, Stanley seemed an unlikely driving force. His background was strongly unilateralist, which had come as quite a shock to Sara Barker, Labour's legendary National Agent, when he was chosen to fight the

Worcester by-election against Peter Walker in 1961. He was also strongly anti-Common Market and, therefore, had all the qualifications of those on the left. But he was also a very loyal Party member, with very close links with the rank and file, and he was deeply disturbed by the growing hostility towards Callaghan, fostered by the NEC.

Knowing me as an out-and-out loyalist, he realised I was just the person to take on the loony left on the NEC. Stanley asked me, therefore, to form an alliance with Sam McCluskie, left wing leader of the seamen's union, Russell Tuck, Assistant General Secretary of the NUR and others to organise a defensive shield for Callaghan.

With Laurel and Hardy very much in mind, I said at the time (and many times subsequently): 'This is another fine mess you've got me into, Stanley.' Nonetheless I did persuade both McCluskie and Tuck to call a meeting of a 'select few' to chew over the difficulties the NEC was creating for Callaghan and the government.

Tuck, quiet but shrewd and hard-headed, was certain to go along with the idea. Instinctively, he knew that only common sense could attract the electoral support of the British people. While naturally cautious, he knew that meant fighting to recapture the Party from the fanatics. A very courageous man, he was the rock on which the fight-back was founded on the NEC by the right wing and their loyalist allies.

McCluskie was a very different kettle of fish. A powerful influence, he was also very shrewd but also held certain very strong left views including support for CND and a violent opposition to the Common Market. Normally, it would have been impossible for me to have talked him into any such meeting – particularly as Sam's close friend and ally, Alex Kitson of the TGWU, was one of the prime movers on the left.

Times, however, were not normal. After Stanley left the NEC, McCluskie expected, as a formality almost, to get the coveted chairmanship of the Organisation Committee. He was after all very powerful, sympathetic to the left, unilateralist, strongly anti-Market and a trade unionist. The idiot Heffer, however, had – according to Sam – contrived with Benn to get himself elected instead.

This election had a profound influence on subsequent events. Heffer himself was a complete disaster. A former building worker and member of the building trade union, UCATT, he appeared to be run from outside. He would take one view in discussion, go to Liverpool and return with another. Either the air on Merseyside was particularly damaging to the brain cells or the Militants and fanatics had got at him.

While Sam retained close ties with Kitson, he loosened his friendly relations with the left wing MPs on the NEC. He believed strongly that he had been stitched up by privileged MPs in the House of Commons and was now ready for the first time to take steps, whenever it was possible, to curb the rise of Benn and Heffer.

McCluskie, however, had so come to hate MPs that he made it a condition that, while he would deal with me as an MP-cum-brother official of the POEU, he would not tolerate my inviting Shirley Williams, Fred Mulley or even Tom Bradley.

In truth, the political right in parliament at this time were an airy-fairy lot. Although they held high office, they were ill-equipped to deal with the taunts and machinations of the lefties. They appeared hurt, bemused and incapable of coping with the bullying of Heffer and his cohorts. While they were more at home debunking the hypocrisy of Benn, they generally appeared lost and out of place in the rough house.

In this atmosphere I thrived, as Stanley knew I would. I was rough, never ducked a fight – with the enemy at least – and had good working class credentials which Heffer, Skinner & Co could never challenge. Just as important, I read every piece of paper that came to me and spent time making sure I understood what the barmies were really after.

The group first met, with Tuck in the chair, at the North Western Hotel near Euston station. In addition to Tuck, McCluskie and myself, present were Alan Hadden (Boilermakers), Syd Tierney MP of USDAW (a member of the Tribune group) and Neville Hough of the GMWU. Gerry Russell of the AUEW – a solid right winger from Liverpool – was invited but did not attend, because he had not 'got time for any of this faction stuff'. He never voted with the hard left, but neither could he be relied on to vote for us. I had to persuade and cajole him all the time.

The meeting was hardly messianic, but concluded that something had to be done to save the Labour Party from the lunacy and ambition of Benn and Heffer. I was made convenor of the Group – it being generally agreed again that I was the only one with enough time to spare. My work as the MP for Newcastle-under-Lyme and Parliamentary Under Secretary of State for Employment they, too, regarded as part-time.

It was a difficult job to manage. Unlike the situation on the left, members of the Loyalist Group did not owe their election to anyone. There were no sticks and definitely no carrots. Everything had to be achieved by persuasion.

Some of the trade union members were, however, totally supportive. Tuck would always do what was necessary. And Hough, the GMWU man from the Black Country, hated the left and would slog in the trenches as long as I wanted him to. The only time he would not vote 'the line' was when David Basnett, his General Secretary, had specifically asked him not to. And when Hough said: 'John, David wants us to vote for this that and the other', I did my very best to deliver – not generally to accommodate Basnett, more out of sheer affection for Neville.

Another who came under the GMWU's ambit was Alan Hadden, when the Boilermakers joined up with them to form the GMB in 1982. For a short time, it looked that either Neville or Alan would be lost to us, but a deal was done to keep them both on the NEC by keeping the two union sections separately represented.

Hadden was a devout Christian who took a strong stand on moral issues. For example, he would always fall out with McCluskie and I (we both came to own a National Hunt racehorse together) over blood sports. I was, however, always careful to avoid too much conflict, as Alan was a key member of the group. His vote could never be taken for granted, so it was always essential to discover his sticking points very carefully.

Syd Tierney of USDAW was easy to get on with despite his membership of Tribune at a time when this signified holding certain left wing beliefs rather than simply harbouring ambition. He had been asked by his General Secretary, who strongly backed the Loyalist Group, to give support. As a natural Labour loyalist himself, Syd readily agreed.

McCluskie's friendships and hatreds on the left made him much more unpredictable. I had to explore his attitude on every issue and discover what room he had to manoeuvre. His position was always important.

I remember once standing in 1980 on the steps of a large hotel at Brighton and being asked by Callaghan where I was going. 'To the dogs,' I replied.

Callaghan, ever the moralist, pulled a face of total disapproval. 'With Sam McCluskie', I continued. 'I need to talk to him.' 'Well, don't keep him waiting,' ordered Callaghan, the shrewd operator, 'Go quickly'. And I went, listened and made suggestions. Sam usually had to look over his shoulder at Jim Slater, his left wing union chief, but he would help when he could – if only by going missing.

Although we met from time to time, the Group's business was not done mainly that way. Progress was made slowly by my listening at length to each member either face to face or on the telephone, formulating a shoddy compromise that all could follow and then persuading them all to do so. Sometimes we met, sometimes not.

Certainly the Kogans' assertion in their book about the NEC – 'the trade unionists tended to come from the north and were not able to have pre-meetings because they could not get to them in time' – is just not true. Meetings were held, but kept very secret.[1]

My job as convenor was simple: to maximise the support for Callaghan and the Labour government. Mine was the job of trying to make sure that loyalists stayed for vital votes on the NEC and then voted as they had agreed. If there was no hope of winning a vote, my job was to prevent a decision from being made if at all possible.

Quite apart from coping with the diverse personalities within the Group, it seemed a thankless task. The left held all the chairmanships on the NEC and controlled the Secretariat and Research Department. Several on the right were either too shell-shocked, disillusioned or busy as ministers to give full support to the fight. And the battle was bitter, causing enormous stress to those involved. Occasionally, however, there were moments from the theatre of the absurd, which provided some light relief at least.

One of my favourites came at a meeting of the NEC's Home Policy Committee held in an unfamiliar room in the House of Commons. 'This won't take long,' said Chairman Benn, as he opened the meeting and the socialists round the table smiled knowingly at each other.

Two hours later the smiles had worn thin. I, being the only Labour member present among the socialists, insisted on giving the contemporary working-class view on every item at very great length. As I went on and on and on – and I am in the *Guinness Book of Records* as a champion filibusterer in the Commons – Benn huffed, puffed and tut-tutted. Heffer meanwhile decided to take tougher, direct action.

'I'm fed up of this f'n idiot. I'm going,' Eric said. True to his word, he gathered his papers and went to what he thought was the door. It was a cupboard and he banged it shut again. He tried again. Alas another cupboard! He then tried again and a broom fell out and hit him! Eric the red was no Robert the Bruce. 'Oh. F' it,' he wailed, 'I'm stopping after all.'

It was not the only such encounter of its kind. Michael Cocks, the Chief Whip, who had to sit through interminable NEC meetings as an observer, remembers the remorse that Heffer felt after one of these episodes. Eric, who had just promised to throw me out of a third-floor window, suddenly slumped on the table in front of him and put his head in his hands. 'And I went to church before I came here to pray to God that he would give me tolerance!' he wailed.

While such unaccustomed fightbacks disturbed some on the left, the Loyalist Group was still easily outnumbered and could, realistically, have little success – particularly as I did not want McCluskie to put his position at risk by too obvious support.

Small victories could be had, however – particularly when Lena Jeger or Judith Hart could be persuaded by Callaghan to break ranks. I once complained bitterly, indeed, that Jim was so used to being beaten, he sometimes caved in even when I had got him a majority!

Generally, however, it was so bad that the loyalists were genuinely surprised when they managed to persuade the NEC to pass a resolution supporting the Labour government on the day of the crucial vote of confidence in the House of Commons! The emergency resolution on the confidence vote, drafted by and in the names of McCluskie, Hadden, Tuck and Hough was carried unanimously even though it was a statement of loyalist rather than leftist belief.[2] We were also able to give valuable support to Callaghan over the manifesto. Although the Loyalist Group was in a small minority on the NEC, it had great power at joint meetings with the Cabinet.

On one issue I was unable to deliver. The troops could not agree with Callaghan's proposal to ditch the Conference policy of abolishing the House of Lords. Cocks had persuaded him that a Labour government would get nothing else done if we got bogged down with this.

For this reason and – perhaps to show electors he was not under the left's thumb – Jim felt very strongly. He abused the messenger (the fate of all messenger boys!) and then dug his heels in, refusing to include it in the manifesto. No one was prepared to take him on and Jim got away with it. This was to have reverberations later.

Although this has never been publicly acknowledged thus far, the creation of the Loyalist Group did give Callaghan greater strength in ensuring that the 1979 general election was fought on a realistic manifesto.

It was our tragedy that having a sensible manifesto was irrelevant to an electorate still stunned by the irresponsibility and thuggery of the Winter of Discontent.

FIVE

The Sad Farewell to Old Labour

The end of 'Old Labour' came on Wednesday, 28 March, 1979 with the defeat of Jim Callaghan's government in the House of Commons. Typically, Old Labour's 'Black Wednesday' began, true to form, with equally black comedy at a meeting of the NEC which took place in the TGWU's boardroom at Transport House.

While Rome burned, a discussion took place on the question – wait for it – of the enormous allowances being paid to Euro MPs. 'They ought to be paid into the Party,' suggested one member and a wave of righteous approval went through the room. 'That's a load of hypocrisy,' I said in my ever gentle, tactful manner. 'MPs at Westminster don't pay their House of Commons secretarial allowance into the Party. Some even pay it to their wives.'

The MPs present, unused to candour on the subject of their perks, changed the subject rapidly. I was about to have another go at the glaring gap between principle and practice on the left when I suddenly found the huge figure of Heffer looming over me. 'Take your jacket off and come outside,' he said. I, five-foot-six and a bit and definitely not Guards material, looked up, not realising that I had upset Eric bitterly because he himself employed his marvellous, long-suffering wife Doris as his secretary.

Just as I was about to explain that I had a doctor's note, I was saved by Lena Jeger. 'Eric,' she said, 'remember, we have a vote of confidence tonight and we need every vote.' Eric closed his eyes in pain, as he remembered how important it was for me to go on living, if only until 10 o'clock. Completely mortified, he mumbled 'F' it' and shambled back to his seat.

As it happened, Heffer could have knocked my block off and it wouldn't have made any difference. After a nerve-wracking day – and a debate in which Thatcher, to quote *The Times*, was 'astonishingly uninspiring', while Jim spoke with ease and conviction – we packed into the division lobbies.

'The result was in doubt until the last moment when the Speaker called for the division lobby doors to be closed,' as the *Guardian*'s Ian Aitken reported. 'Desperate efforts were made by Labour MPs and whips to persuade Frank Maguire, the Independent Republican member for Fermanagh, to go into the lobby on the Labour side. But he stood solidly behind the Speaker's chair rejecting all approaches. In the end he walked back into the chamber to resume his seat as a public abstainer. It was in effect his decision which settled the issue.'

After the vote, the huge Tory whip Spencer Le Marchant, lover of Buck's Fizz, bellowed in his usual fashion: 'The Ayes to the right 311, the Noes to the left 310' and we were forced into a general election. The Scottish Nationalists, who would certainly lose heavily in the election had, to use Jim's phrase, been turkeys voting for Christmas.

For the record, the voting breakdown was: Ayes–279 Conservative, 13 Liberal, 11 SNP, 8 Ulster Unionist, making 311; Noes–303 Labour, 2 Scottish Labour, 3 Plaid Cymru, 2 Ulster Unionist, making 310.[1]

Corals, the bookmakers, priced the Conservatives at 1–4 on to win the poll with Labour at 3–1. If there was any doubt an election was in the offing, it was dispelled by Callaghan, who revealed at the end of his speech in the Commons the generous increases in pensions due in November. Married couples were to get £4 and single people £2.50.

After surviving crisis after economic crisis, it was the self-inflicted wound of nationalism that brought us down. Whilst Scottish devolution had been a major manifesto commitment, the government failed to prevent rebels attaching a condition requiring at least 40 per cent of the Scottish electorate as a whole to vote in favour. The rebels were right in their assessment that this would kill off the project: when the referendum was held in March 1979, although a majority voted in favour, the 40 per cent condition was not met. Devolution hit the dust and the wrath of the Scottish Nationalists descended upon us. We were already extremely vulnerable because the Liberals – who had broken off the Lib–Lab pact – also wanted to go to the polls before the European elections in June and before the scandal of Jeremy Thorpe, their former leader, went before the courts.

Worn out by the events of the winter, Jim was getting more and more fed up and seemed inclined not to soldier on to October anyway – when our five years would have been up – even had we won the vote. He wanted an election in May, because he believed the country was becoming ungovernable. According to Donoughue, therefore, Jim did nothing to try and win the censure vote. Whether that is strictly true or not, he certainly did not pull out all the stops to make sure we won.

Roy Mason, the Northern Ireland Secretary who was the darling of the Prods, was told not to try and buy the Unionists off. Without their votes on the night, we couldn't win, because Gerry Fitt of the SDLP abstained and Frank Maguire, pressured by Gerry did likewise. It was rumoured that Gerry behaved in this way because Mason had refused on one occasion to speak to him on the telephone at some ungodly time in the early hours of the morning. It probably had more to do with his resentment that he couldn't get the necessary 100 Labour MPs to vote for a bill for proportional representation in Ireland.

Despite Jim's death wish, the whips under Cocks did their best and speculation mounted daily as to whether we would survive. Legend had it afterwards that it should have been a draw, but that the whips forgot to send an ambulance to bring a sick MP to the Commons. My friend Doc Broughton, however, had a heart attack the week before, was much too ill to be nodded through and died shortly afterwards.

The fact of an election was greeted with mixed feelings among Labour MPs. The atmosphere at Number 10, too, when Jim threw his farewell party for ministers was weird. Most of us listened, as Jim spoke standing on a chair, as though we were at a funeral. It was hard to shout approval with any enthusiasm.

When he called me over and told me that he had decided to put me in the Cabinet in charge of policy co-ordination if we won the general election, it sounded like someone promising to send you on holiday if they won the lottery.

I felt pleased that my skulduggery had been recognised, but knew that there was not a cat in hell's chance of our winning the general election. In the Department of Employment this view was shared strongly by Harold Walker, who announced that he was not going to leave a drop of the ministerial whisky for the incoming Tories and invited all our drivers and other personal staff to drink it dutifully there and then.

Some ministers were less sure. When I told Harold Lever shortly before-hand in his Eaton Square flat that, from my canvassing, I was certain we would be beaten, he expressed surprise. He told me he never went to his constituency until polling day and certainly never went canvassing in case the lady of the house resented being dragged away in the evening from her dolly tub. I will never know whether I was having my leg pulled or not.

Certainly, he could not have read the papers. At the beginning of April, a poll in the *Observer* gave the Tories a 21 per cent lead. Another, from London Weekend Television, put the Tory lead at a more modest 13 per cent – hardly comforting, though, as it was conducted in 100 marginal seats.

The Battle of the Manifesto

Callaghan went to the country fighting on the government's record and his own election address. Later among the left, the 1979 manifesto – 'the betrayal', as they saw it – assumed almost mythological status. How to draw it up was the issue of the most bitter dispute between Benn, Heffer and the loonies on the NEC and Callaghan and the bulk of the Cabinet. Later, many fictions were created about this process, fabrications later used by the left to try and change the whole basis of parliamentary democracy in our country. So it is time to redress the balance.

The Labour Party constitution laid down the process (and still does) in Clause V. First, Conference would decide by two-thirds majorities what would go into Labour's programme. Then the PLP and the NEC would determine which items in the programme would go into the manifesto. While the constitution was clear that both the PLP and the NEC were to be involved, it did not deal with the situation which arose in 1979 – where the NEC and the leadership of the PLP clashed head-on with irreconcilable objectives.

Benn and Heffer wanted to use the manifesto as a burning declaration of socialist faith, as a compendium of Conference and NEC decisions. In other words, they wanted a 'make-me-feel-good' document setting out their entire political philosophy.

Callaghan, on the other hand, wanted one which would attract public support and which, if elected, he could deliver. This was bound to lead to a much more cautious and realistic approach than that of Benn and Heffer, the Don Quixote and Sancho Panza of the Labour Party.

Bish, the Research Secretary, whose job it was to provide them with mangy horses and bent lances to go into battle with against the government, had already long started drafting the manifesto. Alerted to this, Jim made it clear to Benn that he didn't want the abolition of the House of Lords or a wealth tax in, but planning agreements – between the government and major companies – and industrial democracy should be included.

Heffer's reaction, in turn, was to go on the stump throughout the country demanding a left wing manifesto based on Labour's 1976 policy programme and the decisions of the last Party Conference.

He spelt out the demands of the left: higher public spending, especially on education and health, to bring down unemployment; an expanded role for the National Enterprise Board; an extension of planning agreements and tighter control over the City; abolition of the House of Lords and the strengthening of the Commons; a Freedom of Information Act; democratisation of the civil service; withdrawal from Europe, if changes were not made in the interests of Britain; genuine industrial democracy; and measures to protect the family. It was a popular campaign.

He pressed these proposals at a crucial meeting of the TUC–Labour Party Liaison Committee which took place in July, 1978.[2]

As is often the case, the meeting is best remembered for a violent clash of personalities, not least Eric, the punch-drunk pugilist. Just as he was in full flow over-nationalisation of construction, Jim butted in to tell him to make up his mind whether he wanted the wholesale nationalisation of the industry or just one firm.

This totally flummoxed Eric, who normally didn't bother himself with questions of detail. Jim, clearly on top, added that it was time Eric made up his mind whether he chose to support the Labour Party, with him or without him. Eric snapped back, telling Jim that he wasn't God, just a member of the Party and threatening to walk out.

Benn, almost certainly wanting his vote more than his voice, persuaded him to stay. Following this profound philosophical exchange, the question of the construction industry was dealt with by a fudge, which read simply: 'The public sector needs to create and extend its own capability to facilitate this'.

Callaghan was less successful in opposing Benn's support of the policy document 'Into the Eighties' and amendments tabled by the Home Policy Committee. Despite Scanlon's support for Jim in opposing the expansion of public services and Basnett's vote against more money for the National Enterprise Board, Benn was successful in pushing increased spending. It was also decided, against Jim's wishes, to increase the wealth tax and to abolish the House of Lords.

Benn's only setback was his failure to persuade the meeting of the need for the extension of planning agreements.

By September, Callaghan was putting a brave face on the defeat and consoling himself by arguing that in the coming election detailed policies would not be as important as attitudes and the issues of the day. The 'Into the Eighties' document would form the basis of the manifesto – and employment was the key issue.

To draw up the manifesto itself, eight small NEC–Cabinet working groups provided material for Bish's first draft, which incorporated the various policy decisions of Conference and the NEC. This then provided the basis for a new NEC–Cabinet Group on the manifesto, chaired by Frank Allaun.[3]

This group met almost weekly and had 11 meetings. Callaghan had a majority, but sadly the ministers often failed to turn up, so leaving the left to call the tune.

On 4 December, Bish produced his proposals for the manifesto, 'Keep Britain Labour', admitting that it was 'probably too ambitious, given the pressures both on the parliamentary timetable and on resources'.

On the day of the government's defeat on the confidence vote, the NEC decided to have a special meeting before the formal Clause V gathering to decide the final document. Before it, Jim told the Cabinet he didn't intend being worn to a frazzle by arguing with the NEC and hoped that other Cabinet members would accept some of the burden. He certainly didn't want the NEC to give instructions to a future Labour government and lay down detailed commitments.

He believed that the purpose of a manifesto was to appeal to the electors and give the general direction of policy. He made it clear that he was only going to have one Clause V meeting and that he was going to submit a draft manifesto himself. And abolition of the House of Lords would certainly be left out.

The special meeting of the NEC was held on 2 April, a strange event at which there was much ducking and weaving. Tuck and I, knowing full well that Jim didn't want Bish's document at any price, moved mischievously that: 'This document be remitted to the Chairman of the Party, the General Secretary and the Prime Minister to draw up a suitable draft for submission to the Clause V meeting'.

There was no chance of carrying this, but it started the ball rolling. Diplomatically, Jim said that while Bish's document was 'well-prepared', we really needed a much shorter one emphasising jobs, cutting inflation and dealing with union unrest by negotiation. This would counter the short Tory manifesto, which would focus on cutting taxes, taming the unions and asserting law and order.

And just by chance, Jim had one in his pocket, a third of the length of Bish's, in which the Leader avoided making firm commitments – a point Barbara Castle played hell about! Bish's socialist bible, on the other hand, seemed to include every decision of the Conference, the NEC and its sub-groups. This was despite the fact that Callaghan had told him to draw up the draft manifesto according to the rules, including therefore only those Conference decisions which had been passed by the requisite two–thirds majority.

Brushing the motion from Tuck and myself to one side, Heffer moved instead that Bish's document be shortened. At this Jim looked quite disconsolate. Clearly, we couldn't have two documents and he asked quite plaintively about his own. Following his performance at the TUC, I expected Jim to break out any minute and sing 'I took my harp to a party but nobody asked me to play'.

Things looked black until suddenly Heffer lost his nerve, moved that a small working party be set up and this was carried. Clearly, to stop the barmies, the make-up of this would be vital.

After much pushing and shoving, by 18 votes to 4 it was decided that the membership would be: the Party Leader, Deputy Leader, Allaun, Benn,

Healey, Heffer, Jeger, Tuck and the General Secretary – and that they would meet that very evening at 6.15 pm at Number 10.

Jim particularly wanted Jeger in because he knew he could rely on her when the chips were down. Indeed, he immediately arranged for David Lipsey to invite her to Number 10, place her comfortably in a sitting room, give her his manifesto and a bottle of whisky. After a few drinks and reading the draft she declared it to be completely satisfactory. In this way, Jim went into the meeting with a majority!

In addition, David Lipsey, Reg Underhill, Ron Hayward, Joyce Gould, Jennie Little, Geoff Bish and Tom McNally attended the meeting as observers. The Civil Service being on strike, they had to help themselves to drinks and wait for tea until midnight.

At the gathering, two drafts were presented: a shorter version of the Bish document and one drafted for Jim by McNally and Lipsey. On merit alone Jim's would have been the clear winner, but far more importantly for once Jim now had a majority. No wonder, then, that Bish's document was quickly pushed to one side and the other taken as the master.

While Benn then naturally tried to add everything from Bish back in, he just didn't have the skill to beat Jim who ran rings round him. McNally summed it up superbly by saying that: 'the meeting just went round Benn; he made statements but did not fight his corner, thus giving the impression that he was just making speeches to record for posterity'.

On a handful of subjects there was real disagreement. On the House of Lords, of course, there was a real bust-up with Jim saying he wouldn't budge, followed by Heffer once again parroting that Jim was just a member of the Party. The issue was put to one side, as was the subject of open government and Allaun's views on defence.

At midnight they sang Happy Birthday to Benn, though at this gathering for once he came away with very few presents.

The drafting committee met again on 4 April, but only minor changes were made before discussion at the full NEC–Cabinet 'Clause V' meeting at Number 10 two days later. There, only three issues remained outstanding: planning agreements, the construction industry and the fate of the House of Lords.

The meeting lasted a full eight hours nonetheless. After agreeing the title, 'The Labour way is the better way', Benn moved the inclusion of a big chunk of Labour's 1973 programme, saying that this was the only way to give the manifesto credibility. Jim resisted on the grounds that I strongly opposed this, countering that we had to proceed by agreement.

While this was news to me, I glared at the left in defiance nevertheless. I shifted from glares to grins at these meetings with an ease that would have done credit to Laurence Olivier. After Heffer, Kinnock, Skinner and Judith Hart had spoken in support of Benn, Jim – appearing to make a great concession – declared that he had now decided to include planning agreements. But there could, of course, be no detail because we hadn't reached any consensus on these at all.

Callaghan did, indeed, make many concessions and compromises at this meeting – far too many, I thought. I only discovered many years later that McNally, as Jim's adviser, had acted on the basis that they thought they were dealing with Benn's poodle. He did not know, as I had told Jim, that there were enough loyalist NEC votes in the bag to enable Jim to carry the Clause V meeting on most issues. I blame myself for not making sure that all in Jim's team knew that the loyalists would support him on most occasions.

There was, in any case, no problem with defence. Jim had already reached agreement on Polaris and accepted the words 'that there must be national debate on nuclear weapons'. Benn also managed to get a further commitment on nuclear safety.

On Europe, too, Jim himself was lukewarm and quite content to see Peter Shore and Benn overcome the resistance of David Owen and Bill Rodgers and therefore keep our commitment to strengthen the House of Commons against European legislation.

For whatever reason, Jim also compromised on limiting imports, Civil Service reform and putting in a commitment to a 'fundamental shift in the balance of power and wealth' (but leaving 'irreversible' out!).

And while fox-hunting went out (when it was discussed at the NEC, Castle actually argued in favour of hunting because the night before a fox had her chickens), deer-hunting went in.

Maynard's proposal to have the improvement of agricultural wages included was defeated on the grounds that this would mean statutory wages control and Jim resisted easily squashed proposals on banking put forward by the Militant Tony Saunois.

On the whole, however, the left did far better than I would have liked. Benn himself said at the time: 'It wasn't too bad really. I thought we'd done rather well.' And this from the man who later spoke as though this manifesto was a total betrayal of the Party and the working class!

The reality is that the only issue on which Callaghan flew in the face of the overwhelming majority was over the House of Lords. Those speaking in favour of Benn's proposals were Heffer, Kinnock, Skinner, Atkinson, Orme, Hoyle, Castle, Silkin, John Smith, Foot and Hadden. Only Jim, Shore, Cocks and I were against.

In the end, however, after several attempts the most the left could prise from Jim was a wording to the effect 'that the House of Lords is indefensible with its power and influence'.

I have listened to two theories why Jim was so pig-headed on this issue. McNally believes he wanted an issue on which to fight the left and show the electorate that he was not under the control of Benn and the NEC. Cocks, however, told me how he persuaded Jim that the issue would bog down the first year of a new parliament and was not worth the candle.

Whatever the reason, it was – as Jim later acknowledged – 'a mistake'.

In no way, however, was this sufficient to justify Benn's claim that: 'At the last minute on the night of 2 April, Number 10 had produced a new manifesto draft which the PLP had never seen and we had been told that the Party Leader would resign if he didn't get his way.'

Like other claims by Anthony Wedgwood Benn, it reads well, but it is demonstrably untrue.[4]

The General Election

Despite the Tories' runaway lead in the polls, Jim's personal popularity remained high, well ahead – thanks to Benn, Heffer and their acolytes – of that of his own Party.

He would never apologise for the record of the 1974–79 Labour government and had no reason to do so. Despite all the economic problems inherited from Ted Heath and Anthony Barber, the oil crisis and the lack of a parliamentary majority, the government had implemented a substantial proportion of its election promises.

Jim's letter to Labour candidates on 28 April, 1979 summed up his attitude to politics, which I supported wholeheartedly: 'As long as there are families struggling to make ends meet; men and women without jobs; children in need of better schools; sick people in need of better hospitals – then there is work for a Labour government and work for every candidate'.

And Jim Callaghan fought the 1979 general election well.

Law and order, an issue brought into its own by the Winter of Discontent, was clearly at the forefront of the campaign. It was an issue, indeed, which became even more the order of the day when Airey Neave, Mrs Thatcher's right hand man, was blown up by the IRA in the House of Commons car park just two days into the general election.

During the election campaign, major meetings were targeted by 'Troops Out' protesters, who were joined by other loony groups. On TV and in the press, these chaotic events reinforced the impression that anarchy was on the loose.

A riot in Southall on 23 April, caused by an attempt to stop a National Front march, led to the death of one protester, Blair Peach, injuries to 35 police and 340 arrests. Of course, Jim did everything possible to give the impression that he was in control, but in the aftermath of the Winter of Discontent, Thatcher used the riot as unmercifully as other Tories used the race card.

Jim bravely took the issue of breakdown with the unions head on, underlining the efforts we had made to reduce unemployment. The polls, however, were inconclusive as to whether Jim was making up any ground. He knew, and admitted privately, that the tide was against him.

If the 1979 general election was a difficult one for Jim, it was even harder for me. I was still in a daze, suffering deeply from the trauma of the death of my son Tom in the middle of March. Though I soldiered on in the Department of Employment and on the NEC, when it came to the general election, I only went through the motions of campaigning in Newcastle. There was no way I could enjoy the normal cut and thrust, as I usually did. And, for another thing, the overwhelming personal sympathy of the people in Newcastle made it quite impossible for me to conduct my normal street campaign. Of course, I still did some canvassing and knew right from the start that we were going to lose. There is one sure way to know how an election is going – listen to the children. In their shouts on the street, they reflect what their parents are saying in private.

Despite the ill omens, however, I did have a £500 bet with my Tory opponent Mrs Elsie Ashley that I would win in Newcastle-under-Lyme. At the time, I thought she was well off, but soon realised my mistake as many years later she still appeared to be saving up to pay me out.

As it turned out, I won more easily than I thought possible – by 4,228 votes. For once, watching the votes being counted on the tables was not too tense.

The results generally, however, were dismal. As Llin, my agent, and I listened huddling round radios at the count, we became more and more depressed. Shirley Williams at Hertford and Stevenage and Syd Tierney in Birmingham Yardley, a key member of the Loyalist Group, had both gone – as well as other good moderates Eric Moonman, John Tomlinson, Alan Williams and my travelling companions Bill Molloy and Bruce Grocott.

Not even the disproportionate defeat of left wing enemies cheered me up. Uncharacteristically I felt no glee as Doug Hoyle (Nelson and Colne), Margaret Jackson (later Beckett, Lincoln), Arthur Latham (Paddington), Tom Litterick (Selly Oak), Eddie Loyden (Garston), Max Madden (Sowerby), Brian Sedgemore (Luton West), Ron Thomas (Bristol North West) and Audrey Wise (Coventry South) all bit the dust.

Even if I had been doing the picking, I couldn't have done much better myself. But although they had brought defeat upon themselves, they had inflicted it on us moderates as well.

The Tories won with a 44-seat majority. There was nothing for it, but to go and clear my desk at the Department of Employment, say goodbye to my Irish driver Tess – whom I would miss more than my black car and red boxes – and settle back into opposition again.

The Inquest

The inquest was long and bitter. Indeed, it has not yet been closed by those of us who still comment cynically on the later progress in politics of the very people who helped to bring about Jim's crushing defeat.

Immediately after the election, the General Secretary Ron Hayward –

noting the loss of support among young people, many trade unionists and council house tenants – argued soberly that we needed to look at the views of the average British voter who does not belong to the Party and only supports us.

To those of us in the real world, it was hardly a revelation when he identified the things that mattered most to them: homes, education and law and order. As yet he was not blaming Callaghan's veto on Conference and NEC resolutions; this would come later, when he wanted support from the Party faithful.

A true picture, however, was already available from Bob Worcester of Mori, the pollster, a picture which confirmed Callaghan's assessment a few days before polling day that there had been a 'sea change' in the attitudes of the British voter.

This unforgiving new attitude made it impossible for Jim to win. It occurred because the Winter of Discontent was still vivid in people's minds. Above all, the unburied bodies created utter revulsion. The mass of the electorate became anti-union and sceptical of Labour. They reacted against the mindless fanaticism of the pickets and withdrew their support from the Labour movement as a whole.

People lost faith, too, in collective trade unionism. They were extremely receptive to suggestions that the unions had become too strong, that the union barons were nothing but bully boys and the force of law was necessary to bring them to heel.

But the Tory victory was won not only through revulsion against the Winter of Discontent. In the West Midlands, where people believed firmly in looking after themselves, the skilled – like the car workers – resented the way pay policy had narrowed earnings differentials.

As I was told quite bluntly in Newcastle-under-Lyme, the centre of my universe, there were very positive reasons, too, why the electorate voted for Thatcher. The Tories were united, whereas we were riven. Thatcher offered home ownership, controls on immigration, rolling back the state, sorting out the 'layabouts' and the like. She was masterly at appealing to the aspirations and prejudices of the skilled, respectable working class.

Council house tenants were delighted at the 'right to buy' at knock-down prices and bitter that Labour opposed this. Donoughue and his think tank had actually proposed this to the Labour government, but Peter Shore and others – myself included – had killed off the idea.

The electors had become disenchanted with public ownership and many later jumped at the chance to buy shares in privatised companies. Those of us who fought privatisation – and no one fought harder than I – gained little support.

Likewise, so many people supported the attacks on the welfare state. They believed and passed on the myth of the layabouts, spongeing off the state. Their views on immigration were racist. They wanted strong defence. They wanted a government which had the support of industry and finance. And above all, they responded enthusiastically to Thatcher's promise of 'less tax and more law and order'.

Amazingly, only months after the election, Labour did marvellously at the Southend-on-Sea by-election and in the polls until 1981. But, as the people moved to the right, the Party continued leftward. It was a parting of the ways which was to keep Labour out of power until 1997, when Tony Blair again caught the popular mood completely.

After the 1979 defeat, the first target of the left was, of course, not Thatcher, but Callaghan, the PLP and the right. They had to be scapegoated for imposing the right wing policies which, the loonies claimed, had caused the rout. Vicious, scurrilous speeches were made at the 1979 Annual Conference by the Party Chairman Frank Allaun. The election was lost, he squealed, 'because the parliamentary leadership ignored the wishes of both the TUC and Labour Party Conferences'. General Secretary Ron Hayward, while acknowledging the contribution of the Winter of Discontent, now put the blame squarely on the government.

The analysis of the left, as they poured odium on Jim, was miles from reality. They never explained why the electorate switched so markedly to Thatcher – in England, if not in Scotland. One of the great political mysteries of our time is how the left could conclude from her victory that what the British people wanted was more socialism! And yet that was the message of the left. We had lost, they declared, because we had not been socialist enough. In the Party and in the unions, the left could never come to terms with reality. They lived on another planet. They could not talk to the electorate in terms they could understand. So they could also not persuade people that what Thatcher was doing was wrong.

You only have to look at Heffer's press articles from the time to see their make-believe world. 'If the right wing, laissez-faire policies cannot solve Britain's problems, and I believe they cannot, then it will not be too long before capitalism is swept aside,' he wrote in the *Daily Telegraph*.[5]

The short answer was that it never would. But Eric and the comrades were too isolated to understand that. Instead of puzzling out how we could persuade the working class to support even moderate Labour policies rather than Thatcherism, they were hell bent on taking Labour even further left.

Heffer developed this theme in the *Morning Star* in a piece headed 'Tribune must push Labour to the left.'[6] In this piece of political claptrap, designed to appeal to his Trotskyite puppet masters in Liverpool, he argued that: 'One thing is relatively certain: the Labour Party, the unions and even the Parliamentary Labour Party are bound to move politically to the left. That is not because all the Labour Party and trade union leadership believes a leftward move is necessary – on the contrary, many of them do not – but because the circumstances of the Thatcher government will force them in a leftward direction.'

Heffer was right in one respect – the time of the left had come. But this was not due to any reaction against Thatcherism. It was down almost entirely to personalities within the Party and a reaction against the previous Labour government.

Indeed, even the PLP had moved to the left. At the election, several of the retiring trade union, working class right were replaced by left wingers nurtured in the new polytechnics, while other right wingers were defeated.

Whilst this shift in the PLP was relatively contained, the surge of left support in the unions and the CLPs was huge, boosting the left wing caucuses beavering away from within. Both the CLPD and Militant increased in size and significance.

Another new factional group, the Labour Co-ordinating Committee (LCC), formed in 1978, also took off – providing Benn with yet another platform and an extended web of contacts throughout the constituencies and trade unions working on his behalf. The LCC, under its Secretary Nigel Stanley, campaigned for the left's Alternative Economic Strategy and withdrawal from the Common Market. Its members believed that the Wilson and Callaghan governments had reneged on Labour's 1973 programme and that the Leadership needed to be forced back into the fold.

It gathered together Benn's apostles: Tony Banks, Stuart Holland, MP for Lambeth Vauxhall, Michael Meacher, Bob Cryer, MP for Keighley, Audrey Wise, Peter Hain, Frances Morrell, Chris Mullin and Stuart Weir, later the editor of *New Socialist*.

They were obviously born under a lucky star. Not only did the LCC get a grant from the Rowntree Foundation, but three of them became ministers in the 1997 New Labour government. Whether they ever visit Benn these days, I do not know.

Their newspaper, *Labour Activist*, was run by Benn's entourage – Frances Morrell, Francis Cripps, Bob Cryer and Michael Meacher among others. Benn claimed, indeed, that the LCC had replaced Tribune 'in a way' because it was broader and included people further to the left.

The LCC was an immediate success, confirming the strong appeal of the left wing factions. It attracted 250 people to its first conference in Glasgow and by November 1979 Benn could report that a weekend conference in Manchester had brought together 'a great gathering of the clans', about 600 in all, including Arthur Scargill as well as many of the apostles. Benn was delighted, indeed, that the legendary Chris Moncrieff of the Press Association and others from the media were also there.

By 1981, the LCC had 800 individual members and over 50 affiliated organisations. It was propagandist by nature, rather than plotting and organisational, and held conferences for trade unionists, attracting audiences a thousand strong. Tribune also joined, together with the Institute of Workers' Control, the Independent Labour Party (ILP), CLPD, and MPs such as Robin Cook, together with some of the 'off the wall' tendency like George Galloway.

Another crucial left wing group was the Rank and File Mobilising Committee which brought together an alphabet soup of factional left groups, including Militant, CLPD, Clause IV, NALSO (the National Association of Labour Student Organisations), Young Socialists, IWC, ILP, Broad Left and the Socialist Campaign for Labour Victory. It had a short life, however, because by mid-1981 Benn wanted to replace it with a wider body which brought in MPs, the union left and the constituency grass roots. Benn would find it much easier to exercise personal control over such a group.

But while Benn allowed it to exist, it did make its own singular contribution to the devastation of the Labour Party. It helped particularly to build the strength of the left in the unions. It politicised the small active minority, who enjoyed the buzz and adrenalin of the picket line, always a fertile ground for left splinter groups.

There was also a major move to the left among some of the trade union leadership, particularly in the public sector. Even among those not completely beyond the pale, like Basnett, there were bad memories of the bruising dished out by Healey and the Treasury.

I had, indeed, experienced myself the difficulty of working with Joel Barnett, Healey's number two. One day, in the members dining room in the Commons, he told me that he was going to move in Cabinet to end the Temporary Employment Subsidy scheme (TES), which was my pride and joy.

I pointed out to him its advantages, paying money to employers to keep on workers they would otherwise have to sack. But he was adamant: 'It has to go.' All looked lost until a few days later he told me that a factory, where his constituents but also several delegates to his local party worked, was going to declare massive redundancies. 'Could I help?'. I told him sure, if the TES survived. He responded that officials had told him that the rules of the TES did not cover the situation. I looked at him with the pity of someone who knows that rules can always be altered and promised to make a visit immediately.

It was almost stranger than fiction. I was negotiating on the phone with the factory owners in Chicago, while telling officials that the rules now were irrelevant, because they would be changed – following, of course, all the correct procedures – when I got back to London. In the event, the jobs were saved, the union men continued to support Joel in his local party and he never once raised the question of abolishing TES ever again. Mind you, he didn't need to: it was later destroyed by Brussels.

But not everyone had my luck in dealing with Barnett or Healey. They usually rode roughshod over all opposition. Those battles, involving personality, had important consequences, costing Healey the Leadership because of his brutality. They did not have the same significance, however, as the clash of dogmas. For unionists of the left, such as NUPE's Alan Fisher, the antagonism to the Labour parliamentary Leadership arose out of deep doctrinal differences and the belief that they were engaged in some sort of Holy War.

NUPE, in particular – which never gave recognition to the fact that the £6 wage policy had given them double anything that had gone before – had fought the 5 per cent target and cuts to record public expenditure as crusades. As one NUPE leader put it to Llin (who was a NUPE steward at the time): 'We are going to teach them a lesson.'

This vicious vendetta against the leadership not only cost us the 1979 election and NUPE's membership dear, it also lost Labour several more general elections to come.

SIX

Leave Thatcher, We'll Get Callaghan First

Following the defeat in the general election, we should have picked ourselves up and sorted ourselves out. Instead we stayed on the floor, kicking hell out of each other, while Thatcher walked all over us.

Because of divisions in the Party and the electorate's swing to the right, it was difficult to mount an effective campaign against the Thatcher government.

The Party and the unions' response was totally ineffective. While some measures such as the sale of council houses, the privatisation of nationalised industries and the curbing of the trade unions had considerable support, in other respects her government was a failure. Her record on unemployment was deplorable, taxation rose, she ruled over a divided Cabinet and had to face riots in Brixton, Toxteth, Moss Side and St Paul's in Bristol.

With Callaghan, Labour MPs worked hard in parliament to fight her. Whatever the effort, however, the average Party activist was generally more interested in attacking the PLP and its Leadership than in savaging the Tories. Labour's civil war, of course, was far more newsworthy than worthy speeches from the opposition benches. And voters were simply put off even more by the venom of the left's attacks.

There were serious differences, too, about how Thatcherism should be fought. Callaghan put the view held by the majority of the PLP: that everything must be done constitutionally. The extreme left would not accept this and they said so, in loud, strident speeches.

Thatcher, too, was hardly going to help heal Labour's wounds. Shortly after the election, for example, NEC members met representatives from North East Derbyshire CLP to discuss the Clay Cross councillors, who had been disqualified from holding office. The NEC was persuaded that, on their discharge from bankruptcy, the councillors should be able to hold office again. Daft as brushes, they decided to ask Thatcher's government to back legislation to this end. They might as well have asked her to nationalise the City of London.

As for action outside the law, Benn saw the big hole being dug for him and as always opted for a smoke screen. 'The key to it all' he said, 'was future policy. People want to know what a Labour government would do. Then the question of the law would fade into insignificance, because it wasn't the major issue.'

Other lefties, however, showed that – policy, present or future – the question of obeying was simply of no importance to them. Take Norman Atkinson, for example: 'If you support the law you simply become the agent of the Tories; therefore we have to explore alternatives.' The Militant Tony Saunois put it more bluntly: 'If councils are faced with the choice of being an agent of the Tories or opposing the law, then they should oppose the law.'

Hattersley, Kinnock and Stan Orme made it clear that they could not follow the Militant line and lead people into breaking the law. As ever, Healey put the case most forcefully, pointing out that there were two Conference resolutions making it clear that we should obey the law.

Not that Denis swore by Conference decisions. He regarded them merely as declarations of opinion. For him the practical arguments were crucial – the Tories would deflect public anger against the law breakers and also, if we destroyed respect for the law, then law-breaking would be used against us when we won.

Jim summarised the moderates' argument succinctly: we would encourage the maximum resistance and act with maximum vigour, but within the law.

But it was not only on councils, in local parties and on the NEC that there was division: it was also true within the PLP. Right and left united against Kinnock's decision, as Shadow Education Spokesman, not to commit Labour to restoring free school dinners, milk and transport. But we split completely over Les Huckfield's campaign to secure the re-instatement of Red Robbo, the fiery convenor sacked by British Leyland for advocating strike action.

Robbo's union, the AUEW, certainly objected to Huckfield poking his nose in. The NEC in December, 1979, however, called for Red Robbo to be re-instated, a motion passed against Callaghan's wishes. Thus Labour also came to be seen as supporting the disruption of the car industry.[1]

The Party was also in a sorry financial state and riven by Benn and the left's determination to change the rules for electing the Leader and to clear out the right on the PLP with mandatory reselection of MPs as soon as possible.

Saint Basnett tries again

It was not, however, that we moderates were entirely without allies. David Basnett, in particular, had been doing his busy-bodying best. He revived plans for a special Commission of Enquiry on the big constitutional questions and with Clive Jenkins and Moss Evans brought together the unions to discuss party finances.

As Political Officer of the POEU, I attended these meetings with Bryan Stanley, my General Secretary. I remember this crew sitting on the top table looking like prosperous undertakers. Appropriately, they recruited a couple of helpers, Fred Jarvest of the GMWU and Fred Moss, the Treasurer of the UCW, who spoke in low voices and looked for all the world like pall bearers.

Their job was to sort out the sorry mess by raising more money from the unions and re-organising the chaotic financial controls. They hardly inspired confidence, however, at those meetings in smoke-filled hotel rooms. Not only was there a total absence of charisma at that top table, there was also a complete lack of humour. I remember these meetings as some of the grimmest I have ever attended.

Many on the right despised Basnett and certainly distrusted Jenkins. Jarvest and Moss on the other hand were solid, reliable men, but did not have the flair to deal with the situation successfully. Basnett and Jenkins wanted to fund a massive increase in union affiliation fees and high contributions to political funds. Seeing them forced to retreat was not a pretty sight.

Union opposition stemmed not only from a reluctance to hand over members' money to a crackpot NEC. Influence and control of Labour's

Annual Conference was at stake. Politically, it was unacceptable to those with little money in their political funds – such as the AUEW – to have to reduce the numbers with which they were affiliated, and hence their voting strength, to meet the cost of higher affiliation fees.

There was another very good reason for resisting change. Arguments about the political fund could lead to an increase in the level of members opting out. Bryan Stanley and I were the only union officers at these meetings with recent experience of establishing a political fund. We knew that if the question was raised again, many sane, ordinary members would tell us they weren't going to pay anything to support a Labour Party with Benn there at the top.

As ever, the best approach was 'softly, softly'. And so the Party had to wait. Many union leaders also wanted a softly, softly approach to the constitutional changes pursued by the left. In truth, some of us wanted a 'never, never' approach.

Basnett and his allies shared our concerns at the NEC's readiness to bulldoze through changes for reselection of MPs, election of the Leader and the control of the manifesto by the NEC. They believed all this should be discussed with the unions until a consensus emerged. So the idea of a new Commission of Enquiry was put to the NEC, which was asked to shelve the proposed constitutional changes.

Dennis Skinner and Tony Saunois, thinking it a right wing plot, tried to kill it off from the start. Benn and Heffer, however, knowing it had the support of influential members of the TUC left, were frightened to move against at that stage.

When it came to the NEC, there was the usual manoeuvring. The loyalists failed to get full support; Heffer failed to wreck the project; and it was agreed to meet the General Secretaries. After that meeting the Organisation Committee agreed to an enquiry that would cover Party membership, improvement of finances, general and Euro-election campaigning and organisation of the Party.

The left amended the proposals, however, so that the three big constitutional issues – reselection, the Leadership and the manifesto – would not be left to the Commission but to the 1979 Conference.[2]

Kinnock and Benn added also a provision 'to bring forward proposals to ensure that the Party is open, democratic and accountable at all levels: and to ensure that all levels of the Party leadership, and all aspects of the work of the Party are fully accountable and responsive to the wishes of the membership'.

Despite opposition, it was decided that a paper prepared by Benn and Heffer should be the basis of discussion for the Commission. The left did not want this enquiry but they could not get out of it. It was a case of no enquiry – no increase in affiliation fees. They did, however, put Basnett's nose out of joint by insisting that the constitutional changes should go ahead at the 1979 Annual Conference.

When I think of that Conference, held in Brighton under the dreadful chairmanship of Frank Allaun, I only console myself that I am not back there in reality. It was yet another blow for common sense. CLPD, in particular, had exploited the Party's post-election demoralisation to ensure that delegates and motions alike were hostile to the right. The whole atmosphere was poisoned by the whipped-up hatred towards Callaghan and the parliamentary Party.

CLPD managed, thanks to delegates following their 'slate', to keep a left-wing NEC. Indeed, if anything it became worse, as Jo Richardson replaced Barbara Castle who had stepped down to lead Labour's Euro MPs. Castle had fought Callaghan out of malice for what he had done to her during the 1960s dispute over *In Place of Strife*. But Richardson, Ian Mikardo's sombre, ruthless, hard stick of a secretary, needed no such personal motivation. She appeared genetically programmed to destroy.

But it was not only in the NEC elections that CLPD's left wing fixers triumphed. Hitherto, they had been prevented from getting immediate control over the PLP, via reselection of MPs, by the so-called 'Three Year Rule'. Introduced in 1968, this said that to change the constitution you needed to propose amendments one year in advance and that any defeated amendment could not be raised for another 3 years.

For the left, of course, there was only one thing for it – get rid of the rule. They drew up a battle plan and circulated it to their troops. And Benn was quite ruthless in ensuring that support was given by the left on the NEC to the CLPD's scheming. The Party's Conference Arrangements Committee (CAC) protested that the NEC was indulging in lots of sharp practice. But this made little difference. The NEC continued to present documents making policy to the Conference. And when the CAC declared that the nomination of Margaret Beckett was invalid as she could only be nominated by her own local party, the left on the NEC pointed out that an announcement in *Labour Weekly* had made it quite clear that the former Margaret Jackson had, indeed, moved to live in Manchester on getting married. With total disregard for the rules, the NEC had her declared a valid constituency delegate and therefore eligible for the NEC.

As a result of the combined scheming of Benn and CLPD, bitter debates ended with victory for the left. The three-year rule was abolished and mandatory reselection of MPs introduced. Although they failed to get all they wanted, they had won the crucial ability to pursue their destabilising guerrilla war – to press for change year-in year-out, with all the damage this was to bring.

Clear the Right Out – Mandatory Reselection of MPs

At Conference, the left fixers were particularly ecstatic at winning the battle over reselection. Soon, they calculated, they would be able to throw out all the right wing MPs loyal to Callaghan and Healey and replace them with stooges for Benn, Militant and all the left splinter groups. This design, of course, in those days may well have been helpful not only to Benn, but to others on the left who harboured dreams of Number 10 such as Heffer (you must be joking!) and Kinnock.

A number of arrogant and disloyal Labour MPs had also made it easy for the left to get support. Bitterness among activists had been growing since Dick Taverne was deselected in 1972 and then stood against Labour in Lincoln in 1973. Reg Prentice had joined the Tories and Roy Jenkins and David Marquand had gone to Europe.

The names of Ray Gunter, Christopher Mayhew, Lord Chalfont, George Brown and Richard Marsh were also raised whenever the subject of betrayal was raised. Other MPs caused resentment because they felt little obligation to their local parties or constituencies. Chris Mullin – the co-author of the seminal pamphlet *How to Select or Reselect Your MP* – came to support reselection because his MP, George Strauss, had little contact with the constituency. Mandatory reselection of MPs had long been the left's Holy Grail. As far back as 1974, CLPD had secured two million votes for a resolution at Conference moved by Ken Coates. It was defeated, but they continually organised motions, which were rejected with regularity under the three-year rule.

Three years later, in 1977, the noose tightened further. All the pressure helped get a motion 'remitted' – a halfway house, meaning it was neither passed nor defeated, but left on the table – with an assurance from the NEC that something would be done. At the time the debate was fuelled by the controversy raging over the deselection of Reg Prentice, who had supported the Tory prosecution of the Shrewsbury pickets.

As good as its word, the NEC established a working party, chaired by Bryan Stanley and including Heffer and leading union luminaries, to discuss the question.[3]

On the Committee, Ian Mikardo – who had himself first supported mandatory reselection as far back as 1972 – proposed a middle way, which the majority accepted. Under the so-called 'Mikardo Compromise', constituencies would no longer be allowed just to hold an adoption meeting after an election had been called, but would have to decide well before whether to have a full reselection for their MP or not.

Under the rule, not less than 18 months and not more than three years after the election, they would have to call a meeting to decide whether or not the MP should be selected as the parliamentary candidate at the next general election. If the meeting decided 'yes', that would be the end of the matter, unless new circumstances arose which the NEC agreed merited a fresh decision. If they decided 'no', a full selection conference would be held, at which the sitting MP would be considered with others.

Shirley Williams believed that the crucial thing about the compromise was that all power was taken away from the NEC, except as a ringmaster upholding the rules.

While the majority of the working party accepted this formula, lefties including Richardson, were opposed because it did not force competitive reselection on CLPs.

Heffer ostensibly had other reasons to fight it. He believed CLPs should have the right to deselect their MP at any time and not only when the NEC agreed. This was probably a typical Eric switch. Having arrived at a sensible compromise, Militant on Merseyside will have leant on him to renege and he had to find some other reason for opposing.

In the event the left on the full NEC – under CLPD pressure – supported the minority, threw out the compromise and plumped for mandatory reselection whether constituencies liked it or not.

The left fixers' revenge on Mikardo was swift. At the 1978 Conference, he was voted off the NEC for having proposed his 'middle way' in the first place. But the NEC's line was overturned on the Conference floor, his compromise endorsed and the relevant constitutional amendments carried.

The fly in the ointment, however, was that this only happened because Hugh Scanlon had cast the AEU block vote against the decision of his own delegation and then claimed that he was confused. The Conference chair, knowing that union leaders live their whole lives in confusion, refused to allow another vote – otherwise the precedent would have been horrendous!

The fly, however, was not allowed to stay for long. Benn, like everyone else, treated Conference decisions with total abandon and was determined that Mikardo's compromise should receive short shrift from the organised left. He and the comrades were determined to fight, fight and fight again. It was imperative for his own leadership ambitions to bring the PLP to heel and he knew that the Mikardo formula would leave most right wing Labour MPs in place because they were conscientious, hard working and got on well with their local parties.

The left were helped in their manoeuvrings by a loophole in the 'three-year rule'. While this debarred the same constitutional changes being taken every year, it could be waived if the NEC declared a matter to be of immediate importance.

Although by no stretch of the imagination could reselection be seen as an 'emergency' matter, Allaun got the NEC's Organisation Committee to declare it as such. Although he failed at the full NEC to get this endorsed, it was decided to see what the Conference Arrangements Committee thought of the proposal.

A meeting was arranged, but then deferred because of the general election until 5 July, 1979. In the meantime, however, Tony Saunois, the tiny Trot, and Kinnock decided it was too risky to put it to outsiders on the CAC.

So instead they had passed a pre-emptive resolution at the June Organisation Committee meeting to waive the three-year rule and allow mandatory reselection and the method of selecting the leader to be taken at the coming Conference as matters of immediate importance.

Shirley Williams and I huffed and puffed, but were predictably unsuccessful. Even with the agreement of Kinnock, who did a somersault on this, we failed to get the question of the Leadership excluded and the whole thing went to the full NEC again.

As the NEC had previously decided on talks with the CAC, we hoped that the decision would be deferred until 5 July. No such luck. Despite our continued opposition, this time the NEC endorsed the taking of reselection at the 1979 Conference by 17 votes to 9 and the election of the Leader by 14 to 11 votes.

Why the abrupt *volte face*? Doubtlessly the fixers in the CLPD had put the frighteners on the left, reminding them they were putting their own re-election at Conference at risk. A big change had taken place. In the past NEC members would have been more concerned to placate the union barons with their block votes. Now they were more frightened of CLPD and already haunted by the ghost of Ian Mikardo!

Desperate to elect a Leader under more favourable rules and to clear out the PLP as soon as possible, the left on the NEC brazenly stuck two fingers up to the barons and Basnett's great Commission of Enquiry. Benn, indeed, also wanted control of the manifesto, but hadn't quite yet got a majority for this on the NEC. So Basnett found himself outflanked, as the left knew they could do. Except in films – and in 'New Labour', insists Llin, ever the hyper-loyalist, holding a gun to my head – the softies usually bite the dust first. The left's certainty stemmed from the headway they and their allies, CLPD and Militant, had made in the unions themselves.

In the good old days, for example, the TGWU General Secretary was all powerful. Now, however, it did not matter to the left that Moss Evans had supported the Mikardo compromise, wanted a consensus on the question of the Leadership and was sceptical about NEC control of the manifesto. Whatever Moss had said or thought, the left knew that with the help of his Assistant General Secretary Alex Kitson and Executive member Brian Nicholson, they could deliver the TGWU vote against Evans' better judgement.

CLPD could also rely on a number of other unions including NUPE, ASTMS, ASLEF and SOGAT. At NUPE, Alan Fisher and Bernard Dix not only helped by allowing CLPD to be run from the union's HQ, but also by substantially increasing their affiliation by 100,000 and therefore their vote at the Labour Party Conference.

Without this increase in the NUPE voting strength, indeed, the resolution which proposed changes to the election of the Leader would not have been carried.

The left fixers thus outmanoeuvred not only the right, but also those union leaders who supported Callaghan.

Jim's view that the Commission should first settle the relationship between the NEC, the Leadership of the PLP and the unions and only when this had been done should the Party go on to take decisions about 'election of leaders, control of the manifesto, reselection and so on'. 'These questions', he believed, 'are important but it is illogical, in my view, to take the decisions first and then ask a committee of enquiry to look into them afterwards.'

Blood on the Carpet: the 1979 Conference

Callaghan was right, of course, but he may as well have saved his breath. Logic was not to be allowed to have anything to do with it. The left were determined to take complete and unchallenged control and on that Black Tuesday at Conference, their steam roller was set moving by the delegate from Rochester and Chatham, Gordon Monsarratt, who first moved the proposition to set aside the three-year rule:

'The simple reform we are proposing would make the parliamentary party automatically accountable to the rank and file and thus help to ensure that any further Labour governments shall follow Labour Party policy. And this means policies decided by you, by Annual Conference,' he puffed.

The delegate from Tottenham, Allan Barclay, trotted out the standard line on mandatory reselection: 'You may say, what if the constituency party is happy with its MP? OK, there is nothing to stop that party, its affiliated organisations, making one nomination to the selection conference, and if more than one nomination comes, then it shows they need a reselection procedure.'

'I come from a constituency party which has an MP, Norman Atkinson on the platform, and Norman will be pleased to know and Conference will be delighted that there are no plans to get rid of him.' Sadly, this sentiment was not put to the vote, but it should be recorded that eventually Norman was deselected after boundary changes.

With the hatred that had been whipped up, Conference inevitably agreed to waive the three-year rule. The subsequent debate on reselection would be highly charged with emotion on both sides.

Already, the atmosphere had been poisoned by Ron Hayward. In a wicked, irresponsible speech he said, to applause:

> I still say that we did not – and you over there did not – select, raise the money, work to send an MP to the House of Commons to forget whence he came and whom he represents. I read all the papers. One I read the other day . . . that one MP said: 'If I do not get my way at this Conference, I will resign'. I have got some advice for them. Do not worry about that. I have got a queue a mile long that wants to go to the House of Commons [laughter and applause]. It is a very short queue that wants to be Branch Secretary.

Pat Wall, a Militant from Shipley, appealed strongly to the constituencies. 'Any Labour MP or representative who represents the interests of working people, who stands at their shoulders and fights for them and who fights to change this society, has absolutely nothing to fear from the constituencies or the ranks of the movement.' I have no doubt that Frank Hooley – the hardworking, idealist MP for Sheffield Heeley, who was among the first to lose his seat through deselection – joined with the constituency party delegates in cheering these remarks to the roof.

When the Militant Derek Hatton took the microphone, he was as always dressed to kill: 'Only when the rank and file feel that their elected representatives are accountable with, of course, a socialist programme can the Party really grow,' he crowed.

Mikardo, meanwhile, appeared in sackcloth and ashes, no doubt hoping for forgiveness and re-instatement as a guru of the left, as he spoke out in favour of abandoning his compromise without so much as batting an eyelid. 'If these changes are not made today, they will be made next year. If they are not made next year, they will be made the year after, and if they are not made

Jim before you and I have disappeared from the political scene, they will be made not long after.'

One by one, speakers ranted over the defections of Labour MPs and the 'failures of the Labour government'. As delegates applauded, MPs huddled together in their seats in the hall, feeling more and more resentful at the total misrepresentation of their commitment to the cause. The vast majority had worked hard for Labour all their lives and yet were now subject to vicious attacks from many who had done far less. As I watched their disconsolate faces, my mind went back to a PLP meeting, at which I rammed home the realities of mandatory reselection. Benn, describing me as a 'real tough cookie', noted in his Diary that this was one of the most remarkable speeches he had heard in his 28 years in parliament.

It certainly made an impact. As I revealed with brutal frankness how to get Labour parliamentary candidates selected, the atmosphere in the packed Committee Room in the House of Commons became quite electric. I told how, as Political Officer of the POEU, I had organised – that is to say 'fixed' – more selection conferences than anyone in the room bar the General Secretary and National Agent by 'packing' them.

In Newcastle under-Lyme, I had been selected only because delegates had been recruited and placed on to the GMC solely to vote for me. It was normal practice. Selection conferences were fixed everywhere, although perhaps not as thoroughly as my friend Reg Barnes had done in Newcastle.

Benn reported that laughter turned to gasps of astonishment, when I promised that if mandatory reselection were introduced, we fixers would certainly set about packing all GMCs to ensure that our people were re-selected. I did not want reselection, however, because constituencies would take two years or so to recover from the conflict. The parliamentary Party was already divided into factions and we didn't want that situation extended deeper into the constituencies. I was also concerned about union representation in parliament and promised to protect the union seats from the media men, lecturers and lawyers. I warned, too, that the people who would suffer from reselection were not the organisers, the fixers – who would thrive under such a system – but the idealists. They would not know how to protect themselves. And I ended by proposing that if reselection were introduced, the vote should be given to all the members of a constituency party (as it eventually was), not just the few who got on to the GMC.

In his Diaries, Benn remarked how people laughed as I spelt out the realities of life. If I had been a left winger, he said, the place would have been in uproar. 'But the cynicism was such that that the Party just took it.'

While my speech was appreciated by many, it also upset quite a number. I remember Charlie Morris of the Union of Communication Workers (UCW) telling me immediately afterwards that it was disgraceful. Later, I reminded him of this every time I saw him, because later, after boundary changes, he was carved up by supporters of Michael Meacher. A little more attention to the realities of life would have kept him in parliament.

The speech also upset Michael Foot very much. While he would quite happily 'make arrangements' at dinner and write letters of accommodation to Benn, he didn't like to hear the truth of Labour politics spelt out so starkly. For many, however, the speech was helpful, prompting them to troop one after another to ask me how they should protect themselves. They would, indeed, busily take notes as I sat patiently in the House of Commons tea room explaining how to defend yourself by getting friendly trade union branches to affiliate, recruiting members and ensuring that they became delegates to their local GMC.

Indeed, I held seminars in the tea room on how to change unfriendly GMCs to the advantage of the right, long before Chris Mullin (assisted by Charlotte Atkins, who had been asked by Patricia Hewitt to do it) issued the 1980 pamphlet: *How to select or reselect your MP*, with its tests of purity on MPs' attitudes to EEC membership, pay policy, economic policies following the IMF loan, defence spending, abolition of House of Lords and the Prevention of Terrorism Act.

While incidentally this pamphlet upset Tribune, it pleased me greatly, as by failing on every count I was able to use it to demonstrate my unswerving loyalty to Labour! But this was 1979 and the left were not interested in reality. Even Callaghan did not reveal his great worry that mandatory reselection would be abused by Militant, who had been making great inroads in the inner city areas. He had insisted at the NEC that his opposition to the motion be recorded. But at Conference, he was far more conciliatory than I had been in the tea room.

'I do not believe that it is going to have too much effect on the security of sitting Members of Parliament. It may have some effect in a small number of cases,' Jim said. 'I think most Members of Parliament will win the day – but I think it will mean that GMCs will be much more divided: it will make it much easier for carpet baggers and factions to grow up.'

'If Members of Parliament become more responsive to their constituencies they may become less responsive to the whip in the House of Commons and even to the National Executive Committee,' Jim continued. 'The effect of what you are going to do will be to strengthen local party control and weaken central party control . . . The Party should consider very carefully before it factionalises into 635 pieces.'

Far more forceful speeches were made by moderate union leaders. Norman Stagg of the Postalworkers, a stocky belligerent full time official, pointed out that the left had not accepted the previous year's Conference decision and that we ought to put the issue to a Committee of Enquiry.

It was Bryan Stanley's speech, however, that was to haunt the left in the coming year. Having had the same teacher as I in the POEU, Charlie Morgan, he had checked the rules. He attacked the NEC for setting aside the party constitution and taking ill-thought out decisions. 'You have not followed it through in the rules for the constituency parties, you have not followed it through in the proper, carefully thought out way that the constitution provides for by making provision for one year's delay.' Despite Stanley's warning, Conference decided to take an immediate decision, waiving the three-year rule, and voted by a two million majority to introduce mandatory reselection.

'The right are furious about their defeat,' Benn crowed in his Diaries. 'Even if the election of the Leader is left to the PLP, mandatory reselection changes the whole balance of power in the Party. I don't see why we should be bullied any more by the union leaders. They got it wrong and they have to accept that the Party is entrusted to the NEC. We desperately need their money but they desperately need the Party.'[4]

A Brief Stay of Execution

As always, however, it was the left that got it wrong. Stanley had, of course, been absolutely right. Once again it had been shown that the Party could not be entrusted to the existing NEC when shortly after Conference, at the November Organisation Committee, it was reported that legal advice had supported Bryan's view. The amended rules contained so many inconsistencies and anomalies, that reselection would have to be deferred until the rules had been corrected at the 1980 Conference.

The faces of the left – there in force to re-elect Heffer as chairman – were a picture as they saw the broad grin come across my face and stay there to taunt them. The evil goblin, as they saw me, had triumphed against the odds again. Playing for time, they 'resolved that 'this committee, in pursuit of the Conference decision and being anxious to put it into effect, considers that this item should deferred for one month pending the receipt of Counsel's opinion and also opinions of other Labour members of the legal profession in the House of Commons.'

In other words, they would scour the endless corridors of Westminster trying to unearth a lawyer who would give them a way out.

For the left, matters got even worse when they were told in late November that this frantic search had only succeeded in revealing the fact that, because of the defects in the rule changes, any member de-selected would be able to take the Party to court. On hearing this good news I didn't need to say anything – my goblin's grin told it all.

After more desperate manoeuvring by the left, in February advice from an eminent QC – doubtlessly charging more than Bryan Stanley – settled the matter once and for all.[5] And so the left on the NEC had to face the humiliation of taking new rule changes to Conference. The matter would have to be debated again at the 1980 Conference. It was a respite – a brief one, as it turned out – but in those dark days, we champions of common sense were glad of any breathing space we could get.

Chaos in the Country

In the country in response to Thatcher, meanwhile, the division between right and left was at its sharpest on local councils. Expulsions of lefties from moderate Labour groups became almost commonplace as hardliners defied decisions to set legal budgets. By June 1980, the strife was severe enough for the Party's General Secretary, Ron Hayward, to send a letter full of wishy-washy claptrap urging flexibility by moderate majorities and the use of discipline as a last resort.[6]

After this self-deluding nonsense, the National Agent David Hughes presented another paper to the July Organisation Committee on 'Labour Group Discipline', which included a recommendation that there be no change to standing orders – that it should still be possible to discipline councillors who did not support Labour group policies. Shirley Williams and I tried to get this accepted, but were defeated by three votes to seven.

In truth, we were merely going through the motions because Benn had put in a list of amendments which were designed to undermine council leaders and Labour group majorities. Under his proposals all local government policy would be determined by the local Labour party and it would be for councillors just to implement it.

Additionally, it would be for the local party to choose by secret ballot who to nominate for civic offices and council committees. The left on the committee not only bumped these amendments through but also agreed to a further one put by Tony Saunois that the Leader and Deputy Leader of the Labour group should be elected annually by the local party.

The effect, of course, would have been to pass complete power over to unelected party activists. Had this happened, it would have been a total disaster for Labour in local government. For once, however, the reaction was so violent that Benn retreated and actually moved himself that these proposals lie on the table – which was carried by 23 votes to 1.

As a face-saver, later Benn successfully moved that he, Eric Heffer, Doug Hoyle, Joan Maynard and Shirley Williams plus party officers meet to consider the Model Standing Orders for Labour Groups.[7] Clearly, no-one was in any hurry to pick up this hot chestnut again because in November it was resolved that the sub-committee formed to consider this subject should meet and report back. I cannot remember that it ever did.

Benn had in any case taken another tack, by putting a paper on tolerance within the Labour Party to the NEC, but we will deal with this elsewhere.

The May local election results gave indications of the bleak future facing Labour. The initial reaction was that we had done well: 'Maggie takes a beating,' cried the *Daily Mirror*. By the Saturday, however, we realised that although we had done well in the North and Midlands, we had been wiped out in large parts of the South. Tactical voting for the Liberals had reared its ugly head.

Ron Hayward claimed that the local election results showed that people preferred rates increases to cuts in public services. 'That is our democratic socialist aim and we must not be afraid of stating it. Nor must we be afraid of stating that higher taxation and rates are necessary in order to finance the level of public expenditure we want to see devoted to our community services.'

The public mood, however, was hardly encouraging. The TUC's Day of Action on 14 May was a huge flop and Labour's Special Wembley Conference on 31 May, 1980 on fighting the Tories was an even bigger damp squib.

Indeed, we nearly didn't have it. When the letter from the TGWU – expressing concern about the Tory government's policies and urging a special conference as soon as possible – was put before the March NEC, I tried to make it 'a popular demonstration' and argued that the money could be better spent elsewhere. The vote on this was tied 10–10 and was lost only on the chairman, Lena Jeger's, casting vote. Who had provided the whisky this time, I asked myself!

At this time Benn, Heffer and Geoff Bish were busily preparing yet another policy document which they proudly took to a meeting attended by Callaghan, Foot and Norman Atkinson. On defence, Jim saved multilateralism, but had to agree to oppose the deployment of cruise missiles and the next generation of nuclear weapons.

Overall Benn was cock-a-hoop: 'The statement will include a reference to amending the European Communities Act, import controls, a large section on economic and industrial policy, a pledge on full employment, and the abolition of the House of Lords,' he wrote. 'It really is quite a good draft rolling manifesto; it's the one we should have published last year.'

This document called *Peace, Jobs and Freedom* was to turn out to be one of the most unpopular ever produced. While it did not go far enough for many activists, it persuaded the general public that we were suicidal – peace at any price, spend money you haven't got and deny freedom wherever possible.

Just to make sure that the document stayed unacceptable to just about everyone, at the April NEC it was decided that there was no time to allow the CLPs or unions to put amendments. It would be put to the Special Conference as the only item and the debate noted. It appeared to me that we, indeed, were not going to have a real conference after all – only a very unpopular demonstration!

The trade unions thought, as I did, that the whole exercise was a complete waste of time and money and did not take their full delegations. On the day this not only left a vast number of empty seats in the centre of the hall; it meant that the loonies greatly outnumbered the moderates, because the constituencies were there in force.

To alienate the public even more, most of the constituency contributions demanded that the policy go further. The Trots meanwhile, Ted Knight and Ray Apps, demanded extra-parliamentary action. Knight deplored the fact that the policy statement gave 'no clear call to end this Tory government before its natural period of office'.

The gentler left – including Eric Deakins, MP for Walthamstow, Joan Lestor and Jack Straw – demanded our withdrawal from the Common Market.

As they made their crackpot speeches, the barmies were cheered. The moderates on the other hand were either listened to in silence or booed. Callaghan made a superb speech strongly attacking Thatcher, but it did not go down well. To have received star rating at this Conference, he would have had to attack himself.

Healey was booed even louder than David Owen after pointing out in his usual moderate manner that Labour would not win the next election if it became too tied to the policies of the left-dominated NEC or if it adopted the policies of the 'toytown Trots of the Militant group'.

As the day wore on, it became even clearer that we were spending much needed money to further demoralise good Labour voters.

The same can be said of much of the NEC's response to Thatcherism which consisted of demos, committees and leaflets. In a parliamentary democracy there is little else to do but constantly say 'I told you so' to a punch-drunk public and promise a better world to come.

Because of the public spending cuts, Skinner and I did persuade the NEC to refuse Blackpool Council's offer to hold a civic reception for delegates, but this did not come to be a turning point in the history of our time.

Committees were created which gave people the chance to persuade themselves that they were doing something and feel important. On them, they decided to prepare leaflets and organise days of action, marches and demonstrations.

These leaflets were prepared with great care and distributed at great expense to the homes of Constituency Secretaries, where no doubt they still are to this day. But as the leaflets were rarely distributed, except to the faithful, they probably did little damage.

This was almost certainly true also of a peaceful march, led by the loyalist Gerald Kaufman from the House of Commons to the Department of Environment 5 or 6 minutes away. Although malicious people say that Gerald is still resting to recover from the physical effort of that day, it certainly did no-one else any harm.

The same cannot be said however of the organised traditional marches and demonstrations which were generally a disaster for Labour. These provided a ready source of wealth for Militant and the Socialist Workers' Party which sold revolutionary claptrap to all and sundry and collected thousands of pounds that ought to have gone to the Party. Their appearance on TV news broadcasts drove even more respectable folk to support Thatcher.

Not that these demos were without their brighter moments. I remember how on one march a bag woman came out of the crowd in Park Lane, hugged Benn much to his embarrassment and insisted on walking with him.

On seeing this, someone turned to me and explained how terrible the woman was. 'Don't say that', I replied convincingly, 'that's my mother!' Such was the Party in those days that the story spread at the speed of light a mile or so down the march that my mother had turned out to support Benn. Is it any wonder that the sight of such gullible loonies barracking Callaghan and Healey at the end of demonstrations persuaded many electors that Thatcher should be 'in' rather than 'out'

The rallies against unemployment held in Liverpool, Glasgow, Cardiff and Birmingham should have been great moments, but they were always spoiled by the mob and did us immense harm.

SEVEN

The Darkest Hour

The 1980 Conference held at Blackpool with Lena Jeger in the chair was without doubt our darkest hour. At the conclusion on the Friday morning, groups of left wing political thugs stayed on the floor after the traditional singing of Labour's the 'Red Flag' to raise their arms, clench their fists, sing the revolutionaries' 'Internationale' and give three cheers for international socialism. It was a depressing sight.

This further revelation of the extent to which the revolutionary Trotskyites were taking over put the top hat on a terrible week – a week in which unilateralism triumphed, Conference voted against the Common Market, mandatory reselection of MPs was pushed through and, perhaps most devastating of all, the left succeeded in wresting the election of the Leader from the Parliamentary Labour Party.

Benn was applauded to the rooftops, too, when he announced the three pieces of legislation that Labour would pass immediately on coming to power – firstly, an Industry Act to extend public ownership, control capital and provide industrial democracy; secondly, withdrawal from the Common Market; and thirdly the abolition of the House of Lords with the creation, if necessary, of 1,000 Labour peers. This so bitterly upset Shirley Williams that she gave the Party only until the end of the year to sort itself out.

At the end of a dreadful day, a bunch of rightwingers sat in her room watching the replays on the TV, grumbling among themselves and discussing the possibility of a split in the Party. When Philip Whitehead, a fanatical Party loyalist, asked John Cartwright – MP for Greenwich and key SDP defector – what he intended to do, he was dismayed to hear John reply:

'I'm not sure'. Any experienced doorstep canvasser faced with such a 'don't know' would know that the signs were ominous indeed.

It was all the more galling to watch the triumph of the fanatics and share the gloom of the Manifesto Group – the moderate group in the PLP – because we moderates had gone to Conference thinking that, at last, all would be well.

Back in June, we had read with glee a report in the *Sunday Telegraph* which revealed that Heffer had revealed the 'sad truth' that the left had suffered 'one or two' setbacks since the last Annual Conference with reverses in certain large unions.

> It was the swing to the right in the engineering workers union that had raised the chances of the right being able to maintain status quo at the party conference. This would keep the election of the leader in the hands of MPs, the veto on the manifesto effectively in the hands of the party leader and perhaps even permit a compromise on the mandatory reselection of sitting Labour MPs agreed at last year's conference.
>
> The left is by no means in a full scale retreat,' Heffer said. 'But neither is it . . . advancing quite as firmly as it was. He blamed this on 'a great deal of backstairs manoeuvring 'over the last year between 'some right wing trade union leaders and certain leaders of the Parliamentary party.[1]

Oh, that he had been only half right. In truth, not only were the moderates still plagued by the union feuding over the Isle of Grain power station dispute, but they were also dogged by bad luck and major cock-ups.

The moderates in the AUEW had come to Conference thinking that by organisation they had gained control, by just one vote, of the delegation. Then one of the delegates elected on a right wing ticket was turned over by the left and everything changed.

This delegate, Brother Doug A. Knott from Poole in South Dorset, changed the history of the Labour Party. Had he voted differently, everything would have been different. Crucial votes at the Conference – the election of the NEC, the votes on the constitutional issues – were determined by the way the AUEW voted and that vote was determined by the man from Poole.

Had he voted with the men who had helped to secure his election, there would have been no SDP and we certainly would not have been in the wilderness for so many years. If ever a man deserved a statue in the Conservative Central Office it was Brother Doug A. Knott.

John Spellar tells me that when it became known that Bro. Knott was not going to vote with the moderates: 'Frank Chapple argued strongly with Terry Duffy that such a ludicrous situation could not be allowed to determine the history of a great party. Even though Duffy was in an election, he was prepared to entertain the idea of casting his vote for the moderates, but could not persuade the more conservative John Boyd, the experienced General Secretary'. As a result of the failure to deliver the AUEW, the NEC election results were again disastrous and ensured that we loyalists faced yet another winter in the trenches. But on this front, there would be no ceasefire, no quarter given and no games of football in no man's land at Christmas.

On the NEC, we were skewered on unforgiving bayonets. In the Women's section Lena Jeger – who could be relied upon to support Callaghan on critical occasions – retired and was replaced by the ruthlessly dogmatic left-winger Margaret Beckett (It is rumoured that she is the same person as the sane, balanced, pragmatic Cabinet member in Tony Blair's government – but I find it difficult to believe that the Beckett I knew, and did not love, could appear on TV beside a Japanese flag eulogising the Common Market).

In addition, Fred Mulley of APEX was replaced not by Denis Howell, as we had hoped, but by Charlie Kelly of UCATT, yet another on the dogmatic left. And Emlyn Williams of the NUM was replaced by his union colleague Eric Clarke. Although both were of similar politics, Clarke was not only hard left but also hard-working and had a lot more about him than Williams. Certainly his attendance could be relied upon by those who ran the left. When 'bums on seats' meant everything, Clarke was gold dust to them. His bum always knew which seat it was supposed to be on.

In truth, the blame for the sharp setbacks for the moderates in 1980 can be laid on other shoulders than just Brothers Knott and Boyd. During the year, union leaders involved in TULV, including Basnett and his allies, had become increasingly fed up with Benn & Co's antics on the NEC.

The battleground was Basnett's precious Commission of Enquiry and, in an attempt to escape from the annual wrangles, the unions simply bulldozed the reintroduction of the three-year rule through Conference despite opposition from the NEC.

But what a pity the TULV leaders – Basnett, Moss Evans and Clive Jenkins among them – did not resolve to remove control of the NEC, too, from those they now knew to be inflicting so much damage!

Basnett's Damp Squib

The Commission report was to have played an important role at the 1980 Conference. It certainly made its mark in addressing the party's perilous finances. But on the big constitutional questions, after so much effort, navel-gazing and sheer bloody infighting, it had as much lasting political impact as the bite of a gnat.

What the whole torrid episode demonstrated once again, however, was the left's unrivalled ability to lash the Party down while Thatcher walked all over us.

To kick off there had, of course, been the obligatory almighty tussle about the Commission's composition. There had been a continual wrangle about this. Everyone distrusted everyone and every time I went into the House of Commons tea room or the Division Lobby I would be grabbed by someone who asked me, desperately, 'to stop it'

Over and over again, I had to explain that we would do our best but that inevitably we were fighting a losing battle. We were strong on dogged determination and reasoned argument, but lacking in numbers – and the only thing that mattered was the counting of votes. As Denis Skinner reminded the NEC, 'it was about power' and the left were determined to exercise that power in their own interest.

So the bitterness expressed by MPs, particularly Gerald Kaufman, in the PLP meeting held the day before the NEC, carried no clout at all. Far more important was the left wing caucus meeting held on the same day. Here tactics and the slate were discussed and determined. This made certain that the request by the Shadow Cabinet for a meeting with the NEC before the composition of the Commission was finalised would be brushed to one side and that only members the lefties could rely on would go on to the Commission.

The left were well prepared for the NEC meeting. We moderates were not only less well organised, but at sixes and sevens. While moderate trade unionists went to the NEC briefed by Basnett to press for an immediate start to the Commission, Callaghan unsuccessfully attempted to delay proceedings to try and get strong Shadow Cabinet representation.

'We have got to ensure that the warriors on each side do not slay each other', Callaghan told the press, 'but yesterday's slaughter was all on one side.' Ironically, the slaughter began when Neville Hough, the GMWU representative and the most dogged of moderates, moved that we get on immediately with the Commission and this was carried with only six votes against. A meeting would only be held with the Shadow Cabinet 'so that the position could be explained to them'.

Our lines were seriously crossed and it went from bad to worse. We moderates next gave full support to Basnett's proposal, moved by Hough, that there be 5 NEC, 5 TULV and 3 PLP members on the Commission including the Leader.

But the left were totally opposed to giving separate representation to the PLP. Such was the contempt, indeed, that Heffer countered by saying that 90 organisations had asked for representation and if it were to be given to 'one group', it would have to be given to others!

The inimitable political journalist Tony Bevins accurately noted that CLPD had inspired this flood of these requests and that Callaghan 'had been completely outmanoeuvred – it is understood that Mr Benn and his friends had planned their tactics in detail at a private caucus on Tuesday night.' It would have been more accurate of Bevins to have written 'outvoted' rather than 'outmanoeuvred', but I suppose that working for *The Times* he had to use long words which were difficult to spell.

After a series of skirmishes, Benn successfully moved that the committee comprise five union General Secretaries, five from the NEC, the Leader, Deputy Leader, Treasurer and the Vice-Chairman.

The five from the NEC, furthermore, were to be Frank Allaun, Tony Benn, Eric Heffer, Joan Lestor and Jo Richardson. We could have wept – especially as they rubbed sat into the wounds by deciding that the Commission Secretary be the General Secretary of the Party. Not content with capturing the bridge, the lefties had also taken over the engine room.

The moderate Manifesto Group deplored the slap in the face for MPs. Giles Radice said: 'They have pushed it too far'. But too far for what, was the obvious response. In the main, MPs strangely had no idea how to fight back other than to whinge to union General Secretaries.[2]

It is hard now, in the heyday of New Labour, to convey the bitterness of meetings of the PLP, too, in those dark days. When Callaghan spoke, Heffer interrupted throughout. Jim warned against entryism and the bedsitter brigade at time of reselection. He claimed that he was not for the right against the left, but a peacemaker between the sides.

He railed that the monthly meetings of the NEC were like purgatory where he would be cross-examined and attacked over government policy. As he laid into the left, MPs banged the desks and roared their support. But he also disappointed his followers by saying that there should be no boycott of the NEC, if it rejected MPs' pleas again.

The bitter wrangling about representation rumbled on until Christmas 1979, as the barons, unused to being snubbed, weighed in with threats against the NEC.[3] And after several unsuccessful attempts by the union leaders – Basnett, Boyd, Evans, Jenkins, Sid Weighell, Bill Keys and Bill Whatley – the mood was hardly festive when the NEC last met to consider the issue on 19 December.

In fact, all hell broke loose, as Heffer first launched into a tirade against Weighell. Sid, you see, ten days earlier had written in the *News of the World* of Benn and Heffer: 'These men must go: they couldn't run a fish and chip shop.' To many of us, that seemed to be to be fair comment, hardly provocative at all.

Next Basnett lost his cool at Heffer's outburst, telling him: 'Stick to the point . . . we'll take you on if you want.' Benn then intervened with a piece of astonishing sophistry, claiming the composition was politically balanced. I say 'astonishing' advisedly, because we know that in his Diary he had written that there was a 10 to 4 left majority! Indeed Benn, who had gone to great lengths to ensure that the NEC side was well and truly 'sorted', became indignant about the very allegation of rigging!

That bad-tempered affair broke up inconclusively, but at the next meeting on 23 January 1980, Heffer and Saunois got the NEC to agree not to remove the left wingers Alex Kitson and Norman Atkinson, as the barons wanted, by the narrowest margin, 12 votes to 11. In an absurd twist, however, Kitson resigned anyway, unable to withstand the pressure from his trade union brothers.[4]

The Commission eventually met on 8 February and, in the event, despite protests from the Shadow Cabinet and union leaders, it was almost entirely a left wing affair.[5]

Against Benn's 10-4 reckoning for the left, Tony Bevins made it 9-5 and I, the optimist as ever, scored it 11½ to 2½ – i.e. Callaghan and Duffy, with Basnett the half portion. As it turned out, however, the issue of right and left proved to be of far less importance than Basnett's desire to use trade union power for his own glorification.

Outnumbered, Callaghan nevertheless decided to take the fight right to the heart of the left, proposing a special two day conference for the following year, in the spring of 1981, and suggesting looking at the composition of the NEC and the issue of Militant. Benn reported Foot as saying: 'They, Militant and the composition of the NEC, must be excluded,' while Duffy backed Jim.

Needless to say, however, many of the hot potatoes were left for Neil Kinnock, John Smith and Tony Blair to pick up many years later, such as 'entryism', the union block vote and the issue of 'one member, one vote'.

The Commission ploughed on until from 13 to 15 June when the first 'final Commission meeting' was held at the ASTMS' plush Whitehall College in Bishops Stortford. The grandeur of the occasion may be judged by the fact that Clive had bought goldfish for the pond especially.

All the good, bad and plain ugly were present and, predictably, on the grand constitutional issues, it made little headway.[6]

There was a bitter squabble over reselection. Jenkins wanted mandatory reselection unless 60 per cent were against it; Moss Evans reselection if 60 per cent positively wanted it; while both Foot and Callaghan opposed it altogether. Confusion was heaped upon confusion until it was decided to take a break for people to sort themselves out.

In truth, this just gave Benn & Co time to lean on Evans, so that when the meeting re-convened, it was decided by 7 votes to 6 to go along with Conference and back mandatory reselection. In turn Callaghan raised 'one member one vote' as an issue, got nowhere, announced that he couldn't recommend the decision to the PLP, picked up his papers and left!

Thereupon, Basnett in the chair adjourned the meeting. Heffer refused to accept this, but Basnett and others simply took no notice and departed, leaving Heffer alone with Benn and a couple of their left-wing mates.[7]

When Jim finally returned but on the Sunday morning, Heffer – now in the chair – ruled out 'one member, one vote' on the grounds that it was not included in the previous year's Conference decision. Stalemate again.

To avoid a further row, Basnett proposed that they move on quickly to the question of electing the leader. The way Jim was looking and behaving, they might indeed have needed to look for a new Leader any day now. Basnett's big idea was an 'Electoral College', a National Council of Labour, which would not only elect the Leader but also take responsibility for the manifesto and rolling programme. So carefully had he prepared his ground, however, that at first his grand idea got no support at all.

Callaghan, Foot and Terry Duffy each argued for the status quo. Jim, who saw that this was the only way to avoid a split in the Party, pointed out that the country wouldn't accept an electoral college in which trade unions had 50 per cent of the vote because people didn't want the unions to be running the country. He could not recommend it at all to the PLP.

Bill Keys, who later held much of the responsibility for Labour losing the 1983 election, responded in kind: 'The problems of an electoral college are not insurmountable. We wouldn't wish 50 per cent trade union representation, but the PLP are not the be-all-and-end-all, they are not the Labour Party.'

Needless to say, Benn, Lestor and Heffer were determined to get change. Thinking no doubt of Healey, Heffer argued spouted forth: 'Next time round we could have a Leader, if we weren't careful, who was hated in the country or by the Party.' They should have discussed whether it was better to have a Leader who was hated in the Party, like Denis, or one hated by the country such as Benn but instead broke up to meet in their factions again.

When they returned, Foot's proposal to maintain the status quo was defeated by 3 votes to 9. After a row, a motion moved by Evans and Jenkins to have an electoral college which gave 50 per cent of the votes to the PLP was finally carried by 7 votes to 6.

Later Benn, after yet another furious bust-up with Foot, summed up: 'Looking back on the weekend, Eric, Jo, Norman, Frank, Joan and I stuck together. Clive Jenkins and Bill Keys are just fixers. Moss Evans is absolutely unaffected by the mandate of his trade union. David Basnett is devious and cynical but hasn't got real strength; you can beat David Basnett Duffy is much tougher and honest and straightforward. Jim is angry and cross and on his way out. Michael Foot is hopeless.'

Ultimately the Commission proposed not only to keep mandatory reselection and introduce an electoral college giving 50 per cent of the vote to the PLP, but also that the manifesto be drafted by the NEC and ratified by the College as well!

In the Shadow Cabinet the following week, Bill Rodgers and David Owen laid into Jim, who gave as good as he got. Healey has since claimed that he rejected pressure from the right wing Manifesto Group to break with Jim and lead an all-out attack on the new leadership formula. However, while individuals may have approached him, I cannot recall the group itself ever taking such a decision. Many on the right, however, undoubtedly felt that they had been betrayed at Bishops Stortford.

Oddly, so did the hard left, who now organised opposition through the Rank and File Mobilising Committee in the run-up to the 1980 Conference.[8] Such was the mad house we inhabited then!

On 20 June Heffer, obviously already under pressure, announced that he and some of his colleagues would present a minority dissenting report to the NEC and Conference in October. 'If agreement could not be reached, conference should kick the whole thing out,' he told the press.[9] And that, for better or worse, is exactly what happened. The combined opposition from right and left had made its impact. At its final meeting, in July 1980 the Commission decided to drop its constitutional proposals. Once that happened, it ceased to have any great political significance.

Perhaps that is why there were so many members absent, including me, when the NEC met on 16 July 1980 to consider it.

The Commission certainly contributed towards putting the Party finances on a more even keel (though it by no means solved the perennial financial crisis). At Conference the debate on finance was introduced by Clive Jenkins. And I enjoyed the sight of Norman Atkinson, sitting and listening to Clive, who after helping him to beat Eric Varley for the Treasurership, flayed him alive over the Party's financial crisis.[10]

But after burning everyone to a frazzle, on the big political issues so little had been achieved. Basnett's pet project turned out to be yet another damp squib, indeed.

Not so the wars on defence and Europe, however, where the left's triumph made sure that we not only lost the 1983 general election, but that we went into battle fatally divided, as some of our best footsoldiers simply upped sticks to another camp.

CND's Biggest Branch

A signed photo of Ernest Bevin hangs in a place of honour in our home opposite one of Jim Callaghan. Oh, that Ernie had been at Jim's side during the debates on defence! In the debate on defence at the 1935 Conference, Ernie had destroyed George Lansbury and his pacifist wing in a rough, shrewd speech accusing him of hawking his conscience from Conference to Conference.

Ernie, a true representative of the working class, kept the Party straight and so it stayed until Aneurin Bevan, Foot & Co secured the defeat of Hugh Gaitskell in 1960, passing a proposition which rejected 'any defence policy based on the threat of the use of strategic nuclear weapons.' That prompted Gaitskell's famous cry that he would 'fight, fight and fight again' to reverse the decision.

Despite Bevan, too, later not wanting to go into debating chamber naked, a sane defence policy became one of the casualties of the rise of the left. Of all the issues on which the right and left faced each other in the trenches, the most important was that of the bomb.

In the early 1980s a deep split emerged between the PLP and Shadow Cabinet on the one hand and the NEC and Conference on the other. While the Shadow Cabinet remained committed to multilateralism, the NEC predominantly supported the unilateral renunciation of nuclear arms. And, sadly, this included several in the Loyalist Group.

For the majority of the Shadow Cabinet who supported multilateralism, 1980 began badly and steadily got worse. Personally I knew little about defence and took even less interest. I was not present at the joint meeting between the Shadow Cabinet and the NEC in January, but on reading the minutes again, I can easily visualise the scene – two implacably opposed sides glaring wildly at one another.

The left, jaundiced and truculent, accused Shadow Defence Secretary Fred Mulley of preparing the way within a secret committee for weapons of even greater potential for destruction and Shadow Cabinet members of supporting Thatcher's policies.

One after another, like well-trained parrots, they demanded that the Shadow Cabinet support Party policy – read our lips, no new nuclear weapons. They demanded a veto, indeed, over all American weapons.

The Shadow Cabinet sat glumly, resenting every wasted minute doggedly defending themselves: the British people wanted strong defence, Rodgers, Owen and Shore lectured the left. Healey, as ever, could not be bothered with the formalities and laid into them hard. Roy Mason baited them over all the commitments we had kept.

Callaghan as ever tried to bring peace, while hitting Heffer over the head with the hardest part of the olive branch. 'The Party,' he said, 'has to move together.' What a forlorn hope!

Throughout 1980 there was strong growth in support among CLPs for unilateralism and the Campaign for Nuclear Disarmament (CND). Labour became, in effect, CND's biggest branch. The bomb pretty much dominated the special Wembley Conference on 'Peace, Jobs and Freedom' at the end of May.

Benn reports joyously of the time he 'watched Robin Cook and Mary Kaldor, the Labour Party's adviser on defence, talking about nuclear weapons on a marvellous party political broadcast. It was principled, serious, straight, with no rhetoric; I felt it was tremendously effective.' Inevitably, this meant that it was a vote loser.[11]

The NEC also lost us votes by becoming involved in the big anti-nuclear marches of the year. On 22 June, 1980 they even led a rally under the banner 'Nuclear arms No; Peace Yes.' It pleased me that the rain bucketed down on all of Benn, Foot, Orme, Heffer, Skinner, Maynard, Richardson, Allaun and Atkinson as they paraded along.

At July's NEC, amazingly we managed to deflect sending a deputation to the Defence Secretary on the hot issue of American cruise missile bases in Britain (by the casting vote of the chair on an even 10-10 split).

Having squeaked that one, we lost the next – over an anti-cruise missile march on 26 October organised by CND. Shirley Williams, supported by

Jim, said we shouldn't have anything to do with CND. The vote, however, went 15 to 9 to attend – with Jim stomping that he'd never agree to unilateralism, whatever the Party said.

I still do not know how we managed to get even the nine votes.

Over the summer, the unilateralist motions for the Annual Conference poured in. Of course they were 'plants', but the sheer volume and organisation was still both impressive and very depressing.

The atmosphere, as the motions were put to Conference, was enough to make the level-headed almost suicidal. Two of the motions would have been difficult for any government to handle. One called for negotiation and persuasion to bring about a nuclear-free zone throughout Europe; the second called for a Campaign for World Disarmament.

Two others, however, were a total disaster – unilateral disarmament, 'No to Cruise' and 'Polaris into ploughshares', as it were, all rolled up into the first; closure of all nuclear bases, British and US, and effectively renouncing NATO, in the second, proposed by the ever troublesome Bill Keys of SOGAT.[12]

Knowing the votes were already stacked against him, Callaghan nonetheless made a powerful plea in support of multilateralism. In his speech, he not only spoke eloquently of the horrors of nuclear war but also of the build-up of Soviet armaments and the efforts of Helmut Schmidt, which had just resulted in talks scheduled in Geneva in mid-October between the USA and USSR.

He listed the concessions which had already been made – the B1 bomber and neutron bomb – to which the Soviet had not responded. It was the cohesion of the West, not concessions, that had brought the Russians to the negotiating table, he argued. On the floor, the multilateralist position was put by Bill Rodgers who argued that single-handed renunciation of nuclear weapons would be rejected overwhelmingly by the very people whose support Labour needed to win.

'We in our movement have a very great respect for those of pacifist convictions, but go into the pubs, go onto the shop floor, go onto the doorstep and you will find a great majority of people who deeply want peace and deeply want disarmament but who believe you cannot win the peace unless you are prepared to say will defend yourselves,' Bill argued passionately. 'No trade union would go into negotiation and say beforehand it will not exercise the industrial power it possesses. You cannot win a negotiation if you give up in advance the authority and power that you possess.'

I despaired at the logic of supposedly sane, intelligent people who wanted to change Britain's defence policy, but who were prepared to lose to Thatcher, to go to the wall over the bomb. If we had to have a death wish, so be it, they shrugged.

Bill Keys: 'Friends, it has been argued by some that if this great Party of ours comes out in favour of nuclear disarmament, it would probably stop the return of a Labour government. I say to you I do not accept that argument. I equally say to you that if that was true, it would not be too high a price to pay for civilisation.'

And Robin Cook: 'I will not bandy words with Bill Rodgers as to whether his position or my position will be the better electoral asset. I cannot think of a more frivolous position on which to make up our mind on the central issue facing mankind.'

It was bitterly upsetting to many of us that they were prepared to sacrifice the interests of the British working class for the sake of CND. We did not believe that the welfare of working people was a frivolous issue, at all.

Some of us still believe that 18 years of Tory government was too high a price to pay for the emotional maelstrom that people like Philip Noel Baker, Keys and Cook could stir up Conference. The speeches harked back to the heyday of CND in the 1960s, the Aldermaston marches and the great battles with Gaitskell.

They fought on an easy wicket. The Tories had issued some stupid advice on Civil Defence in the case of nuclear attack – teabags under tables and the like – which was so easily ridiculed. Cuts in welfare, too, highlighted the exorbitant cost of arms expenditure – £11 billion, some 5-7 per cent of GDP.

It all went down badly with most of the MPs, huddled together in their square as ever in the face of the onslaught. Some were too shell-shocked by now to show any sign of emotion. While the left went wild with joy, others vented their outrage only too clearly as the results were announced.

Some MPs had fought a rearguard battle, but lost – overwhelmed by the wave of unilateralism that had swept the Party. The demos, marches and lobbying had paid off. While Foot, Kinnock & Co. congratulated themselves on the top table and hysteria broke out among CND, some of the right wing looked as though the end of the world had come. Stalwarts like George Robertson, John Spellar and John Gilbert would taste a Labour victory finally in 1997. But for the likes of David Owen, Bill Rodgers, Peter Shore, Roy Mason, Denis Healey, this was the most dreadful of defeats.

The propositions which were carried on a show of hands ensured that Labour lost the 1983 general election and went into the wilderness. They should be writ large on the tombstone of Old Labour.

Jim Callaghan went, the Social Democrats went and the policy landed the Party with an unelectable Leader supporting a defence policy rejected by almost all of the British public. There was nothing left but to lie back and think of little England.

Stalling on the Market

In the Labour Party, there were certainly many little Englanders who violently opposed our membership of the Common Market. At the referendum in 1975, I had supported it partly because it promised protection to British pottery and partly perhaps because, although for me Nelson was a hero, I had always preferred Napoleon to the English aristocracy.

It was one of those subjects, like defence, on which knowing little I adopted a 'me too' policy and followed the tiny band of mostly right wing pro-marketeers. We were and remained a tiny, little band.

At one NEC much later, indeed, when an increase in farm prices led to a vote confirming 'the wisdom of Labour's policy of withdrawal from the EEC' only Betty Boothroyd, Denis Healey, Shirley Summerskill and I voted against. Gwyneth Dunwoody, Syd Tierney and Gerry Russell voted with the left. As I've said, it was a lonely life supporting the EEC.[13]

Even as a supporter, I had experienced how the Commission could make life difficult in government when one black day I was told it had outlawed my beloved Temporary Employment Subsidy scheme.

When I asked what would happen if we just ignored the ruling, I was told politely that the government Accounting Officer would refuse to sign the cheques. Under the law, it would be illegal to do so. I then had to face the TUC General Council to break the bad news and, as always happened when

I was the messenger, be kicked from pillar to post (a process described by Albert Booth as 'taking the shine off the ball').

Faith in the Common Market was forever challenged by Conference and the NEC. In 1978 after the Conference had carried an anti-EEC proposition, the NEC waged continual war against the policies of the government, even though Callaghan and Healey themselves were sceptics and Joel Barnett even more so.

When Healey published a memo on the European Monetary System, the NEC's Home Policy Committee – in its role as the 'Socialist Government in Exile' – prepared its own document for Labour MPs and affiliates to incite rebellion against their own government. The left delivered their tirade and Denis replied in his normal manner, not bothering to mop up the blood as he went.

He made clear the government's position. It was rather like the single currency today: we would only join if the disadvantages did not outweigh the advantages. But he might as well have saved his breath.

As soon as he had left to do something more useful than try to bring enlightenment to the NEC, the comrades behaved true to form. A resolution, already drafted by Benn and slipped to Heffer, Kinnock and Allaun, was passed calling on the Labour government to take the necessary steps to stop the EEC from adopting EMS and to allow MPs to vote for Party policy against the government.

The insistence on MPs being allowed to vote against the government derived partly from an alliance, including Benn, against the EMS between the left wing socialists and right wing Tories. Benn claimed he was opposed to EMS because it would lead to federalism, loss of control over our own economic future and reliance on Germany. Although a Cabinet minister, Benn described EMS as 'a treachery to my country' to Neil Marten, a right wing Tory, who in return revealed that he, Enoch Powell, Douglas Jay and Bryan Gould (the mind boggles) met every Monday to discuss strategy on Europe. Benn asked Marten to gain Thatcher's support against any move by Jim to get EMS through. Is it any wonder that Benn went to Powell's funeral and so honoured one of the most evil British politicians of our time?

Gould, with Benn's goodwill, then worked hard among Labour back-benchers to help Thatcher undermine the government by obtaining 114 signatures on a resolution against the EMS. But all the time Callaghan and

Healey could hardly be described as enthusiastic pro-marketeers – they were not.

The 1979 general election manifesto was very critical of the European Community. It proposed fundamental and much-needed reform and looked forward to enlargement of the community to provide opportunity that for reform. Top of the agenda, then as now, was the Common Agricultural Policy, with the threat of a British veto on any further price rises while food mountains persisted.

The manifesto opposed federalism and defended the right of countries to determine their own industrial policies, such as import restrictions to protect vital national economic interests. It opposed the EMS and sought cuts in Britain's European payments.[14]

In the mood of the time, however, we lost the Euro-elections very badly in June with an equally negative manifesto. The campaign, indeed, was hardly fought with conviction. Benn didn't want Europe and believed democratic elections would strengthen it. And during election, the NEC objected so strongly to a leaflet under the slogan 'Labour for Europe' that candidates were told not to distribute them.

In truth, the manifesto drawn up when the Home Policy and International Committees came together under Benn's chairmanship in January, 1979 could well have been called 'Labour against Europe'. Our divisions then almost exactly mirrored those of the Tories in the 1990s.

As ever Shirley Williams and I repeatedly recorded our dissent as the committee went through the draft. In vain, naturally, as the document was endorsed and submitted to the NEC. There, despite opposition again from the old firm of Williams and Golding, a request for prior consultation from the PLP was snubbed. Instead, they would only deign to talk to the PLP after endorsing the manifesto and then proceeded to tack on amendments concerning a 35-hour working week.

At the end, Williams and Tom Bradley had their objection recorded, but I didn't because I knew that – as the ultimate party hack – I would soon find myself campaigning in its support. My discipline, indeed, was better than Callaghan's. When the document was launched at the press conference he said under his breath – so that everyone could hear – that it certainly wasn't his manifesto at all!

The Euro-election results were a total disaster. On a 30 per cent poll, Labour gained only a third of the vote, winning just 17 seats compared with 60 for the Tories.

In the aftermath, at the 1979 Conference, Callaghan once again laid into the waste of the CAP, but warned the Party not to 'throw the baby out with the bath water'. Common problems, in industry especially, needed co-operation Europe-wide.[15]

Not content with winning a vote critical of the EEC at Conference, Benn of course just ignored Jim and was soon pushing for total withdrawal from Europe. As for the right wing pro-marketeers, they were to be isolated in the Party and Shirley Williams was roundly defeated in her attempts to pull the NEC back from total disengagement with the EEC. Little did we know it then, but the path was being well and truly laid for the breakaway of Shirley with the SDP.

Antagonism to the EEC was also underlined at the Wembley Special Conference. There, even Eric Deakins, Joan Lestor and Jack Straw of the 'more gentle' left (how could I dare describe Jack as 'soft') demanded our withdrawal from the Common Market. 'Peace, Jobs and Freedom' would be achieved by little England alone.

By the time we got to the 1980 Conference, then, as far as the comrades were concerned, we were well on our way out of the Common Market already.

And as everything else went wrong at that Conference, there was no reason to hope that we would emerge with a credible policy on the EEC. Indeed, we adopted a hardline policy of withdrawal in yet another major setback for leading figures on the right. While Callaghan and Healey were sceptical, for the 'Gang of Three' – Owen, Rodgers and Williams – membership of the EEC was an article of faith.

The anti-Europeans argued, in the best tradition of international socialism, that rather than investing in our industry, we were spending our North Sea oil and gas revenue to subsidise Franz Joseph Strauss's fat cows in Bavaria. And as an afterthought to these appeals to self-interest, they complained that the EEC was not democratic, either.

Of course, these speeches were cheered to the rafters. To the delegates it was all so simple: they followed the left in whatever they said. For us on the

EEC's side, it was far from easy. It took real courage for Bill Sirs of the Steel Workers to go to the rostrum and tell the baying hordes that, though we were disappointed, we still needed to support the EEC and be on the inside track.

Owen also put the marketeers' case, which unfortunately was not helpful, pointing out that the Community was already our dominant trading partner. If a Labour government wished to come out, it should commit to a referendum.

Peter Shore knocked that right on the head, after Benn arranged it with the powers that be to specially extend the debate for Labour's parliamentary spokesman to make a 'Churchillian-type of anti-market speech'. 'I do not believe,' Shore argued, 'that, if we state fairly and clearly in our next manifesto what our policy is, we have any necessity at all to resort to yet another referendum.'

Given the reaction of the delegates so far, there was no need to bring in any big guns – if you can refer to 'pop gun Peter' this way – to win. Indeed. not even Heffer, who wound up the debate for the NEC, could lose it.

As a result, the ASTMS' Composite Resolution 15, urging withdrawal as a priority for Labour's next general election manifesto, was carried by some 5 million votes to just 2 million. It was a 'sensational, a fantastic victory,' Benn said.

We were on our way out brothers. And so were the right, if not by defection like the Social Democrats, then by deselection – in the minds of the comrades, at least.

Deselection Rears its Ugly Head Again

The reselection issue rumbled bitterly on, as the left made fools of themselves, as we have seen, over changing the rules.

At the 1980 Conference, of course, we moderates tried to capitalize and recover the situation, with Denis Howell and Bryan Stanley putting a motion to resurrect the 'Mikardo Compromise'.

Howell highlighted the bungling, twists and turns in the NEC's position. And Stanley once again spelt out that the Prentice situation had been dealt with and how optional reselection was preferable because of the damage that mandatory selection would do to the constituency parties. It was also more democratic, not forcing divisive contests, when a constituency was over-whelmingly satisfied with its MP.

Joe Ashton, the MP for Bassetlaw, once a leftwing firebrand, also created uproar in a well-remembered speech, pointing out that 'if you sack MPs, they will fight back . . . they get £12,000 for standing and losing . . . If Roy Jenkins wanted to form a party of 25 sacked MPs now in this parliament, they could be in business in six months.'

It was not the opponents to change who electrified Conference delegates however. On this occasion, that distinction went to my mate Sam McCluskie. Hating MPs since failing to chair the Organisation Committee, he wound up for the NEC with the most vicious attack possible – oblivious to the fact that he was putting his enemies Benn and Heffer on the road to power.

He started quietly and very reasonably: 'I recognise that there are problems which are created by mandatory reselection, not so much in the constituencies but in parliament itself, because the history of the last Labour government was that at the end of the day they had to do a deal with the Liberals to get through some of their legislation that we, as trade unions, we, as a Conference, wanted put forward.'

'Let us assume they had a small majority and let us assume that during that period of time reselection conferences took place, and let us assume that certain members lost their seats and that other people were re-elected in their place,' he continued. 'What is going to be the position of the sitting MP who is not being re-elected for his constituency? That was the worry I had and still have.'

The delegates shifted uneasily in their seats, while the MPs settled back comfortably in theirs. Then, two seconds being a long time at Conference, Sam dropped his bombshell. 'But I will tell you,' he said. 'I am convinced now by the arguments that mandatory reselection is the answer.'

And then came the rush of blood to Sam's head. 'I say to you that mandatory [reselection] . . . if it helps anything, it can control the arrogance of the MPs in their relations with the constituency parties. Because it is that arrogance that the MPs know better than the constituency party and that only they, and they alone, can solve the problem of the Labour Party.'

At this constituency delegates, for once having no difficulty understanding Sam's broad Glaswegian accent, whooped, cheered and applauded him to the skies. Had they had sufficient strength to lift his massive frame, they would have carried Sam down shoulder high right there and then.

Needless to say, this speech bitterly upset my colleagues in the PLP block. One after another, knowing my close relationship with Sam, they trooped to express their disgust. As I had often praised Sam at the right wing Manifesto Group, it was a difficult situation. If I had not been such a glutton for punishment, I would have hidden in a nearby betting shop. Being skinned by the bookies is preferable to being skinned alive by parliamentary colleagues.

It was a difficult situation. The problem was that many of my moderate trade union brothers agreed with Sam. They looked at the parliamentary block, saw the undoubted arrogance of some MPs and resented it. Other union officials told me that as they were subject to election every five years, they didn't see why MPs should not be also.

Additionally, Harry Urwin of the TGWU argued that it was difficult for his union to oppose because – having had trouble with George Brown – they had introduced mandatory reselection for their own parliamentary panel.

While Sam's anti–MP sentiments horrified the PLP, they certainly hit a chord with the delegates. MPs were hated and despised by Party delegates, as debates from the period show. Now Sam had shown them how to hit back.

And so, in 1980 new rules providing for mandatory reselection were carried. That was not the end of the controversy, however, and the rest of the long-running battle is perhaps dealt with here.

The right's rearguard action took place because it was still possible within the rules for parties to circumvent a competitive selection by putting just the MP on the short-list. And in a famous victory at Conference in 1981, the left failed to secure changes outlawing short-lists of one.

The fight-back began, as so many did, with the soft left agreeing with me in Committee, being nobbled by CLPD or some other left watchdog immediately afterwards and then reversing their position at the NEC.

On this occasion, I was dumbfounded, with no other moderates present, when at the Organisation Committee in December, 1980 I was able to move successfully that: 'It is within the rules to have a short-list of one.' The shock of success didn't last long, however. All reverted to normal at the December

NEC when the Lefties carried Margaret Beckett's motion to refer back the decision they had voted for previously!

The Organisation Committee in January, 1981 duly passed a proposal allowing short-lists of one, if nobody else's name had been put forward. At the time, I described the decision as 'very bad'. 'What it means,' I said, 'is that the left are trying to ensure that there is going to be conflict and confrontation in every constituency. This can only help the Tories.' It certainly was of no comfort to sitting MPs. The left, namely, could always procure another name and moreover the proposals gave GMCs, stuffed full of left wing activists, discretion to add another name at the final stage and delete the MP's!

When the issue came back to the full NEC, however, the left were in for a rare shock. While CLPD had great influence, Foot could also from time to time call on great reserves of loyalty. As as a good parliamentarian, Michael had continually supported fellow MPs of whatever faction on this issue. And now he persuaded Judith Hart, Neil Kinnock, Joan Lestor and Renee Short to join with him in helping me and the moderates to send the decision back yet again to the Organisation Committee.[16]

There, however, Michael failed to beat Benn and Tony Saunois when an amendment was carried 7 votes to 7 by Heffer's casting vote that: 'The reselection procedure should follow the practice normally adopted for ordinary selection conferences except for the provision laid down by Conference that the sitting MP must be invited to attend the meeting . . .'

As it happened, this was meaningless and unenforceable and so we let it be. The supporters of mandatory reselection, including McCluskie, tried to recover a situation which was quickly slipping away from them by taking a decision now to advise CLPs, instead, that they should not have a shortlist of one, rather than preventing them outright

My local newspaper the *Sentinel* summed up my position well.

Some left-wing critics of Mr Benn were disposed last night to make light of their defeat over reselection. Mr John Golding . . . .was less sanguine. He described the decision to issue new advice to CLPs as monstrous. Constituency parties are within the rules and within their rights to have a short list of one when they are totally satisfied with their MP, he said last night.[17]

The majority on the executive is now trying to bulldoze constituency parties out of their rights. They are totally out of touch with the feelings in the constituencies where ordinary members want to get on with the job of fighting the Tories.

We did better in July when a move by Skinner to change the rules again to outlaw a short-list of one was defeated and even better at the the 1981 Conference when the constituency amendments condemning short-lists of one fell.

And so, mainly due to Michael Foot's support of MPs, we had one success, at least.

My forecast of the disaster facing idealists was confirmed, by the way, when Frank Hooley (the left wing MP for Sheffield Heeley) was deselected. He sent us a letter setting out his views on his failure to be reselected. In this letter he explained how he had been a very conscientious constituency MP and active in the House of Commons.

I am fully in agreement with the mainstream of Labour policy on the Common Market, nuclear weapons, the Alternative Economic Strategy, and constitutional reform. In the wider sphere I have campaigned actively in the anti-apartheid movement against the brutal racism of South Africa, and within the United Nations Association for international co-operation, disarmament and peace keeping.

Now he had been de-selected and was saying that in such circumstances a constituency should give reasons. If they were not good enough, the NEC could step in. I had no sympathy, he had helped sharpen the sword with which they cut off his head.

Ironically, when it came to my own reselection, we decided it would give me greater strength to be seen beating off the opposition. But that story, and that of the dead cat, must be told another time.

EIGHT

Blunders, Bloomers and the Leadership

There was no blacker moment at that awful 1980 Conference than when we lost the vote on the issue of how the Leader of the Labour Party was to be elected. It was another calamitous cock-up. The truth is that we expected to win and should have won. When, however, we learned that there had been a major upset in the Boilermakers' delegation we knew that things were tight, if not doomed.

Writing this, I can still feel the stress etched on my face, as I listened to how at their delegation meeting, the General Secretary John Chalmers along with Alan Hadden had secured a decision to vote against any change to the method of selecting the Leader and then left to attend to something else.

Then, having happily waved them goodbye, the left members of the delegation, supporters of the Rank and File Mobilising Committee, simply re-opened the issue and reversed the decision. It was a diabolical thing to do, but this was war. And more importantly, it succeeded.

The issue over the election of the Leader and Deputy Leader of the Party was opened by the left in the early 1970s in a Tribune pamphlet written by Frank Allaun, Ian Mikardo and Jim Sillars, who later reneged and joined the Scottish Nationalists.

The campaign to have the Leader elected by the Party as a whole was given a powerful fillip by the election of Callaghan as Wilson's successor in 1976 by the PLP when he beat Benn, Tony Crosland, Denis Healey, Roy Jenkins and Michael Foot. Although Foot did far better than expected, getting 137 votes, the left in the Party were furious. In previous elections, Attlee and Wilson had both defeated their right wing opponents, Herbert Morrison and George Brown.

The left found it difficult to accept Callaghan, the first Leader elected from the centre right since 1931. In 1975, troubled with health problems, Jim had settled back, never believing he could be Prime Minister. He hardly over-exerted himself, appearing too busy in his spare time thinking of his cows and his farm to pursue the ultimate prize.

But when the time came, with the surprise resignation of Wilson, he won easily because a very large group in the PLP, who were not high flyers but whose votes counted equally with the high and the mighty, felt comfortable with a solid Labour man. They much preferred to have the keeper of the cloth cap than those who preferred a cap and gown.

This group, marshalled well by Jack Cunningham, included many shrewd organisers who had spent their lives 'delivering votes' in union elections from the shop floor. While the academics supporting other candidates discussed the finer points of policy, we collected the vote in for Jim. From a fixing point of view, it was a job well and truly done.

There were, indeed, black comic moments such as when some of us on Jim's Campaign Committee hid our faces from the cameras as we left the House of Commons courtyard from a so-called 'secret' fixing meeting one Sunday morning. Unfortunately, this added to the feeling that the Leadership was being stitched up in smoke-filled rooms, which so antagonised many in the Party outside, who would have preferred Foot as Leader.

Certainly, after Jim's election there was a strong demand for change which was not just confined to the loony left.

Passions ran high at the 1979 Conference. Norah Websdale, the delegate from the highbrow Hampstead CLP, expressed some of the wider Party's frustration when she moved composite 18 at the 1979 Conference.

This issue has been before the Party Conference since 1976. It is not a new issue, and it is nothing whatever to do with personalities. Let us get that one out of the way. [applause]. Those within this movement who seek, for their own ends – young Pretenders, Old Pretenders – all of them to pin their colours to the mast of any of these issues, their personal colours, do this Party and this movement a great disservice.

What we in this resolution are looking for . . . is a greater say in the running of the Party and a wider democratic base from which to operate. Many of the delegates here today live in constituencies which return no Labour MP. They are loyal, hard-working Party members, and they are loyal hard-working members of their union branches, and yet they are denied a say in the election of their Leader. At the moment less than half the constituencies here have, through their MPs, an effective say in who the Leader or the Deputy Leader of this party shall be.

It was an extremely effective contribution. Christopher Palme (of Newham North East CLP) also appealed to the activists: 'It is no longer good enough to offer constituency workers the jobs of addressing envelopes. They need to be involved in a political party and that means they need to be involved in the selection of the Party Leader.'

Michael Meacher, whom I distrusted immensely, had the gall to raise the question of trust. 'To be certain that party policy was implemented,' he argued, 'you had to elect the Leader.'

After Meacher, regarded by many as daft as a brush, had returned to his seat we had a breath of fresh air from Frank Chapple who argued that the Party Leader, if he were the next Prime Minister, had to be accountable to the whole of the British electorate.

This debate is not about democracy and accountability . . . it is not about extending the size of the NEC or broadening its composition. It is not about involving the mass of Party members, or developing closer links with the grass roots views of Labour voters. It is not about giving greater say to the constituency parties.

If it were, the NEC could not have avoided . . . questioning the block vote system; nor could it tolerate allowing delegates to attend this conference on the patently untrue basis that they each represent 1,000 party members. Nor could it allow the Militant Tendency to continue to act as a secret cabal within the party – [applause] – meeting before meetings, deciding resolutions in advance [interruptions].

Why did the NEC not suggest a ballot vote of all Party members to elect the Leader? It is good enough to elect trade union general secretaries . . . Why do they now suggest an electoral college, as unrepresentative as the present system? No this debate is not about democracy – it is about power and about policy.

And, indeed, it was. The left's first attempt to change the procedure for electing the Leader had misfired. While they were successful in 1978 in creating for the first time the formal post of Leader of the Party (rather than just of the PLP), the Conference left the choice of that Leader with the PLP and rejected election by either Conference or an electoral college.

Although many on the left were disappointed, others like Jo Richardson rightly believed they had made progress: the Leader would now feel a responsibility to the whole Party and in time must come to be elected by the whole Party.

Under the three-year rule, that should have been that and the issue left to lie until 1981. But what if Jim retired before this? Benn would simply not have been elected Leader. And when it came to the ambition of Anthony Wedgwood Benn, rules and Conference decisions were never allowed to stand in the way. And so, as we have seen, the three-year rule was scrapped.

Despite a great deal of to-ing and fro-ing between the left on the NEC and CLPD (which preferred an election by Conference, but was prepared to accept an Electoral College in order to carry the support of some unions), in 1979 two left wing propositions calling for changes to the election of the Party Leader were again defeated.

Once again the Benn, Tribune and the left and they had been given a black eye. But did they give up? Of course not and why should they? They had been encouraged to soldier on by two speeches, in particular.

During the 1979 debate, Jack Ashley – a right wing, GMWU-sponsored MP, who would himself have been a strong contender for Leader had he not become deaf – declared:

> I think we are now all agreed, the whole Labour Party, on the need for change and on the need for constitutional reform. I think that is quite beyond dispute and the whole Party really wants it and the real question at issue is whether we are to leave it to the (Commission of) Enquiry or push through decisions today.

David Warburton, a right wing stalwart speaking for the GMWU, further cheered up the left and depressed his fellow moderates by declaring that:

There needs to be a change and it needs to be looked at. However there were many ramifications, the choice before the Conference was not sufficient – it needed study by the Commission of Enquiry which the GMWU had asked for in 1987.

David would never, left to himself, have made such a speech. These were the words, in reality, of Basnett – as ever sleepwalking the Party to disaster. And so it came as no surprise when, shortly afterwards, Basnett allied himself on the Commission with Bill Keys and Clive Jenkins, leading members of the TUC left, and committed himself to change.

Faced with this alliance Callaghan, Foot and Terry Duffy capitulated and themselves agreed to go along with the change. This was greeted by astonishment, dismay and disgust by many in the PLP. They thought the way was being paved for the election of Benn. In the event, as we have seen again, the Commission made no recommendations for constitutional change, but the damage had been done.

By June 1980, Benn had decided – in the tortuous discussions and manoeuvrings over the share of the vote that each element of the Party was to have in a college – to go for the formula proposed by CLPD: 50 per cent for the unions and 25 per cent each for the local parties and the PLP.

He opted for this on the grounds that it had the best chance of success and would avoid conflict with CLPD. He had a problem, however, persuading Heffer, Kinnock, Lestor and Richardson to go along with him. The Tribune group, of which Benn was not a member at this time, had opted for equal proportions for each.

At the July Organisation Committee, after Shirley and I failed predictably to retain the status quo, Lestor and Heffer were easily beaten by 7 votes to 2 when they pressed Tribune's case. Instead, by six votes to two, it was decided that Benn's preference should go forward to Annual Conference.

This defeat of Tribune by Benn was to have great repercussions later, not only losing him the Deputy Leadership election, but also helping to split the left. For the moment, however, when pressed, he managed to keep most of the soft left with him.

So when at the full July NEC, Shirley and I tried to overturn Benn, we lost by 11 votes to 14. It was hard-fought, however. Foot, for one, asserted the rights of the PLP. Callaghan pointed out, too, that Conference had already voted on the issue twice in 1978 and 1979. Maynard, however, evoked the ghost of Hugh Gaitskell, declaring that supporters of change would fight, fight and fight again. Kinnock, meanwhile, continued to support Tribune against Benn and CLPD's way, referring to the fact that the trade union votes could be easily manipulated.

In the run-up to Conference, the left ensured that the issue would be put again and delegates given a choice between the CLPD and Tribune formulas.

When the result was announced, we found that the Boilermakers 'cock-up' proved to be fatal. The switch of their 75,000 votes had been decisive. The proposition approving the principle of extending the franchise was carried by just 3,609,000 to 3,511,000.

While the left went crazy with delight, there was utter dismay on the part of the moderates and most MPs. The spectre of Benn loomed large. Healey and Owen, possible heirs to Callaghan, sat shell-shocked.

As the news spread about the cock-up, the popularity of the union block vote slumped even further among Shirley Williams and her friends. Those of us who managed the machine huddled together for comfort, until we pulled ourselves round and got to work to salvage what we could from the wreckage. The life of a fixer is very hard when things are going so spectacularly wrong!

People hardly noticed when a proposal to consider the method of election at that Conference was then carried on a show of hands. They did notice, however, when quite unexpectedly both amendments which would give effect to the decision were defeated on card votes. No amendment carried meant that there could be no election!

All hell broke out during the votes. In particular, there was an enormous row in the AUEW delegation as Terry Duffy voted against 'a third, a third, a third'. Several delegates had to be escorted off the floor. The Tribune formula was defeated by 3,737,000 votes to 3,322,000.

There was even greater pandemonium when the '50/25/25' formula was defeated by 3,557,000 to 3,495,000. Constituency delegates, believing victory had been snatched from their grasp, were in uproar. They knew that if Callaghan left quickly, the PLP would still be able to select his successor and that it would not be Benn. The smiles of the left leaders changed to scowls, while we moderates were positively beaming.

As the *Daily Mirror* reported: 'Mr Heffer's smile turned to anger, while Mr Callaghan gave a broad grin and an approving laugh.'

Following this excitement, the NEC met at six o'clock that evening to decide what was to be done. Naturally the left steamroller was trundled out and it was decided by 16 votes to 8 to prepare a list of options for consideration by the NEC, which would convene again at eight o'clock the following morning.

For good measure, this emergency session also rejected a Basnett proposition to re-introduce the three-year rule. After this, while we mods had an easy time – winding up the General Secretaries with the news that the NEC had spurned their appeal about the three-year rule – the left had a night of pure farce.

We were told later that at 11pm a left wing caucus, including Benn, Heffer, Saunois, Maynard, Allaun and Skinner had agreed to compromise and give 40 per cent to the PLP. When CPLD's leaders – Jon Lansman, Victor Schonfield, Vladimir Derer – were told, they went berserk and insisted that the unions had the 40 per cent.

Morrell was despatched in the early hours to tell Benn in his bedroom. The picture of him receiving his instructions from Francis Morrell, whilst his wife Caroline was trying to sleep in the bed, will always be a compelling one. Jo Richardson was found in a bar and they accosted Dennis Skinner next morning in a lavatory.

When the NEC met at 8 am next morning in the Imperial Hotel in Blackpool, only Alex Kitson and Emlyn Williams were missing. Everyone else on the left having been brought to heel, a decision was taken by 13 votes to 7 to follow CLPD midnight's decision – 40 per cent for affiliates, 30 per cent for constituencies and 30 per cent for the PLP.

It was decided to ask the Conference Arrangements Committee to make time on the Conference timetable for the proposition that day and that Heffer would introduce it.

Even as NEC meetings went, this was an extremely rough one. Heffer argued not to get a decision would lead to a lame-duck Leadership in October. Jim, still smarting from Benn's attacks on him and the manifesto the day before, responded that if Benn were elected, they would have no lame duck Leader but the biggest fight ever on their hands.

After Benn's assault, there could be no unity in the Party, Jim said, and he would withdraw his Conference appeal for unity. He threatened that the Labour Party could end up with two leaders if the left gave the PLP only 30 per cent of the vote. If Benn was foisted on MPs as Leader, they would simply not accept it.

Benn responded by stating that Jim only spoke for himself. The General Secretary told Benn that he was declaring open war and Benn shouted back 'rubbish, rubbish' before they both backed off. It was enough to put anyone off their grilled kippers. The Conference session was equally rough, as can be seen from these edited highlights of what was undoubtedly the match of the week.

Heffer: 'My belief is that yesterday the intention of the Conference was quite clear [applause]. They wanted – or you wanted – an extension of the franchise and you wanted to do it through a constitutional amendment this year to get it out of the way. [applause]. If we do not get it out of the way, we can have another argument next year and that does not help in our fight against Thatcher [more rousing applause].'

'Some of us, particularly those who were on the Commission of Enquiry, are up to here with constitutional issues. Every time we met we actually had to give a press conference in order to tell the press what was happening because they were around all the time [laughter]. We did not ask for a constant constitutional battle, and I am asking this Conference to decide now and to decide on the basis of the recommendation of the NEC [cheers and wild applause].'

Tom Jackson, the great UCW loyalist [applause and loud boos]: 'Comrade chairman and comrades, I come to oppose the NEC proposal and I do so because I have no opportunity whatsoever to consult with the people who sent me here about changes which are being proposed time after time [applause].'

'The NEC are producing constitutional changes with the speed of a conjurer producing white rabbits from a top hat [applause]. That is not the way our Party should do business. We have an entitlement in a democratic organisation to consult with our constituents, to take their advice and to come before this Conference with their backing. That is being denied us [applause again].' 'Today we face a constitutional change which has had one hour's consideration by this lot up here between 8 o'clock and 9 o'clock this morning [applause]. Look at paragraph 4, if you want to see an abortion. He had to explain it to us. He said that when the general election was on and the Party Leader died, they would consult with the Parliamentary Labour Party, which is not even in existence at the time of a general election [applause].

'Friends, if you do not defeat this and give those back home the opportunity to consider it, you are doing a great disservice to the democracy, brotherhood and comradeship which should exist in our organisation. Madam Chairman, I oppose.'

Andrew Faulds, MP for Warley East: 'I represent the true Labour Party in Smethwick, not the Workers' Revolutionary Party nor the Militant Trots [applause]. They have infiltrated so many constituency parties as you know [more applause]'.

'Madam Chairman, the baying of the beast betrays its presence: you can hear them . . . we have had a great one [leader] in Jim . . . There is a real quandary. We know where most of the leadership contenders stand: there is blunt, pugnacious Denis, there is forthright Peter Shore, there is outspoken John Silkin and we all know clearly where Shirley stands. None of them has welched on a Labour Government they have served in. But what of the Rt. Hon Anthony Wedgwood Benn? [cheers]'

Chairman: 'Andrew, I must ask you for no personal attacks [interruption]. No, Andrew no personal attacks. We are dealing with a National Executive statement.

Faulds: 'That is right. Madam Chairman, I am raising the matter because how we rig the proportions in this electoral college is very important. That is why I want to examine, if you will allow me – that is what this Conference is about – the record of some of the gentlemen involved.'

Chairman: 'No that is not in order. You can only examine the National Executive's statement on the election proposal.'

Faulds: 'If you are silencing me, Madam Chairman, I will withdraw.'

Chairman: 'No, I am keeping you in order'.

Faulds: 'I would have thought the record of the men we are voting about was relevant to the proportions of the college we decided to set up. If I have been ruled out of order I retreat, but under protest. I think it disgraceful that I am not allowed to make the comments on this particular gentleman.'

On winding up for the NEC, Heffer cheekily asked those not mandated for change to sit on their hands and then blundered into one of his infamous gaffes. 'I think if I remember rightly, during the speech of one of my parliamentary colleagues, he was attacking the rabble over there,' pointing dramatically to MPs (though denying it later). 'What about the rabble over there?', he roared to tumultuous applause from the cheaper seats and the gallery.

There was little sitting on hands, however, and the NEC's rabbit was defeated by 3,910,000 votes to 3,235,000.

Basnett, who had argued for a Special Conference in January to give time for consideration, moved a proposition to that effect, which the unions carried massively by 6,004,000 to 985,000.

'Jim Callaghan with the skill of a ring master', the *Daily Mirror* said at the time, 'rose to loud cheers'. In his speech, Callaghan made it clear that the PLP must elect someone as Leader before the Queen's Speech to follow its own Standing Orders, but would naturally take notice of Conference decisions when it did. It was an election which might be changed later. 'Jim did not make it clear, yet again, whether he would stand again but the Conference was satisfied,' the *Mirror* reported.

I knew myself, however, by this time that Jim had finished. On the platform when I chatted to him about the dismal week we had had, he made it clear that he was determined to go. 'There's no point in my staying,' he said, 'there are better things to do.'

He told me that Audrey kept on telling him that he didn't need all this nastiness and would be better off being with his grandchildren. Looking at the characters on the platform – Frank Allaun; Stalin's Granny, Joan

Maynard; the Black Widow, Audrey Wise; Benn; Skinner; Heffer – who was I to argue?

Callaghan was surrounded by unbalanced fanatics, who had not done one hundredth of his work for the Party or felt so keenly for working people, but who continually hurled abuse at him. Why should he plod on, putting up with the disloyalty of some party officers, the dangerous fanaticism of Benn and his cohorts, the Sieg Heil mentality of the Trots with their outstretched arms and clenched fists?

I remembered how one night in the Commons, long before he was Prime Minister, he had showed me with pride the pictures of his cows that he was looking forward to caring for in retirement. Grandchildren were certainly a big improvement on cows and worth retiring for.

There was nevertheless much speculation about what Callaghan would do. While many on the right wanted him to go immediately, to let them put Healey in, others thought that he should hang on until January to avoid the possibility of having the PLP elect someone in the autumn, who would be removed by an electoral college the following year. That, unsurprisingly, was the view of the left.

However, Jim moved quickly and resigned on 15 October, 1980. It was the end of an era. But was it Benn's great opportunity?

Throughout the early months of 1980, Benn had bounced up and down like a yo-yo on the subject of the Leadership. Lestor was one of the messengers who from time to time delivered bad news. It was she who told him that Neil Kinnock was canvassing for Foot and later broke it to him that press hatred of him was such that people already thought that he would lose them the general election, if he were Leader.

Benn, however, was determined to soldier on. When asked to give the annual Herbert Morrison Lecture, he decided on 'The Collective Leadership of the Labour Party' as the title and to make it his manifesto for a Leadership election.

In a typical Benn statement, he noted in his Diary: 'I shall make it clear that I am only interested in a Labour Party, which is collectively led. In that case it wouldn't matter who was Leader, but I would be one of the candidates.'

Things don't appear to have gone well, however, and by July 1980 Benn was writing 'the more I think about it, the less wanting to be Leader of the Labour Party is relevant.'

Irrelevant or not, when Tony Banks telephoned in August to say that he thought it would be useful if he, Mullin, Meacher and Benn met soon to plan a Leadership strategy, there was no hesitation. If there was one thing which Benn enjoyed more than any other, it was meetings at which plans were drawn up to advance his career.

For a moment he assumed the power of the Prime Minister himself and mentally distributed portfolios to his 'collective leadership'. Mullin was given the responsibility for the constituency left, Banks for the unions and Meacher the PLP, with others to be brought in later.

Benn was full of praise for Banks, in particular. 'He knows the trade union movement better than anybody else' – a statement which still strikes me as, even by his standards, mind-boggling in its inaccuracy. It appeared that Tony had organised all the parties, brought people up to see him, organised the media, got taxis, and so on. And may I say that although I have doubts about Banks's knowledge of the unions, I have no doubt that he was totally skilled at getting taxis.

One of the first moves was to go sniffing around for votes at the TUC in September. But Benn's relations with Len Murray were never close. As TUC General Secretary he was party to a move stopping Benn from going on to the TUC Economic Committee and the TUC–Labour Party Liaison Committee back in 1979.

On Sunday 12 October, when Jim's retirement was in the offing, Benn gathered his clan at his house in Notting Hill Gate – Norman Atkinson, Geoff Bish, Chris Mullin, Frances Morrell, Vladimir Derer, Tony Banks, Audrey Wise, Martin Flannery, Jo Richardson, Reg Race, Ken Coates, Stuart Holland and Julie Clements. All the usual suspects, and a few more besides, were there.

But things hardly went well for Benn. Richardson moved that if Foot stood no one else, meaning Benn, should and Stuart Holland supported her. They almost certainly would have chatted about this before they arrived and tossed up to determine who was to tell him. Mullin made it clear that he too believed that Benn shouldn't stand and asked him outright if he was going to do so.

Benn struggled with this monster of a collective leadership that he had created for himself, but which had now turned against him.

He tried to persuade them that they should all go for the Leadership, the Deputy Leadership and the Shadow Cabinet appointments. 'The Party needs a strong Leader now and, if the left abstains, there will be continued personal conflict with the left Leader-in-waiting and the incumbent will win in the electoral college. I don't think I could fight and win the college if I abstained now.'

He, specifically, was the strong leader who must fight now to win or they would have to face a bleak future without him.

But his group was a pretty tough bunch, little given to sentiment. The St Valentine's Day massacre always springs to mind when I read their names, and Benn could not shift them. They remained of the view that he should not stand in the election that the PLP was insisting on having, but wait until the electoral college was established.

His leadership yo-yo was going neither up nor down but had twisted itself into an awful tangle!

Having failed to get support to stand in this election, Benn then drafted resolutions – which the others now supported – for the NEC and PLP, demanding that no contest take place until the electoral college was established. The total cynicism of it was breathtaking – on reflection, indeed, apologies are due to all the gangsters responsible for the St Valentines Day massacre.

Benn's next step was to persuade the NEC to support his resolution, asking the PLP to suspend the election of Leader. The PLP, however, threw this out after a most bitter meeting and pressed on regardless. The rules were clear and they were going to stick to them. The resignation of Callaghan had left the door open for an old fashioned PLP Leadership contest.

The election began with great uncertainty about who the candidates would actually be. On the right, it was clear that Healey would stand and would be the clear favourite. Hattersley wanted to throw his hat in the ring, but no one would support him against Denis.

In the absence of Benn and Heffer, John Silkin saw himself as the candidate of the left, but he was almost alone in this. There was a vacuum there, which Peter Shore, once left wing and still violently anti-Market, tried hard to persuade Foot to let him fill and have a clear run against Healey. Michael wouldn't play ball, however. He had from the outset refused to stand himself, saying that Denis would make a good Leader. It looked as though Denis would have a clear run.

This put the frighteners on some badly scarred union barons, however, and great pressure was put on Foot at the last minute by Basnett and Jenkins to keep Denis out. Basnett had had great rows with Healey and the Treasury and believed that he was incapable of healing a divided Party.

When Michael agreed, many on the left were relieved to have got a credible candidate, as they didn't believe Silkin could win and they wanted to avoid Benn at all costs. They thought that Foot could win as a healing force and they were right. Never in a thousand years, though, could he win a general election.

Healey began as the favourite – and he should have won – but Foot beat him by 139 votes to 129. There have been many explanations advanced about the upset. Healey attributes it partly to the cowardice of individual MPs frightened of their constituency parties. I do not subscribe to this, however. This was a secret ballot and they were quite capable of voting one way and reporting that they had voted another.

There was more truth in his belief that members voted for Foot because they knew that there would soon be a Party ballot in which Healey would be beaten anyway. They might as well vote for someone who would stay. Foot, too, would stop Benn in a Party ballot, but it was uncertain that Healey would.

Had he been able to fight on his own terms, however, Denis could have won the 1983 general election. The problem was that there was no chance that the Party would change on defence, the Common Market and economic policy beforehand.

With shades of Tory leadership elections in the 1990s, many in the PLP argued that there was not much point in choosing a Leader who disagreed with almost all the main planks of Party policy.

Worst of all, some very shrewd operators who were already thinking of establishing the SDP voted for Foot as the man most likely to fail. They were wrong to leave the Labour Party, but they were right to make the judgement that they did.

Whatever the rights and wrongs of these arguments, the truth is that Healey may have made a good Leader but he was an awful candidate. Not only was he loathed by some trade union leaders, he had also upset many of his natural supporters in the PLP.

In addition, he hadn't a clue about fighting campaigns. He had done badly in the 1976 Leadership election, polling only 38 votes in the second ballot against 133 for Foot and 141 for Callaghan. In truth, having polled only 30 votes in the first ballot he should have withdrawn, along with Roy Jenkins who got 56 and Benn who had 37.

Healey tells how Callaghan had been alerted by Harold Lever a few months before Wilson's resignation and how Wilson had told Jim directly on March 11, 1976. Healey, however, was told by Wilson only a few minutes before the rest of the Cabinet on March 16.

Not that it would have made any difference. Even when he knew there was going to be a contest, Healey had no idea how to go about standing. Whilst thinking about it, indeed, he asked for advice from his deputy at the Treasury and was surprised to learn that he was supporting Callaghan.

From tales told to Benn by Healey's close supporter Dick Mabon – MP for Greenock and, with Bob Maclennan, one of only two Scottish Labour MPs later to defect to the SDP – it was obvious that in this election Denis was not going to be caught out a second time. Dick claimed that he had already been made Denis's campaign manager in 1977/8 and – an unlikely story, this – that Healey would appoint Benn as Deputy Leader. Again, in March 1980, Benn relates how Healey had Barry Jones of East Flint, John Smith and Dick Mabon all competing for the privilege to be campaign managers, with Joel Barnett doing the work.

From my memory, however, the great enthusiast and Healey campaign worker was Barry Jones. Denis's main team also included Eric Varley, Giles Radice and Roy Hattersley. The Callaghan 'machine men' were not used – Denis had no love for what he debunked as the 'trade union mafia'. It was a great mistake.

Denis' supporters began with great cockiness – almost arrogance, even – but were soon deflated. Canvassing in the tea room, the corridors, the lobbies and the Strangers Bar (aka the 'Kremlin'), they met resistance from people they thought were certainties. In addition to believing that Denis was incapable of leading a split Party, some refused to vote for him – as, in an earlier contest, some would not vote for George Brown – because he had been unbelievably rude to them in the past.

Others were upset because it appeared that Denis couldn't even be bothered to issue an election address. When Foot supplied a thousand word, beautifully written article for the *Guardian*, Denis sent round a curt 'Everyone knows where I stand' note. His 'take me or leave me' attitude hardly appealed to people who did not like to be taken for granted, especially where there were many issues to be decided.

The truth is that Denis had decided to keep a low profile on 'issues', so that he would not become the disunity candidate. Therefore, he did not come out against the constitutional changes, indicating only that they would be made to work fairly. He made no great statements in support of multilateralism and the Common Market. He just said that he was available at any time of night or day to answer questions.

After a rough meeting with the officers of the right wing Manifesto Group, when asked why on earth they should vote for him, Healey simply said: 'Because you have nowhere else to go.' Some of those thinking of deserting to the SDP, however, clearly did. They voted for Foot, knowing that if he won, Shirley Williams would go with them.

Despite the worsening mood among Healey supporters, his team still expected him to win. They were distraught when it was announced that Foot had been elected, while Neil Kinnock did a war whoop.

To us, Michael was no ogre. He had been an excellent Secretary of State for Employment and a great loyalist in the Labour government. That we were down in the dumps was due to his faction, his friends and their policies not his personality.

Healey himself had no difficulty in immediately indicating that he would be prepared to be Deputy Leader and that was that. Labour's traditional right wing was never the same again.

NINE

A Second Own Goal At Wembley

Though I have been involved in my own fair share of conspiracies, I have always been a fervent subscriber to the 'cock-up' theory of history. Indeed, we have already seen how we moderates allowed the left to change, in principle, the rules governing the election of the Leader following a giant cock-up on the right.

And now this view of history was to be given yet more credibility by the Wembley Conference – convened in January, 1981 to determine how the Party as a whole, not just the PLP, was to choose its Leader under an entirely new system.

At the Conference, the right cocked it up again – through lack of organisation and some peculiar decisions on the part of individual unions, which gave the hard left everything they had worked for in terms of an 'electoral college'. In turn, this gave the Social Democrats even more reason to break away.

But it also pushed the right, at long last, into organising effectively, which in time led to the demise of the hard left. This happy day was hastened because the loonies, by forcing the pace, so antagonised the soft left Tribunites that it contributed to a split on their side.

CLPD and Tribune fought, in particular, over the precise proportions to be allocated in an electoral college to the trade unions, CLPs and the PLP. Of all the cock-ups at this Conference, none was so ironic as the fact that the successful CLPD formula turned out to be instrumental in denying Benn the Deputy Leadership. The defeated Tribune formula, on the other hand, would have given him victory.

All this, however, is hindsight – the cherished possession of armchair critics. At the time, the Conference could only be seen as yet another great success for the left. From a house in Golders Green, the CLPD's Vladimir Derer and his wife Vera, Victor Schonfield, Peter Willsman, John Lansman, Francis Prideaux and Audrey Harrris conducted a brilliant campaign.

In the unions they were helped nationally by ACTT, the train driver's union ASLEF, ASTMS, the TASS and Construction sections of the AEUW, FBU, NATSOPA and NUPE. Key national officials of other unions who also lent vital support included Ron Todd of the TGWU, Eric Clarke of the NUM and Bob Wright at the AUEW. Throughout the unions, too, CLPD attracted support from individual activists and their branches.

This time CLPD left absolutely nothing to chance – they wisely set about rigging everything. To ensure that there would be no unexpected lurch to the right, under pressure from CLPD, the NEC decided that Wembley would be a Special Conference limited to those who had attended the previous Annual Conference.

CLPD also decided that the NEC should send out a basic 'model' constitutional amendment as guidance, which would help constituencies and unions to submit valid propositions to the Conference in line with its own proposals.

To say there was strong reaction in the PLP against the decision to have a model amendment would be more than an understatement. MPs were livid. A general view expressed in the Commons tea room, which I did my very best to encourage, was that the NEC was on the fiddle again, forcing us into an electoral college while leaving only the proportions to be filled in.

This bitterness overflowed at a rough meeting on 4 November, where Heffer was barracked unmercifully and responded by telling MPs that their sneering attitude would be 'noted'. Come the revolution, I would certainly be top of his black book.

At this meeting Jack Straw, who as everyone knows is an incurable softie, argued that the PLP should accept the proposals for change. He attacked the notion, being seriously peddled in the tea room, that the PLP should declare UDI. Joe Ashton also opposed UDI but suggested that we abandon the Conference and hold instead a one member, one vote (OMOV) ballot to confirm or otherwise the choice of Foot as Leader.

For my part, I warned that the NEC had opened a Pandora's box, which it would truly regret. Had we known that the changes would lead ultimately to a PLP with Tony Blair as leader and Benn a lonely, ineffective back-bencher, we might not have got so upset.

The day after, the Shadow Cabinet met. While the left on the NEC agreed that there should be an electoral college (with only the proportions to be decided), the right in the Shadow Cabinet were divided. Healey wanted a one member, one vote cast in secret at a Special Conference. Hattersley advocated a compromise: the PLP would be given 55 per cent and there would be an OMOV postal ballot of CLPs and trade unions.

Hattersley's plan was adopted by 8 votes to 7 at the Shadow Cabinet on 11 November and by 68 to 59 at a thinly attended PLP the following day. Full OMOV, strongly supported by Bill Rodgers and David Owen got nowhere and Owen, in a fit of pique, decided not to stand for the Shadow Cabinet elections.

While the PLP huffed and puffed and the Shadow Cabinet fell out, CLPD worked determinedly on 'fixing' the Conference.

Their next dodge was a real winner. They decided to shelve the established practice at Labour Party Conferences whereby it was possible to reject any proposition – because they realised that all the proposals might be defeated, just as at the last Annual Conference. Instead, they decided that a change would definitely be carried as the result of an elimination ballot with delegates voting in order of preference until one proposal emerged as winner.

At an NEC held on the 3 December we fought over the nuts and bolts – how the vote was to be taken by post or in Conference, the number of nominations from MPs each candidate required, how CLPs should take decisions. There was little principle involved – just manoeuvring for factional advantage. It was clear that whatever else this exercise was about, it was nothing to do with giving members of the Labour Party a real say in who should be their Leader.

Then the NEC staged its own eliminating ballot to decide proportions in an Electoral College. I, with Neville Hough's support, moved a formula which would give the PLP 50 per cent and the CLPs and trade unions 25 per cent each. With only Foot and Russell Tuck giving support, it was swiftly eliminated. So, too, was a motion giving 40 per cent to the PLP, 30 per cent to CLPs and 30 per cent to affiliates, which was supported only by Kinnock and Lestor.

The PLP had been put firmly in its place and in the final ballot the Tribune proposal – of one third each, moved by Allaun and Heffer – was also defeated. The CLPD formula, moved by Benn and Doug Hoyle, giving 40 per cent to the unions and affiliates, 30 per cent to the PLP and 30 per cent to CLPs carried the day as the NEC's recommendation.

Then it was agreed that Heffer be the NEC's speaker. This was regarded by some of us as our last and only opportunity to sabotage the whole event!

The Special Conference kicked off at 10 o'clock on 24 January, 1981 with Alex Kitson in the chair.

The shenanigans started straight away, with John Boyd of the Engineers moving a 'reference back' as the new voting system made it impossible to vote against every proposition, if necessary, in the time-honoured way. This was important to the AUEW, which had been mandated to vote against everything that did not give the PLP an overall majority. This was defeated by 1,936,000 to 5,060,000, however.

And so Wembley went on to debate the five bewildering options set out in the report to Conference: an Electoral College at Party Conference, a postal Electoral College, a separate Electoral College, a Ballot of Individual Members, and the last unbelievably headed 'Miscellaneous'. Following debate, an eliminating ballot would be taken until one method gained more than 50 per cent of the vote, as CLPD wanted. Conference would then vote on the precise rules applying to whatever method was chosen.

As often, I slept through Heffer's boring, opening speech proposing an electoral college. I was, however, rudely awoken by the barracking of Frank Chapple, advocating OMOV, which was much more lively.

'It is quite wrong,' he said, 'that the Leader of this Party, and a possible Prime Minister of the country, should be appointed by a combination of a caucus vote in the constituencies and wheeling and dealing by trade union leaders and the say-so of people who are not even members of this Party.'

Two political lemmings – MPs shortly to join the ranks of those not in the Party – Bob Maclennan and David Owen both attacked the block vote, supported OMOV and gave due warning that an electoral college would split the Party i.e. they would pack their carpetbags and depart.

Owen spoke with great realism and candour: 'The votes have been cobbled up. The arrangements have been made. An electoral college is going to be done. But I say to the Party this: The day this system is used to elect a Prime Minister, the whole of the country will be watching the procedures, and then these procedures will be shown to be totally undemocratic. They will be shown to be totally illegitimate.'

'Why change for a system now which you know will split the Party, which you know is unfair, which you know is undemocratic? . . . To allow the block vote to choose the future Prime Minister of this country is an outrage. It is a disgrace. This Conference ought not to accept it.'

John Morris, the former Secretary of State for Wales, who thankfully stuck with us and was never tempted to go with Owen & Co., also put the case for OMOV: 'Ultimately it will come, but today, Mr chairman, we must ensure that whatever we agree, whatever form the electoral college comes to, that it minimises conflict in the future.'

Bryan Stanley, of the POEU, put the Hattersley compromise, giving MPs a continuing role and providing a vote for members. Weighell supported him, ironically remarking: 'I know the block vote is suspect – I have one in my hand.'

The vicious attacks, of course, came from the loony left. Pat Wall, the Militant, attacked OMOV, arguing that 'the multi-millionaires who control the media would have the greatest influence'.

Moss Evans, the General Secretary of the TGWU, meanwhile spoke with the confidence of someone with 1,250,000 votes in his pocket. Supporting an electoral college, he laid into the 'practicality of OMOV'. 'Imagine that with a close-run election,' he said. 'It would not be a very strong basis for a Labour Prime Minister to go to the Palace on, would it?' For a Labour Prime Minister to go to the Palace with the Party in the state it was in would have been a near-miracle!

The result was an overwhelming victory for an 'Electoral College at Conference'.[1] The Conference then went on to decide the sticky question of the shares each section - trade union, PLP, CLPs and others – would have.

From a moderate trade union point of view, we were hamstrung from the outset in that the AUEW was committed to a formula which gave 75 per cent to the PLP, 10 per cent to the trade unions, 10 per cent to the CLPs and 5 per cent to other affiliates. It was a formula which had not a cat in hell's chance of being carried, but which Terry Duffy had put to his National Committee whilst having a rush of blood to the head.

Worse still, trying to avoid the cock-up caused by Bro. Knott at the Annual Conference, he had also got a decision from the National Committee binding on the delegation that they vote for nothing that did not give MPs a majority.

In this way, he found that he had not only stopped the left from forcing the delegation to vote for the CLPD motion but also ensured that he could not himself vote for the GMWU motion which would give MPs 50 per cent.

In the morning Joe Gormley had warned: 'Let me say to those of our colleagues who seem to be tied up by decisions and constitutions, that I do not think you are entitled this afternoon to opt out of responsibility of voting for something. This is too serious for that.'

Given the decision of the National Committee and the eagle eye of John Boyd, however, there was no way in which Terry could have voted. Many blamed Terry and Terry alone, but it was not just his fault. That belonged to all of us on the right who had not done our homework, produced an acceptable formula and organised behind it.

Not only had we lost the AUEW in this way, but more importantly in many respects USDAW, which had been gulled into submitting the proposition supported by CLPD. This came to have two main rivals – Tribune's PLP 33 per cent, trade unions 33 per cent, CLPs 33 per cent, Co-op etc 1 per cent; and the GMWU's 50 per cent to the PLP, 25 per cent to the trade unions and 25 per cent to the CLPs.

The GMWU proposition, moved by Basnett, started as the front runner. Tom Jackson, seconding, tackled the problem of the threatened SDP split head on. '[We] want to reassure the parliamentary party of a continued substantial influence in the election of the Party Leader. We want them to know and to understand that as our representatives in parliament they have our confidence, and we want them to stay with us. I do not believe that this Party can afford to lose the talents which we are in danger of losing. I believe it absolutely essential that this proposal, rather than the proposal which will reduce the status of the Parliamentary Labour Party, should be carried,' he said.

Bill Whatley, USDAW's General Secretary, was a strong moderate and would have been happy to see the defeat of his own union's proposition so that he could move his delegation's support behind Basnett.

The left's tactic, however, was clearly to prevent this from happening by piling up votes behind it. Clive Jenkins, for one, never missing a chance to be in the limelight, withdrew his own union's amendment early on in favour of USDAW. This was a tactical move, copied by others, which was to give success to the hard left

Before the Conference, CLPD had been very active. Although they set out with less widespread support than Tribune, they set out to win over to their formula those delegates with propositions which were bound to fall. To this end they contacted delegates, issued newsletters and held fringe briefing meetings. One message was clear: to beat Basnett and the PLP, all must swing behind USDAW.

Tony Banks, then representing Tooting CLP, rammed the message home from the rostrum, announcing that the agricultural workers were the latest to line up behind USDAW.

'It is an open secret that USDAW have said that if their resolution, Amendment 76, goes down, they will support 50 per cent for the PLP, 25 for the unions and 25 per cent for the CLPs,' he said. 'Therefore we have a great vested interest in encouraging USDAW's amendment to be at the top of the ballot right the way through, so that we are not left with a far more reactionary proposal.'

Banks's message was received loud and clear. The issue had been settled. Now there was no chance of USDAW switching, which Whatley would have done, given half the chance. Now, Conference paid more attention to telling the 'Gang of Three' how much they were definitely not wanted!

The only thing that remained was to put the right card in the box. A great buzz developed as everyone advised everyone else how to perform this simple task and then came the nervous wait for the results of the card votes.

In the first round, the Basnett '50 per cent to the PLP formula' obtained 2,368,000 votes and both Tribune and CLPD got 1,763,000. The AUEW formula received 992,000 and was eliminated with all the other no-hope options.

Then we voted again and waited, albeit without much hope. In the second ballot, the GMWU obtained 2,685,000 and CLPD 1,813,000. Tribune, with 1,757,000, was eliminated and the final ballot held between the GMWU and CLPD formulas.

At this point, it was quite clear that without the AUEW vote we could not win. On the third ballot Basnett's vote rose to 2,865,000, but CLPD's surged ahead to a winning 3,375,000. A final card vote endorsed the decision by 5 million to 1.8 million.

Benn's reaction was predictable 'No praise is high enough for the enormous skill of the CLPD, who worked tirelessly to get constituencies and smaller unions to vote for the 40–30–30 option.'

From the point of view of fixing, I totally agree. Although CLPD had been beaten at the NEC, they refused to give up but went on to win at the Conference. And the main reason that they won was good organisation. That it turned out to be a Pyrrhic victory should not detract from our admiration for a job well done.

It was Pyrrhic because the outsmarting of Tribune – with Benn telling them that 'we will go on until we win' and Heffer calling Benn and CLPD 'saboteurs' – split the left in a way that made them vulnerable when the right finally united and got its act together.

In another sense, too, this CLPD victory contained within itself the seeds of Benn's destruction. Had Benn and CLPD accepted the Tribune formula, Benn would almost certainly have become Deputy Leader. By giving the unions more votes than the CLPs, however, they made sure that would not happen.

By outmanouevering the moderate trade unions so decisively and humiliatingly at every turn, too, they brought into play one of my fundamental laws of politics – that every action produces an equal and opposite reaction. The moderates, realising that they could no longer go on like this, finally sorted themselves out.

It was not enough to rely on moderate MPs and their Campaign for Labour Victory, which was well-meaning but ineffective and had managed to issue just one broadsheet on OMOV in this whole battle.

While there were crumbs of comfort, overall the result was disastrous in so far as it was to be the excuse for 'The Gang of Three' Social Democrats at last to leave. Bryan Stanley told it to me in this way:

As the Conference was moving to its conclusion, Shirley Williams approached me in my seat at the end of the row of POEU delegates and asked if I could have a word with her.

Since I held the union's voting card, I was reluctant to move far away from my seat, and therefore Shirley and I sat on the stairs at the back of the hall where I could still keep an eye on proceedings. Shirley's message was clear. Owing to left wing control of the NEC and Trotskyite infiltration in the trade unions and constituency parties, the Labour Party was unelectable and it was time to look anew at a party based on social democratic beliefs.

Shirley then asked me if I would be prepared to support such a move. I was deeply disappointed to hear these ideas coming from Shirley, as we had worked together on the NEC in opposition to the crazy ideas of some of the more extreme left wing members. I respected her intellectual ability and I did not want to see the Labour Party losing her support.

I told her that I had been a member of the Labour Party for over thirty years and that I would never leave. There were things that were wrong at this time, but that we had to work together to change things for the better. However, she took the view that it was already too late, and pointed to the absolute chaos so evident that day at the Conference and expressed grave doubts about whether moderate trade union and Party Leaders would ever be able to work together to save the Labour Party from further disintegration and decline.

It was at that time and as a result of the Wembley Conference that I made up my mind that I would do my utmost to bring together leaders of the Labour movement to combat the organisation and manoeuvring of the left wing factions within the party.

Since 1978, the Loyalist Group on the NEC had nipped away at the ankles of the left, ever faithful to Jim Callaghan. But, as we have seen, apart from mandatory full reselection of MPs, the left juggernaut simply rolled on. Soon it was to be time for us to finally get out act together on the right. Again Bryan Stanley would be a leading inspiration – and John Spellar, Roger Godsiff and I the more than willing footsoldiers. But first we had to endure the return of the 'prince over the water', the Limehouse Declaration and the sad loss of so many loyalists to the SDP.

TEN

Shirley Throws In the Towel

The defection of the 'Gang of Three', David Owen, Bill Rodgers and Shirley Williams, from the Labour Party, together with many other moderate MPs, lords and Party activists in 1981, proved to be a body blow for the Old Labour Party from which it never recovered.

We did not win until 1997, when New Labour fought on policies which Owen described as more right wing than even he had wanted.

The Social Democrats left, I believe, not just because of the dreadful outcome of the Wembley Conference but because they could not get support from within the Party for the causes they espoused or, in the case of Owen, for their own personal ambitions.

For those of us who also advocated sane policies, it was a great misfortune that so many of the leading moderates appeared so personally arrogant and superior – and none were more so than Owen and Jenkins.

In Jenkins's case, it was not just pet causes and ambition, but pure pique that led to his leaving. He had blighted his career in March, 1972 with a massive political miscalculation – by resigning as Deputy Leader, when he thought the PLP was going to support a Shadow Cabinet decision calling for a referendum or a general election over the Common Market.

I say 'miscalculation' advisedly. Because I know from Jim Wellbeloved, who sat at the desk next to me in the Labour whips office, that the pro-Jenkins camp had blundered on their count. The pro-marketeers were actually going to win and Jenkins, to his disgust, had thrown it away. The reaction, however, to Jenkins's resignation was so marked that the vote was, in the event, lost!

It was no surprise to me. I knew Roy Jenkins as arrogant, superior, remote

– I was his regional whip for over four years but he spoke to me only once in all this time. This may have shown exemplary taste on his part, but it was a serious misjudgement for someone who required votes from lesser mortals.

Jenkins's aloofness came home to roost on Wilson's resignation, when he was beaten so easily by Callaghan for the Leadership. Then Jim decided not to make him Foreign Secretary, but Home Secretary instead. As a result, he quickly decided that, when the opportunity arose, he would go to Europe.

This he did on 8 September, 1976, with David Marquand joining him shortly afterwards. He did not do so well, however, in Europe and it wasn't long before we started to hear rumours that the 'prince over the water' was plotting his return.

These rumours flew thicker and faster when he gave the annual Dimbleby Lecture in November 1979, with the giveaway title 'Home thoughts from afar', in which he flew the kite of a realignment of the centre, called for proportional representation and advocated coalition politics.

The lecture certainly caused a stir. Indeed, Benn recalls that when Tom Bradley for one told him of Jenkins' intended return, Bradley remarked of the lecture: 'You should have seen the bits he left out!'[1]

By mid-January, 1980, obviously puffed up by the response from the chattering classes, Jenkins grandly declared that he would make himself available for a radical initiative in British politics.

Having seen Roy at work, I did not shake in my boots. A small group of fanatical supporters duly formed to prepare the way for the less than bonnie prince, but they did not attract very much support.

The greater threat came from Rodgers and Owen, although with me the penny dropped slowly that they were going. My vendetta against a group of right wing Labour fanatics, the Social Democratic Alliance (SDA) – of which more later – ensured that any members thinking of abandoning ship told me as little as possible.

After the split, one newspaper wrote about me as 'the one who got away', but the truth is that they never cast so much as a single fly in my direction. I was part of the trade union establishment from which Owen, at least, was trying to escape. It appears that it was John Horam – a man, now a Tory, who holds the distinction of ratting on two parties in his miserable career – who first put the idea of a separate party to Rodgers on the day that Jenkins was making his Dimbleby Lecture. A few days later, speaking at Abertillery, Rodgers himself referred to the need for a radical centre.

Now the real cancer had set in. At first both Owen and Williams resisted the idea. Both had made a big contribution to the Party, which had given them an enormous amount back in return. During the spring of 1980, Owen was still adamant that he would not leave the Party and attacked anyone who suggested it.

He believed that it would take 'a ten year slog' to get the Party back but thought the effort worth it. In late May, when he attended a Campaign for a Labour Victory meeting in Birmingham attended by both 'stayers' and 'splitters', Owen was clearly on the side of the 'stayers'.

After the Wembley 'Peace, Jobs and Freedom' fiasco, however, he had certainly joined the 'splitters', following the discovery, too, that John Silkin was going to re-open the question of Europe again.[2]

At the beginning of June, the issue of a split became a live one when the *Daily Mail* came out with the headline 'Centre Party to be formed on Monday', reporting that Jenkins was going to resign as President of the European Commission within a month and return to British politics.[3]

The piece was premature, but reflective of the tragedy to come. Just days later, Shirley Williams announced that whether she sought a seat in the Commons again depended very much on Labour's stance on Europe. With Rodgers and Owen, she issued a statement, too, to the effect that they could not remain in the Party if it decided to support withdrawal from the Common Market.[4]

Some, including Peter Shore, made it clear they would hardly weep at the prospect, but there was much dangerous gnashing of teeth among sympathisers in the PLP, many of whom wanted to declare UDI from the Party at large.

All the time that Jenkins sat in Europe dreaming of lording it at Number 10, the debate raged at home in the Labour Party. From the left and right, Heffer and Williams made most of the running, making speeches and writing articles. They became the Mutt and Jeff of the controversy, sparking off each other, as though they were conducting a lovers' tiff.

It was, indeed, the most beautifully choreographed of public spats. It began on 3 February, 1980 when both made widely reported keynote speeches simultaneously, Heffer at a Young Socialists Rally in Central Hall, Westminster and Williams at a Campaign for Labour Victory meeting in Leicester.

'Let me make it clear,' Eric told the true believers in fake benign fashion. 'I am not one of those who wants to throw anybody out of the Labour Party. The Party, in the best Anglican tradition, is a broad church and it must remain one by being tolerant to all the varying strands that go to make up the Party.'

Then he plunged the knife. 'But if some people feel they cannot accept Labour's socialist principles, aims and objectives; if they cannot accept Clause IV and the constitution, then they really ought to join some other party which is more to their taste. This would be good for them and good for the Party. Such people who have no real sympathy for Labour's basic views should not act as a fifth column in Labour's ranks. The words of the old song seem very appropriate: 'We don't want to lose you but we think you ought to go.'[5]

In Leicester meanwhile, Shirley was pulling no punches, calling for Militant and the other extremists – that is, most of Eric's audience – to be drummed out of the Party.

'The Party cannot turn its back on its internal rows. We cannot because hundreds of our best party workers are leaving the party. We cannot afford to lose them. The legitimate left members of the National Executive and of the parliamentary Party know this too. How long will they watch while the Party is being eaten away,' Shirley rightly warned.

'Speaking for myself, I do not want a new centre party. I want a Labour Party, the Labour Party, refreshed by new thinking and able to offer a convincing and attractive alternative to the Tories.' 'But if nothing is done by the legitimate left to fight the depredations of the Militant Tendency, the Labour Party will split or the support for a party of the centre will grow and grow. Our survival is in our own hands.'

Like any other lover from Liverpool, Heffer constantly blew hot and cold. One day he was attacking the 'Gang of Three' for voting with the Tories to go into the Common Market in the first place. The next, he was in conciliatory mood, asking them 'to think again' and talking of a 'united front' – quite possibly because he still laughably saw himself as successor to Callaghan.[6]

'It would be most regrettable if people who are pro-Market decided there was no place for them in the Labour Party. We have got to be prepared to recognise that there are varying points of view. There must be greater democracy within the Party.'

Over the summer, barely a day went by without more stuff and nonsense from Marching Eric. He was never out of the papers, declaring that a new centre party led by Jenkins had as much chance of success as a 'snowball in hell' and calling the Gang of Three 'one-issue fanatics'. Wrongly too, as usual, he pronounced a new party as unlikely to get off the ground.

On 1 August, Williams set out her views again in an 'open letter' in both the *Guardian* and *Mirror*, whereupon Mellow Eric replied more in sorrow than anger through 'The Thunderer' that their differences were not great and should be settled.[7]

It was not only Eric, however, who blew hot and cold. At one point, addressing the prospect of a third-party split, Williams responded that 'such a party would have no principles, no value and no backing'. At the end of September, however, she re-iterated that she would indeed quit if Conference voted to leave the Common Market.

The twists and turns in Shirley's mind are thrown into sharp relief during a mirror image guerrilla battle I, in particular, was pursuing with some other loonies – not Eric's Merseyside Militants this time, but the so-called Social Democratic Alliance on the Party's right.

The people who ran the SDA – Roger Fox, its chairman, and Douglas Eden and Stephen Haseler, the joint secretaries – were as arrogant as Owen and Jenkins at their best. They had founded the SDA in June 1975 to bring together those prepared to fight back against the steady advance of the extreme left. From just 42 original sponsors, by 1979 its membership numbered 800 and its Executive published newsletters, provided assistance against the left and publicised the growing influence of extremism in the Labour movement. Had the SDA confined itself to internal organisation, it would have been highly commendable. Unfortunately, however, it spent much of its time going public in ways embarrassing to others of us who were fighting the left. It did not help, for example, when, just prior to the 1979 general election, the SDA published *The Mutation of Labour*, warning Callaghan that he would lose. They demanded a pledge, too, that Jim would refuse to appoint any known left-winger to ministerial office including Benn, Foot, Allaun, Stan Orme, Norman Atkinson and 39 others who had allegedly consorted with extreme Marxist groups.[8]

The SDA then blotted its copy book completely during the Euro-elections on 30 May, when it declared that the candidacy of Terry Harrison, a member of the Editorial Board of *Militant*, was 'an affront to the voters of the Liverpool constituency. In these extraordinary circumstances it is not possible to advise the people of Liverpool and Bootle to vote Labour at this election'. Many did not and the consequent swing against Harrison was twice the national average (nearly 11 per cent) and Labour lost its tenth safest seat in the election.

This action was totally unacceptable and action against the SDA leaders inevitable. Heffer declared that he did not intend to get steamed up 'about the organisation, but the three officers had put themselves in an increasingly impossible situation'.

My view was harder, believing that it is just not possible for a serious political party to ignore members who are doing their best to ensure that your candidates are not elected. They could not remain members if they were going to help the Tories.

Whilst I was quite clear that we must take strong action against these right wing 'nutters', the left on the NEC found themselves in a great dilemma. The proposals to expel Haseler and Fox coincided with one to expel Ted Heslin of the Workers' Socialist League. The left, therefore, was forced to apply a similar outrageous, nonsensical formula to the SDA that they had devised for Heslin: 'That the NEC condemns and repudiates the action of Dr Haseler and Mr Fox and dissociates itself completely from their critical statements made by them about the Party; and in the light of this to uphold their appeals against expulsion.'

Judith Hart, elected by the unions and therefore not totally in the grip of the left caucus, challenged this nonsense, but lost. I was more successful, however, at the NEC in June when I challenged a similar decision over Eden.[9] I did so because during 1980 membership of the SDA became increasingly incompatible with that of the Labour Party and there was every reason to outlaw it. Not only did it become more strident, it also changed its essential character, ceasing to recruit solely among members of the Labour

Party, forming its own branches, affiliating sympathetic organisations and justifying this on the basis of the increasing numbers of moderates forced out of active Labour Party membership by the left.[10]

The SDA also announced a list of candidates, which included Fox, Haseler and Eden, to stand against the Labour extremists. A certain Councillor Roy Morris was to oppose Benn and other NEC left-wingers on the hit list included Heffer, Kinnock, Skinner, Lestor and Renee Short.[11]

Benn and his fellow lefties, however, continued to uphold the appeals of the SDA leadership, quoting the NEC resolution on 'Toleration within the Party'. This completely intolerant lot were worried, of course, in case I got at Militant and other ultra-left groups through action against the 'Social Democrats'.

Despite Benn's opposition, I persisted and in the autumn the National Agent, David Hughes, presented a paper recommending that the SDA be ineligible for affiliation to the Party i.e. that no SDA member could remain in the Labour Party.[12]

Then the focus of debate turned to the list the SDA had published of Party members willing to stand against left wing candidates at the general election. And at that stage, in September, Williams was quite prepared to move a resolution ejecting members, whether Militant or SDA, who stood against the Party.

In the event, she was defeated by Benn & Co., who gave those on the SDA list a month instead to deny their intentions before being chucked out.[13] Undaunted, however, the SDA refused to be intimidated by the NEC, warning it would press ahead if the Party went unilateralist at the 1980 Conference and the left pushed through the constitutional changes it wanted. To add insult to injury, the SDA invited Callaghan to break off all links with the left and lead the moderates instead. Of this, there was no chance – whilst Jim was fed up to the back teeth with the NEC, far from being Jenkins he was a Labour man through and through.

The SDA refused to co-operate with the NEC until it dealt with the likes of Militant, the irony being that it was shielded by the very same people it wanted out. I finally nailed the SDA in Benn's absence at the December meeting of the NEC's Organisation Committee when a report from Brigg and Scunthorpe CLP, of all places, that they had opposed an official Labour candidate in a Borough Council by-election, brought the issue to the crunch.

In the end it was all so simple. My resolution expelling the SDA was carried by 6 votes to 1. And as a consequence, it was finally decided that Douglas Eden could not be a member of the Labour Party.[14]

By this time, however, Williams and her close ally Tom Bradley had gone strangely missing. Later, indeed, in her absence I had to move motions which Shirley herself had prepared during November.

The first, expelling anyone who stood against us in the general election, was pretty much identical to the one she had put before. This time, it was passed.[15] The second, in their absence, hadn't a cat in hell's chance of being seconded. It specifically lumped Militant in the same boat as the SDA, with their own separate organisations against the rules.

But apart from me, there were only lefties there to vote – Kinnock, Heffer, Frank Allaun, Les Huckfield, Charles Kelly, Joan Maynard, Jo Richardson and Tony Saunois – and they had already decided not to move against Militant.[16]

By this time, indeed, Shirley had done a complete *volte face* as regards the SDP's future allies from the SDA. The writing was clearly on the wall. Ironically, too, after so many years of struggle against the left, the only expulsions I had notched up were against 'fellow travellers' on the right! In many ways, however, the SDA was identical to Militant – a party within a party. And like Militant they had been protected by Benn and his cohorts. With Benn missing, the SDA had lost its best friend and were shown the door.

At the following NEC, on 17 December, 1980, a request from the SDA to have a meeting with the NEC that morning was refused. Williams and Bradley then tried to overturn the decision to outlaw the SDA and so expel Eden, Fox and Haseler, but they were completely on their own.

And so we broke with the SDA, which only a short time before Shirley and Tom had been willing to expel. It would not be too long before they, too, would be on their way.

Throughout the autumn, indeed, the atmosphere within the PLP had become thoroughly nasty. During September a group of 12 MPs, dubbed the 'Dirty Dozen' and led by Mike Thomas, the MP for Newcastle-upon-Tyne East, published a radical plan for the Party which included 'one member, one vote', separate leaders for the PLP and the national Party and reform of the NEC.

Besides Thomas, this dozen comprised George Robertson (MP for Hamilton), John Cartwright (Greenwich and Woolwich East), Tom Ellis (Wrexham) Alan Fitch (Wigan), Willie Hamilton (Fife Central), John Horam (Gateshead West), Eric Ogden (Liverpool West Derby), Arthur Palmer (Bristol North East), John Roper (Farnworth), Tom Urwin (Houghton-le-Spring) and Ian Wrigglesworth (Teesside Thornaby).

Immediately after the 1980 Conference, Rodgers went a step further, calling on Callaghan to resign and for the PLP to stand up for itself. While Jim did quit on 15 October, it is debatable whether the PLP was capable of standing up for anyone by then, never mind itself![17] That abysmal Conference had demoralised many on the right and the fat spat further on the fire when Foot was elected leader on 10 November.

The pace quickened. Owen and Rodgers clearly signalled that they were on their way out when they attacked those Labour MPs, including Hattersley, who had demonstrated in the House against Tory council rent increases. On 21 November, Owen then announced that he was not going to stand for the Shadow Cabinet because of profound policy differences, including the Common Market and unilateralism. A week later, Williams declared that, although she was still against the creation of a 'Third Party', she had decided not to stand again for Stevenage. By then, she had become disillusioned with talks with both Healey and Foot and the end was near. As we have seen, with Tom Bradley, in November she was drafting a proposition to expel not only Militant but also the SDA, but by December she was leaving me to hold the baby.

The New Year was to be far from happy. On 12 January, Bradley informed Benn that there was going to be a split. This was confirmed for me, too, at a historic, bad-tempered meeting of the right wing Manifesto Group two days later. Then, I recall Owen saying: 'Don't let's fall out. Perhaps in ten years we will be together again.' As he ended up backing John Major, however, that prophecy had no chance of being fulfilled. I can't say that I was happy with the thought anyway, that I would have the ten-year slog he had predicted – only to hand over the better Party to him when he predicted our paths might meet again!

On 16 January, the press was alive with reports that Foot had sent Heffer to talk to Shirley. Sending this kamikaze on such a delicate mission was just as big a blow to us moderates as hearing, two days later, Owen telling the influential interviewer Brian Walden on weekend TV he would leave if we went ahead with an electoral college. That made it a dead certainty.

Our gloom deepened when the great loyalists Ken Weetch, Giles Radice and George Robertson met Rodgers the day before the Wembley Conference, but made no headway. It is only justice that, after New Labour's 1997 victory, Rodgers had to watch Robertson become the new Secretary of State for Defence. I hope it hurt him!

The Special Conference at Wembley was held on the 24 January and was followed the next day by now infamous 'Limehouse Declaration'. So-called because of the area in London's Docklands where Owen lived, this called for the establishment of a new 'Council for Social Democracy' and a realignment of British politics. It was a rallying cry to defect and it was against a background of immense hostility and suspicion, to say the least, that Williams and Bradley attended the next meeting of Labour's NEC on 28 January, 1981.

Shirley was obviously extremely uncomfortable and behaved very strangely. She read a confused statement stating that she was not going to answer any questions until the issue of Militant had been dealt with. Thereupon Joan Lestor, looking to the skies, summed it up by saying that Shirley did not know whether she was going to stay in the Party or not. Earlier, too, Shirley had done a clog dance with meaningless amendments to a draft statement from Michael Foot on 'Working Together for a Labour Government' and was left out on her own even by Tom Bradley.

On 9 February, Williams resigned from the NEC. Ironically, in that very month the tide in the unions at least had just started to turn, with the right dominating the powerful engineering union delegations.[18]

For effect, the names of the Gang of Three's supporters, mostly defectors, were announced in stages. On 5 February a list of 100 'Council for Social Democracy' supporters was published. A fortnight later, Ian Wrigglesworth, Tom Ellis and Richard Crawshaw resigned from the Party and Bradley announced he was not standing as a Labour candidate again.

Then on 2 March, 12 Social Democrats resigned the Labour whip. The following day they were followed by Owen, Rodgers and Williams, in conjunction with Jenkins, George Brown, Alf Robens, Hartley Shawcross, Dick Marsh, Ray Gunter, Herbert Bowden, Edmund Dell and Jack Diamond. These were the heavyweights. Each had played an important part in Labour governments. They were top of the left's most hated list.

At the NEC on 25 March, a document was produced which showed that the new party had already been under active preparation in November, 1980. The paper discussed whether to form a Social Democratic organisation which would avoid proscription or a new party; whether the break should be swift (after the Special Conference) or slower (after the next Annual Conference).

'Keeping the people on the NEC and Shadow Cabinet is a perfectly tenable strategy,' it stated in black and white. By moving quickly, 'we would, however, opt out of the left-right Labour Party row and instead concentrate on putting across a positive image of what we believed in', it added.

A suitable resolution expressing disgust was passed by the NEC and on 26 March, 1981 the SDP was launched. Labour's prospect of power was shattered for a generation.

Publicly, I made my contempt for the 'quitters' quite plain. 'I have no patience with people who resign because for the moment they have lost an argument,' I told my local *Sentinel* newspaper in March. 'There is no way that I would ever leave the Party to join a new Social Democratic grouping. I have been in the Labour Party for nearly 36 years and I have no intention of letting anyone barge me out of it.'[19]

The SDP were, I said later in the year, a 'mixture of the posh set and a convalescent home for Labour MPs who have caved into the rough and tumble of constituency politics.' 'I don't think we have seen the end of the defections yet. Most of the Labour MPs joining the Social Democrats are those who would lose their seats either at reselection or by changing boundaries. It has turned into a rag bag party'.

In fact, we did lose others I wished had stayed: John Grant, Ron Brown, Llin's cousin Jeffrey Thomas MP – 'bad blood', I called it – and (but not to the SDP) George Cunningham. Whatever my caustic comments at the time, I wished that good people such as Jim Wellbeloved, Bob Mitchell, James Dunn and Tom McNally had not been among the deserters.

Those of us on the right not only lost their support and companionship, but also became tainted by their treachery. However they had gone, becoming for those Labour moderates who had stood firm yet another gang to fight against. Now was the time for all good men to come to the aid of the Party and come they did, at last, in the shape of the St Ermin's Group.

ELEVEN

The Moderates Fight Back

It was not only policy differences over Europe and the bomb and the twisting of rules on the NEC that led to the creation of the SDP. One of the main reasons for the departure of the Gang of Three was that they thought that the Labour Party had been lost forever to the left and that consequently that they had no future in it.

They had deplored the fact that Callaghan had capitulated over the method of choosing the Leader at Bishop's Stortford. They were bitter that Foot had beaten Healey even though it is clear that some of their supporters had voted for him. This led them to lose faith even in the PLP itself.

The moderate Manifesto Group, which had operated since 1974–75, enjoyed considerable success in PLP elections, but had little influence outside the House of Commons. It was left to the Campaign for a Labour Victory (CLV), established in 1977 by John Cartwright and Ian Wrigglesworth, to organise the moderates outside. Run by Alec McGivan and Roger Liddle, however, rightly or wrongly it was perceived as elitist and achieved little at grassroots level.

The Gang of Three, together with Roy Hattersley, made various lofty pronouncements through it from time to time, but the organisation carried far too little weight in the Party at large.

The CLV did try, at least, to mount an opposition to the left and constantly called for changes in the NEC. Picking up the democratic gauntlet, in February, 1980, it issued a manifesto calling for one member one vote, an initiative taken up by 30 backbenchers, too, in an appeal to the Party Leadership.

They were, however, unable to create a machine able to match the ceaseless activism of the left. Shirley put this failure down to the fact that, unlike the loonies, they did not commit their whole lives to the Party. I only wish I had known this at the time!

As David and Maurice Kogan relate in their influential book, *The Battle for the Labour Party*, she also complained of intimidation, lack of financial resources and barriers to good, old-fashioned plotting – right wing trade union members in particular, were allegedly unable to have pre-meetings because they had to travel down from the North.

While there was truth in the point about intimidation, however, the account given in the Kogan book is of very limited value. Pre-meetings of loyalists were organised, but on Sam McCluskie's insistence Williams was barred from attending. Nor was money a hindrance, certainly not after we had got ourselves organised.

The failure to make headway in the constituencies arose mainly because the right wing Leadership were seen as elitists, supporting unattractive policies – the Common Market, Nuclear Defence and Wage Controls.

The messianic message of the left promising to give the active rank and file a share in the running of the Party was more attractive than the CLV message asking them to defend the privileges of MPs. It was the difference between trying to sell Eskimos thermal underwear or bikinis.

One type of activist could have been organised better by the right – local councillors. However the parliamentary Leadership put too little effort into mobilising this source of right wing strength. In any case, too many coun-cillors had neglected the Party machine after election or had made it easy for the left by deliberately keeping membership low – i.e. to friends and family whom they could rely on at selection time! Others were just too busy.

The situation in the unions had also been grim. It was not only that the traditional support for the Leadership had been weakened by the emergence of new leaders. Too little attention has been paid by academic commentators to the significance of the Isle of Grain dispute which led to great and crippling antagonisms between Basnett on the one side and Terry Duffy and Frank Chapple on the other.

Originally this was simply a pay dispute with the Central Electricity Generating Board (CEGB). When, however, scaffolders went on strike, laggers – belonging to the GMWU – were laid off. At the end of the strike, not all the laggers were re-instated and so they in turn went on strike. When they were then dismissed by the contractors, work stopped on two boilers, putting others out of work. The craft unions then asked for the intervention of the TUC.

The complex dispute escalated dangerously and absurdly, however. The other unions accused the laggers of jeopardising the jobs of 1,600 workers, so if they would not reach an agreement, other unions would do the work. The TUC then negotiated a settlement which included a provision for laggers to go above £4.60 an hour to help restore earnings. This threat to differentials was unacceptable to the CEGB, EETPU, the AUEW and the Boilermakers and the other unions started lagging instead.

Is it any wonder that the general secretaries were constantly at daggers drawn? The industrial costs were heavy, but the political consequences to the right were catastrophic. With the TGWU lost to us, we desperately needed the support of both the AUEW and the GMWU. As it was, we could rely on neither.

After Terry Duffy replaced Hugh Scanlon as President of the AUEW, we had great hopes. But life is never as simple as that. In those days there was always open warfare in their Labour Party delegation. It was not possible for the President simply to have his own way any more. What made it worse, too, was that the AUEW was tied to an electoral system which had a bad habit of producing left wing delegations totally unrepresentative of their craft membership.[1]

In 1980, we rejoiced when the right wing caucus gained a majority of one in the delegation. We wept when it all turned out so differently, as we have seen, with the delegate from Poole switching his allegiance to the left. We wept, too, when we learned that the Boilermakers' delegation had switched against us over the Leadership because their leaders left the meeting early.

It is not surprising that Shirley Williams would not believe the tales of hope that I and others told her. She made it clear she was fed up with waiting for Basnett and Duffy and so she picked up her hockey stick and left. Her departure was hastened, too, when the AUEW at the Wembley Conference, to use John Spellar's words, 'sat on their hands over some convoluted interpretation of a decision of their National Committee.'

As indicated earlier, the irony was that, on 23 February, 1981, shortly before she quit with the SDP, the right finally gained control of the union's Labour and TUC delegations and the AUEW's National Committee. Duffy's long, courageous fight back had paid off. He had stood his corner in Birmingham against the bully boys of the left.[2]

Because Terry's cavalry had arrived just too late to hold Shirley and the other deserters back, however, we had to cope with the enormous problems they left on our own.

The first thing to be done was to try to bring together those moderates who had stayed loyal. We achieved this, albeit very slowly. In January, more than half the PLP signed a statement disagreeing with the new electoral college, but rejected moves to form a new centre party.

In mid-February, over 100 MPs met in Westminster to form a new group, the Labour Solidarity campaign to pull the Party back from the brink of self-destruction from SDP defectors and the ultra-left.[3] Healey attended and Foot, although he had been told, did nothing to stop it.

The meeting was chaired by Roy Hattersley and it agreed a programme of constituency meetings and a newsletter. A steering group of 14 was appointed, including representatives of Tribune, the Manifesto Group, Labour First and MPs belonging to no faction. It comprised Stanley Clinton Davis, Joe Ashton, Martin O'Neill, Donald Dewar, Arthur Davidson, Denis Howell, John Grant, Ken Woolmer, Frank Field, Gerald Kaufman, Austin Mitchell, Giles Radice, Roy Hattersley and me.

This gang was a grand gesture but without effective constituency organisation it was of limited use. Neither had it much appeal to many union moderates. The truth is that the departure of Callaghan had left an enormous gap. There was no leadership from the PLP. Healey never knew the time of day. Although he attended a couple of meetings he didn't want to be involved in factions. And Hattersley and Peter Shore were to my mind incapable of meaningful leadership.

In the atmosphere created by the defection of the Gang of Three, it would have been understandable if we had retreated into our unions and allowed the left to continue without opposition their destruction of the Labour Party.

That this was not allowed to happen was in large part due to the tenacity of a number of trade unionists – particularly Terry Duffy of the AUEW, Sid

Weighell of the railwaymen (NUR), Bill Sirs of the steelworkers (ISTC), Bryan Stanley (POEU), Frank Chapple (EETPU), Roy Grantham (APEX), Hector Smith of the Blastfurnacemen (NUBF), Bill Whatley (USDAW) and Tom Jackson of the postalworkers (UPW). Joe Gormley and Sid Vincent in the NUM also gave great support.

By coming together and organising the fight against the left they saved the Labour Party. Their names should form a roll of honour that ought to grace the walls of 10 Downing Street whenever there is a Labour Prime Minister.

In February, 1980 it was this group which, rather than give in to the left and follow the Social Democrats into oblivion, raised the moderate standard at a meeting at the Charing Cross Hotel in London immediately after the Wembley Conference.

As Bryan Stanley recalled it:

We found ourselves at a meeting in the Charing Cross Hotel with the common objective of finding a way to save the Labour Party and to make it electable again. I clearly remember that it was a cold night in February and after we left the meeting, which was supposed to have been held behind closed doors with everyone present refraining from publicity, at the front of the station, a newspaper seller had a poster bearing the message: 'The March of the Labour Party Mods'. I bought a paper and found that it was reporting the proceedings of the meeting I had just left.[4]

Remarkably at this meeting, Healey made one of his rare appearances at such a gathering. Denis Howell, always a tower of strength, was there too. Basnett, true to form, did not turn up but Frank Chapple, who would always stand up and be counted, made a momentary appearance wearing a spectacular bow tie. Roger Godsiff, John Spellar and I were there as political officers and fixers.

Healey, sadly, did not come out spoiling for the fight. His job, he saw, at that time was to argue for unity. He did not want to see a split in the unions like that dividing the PLP. Fortunately, Terry Duffy's attitude was what was needed. Enough, he said, was enough. And we would not invite unions who blew hot and cold about the left.

To my relief, the meeting decided to regain control of the NEC by organising the union vote at Conference and bolstering moderate unions in the constituencies to help in the reselection of sensible MPs.

Nobody believed that it would be easy. All sorts of custom and practice – the be-all and end-all of the union movement – imposed constraints at the NEC. Unions, for example, felt bound to support their own nominee even when the political complexion of the union changed. They had little room to manoeuvre even if that officer was left wing. Moreover, traditional alliances often stopped unions voting for a slate made up entirely of moderates. In the same way, the biggest unions traditionally voted for each other – making sure that each of them would be represented.

There were other situations where unions voted for each other as a matter of course, e.g. the historic 'Triple Alliance' of steelworkers, railwaymen and miners; unions in the same industry; those in merger talks such as APEX and ASTMS; and unions which traditionally made deals to share out TUC General Council and Labour NEC seats.

We also faced the increased membership numbers, with which left unions – including the TGWU and NUPE – affiliated, giving them more votes at Conference: the reduced affiliation of EETPU for ideological reasons; and the inability of the AUEW for financial reasons to increase theirs.

And we also had to confront an organised left group on the TUC General Council which had full-time organisers at its beck and call. These included Alan Meale (now MP for Mansfield), a lovely fellow who would have been better suited waving a magic wand for some charity, than wielding a hatchet for the left. But he got results – at least until we counter-attacked.

Fixing the constituencies was no easy job, either. I spent a lot of time doing this for the POEU to obtain sponsored MPs. One key rule that few seemed to understand was that a union branch could affiliate to any constituency in which it had members. We had to work hard to get the message across as to how important it was to increase branch affiliations – except where they were politically unreliable. And then we had to persuade union moderates to join the Party and sign up as delegates.

Ironically, as we shall see later, one of the easier places this was arranged was in the temple of the messiah, Benn himself, in Bristol.

The rescuers, the General Secretaries or their emissaries, met again at the St Ermin's Hotel, London on Wednesday, 4 March 1981. It is a day etched on my mind, as we now became known as the St Ermin's Group. And from thereon Roger Godsiff kept meticulous notes of the meetings.

Just nine people were present at this second gathering. Terry was firstly taken to task about leaking. 'Fixing' was far better better done in secret – indeed, that is why John Spellar had qualms about my writing this book at all. In future, it was agreed, confidentiality would reign supreme. Documents considered would be collected up at the end. All correspondence would go to home addresses. As a result, except for two minor breaches, while documents from the left were constantly provided to this group, the left did not receive those of the moderates.

After we had donned cloaks and unsheathed daggers, Dennis Howell, then MP for Birmingham Small Heath (and later ably succeeded by Roger Godsiff), reported on the Labour Solidarity Campaign which had also been set up with the support of 120 MPs as a loyalist vehicle. Labour Solidarity will receive scant mention in this book. While it tried hard, it had neither the resources nor the leadership to be successful. Roy Hattersley and Peter Shore were frankly incapable of inspiring moderate party rank and file members to go into battle in the numbers we needed.

We in the St Ermin's Group were far more successful in our work with the unions than Labour Solidarity in the Party. Within the Group, the main responsibility for the fight back lay with the Steering Committee for voting at Annual Conference and with the Political Officers group.

While the latter built up our network in the union machine, the former compiled and delivered the votes for our slate of NEC candidates. The two quickly merged and took on a life of their own, without having to troop back and forth to the General Secretaries. The core of St Ermin's consisted of Bryan Stanley, John Spellar, Roger Godsiff, Sandy Feather, Denis Howell, Charlie Turnock and me.

What is remarkable, looking back, and comparing our meetings with those of the left, was the degree of unity and the lack of conflict. Certainly Spellar, an energetic driving force, sometimes thought that Godsiff and I were too prone to compromise with the forces of darkness. We tolerated this, of course, as par for the course because of the hardline attitude of the EETPU in those days!

Spellar made a major contribution in providing a long-term strategic perspective, continually pushing hard, ensuring Godsiff and I kept our noses to the grindstone and persuading the hard right to agree deals from which they got little immediate benefit. He also paid great attention to what the enemy was up to, reading every way-out, loony left wing publication.

If Spellar was the long term thinker and short term progress chaser, Godsiff was the master of calculation. With the maths in his mind all the time, he would always be working out what were the deals to make. In Spellar's own words: 'the left . . . were hampered by never having an experienced number counter. We had the best one in the business in Roger Godsiff . . . Roger's key understanding was that winning seats was more important than the size of the majority, except to individual egos.' One of our opponents, Doug Hoyle, paid another tribute: 'Roger Godsiff would put deals in an absolutely honest way – you will get more votes, but you won't get on.'

My role was to support Spellar and Godsiff by acting as a link with the NEC and an emissary to union officials and others. Often we found that I got access where others would fail. Although portrayed in the party as 'the Hammer of the Left', I was seen by many in the trade unions in a different light after helping them from government days.

I kept up my links with 'the brothers'. In this, I was 'Old Labour' at its most blatant; some would say at its worst. So often it was a case of: 'you scratched my back and, now no-one's watching, I'll scratch yours'.

St Ermin's was not just a three-man team, however. Sandy Feather kept contact with a number of smaller unions; Charlie Turnock was also important and again Bryan Stanley, who was one of the few people on earth that Basnett would deal with. I say 'on earth' because Basnett thought himself on best of terms with all the saints.

One key role was to maximise our strength on the Conference floor – bolstering affiliations, right wing delegations and agreeing 'the slate'. The last was not always easy. It was like drawing up the list of invitations for a kids party: 'Do we have to have him?' 'Yes, remember, he asked you last year' 'Why can't we have her?' 'Because six others won't come, if we do!'

There came a time, for example, when it was apparent that no EETPU nominee was at all electable and yet the EETPU vote was essential. Even though Spellar was its political officer, it was by no means easy to persuade such a big, proud union that it was in the right's best interest to vote for a list leaving them without influence.

It was never possible to hope for 100 per cent success. The aim was to draw up a list to elect as many supporters as possible. Here, Spellar often diverged from Roger and I. He would always look longer out than us, preferring to wait for the person who would give us 100 per cent, rather than just half what we wanted. Reflecting the EETPU's views, Spellar would also often take a similarly polarised view of policy.

We in turn would often aim for temporary alliances of convenience to give us the votes we needed. My motto was always: 'a bird in the hand is worth two in the bush, even if the bugger sometimes hops off and disappears back into the bush'!

Spellar was nonetheless a good team player and only his facial expressions told us when he thought us total softies. Being regarded as softies by the hard right, however, was a small price to pay for progress.

Once people on 'the slate' had been properly nominated, our job was to turn out the vote. With some unions – my own POEU for example – it was a simple case of 'give us the list and I'll bump it through'. With others, the task was more complicated. If they couldn't deliver the whole slate, I would always get whatever I could and be grateful for it – always working to Godsiff's plan to ensure individual votes were most effectively used.

When the left did not have a full slate, the skill was to get left-dominated unions to give their votes to someone on the moderate slate who was unlikely to get elected without them. So you did not want votes for the AUEW or GMWU candidate, who would whistle home anyway. It was better to direct other votes elsewhere.

After 1983, too, Godsiff learned to persuade individual left wingers to look after themselves by doing deals with us and ratting on deals with the left. That, however, only came after two years hard slog to regain the ground we has so painfully lost.

It was on 4 March, 1981, I remember, that I gave the Group's first progress report on drawing up our slate. Betty Boothroyd, Shirley Summerskill, Diane Hayter and Gwyneth Dunwoody had 'picked themselves' for the women's section. The fifth place was left vacant until we found out from USDAW whether they had a nominee we could support. They couldn't and, failing to find someone ourselves, we added Judith Hart.

She would be elected anyway, so any votes given to her would not make it harder for our candidates!

In the union section, the nod was given to me, Allen Hadden, Neville Hough, Gerry Russell, Sam McCluskie, Russell Tuck, Syd Tierney, Denis Howell and Alex Kitson, with three vacancies 'pending further enquiries'.[5]

At each meeting there would then be progress reports on each union in which a list had been planted. Unions having difficulty with any individual name were urged to get in touch with Godsiff or Bryan Stanley.[6]

It was not only the NEC about which we were concerned. Though we were unable to settle on a candidate at our first meeting to succeed Ron Hayward as the Party's General Secretary, we quickly settled on Eric Varley as Treasurer. Like the left, we also paid close attention to motions, settling in particular to try and change the composition of the electoral college to 50–25–25 in the PLP's favour.

As 1981 progressed, however, all of this was put to one side as events in Benn's battle with Healey for the Deputy Leadership overtook us.

TWELVE

Toad Fights Badger

The conflict between Benn and Denis Healey dominated Labour's 1981 Conference and was crucial to the battle for the Party's soul.

The decision at Wembley to create an electoral college dominated by the unions had been initially seen as a great victory for Benn. Later, however, he came to realise that taking the decision out of the hands of the Parliamentary Labour Party greatly strengthened the power of the Leader. Indeed, it paved the way – with the introduction of one member, one vote – for the Party's new presidential style of government.

Had Benn settled for the soft left Tribunite formula for equal shares in the college, he would have become Deputy Leader. I will never understand why he and the left wing fixers did not see that they would benefit most from the formula which gave the greatest possible weight to the constituencies. As Neil Kinnock clearly warned them at the time: 'The trade union vote could be manipulated.'

Certainly these considerations were far from Benn's mind when, straight after Wembley, he held one of his 'ad hoc house meetings' with the Deputy Leadership in mind. Most of his acolytes were present: Tony Banks, Michael Meacher, Chris Mullin, Audrey Wise and her daughter Valerie, Jo Richardson, Ken Coates, Vladimir Derer, Stuart Holland, Frances Morrell, Reg Race, Victor Schonfield, and Stephen and Hilary Benn. They gathered in an excited mood: they had just triumphed not only against the right and the trade union barons, but also against Tribune itself.

How the devil had cast his net – had Comrade Beelzebub attended, he might well have chaired the 'Benn Mafia', this motley collection from the dark side.

Only Ken Coates appears to have had doubts about the wisdom of Benn's strategy. The others were enthusiastic, to say the least. Banks suggested they create a hue and cry from the rank and file that Benn fight Healey. Straining at the leash, Mullin drafted a model resolution there and then for CLPs and Schonfield wanted to arm-twist MPs through pressure from constituency activists.[1]

Reg Race, whose only positive contribution to the Labour movement to my mind was to remove Norman Atkinson from parliament, suggested getting Benn into Tribune to maximise the vote among the PLP. Audrey Wise, too, supported this most cynical of moves, rightly pointing out that their votes were needed. Equally correctly, Coates and Holland had reservations, knowing how antagonistic some Tribune members – for example Robert Kilroy-Silk – were to Benn.

Benn's reluctance to join Tribune proved well-founded. When he paid over his £50, he found a majority, of course, were utterly fed up with him because he had helped to defeat their formula at Wembley.

Forgetting that he should be waiting for the cry of the populace, Benn simply told his fixers that he would stand. The right thing, he suggested, would be to start by ringing up key people. He knew, of course, that Scargill would be OK, but still wondered about the likes of Ron Todd or Jack Dromey in the TGWU.

In March that year we find Benn writing that Foot's attack on Militant meant that he would be driven to campaign for the Deputy Leadership. This, however, is just the usual economy with the truth. The reality is that Benn had long decided to run and do what was necessary to win, whatever the wrecking effect it had.[2]

He was, indeed, keen to precipitate the departure of the Social Democrats and announce his candidature, despite warnings from Foot that it would split the Party. Others warned about the vitriol from many in the PLP about his latest stunt – a loyalty oath for the NEC drafted by Geoff Bish. As ever, however, he put on his blinkers and concentrated on the one thing really important to him: his own ambition.

Joe Ashton told him Tribune wanted him to wait, but Benn was in no mood to listen: he announced his candidature in a statement put into the Press Gallery of the House of Commons at 3 am in the morning!

The news not only split the Party: fatally for Benn, it also divided Tribune. A week later Benn believed that Kinnock was even getting a round-robin signed by Transport House staff, urging him to think again. He knew that no one in the Shadow Cabinet supported him and that many left wing MPs were doubtful, but he still went on undeterred.

While he was able to pull some around, such as the impressionable Alf Dubs, many in Tribune, including Robin Cook and Jeff Rooker, simply could not come to terms with it. John Prescott, indeed, is understood to have declared that: 'Tony should back down or we should disown him'.

From Tribune's ranks, it was Heffer who would have been expected to stand. The rumours buzzed around, but the poor lamb had been warned off by his constituency party under Militant influence. And so Eric was forced to support the aristocratic Anthony Wedgwood Benn.

In the end, the antagonism Benn created within Tribune was to prove his undoing. But, as ever, he thought he could ride roughshod over them and get away with it. He had total confidence in his outside fixers and their vast web of left wing intrigue.

And well he might. Just before Conference, a Labour Co-ordinating Committee meeting attracted 780 of the comrades in support of Benn and Peter Hain was arranging another LCC meeting for trade unionists which they hoped would be equally successful.

The Rank and File Mobilising Committee issued a statement, too, calling for support for free elections in the Labour Party and welcoming Benn's candidature. By free elections, of course, they meant putting the screws on individual MPs worried about their own reselection.

There was a formidable left machine at work, which commanded considerable resources. Benn had no qualms at being a machine politician – indeed he might have been more at home, and ultimately more successful, in Chicago.

All the left groups would be harnessed together – CPLD, the LCC, the Institute for Workers' Control, the ILP, Socialist Campaign for a Labour Victory, Labour Party Young Socialists, Clause Four, NALSO and, of course, Militant. From Benn's point of view, the more who joined the campaign the better – this was not the time to question whether it was right to ally oneself with thugs and totalitarians.

On 31 May, the loonies came together to announced a common '5 point programme' that reprised all the bloody struggles we had fought for years. The machine was going to be formidable.[3]

The night before, Benn had held yet another house party for the usual suspects and others such as Hain and Dawn Primarolo. As Benn saw it: 'these were the people who had formed the Rank and File Mobilising Committee and, when the time came, they would be the people who would organise the Benn election campaign'.

Simon Hoggart, now the doyen of sketch writers at the *Guardian*, summed up the left's tactics beautifully. Under the catchline 'How 'no hope' Benn came in sight of victory,' he wrote.

> The campaign has been organised by the Rank and File Mobilising Committee an umbrella for most of the party's left wing groups. They have met most weeks at people's flats, the Commons, County Hall in London or Benn's house in Holland Park. But they have no central headquarters. Chris Mullin, a leading Benn amanuensis, said: 'We're like the Vietcong.'
>
> What the Benn team have got is a large and impressive card file index containing the phone numbers of Benn supporters all over the country, in every union and almost every constituency. News and information sent in by these people is monitored in precise detail . . . When pressure has to be exerted, it always comes from a supporter in the relevant area or union. An unknown voice from London is of scant use compared to an old acquaintance from the same part of the world. The magic card index contains hundreds of such names.

In the meantime, the Healey campaign was conducted on traditional lines and relied mainly on personal contacts and persuading unions to have ballots in the belief that these he would win. This proved correct except in the NUM, where even the Nottinghamshire miners, later to break from Scargill, went for Benn.[4]

Whether unions held ballots or not, the moderate machine men beavered away pointing out the blindingly obvious: that the election of Benn would be an electoral disaster. Think what the Tories would do to a combination of Foot and Benn. It was, to those desperate to escape from Thatcherism, the only argument that mattered

We kept in contact with MPs, too, region by region. In July, we were issued with a check list asking us to identify the voting intentions on first and second ballot of each MP. Who, too, were the Healey waverers? Should he call them or should someone else? We were asked, too, for phone numbers. For a serious campaigner the questions were basic, but I knew that many of my colleagues had never fixed anything in their lives and had no idea of how to go about it. But we did the 'ring round' anyway, without which no fixer feels life is complete.

Within the unions and PLP, we had a great deal of success. But we failed almost completely within the constituencies, where the left had massive support and far superior organisation. A few went to Healey – in the areas of moderate strength, such as the North East and Wales, and where ballots were held, like Newcastle-under-Lyme – but most did not. Benn's organisers ensured that the vote of most constituencies was determined by GMCs under the influence of the loony left.

I remember receiving my ring-around list in the West Midlands. Later it made pretty dismal reading. Of the 56 constituencies on the list, the single word 'No' is written against 29, with just 6 as 'Yes' or 'Should be OK' and 8 'worth a try'.

While Benn had the constituencies sewn up, however, he still needed to pressurise MPs and make ground in the unions.

His union campaign started with a serious setback. Alex Kitson – part of the left group on the NEC and Assistant General Secretary of the TGWU – responded to the announcement of Benn's candidature by issuing an open letter to the media urging him to back down. Nonetheless, Tony Banks, along with other fixers, was given the job of delivering the union vote for Benn.

They put in an enormous effort and, indeed, were successful in securing votes for Benn in the face of opposition from key union leaders on the left, including Moss Evans and Clive Jenkins. Not only did they want stability in the run-up to a general election, they had serious reservations about Benn's style. They also realised that a contest with Healey would give the SDP a perfect launch platform.

In mid-April, indeed, Jenkins tried to talk Benn out of standing and presented him with a loving cup inscribed 'Elections can be poisoned chalices, Tony' on one side and 'Don't do it, Tony' on the other! Where Benn, or his fixers, failed to get the support of the union leaders directly, however, they appealed over their heads to Union Conferences. On 15 May, the tremendously hard work paid off when SOGAT came out in favour of Benn. Three days later it was Jenkins's turn to eat humble pie: by 146,840 to 140,340 votes – a narrow margin, but even one vote is enough – the ASTMS rejected its leader's advice and backed Benn, who had performed brilliantly at a fringe meeting.

All this frenetic activity, however, created a backlash. And at the beginning of July a group of left wing union leaders visited him in the company of Tony Banks and Alan Meale to warn him against upsetting other General Secretaries.[5]

Far from going softly-softly, however, the left wing fixers spurred themselves on to even greater effort. This was a bitter, no-holds-barred fight-to the-death campaign. Both sides hated each other and made that clear in public. The cynicism on both sides was truly professional. One of my favourite war time recollections occurred at the NEC on 24 June when Healey outflanked the left by jumping in smartly to second a resolution calling for less personal and more tolerant campaigning!

On the same day Benn records going to address a meeting of Labour First, a 35-strong new centre group set up – or so he thought – by MPs 'who are dissatisfied with the Manifesto Group, which is right-wing and pro-Common Market, and with the Tribune Group, which they think of as dangerously left wing'.[6]

Quite a few turned up from both wings, including Gerald Kaufman, Jim Wellbeloved, Joan Lestor and David Clark.[7] In truth, the moderate members of Labour First were far from dissatisfied with the Manifesto Group. Instead, they helped create Labour First as a meeting point for Tribune members fed up with Benn and Heffer.

Indeed, there were few votes for him to win in the House of Commons at all. The antagonism had gone too deep despite his temporary absence from the fray due to illness at the end of summer. Later on, in September, when he went to Wales, Ann Clwyd told him that not a single Welsh MP would appear on the platform with him.

His Campaign Committee, including Meacher, Banks, Mullin and Race, though had more to cheer about when nominations published in mid-August showed Benn to be well ahead of the field.

Despite the Welsh setback, Benn's momentum continued into September. Joe Gormley, while making it clear that if it were down to him he would vote for Healey, not only said he thought Benn would win, but also tipped him as a future Leader.

Stan Pemberton, chairman of the TGWU, even gave Benn hope he might swing the country's biggest union on the first ballot: 'The best of fucking British luck to you, comrade. Just keep your head down this month and you'll be all right,' he told Benn.

Others were less generous, as the slanging continued. Callaghan attacked Benn's doctrinaire dogmatism and Meacher subsequently slagged Jim off on the TV news. The media coverage was huge and intensely harmful to the Party.

At the TUC, too, Foot attacked sectarian dogmatism, which was rightly interpreted as an attack on Benn. Driven by Banks, the messiah went from Congress to Newcastle-upon-Tyne where he took a swipe at Foot's 'infantile and trivial critique' in front of an audience of over 2,000. At the meeting, chaired by Tom Sawyer, he got the most prolonged ovation he ever had in his life.

In mid-September, at a Birmingham rally on unemployment, Benn was cheered to the skies and Healey completely drowned out by booing. The Sunday papers loved it. 'I was appalled,' one of them quoted me as saying. 'I was on the platform while Denis Healey made his speech and it just appeared totally organised. There was chanting, singing and the clenched fist. It's like the Hitler youth.'

In fact, at that time it was like manna from heaven. With the Deputy Leadership election right upon us, it was bound to put some trade union delegates off. I rubbed salt into sores, putting down an emergency resolution at the NEC, demanding an inquiry and calling for the expulsion of anyone organising barracking at rallies.[8]

Abuse, however, became the order of the day and Healey was by no means the only target. The organisations Benn had become mixed up with had not only a common hatred of the right – and hatred, not love nor hope was the main motivating force of many of these political louts – but they often reviled each other as well.

On one occasion, Peter Hain chaired a debate – billed as the debate of the decade – between left wing groups at Central Hall in London. There, Benn was shouted down by the Irish, the anarchists and the revolutionary groups and Tony Saunois of Militant by the other thugs on the ultra-left.[9]

Now, however, the target was Healey and Benn would get the blame. That at least was my hope as I returned home from that Birmingham rally. But Denis, in a moment of disaster, blundered completely. On *Weekend World* with Brian Walden, he accused CLPD's Jon Lansman of orchestrating the booing and heckling at Birmingham and, for good measure, at an earlier event in Cardiff.

The only problem with this information – given to him, no doubt, by one of the eager young advisers 'the chocolate soldiers' – was that Lansman was on holiday in Italy during the Cardiff rally and in Wales, not Birmingham this time. Embarrassingly, Denis was forced to apologise: 'If I made a mistake it was unwise on TV.' It certainly gave Benn great heart. To say that Denis then got a bad press is a bit of an understatement – the TV and the newspapers lapped it up.

On Tuesday 22 September, 1981, Benn had another enormous meeting – this time in Leeds when over 2,000 turned out again. His bandwagon was rolling. The TGWU Executive also decided that their delegation should vote for Benn on the second ballot – if that were so, and NUPE voted for him too, he was home and dry.

The Friday before Conference brought mixed tidings, however. Benn's team told him that NUPE could not be taken for granted. The TV pundit Vincent Hanna calculated, however, that 40 MPs might abstain, but that Benn would still win. 'It now depends on two things,' Benn told himself. 'On NUPE and on whether left MPs are prepared to abstain. If they all vote for me, it will be all right.'[10]

The tension was palpable as Benn turned up in Brighton where Richard Balfe, now a London MEP, set up an office for him in the Grand Hotel. Benn's recorded thoughts at this time provide a good illustration of the anxieties and calculations of a candidate in a situation where he knows the result will be close, but he can do little by that stage to affect the result.

'Joshua was working on his computer and if the T&G and NUPE vote for me, then I'm home comfortably, even with forty abstentions and only 480 constituencies,' he recorded in his Diaries. 'If NUPE vote for Denis Healey but the T&G vote for me, I could just win if I scrabble together a few more MPs and a few more constituencies. If NUPE abstain, I could probably still win on forty abstentions and 480 constituencies or it could be neck and neck. So there is clearly a sense of confidence about it which I have never had before . . . NUPE is in the balance. I don't know.'[11]

Rumours, most of them inaccurate, ran amok on the day of the election. NUPE's position in particular, of course, excited great fear and anticipation on both sides.

An article from the *Observer* was avidly read throughout Brighton.

The NUPE result, which is said by both sides to be very close, had been expected to be announced last Thursday. But the union's leadership decided to delay the announcement until just 90 minutes before tonight's election. The Benn camp appeared last night confident that they would win . . . provided the NUPE vote went to them, as they seemed to expect.

The moderates talked of a fiddle and the Benn camp pointed out that the Branch consultation had not been completed by Thursday. The NUPE results were said by its officials to be locked in a safe at head office in a sealed envelope, the only key being held by Mr Fisher. What the Denis Healey campaigners fear is that when the NUPE delegation meet this afternoon they will be told that the result of the ballot is so close that it is not binding on them, and it is up to the delegation to decide.[12]

On either side hope sprang eternal. The moderates dreamed of getting the TGWU and UCATT. Benn's team hoped to get the Steelworkers.

A bitter feud had been fought out within the TGWU since April when the left winger Jack Dromey (we are talking Old Labour here!) told Benn he would get the vote. The battle was fought not between the right and the left but between personalities – Moss Evans, Alex Kitson and the union's Finance and General Purposes Committee on the one hand and Stan Pemberton, the 'Best of British' chairman and Walter Greendale, the vice-chairman, and the union's General Executive on the other. Due to machinations on all sides no deal was reached, as some had hoped, to support John Silkin as a compromise candidate, at the union's biennial Conference.[13]

Armed with a TGWU General Executive recommendation in favour of Benn, the left went to Brighton in fine spirits. At the Conference, however, the 38-strong delegation – at its meeting at the Old Ship Hotel – divided 18 votes for Silkin with 10 each for Benn and Healey. A ballot then took place to determine what should happen if Silkin were eliminated. For now, they were going to leave this uncounted, until it was pointed out that it might be a tie. It was. Both Benn and Healey had 17 votes and there were 4 abstentions. There being no time for a run-off, the delegation went to the Conference intending to continue their meeting outside the hall. As soon as they arrived, however, they learned that the Deputy Leadership ballot was to be taken inside.

The atmosphere was electric, all the more so when the TGWU delegation rushed in to vote for Silkin. They were joined by the Boilermakers, the Agricultural Workers, the National Union of Seamen, the Boot and Shoe people and the Labour Lawyers.

While everyone was anxious about the TGWU, they knew it was NUPE who could settle the matter on the first ballot for Benn. NUPE's left wing delegation, however, had no choice but to grit its teeth and vote for Healey. After all, 70 per cent of their members had voted in a ballot, coming out 267,650 for Healey, 188,571 for Benn and 28,568 for Silkin.

There were other reverses for Benn, as the Firemen and Musicians trooped through for Healey along with the more predictable Engineers, Steelworkers, Railwaymen and Shopworkers. On this first ballot, Benn's supporters included the Bakers, the Dyers and Bleachers and the Royal Arsenal Co-op. The Blind and the Disabled abstained, as did the Fabians.[14]

The results, announced to great anticipation in the hall, left Benn trailing a poor second with 36.6 per cent. Crucially, however, with 45.4 per cent, Healey was short of the required 50 per cent to beat Benn on the first ballot. Silkin, with just 18 per cent, was eliminated. It would go to a run-off. Healey was well ahead in the unions, had half the PLP in the bag but was slaughtered in the constituencies. All eyes now, however, were on where Silkin's vote would go.[15]

The moderates hoped that the TGWU, with their one and quarter million votes, would abstain. Instead, however, they took a vote by passing a sheet of paper round the delegates in their seats and decided by 20 votes to 15 (with 3 abstentions) to support Benn. The Boilermakers, Seamen and the Boot and Shoes also now switched to Benn, while the Labour Lawyers voted for Healey.

Surprisingly, the Agricultural Workers, with 75,000 votes – which traditionally had been Joan Maynard's base – did not follow the TGWU but abstained. The Blind and Disabled and the Fabians continued to sit on their hands. Eric Ogden MP, meanwhile, had gone off to the Falklands rather than vote for Healey, whom he had nominated. Such were the ways elections might be swung in Old Labour.

In fact, abstentions played a decisive part in this election. Because so many Tribunites had announced that, if Silkin was eliminated, they would not vote for Benn at any price, they had been sent a threatening letter by the left. They huddled together, however, and held their nerve. The left bully boys had overplayed their hand. 'I am appalled to read of the threats which are being made to my own good friends that they should sink their consciences and vote for someone whom they regard as unsuitable, because if they do not it will be counted against them in the future,' Silkin told the *Observer*, putting the boot into Benn.

The intimidation cost Benn dear. Kinnock, Joan Lestor and Robert Kilroy-Silk were among the 37 Silkin supporters who abstained in the second ballot, while two – Frank Field and Oonagh McDonald – switched to Healey.[16] In all, 137 MPs voted for Healey and 71 for Benn. Of those, 60 voting for Healey did so although their constituencies voted for Benn. Of the MPs only two, Michael Meacher and Don Dixon, voted for Benn when their parties had backed Healey.

As a result, Healey was elected by 50.426 per cent to 49.574 per cent. Benn had been defeated by less than 1 per cent. Benn says that he was told several times that he had won. Giles Radice, Healey's staunchest lieutenant, was in total despair, too, thinking that Benn had carried the day, as did most of the media. Roger Godsiff, however, laid back as ever, told Giles that his figures showed Healey to be the winner. It first dawned on me, too, that Denis had done it, when the General Secretary told me not to go over the top when the result was announced.

I wasn't, however, in the mood to take any notice. Having spent so many months in the trenches, there was no way that I would take advice from a General Secretary who had installed Andy Bevan, the Militant, in Transport

House at a critical moment. The commentator Peter Jenkins – whom I always rubbed up the wrong way by treating him as a middle-class irrelevance – reported that: 'apart from right winger John Golding having a victory seizure on the platform, both the winners and losers behaved with uncharacteristic restraint'.

Radice, suave and ever placid, also went bananas. And Denis was hardly moderate in his comments about the time wasted by the election and the damage it had caused to the Party. Benn, he hoped, would not pursue issues to try and exhaust people into submission. A forlorn hope!

As the consequence of the abstentions sunk in, the left went beserk. Despite a messianic campaign, these soft left 'traitors' had led Benn to lose. Margaret Beckett was just one who bitterly attacked the abstainers.

The Tribune Group meeting afterwards must have been pure joy. According to the *Guardian*, Joan Lestor – with whom it still rankled that Beckett had taken her job as an Education Minister when she had resigned – said, for one, that that she was not prepared to 'accept lectures about unity on the left from those who were prepared to go into office in the place of a fellow left-winger and implement cuts in education.'

At the annual Tribune rally, Kinnock was both cheered and booed. Meanwhile he complained that:

Labour's internal war blanks out our policy. The next election is lost and I will have wasted all my time on education. We are in big trouble. Unity is the only basis. Some people want us to lose the next election but fifty years of Callaghan is better than one year of Thatcher . . . I abstained in the Deputy Leadership election to give me a platform from which to say what I want.

Anxious to mend fences, after the Conference Benn concluded that 'you can't fight with everyone all of the time'. He discussed the future of the LCC with Peter Hain, Nigel Stanley and John Denham and concluded that the Rank and File Mobilising Committee should be wound up.

The left fixers fell back to regroup, with Chris Mullin morbidly mulling the future in yet another pamphlet – *The left after Brighton*. The CLPD veteran Vladimir Derer, too, was on the run: 'Constitutional campaigns have waned and our support is weaker now,' he said.

Ruing, no doubt, their decision to hand the unions the biggest slice of the college they vowed to put the block vote in their sights next time round. Ironically, in their desire for union reform, they were at one with Hattersley, who argued immediately after the Deputy Leadership election that we must switch to 'one man, one vote'.

The left were licking their wounds now, however, not only because of this wonderful defeat but also because of the results of the NEC elections at Conference.

Norman Atkinson was replaced as Treasurer by Eric Varley. To achieve this Terry Duffy had to persuade the AUEW delegation to withdraw their support from one of their own members. It is said that the abuse, protests and squeals from the lefties could be heard as far away as Fleetwood – and the Conference was in Brighton.

The uproar continued when they heard the results of the NEC elections. When Renee Short of the soft left lost her seat, the cry went up: 'This is all your fault, Terry Duffy'. 'Guilty,' Duffy cheerfully shouted back.

It wasn't all down to Terry, however. He was just an important part of the conspiracy. In 1981, the NUR did not vote for the TGWU although the TGWU voted for them. In consequence, the hard-left were hit even harder. Bernard Dix, Charlie Kelly and Margaret Beckett, who had savaged Kinnock, were all removed from the NEC.

The right meanwhile were strengthened enormously. Not only did battling Betty Boothroyd keep her place but she was joined from the Women's Section by the formidable Gwyneth Dunwoody – a sort of veritable Mrs Badger – and Shirley Summerskill, a rabbit, but at least our rabbit.

The results of the NEC elections came as a shock to many, although not to those close to Roger Godsiff, whose counting was once again immaculate.[17] On the basis of Roger's advice, I had a bet with Callaghan that we would make at least four gains and received a cheque made out to me as champion tipster. I suppose, like others of my political bets, it was a clear case of insider dealing. Never having cashed the cheque, however, I counted myself safe from the Fraud Squad.

And so Benn was down for the moment. He had lost the Deputy Leadership battle and been routed in the NEC elections. Had Foot been a student of Machiavelli's *Prince* rather than Swift's *Gulliver's Travels*, he would have seen him off there and then. But that was not to be. Instead, Michael now declared that what he wanted was to see a fresh Labour Shadow Cabinet in which Healey and Benn would play leading roles.

It was, he said, the duty of everyone to work towards that end. My typical response to this political stupidity was: 'How daft can you get?'

THIRTEEN

Hope and Despair

The knife-edge result of the Benn–Healey contest left us elated, yet shell-shocked. The razor-thin victory for common sense meant the 1981 Conference was going to be yet more hell for us moderates.

My reaction, nonetheless, for the sake of the troops, was always to 'accentuate the positive', as the old song had it. So I went onto the *Today* programme with Brian Redhead at 8 o'clock on the Monday morning determined to rally our battle-weary footsoldiers around the flag.

On coming out of the BBC radio car, I was greeted by George Westwood, husband of Freda Westwood, the West Midlands Regional Organiser. 'Where do you think you are, John?' asked George. 'Why?' said I, playing for time. 'Because,' George said, knowing I hadn't a clue, 'you've been talking to that Brian Redhead about the week ahead in Blackpool and we are in Brighton!'.

Wherever I thought I was, though bad for Benn personally, the 1981 Conference was yet another good result for the left as a whole. While he had failed to become Deputy Leader and his constitutional changes were stopped in their tracks, the left landed us with policy after policy which was totally unacceptable to the electorate.

But, as Llin always used to say, let's talk about the good news first. And the good news was that the left failed to strengthen the mandatory reselection procedures for MPs, when amendments were blocked which would have outlawed short-lists of one. So it was still possible to avoid the bitterness and trauma of a full reselection by just considering the sitting MP.

It was also a huge relief to see the three-year rule being re-introduced by a huge majority – reflecting the desire of both the unions and, amazingly, the constituency parties, to stop the endless constitution wrangling and to get on with the job of fighting Thatcher.[1]

The left's long-held desire to grab control, via the NEC, of the manifesto provided the ground for the next familiar pitched battle. This was a long-running sore, since Callaghan had outflanked Benn and Heffer before the 1979 election, and in Brighton this time they used every crooked argument they could lay their hands on.

The trench warfare was preceded, of course, by the usual bloody skirmishing on the NEC. Benn & Co used the latest product of Bish's potty pamphlet machine – *Drafting the Manifesto: the record and the lessons* – to great effect in arguing that the Leadership had become too divorced in policy-making from the Party.

They could not, of course, acknowledge their own blind incompetence when they took Jim on, so they had instead to perpetuate the myth of sharp practice on Callaghan's part.

Their solution, pushed through the NEC before Conference by Heffer and Kinnock, was to change the rules and constitution so that it would be the NEC alone – after 'consultation' with the Party Leader and the PLP – which decided what would go into the manifesto.

In his Diaries, Benn wrote of this meeting: 'John Golding disagreed. He thought the Cabinet and the PLP were respected and credible in the country but the NEC was not. Dennis Skinner got very angry with Golding and in the end he left the room to calm down. John concluded that the NEC was not fit to decide the manifesto.'[2]

I had no qualms about upsetting Dennis. According to (Lord) Tom Sawyer it was Dennis who had tyrannised him and the left group on the NEC into submission. And it was Dennis, certainly, who frightened the middle class moderates. It was high time he received some of his own medicine. He could never stir me. Whenever he chuntered on about the 'movement', I would remember stories of his parliamentary training being spent doing imitations of Elvis Presley round the clubs, while mine had consisted of trudging door to door canvassing.

A couple of months later, I was saying equally hard but truthful things about Benn's plans for a 'rolling manifesto', based on Conference decisions, approved by Conference annually and so ready to be 'rolled out' at all times.

In this new scheme of things: 'The Leader and Deputy Leader should play their part, as full members of the NEC, in the final stages just before a general election but neither should have a veto.' This time it was Kinnock who was peddling the theory that Callaghan had in effect altered the constitution by his use of a veto and that the last manifesto was 'useless'.

For myself, I had come to hate votes being taken all the time, when I was always on the losing side. So I focused my fire on the plain and simple. To quote Benn again: 'Golding maintained that in reality elections were fought between two sets of Party Leaders, and if Leaders were thought to be against the manifesto it would be difficult to contest an election credibly.' Hurrah! (even if he concluded from this that I thought the Party was just 'a fan club for its Leader').[3]

Barbara Castle, for one, shared my views on the unreality of Conference as the fount of the manifesto. She described it as a 'jamboree' and so opposed Bish's daft paper. One of her great ideas was of having a blackboard on the platform at Conference on which should be written the amount of money available to spend. As each resolution was carried, it would be costed and the amount deducted. When all the money had been spent – by Monday probably – we would all go home![4]

Sadly yet again, the plain proved too much for the simple. So, citing Benn again: 'When it was put to the vote, the paper was carried by nine votes to two – with Michael Foot and John Golding voting against it. What a combination! Barbara abstained. A tremendously important decision.'[5]

It would, indeed, have been 'tremendously important' had not the NEC just before Conference decided to do an about-face on getting control over the manifesto. This time Kinnock, Alex Kitson, Doug Hoyle – doubtless under the influence of Foot – voted with the goodies.[6]

On this score, Foot had always been on the side of reality and moderation. In 1979, he had angrily denounced Benn's self-serving interpretation of the writing of the manifesto as a pack of lies. He clashed even more bitterly with Benn over the future, rubbishing his plans for a rolling three-year manifesto. 'Conference is not the best body to choose between priorities, especially in the field of expenditure. Conference will go on producing resolutions and it will not add up the bill. The language of priorities is the religion of socialism, as Nye Bevan said.'

Callaghan and Healey, of course, had also rounded on Benn, but in 1980 the NEC had carried on regardless to produce a draft manifesto: *Let Us Face the Future*. The forces of darkness were already preparing for a victory they thought inevitable. And in doing so, they were quite prepared to ride roughshod over Foot as Leader.

This draft was all-embracing – 26 pages offering all the goodies in the world. There were tax cuts for poor and rises for the rich; all sorts of increases in public spending; a 35-hour working week; more public ownership – everything, in fact, except guaranteed free ice creams from Benn.

At the 1980 Conference, the lefties were out in force – and against Foot – to support the NEC taking sole control of the manifesto following 'consultation' with the Leader.

Typical of the delegates laying into the former Labour government was Patricia Hewitt, who later became Kinnock's press adviser and a Cabinet Minister in Tony Blair's New Labour government. In 1980, however, with no responsibility, it was all so easy to her and others. They repeated all the distortions about 1979 and demanded the simple panacea – NEC control of the manifesto.

In 1980, by the slimmest of margins, however, Benn and his acolytes tasted rare failure. He was defeated on a card vote by 3,508,000 to 3,625,000. In terms of victories at Conferences it was now 1-1. There being no provision for a penalty shoot-out, Benn would bounce back like a rubber ball and get ready for 1981.

At the 1981 Conference, in an outstanding speech, Foot stated that the central question which he had been elected as leader to solve was the balance between the PLP and Conference.

There had to be a partnership 'in which the Parliamentary Party does not presume the right to dictate to the Party Conference, and the Party Conference does not presume the right to dictate to the Parliamentary Party.'

He also, by the way, went on to repudiate the doctrine laid down by Wilson that individual Labour MPs in the PLP were there on dog licences issued by the Prime Minister. 'No dog licences for Members of Parliament, their right to exercise their own judgement on these matters, their own conscience, their own political knowledge and experience – that must be part of our democracy too,' he said.

As far as the manifesto was concerned, Foot pointed out that Conference had given 'a whole list of items which we are going to present to the nation.' 'But we have to persuade the nation that we are capable of discriminating between the things we can do first, the things to which we give the highest priority. That is what Aneurin Bevan meant when he talked about the language of priorities being the religion of socialism. We have to choose. You have to choose all the time. Mendes-France says 'to govern is to choose'; of course that is correct.'

It was against this background in 1981 that the debate took place on whether to vote yet again on the control of the manifesto. All the well-worn, hackneyed, vicious, vitriolic arguments were trotted out against the satanic influence of the PLP.

Robin Cook added to all the myths and distortions about 1979. 'The reason we failed to persuade the electorate', he argued, 'was because we confronted the electorate with a manifesto which was the least incisive, the least imaginative and the least radical of any of the four manifestos on which I have stood as a candidate.' There was no mention of the Winter of Discontent. Could Cook really have spent that winter travelling just between Perth and Kelso and never looking at the telly!

Healey's stalwart, Giles Radice went on the counter-attack: 'The main argument for change . . . is that representatives of the PLP use the Clause V meetings to exclude policies they do not like. Indeed, Tony Benn told us last year that certain policies were ruled out of the manifesto. This is really not true, Tony. If you had read the 1979 manifesto you would find that it contained all those policies that you spoke about in your brilliant speech last year – restrictions on capital going abroad, increases in public spending, cuts in arms expenditure, the introduction of a wealth tax and selective import controls. They were not ruled out at all. They were all in the 1979 manifesto.'

This time, Benn did not speak and Foot took the rostrum, on behalf of the NEC, to oppose the plans. Again, he laid into the myths that the 1979 manifesto was a creature of Callaghan alone.

'I know what the arguments were. I was present at all of them. There is no such thing as a personal veto. No Leader of the Party has a personal veto. No, he has not,' Foot berated delegates.

Having spoken so passionately twice, Foot was then devastated to find that on a card vote he had lost. And so it was decided to vote yet again on the issue of the control of the manifesto.

Given the vote that had just taken place, everyone clearly thought the result was a foregone conclusion. Certainly Foot was subdued, as he readied himself to reply once again. Imagine the shock for us all then, when the result was announced, that the moderates had won – defeating the plans by 3,791,000 to 3,254,000! At Conference, everything was possible.

In the interval a pivotal group of unions shifted their ground. Other delegates had simply returned to the Conference floor from the bar. Some later pleaded 'confusion'. Bill Whatley, USDAW's general secretary, admitted to the *Guardian* that there had 'been a spot of bother on his delegation', but that he had put the vote right second time round. Roy Grantham of APEX simply chose to ignore his union conference.

And so in 1981, after Foot's magnificent fight and a spot of union 'confusion', the score over the manifesto became 2–1 in our favour. That's the good news. Now for the bad. We had kept the right of the Leader effectively to control policy, only to wake up to the fact that our Leader supported policies on which we could not be elected.

Except for rejecting 'troops out of Ireland' and barmy plans to nationalise banks, building societies and insurance companies, on policy matters we had little success. The key policies on defence and the Common Market remained like albatrosses around our necks.

Foot certainly saw to that. Callaghan had the sense, when speaking at Conference in front of the TV cameras to ignore delegates and use the opportunity to address the nation. Foot, however, bothered more about the Party. He had to persuade the left that he was still one of them while being conciliatory towards the right. He had to show that his old socialist oratory was as strong as ever.

And on the platform Michael was good; he was very good. And in paving the way for the massive defeat of the right on defence and the Common Market, he saw to it that we would be massacred at the next general election.

The debates, the clashes, the taking of the card votes and the announcement of the results — this was a battleground on which, in 1981, the left were still winning.

Is it any wonder, then, that at the end of the Conference after the official singing of 'The Red Flag' and 'Auld Lang Syne', the hard left gathered again in clusters and sang the Communist anthem, 'The Internationale', with fists clenched and arms outstretched.

This year, indeed, a new albatross was added, despite opposition from Gerald Kaufman, which encouraged councillors to refuse to make government budget cuts.

It is difficult to know what we, on the right, could have done to change direction. These decisions were not unrepresentative. A *Guardian* poll published the previous Friday had shown that 80 per cent of Labour Party members supported left wing policies.

They certainly supported the socialist Alternative Economic Strategy, which would be nigh-on unthinkable these days – with its import controls, nationalisation and all. Indeed, we nearly all supported it.

King Canute demonstrated to his courtiers many years ago that the tide cannot be stopped from coming in. This lesson, however, was lost on the NEC in 1981. It ignored all the lessons of history not enunciated by Marx or Engels and none more so than with its policy to withdraw Britain from the Common Market.

To be fair – though I do not wish this to become a habit – the NEC had the support of the vast majority of Labour and union activists. Most of the influential pro-Europeans had left to form the SDP. The opposition to the Common Market came not only from the hard and soft left like Beckett and Kinnock, but also people of usually sound judgement such as Bryan Stanley, Gwyneth Dunwoody and Alan Hadden.

Indeed, there were not many of us left who had supported the EEC and we were only a handful on the NEC. Unable to meet our opponents head on, the best we could do was go for a referendum, hoping that the people would have more sense than the NEC – and confident in the knowledge that they could not have less.

My subversive attempts before Conference, however, only gained the backing of Healey and Betty Boothroyd. The rest, hard left, soft left and moderates alike were solidly anti-European. As far as they were concerned, when we won the general election, with Europe that would be that.

Those of us who supported the EEC were forced to argue for a referendum because we hadn't a cat in hell's chance of winning the Labour movement over to this view. Only defeat at the 1983 election and Thatcher's refusal to allow union leaders to negotiate in Whitehall, so driving them to Brussels were to do that – along with that great healer, Old Father Time.

Indeed, as I sat putting up with the jeers and sneers of the left, I could never have envisaged Kinnock as a European Commissioner nor Margaret Beckett appearing on TV alongside a Japanese flag eulogising Europe. In those days, the only safeguard from the virulent Europhobes on our side was to let the people decide.

Those of us who presented the case for a referendum – notably steel union leader Bill Sirs – harked back to Wilson's promise of a plebisite at Labour's 1973 Conference, which the left – including Foot and Benn – ensured took place. They got their referendum in June, 1975, campaigned strongly against the Common Market and were soundly thrashed. Indeed, the result – 17,378,581 'for' and 8,470,073 'against' completely demoralised them. Never again should they have been able to claim a special knowledge of the hopes and aspirations of the British people!

Bill Sirs reminded Conference of just that: 'Tony Benn said of the referendum that he had done so much to achieve, that the British people had spoken and we must tremble before their voice'. It was no surprise, then, that the antis decided not to make the same mistake again. So a referendum was unnecessary. 'At the next election,' Heffer told Conference, 'the electorate will be faced with a clear choice: to vote Labour and take us out, or to vote Tory, Liberal or SDP and keep us in.'

Apart from presenting the arguments in favour of a referendum, Sirs supported by Owen Edwards of Merioneth and Derek Enright, then an MEP, fought a valiant rearguard action putting the case for the Market. They emphasised the need for an outlet for our products, the dream of 'one world', help for the Third World, how weak Britain would be outside and the failure of the NEC to say what would happen when Britain came out.

Several brave souls, including Enright, did their best against the whipped-up tide. I knew only too well how tough it was to face a sea of hostile faces – the hatred, bitterness and intolerance of people who preached the brotherhood of man. In this atmosphere, the antis were bound to dominate. There was no contest, as speaker after speaker – including John

Silkin, Manny Shinwell, Alan Sapper of the ACTT and finally Heffer – were called to the rostrum to rub it in.

So what was it that led not only the loonies but sensible moderates beside to adopt policies which sank without trace after their overwhelming rejection by the electorate? The effective speech made by Silkin – always an attractive, smooth operator – gives us a good insight into their sloganism. He railed – 'oh woe is me' – against years spent trying to secure reform of the Common Agricultural Policy and simply concluded this was impossible. This antagonism to the CAP was shared by all – pros and antis. There was deep resentment that we were forced to pay out so much.

But Silkin also went to the heart of the matter when he pointed out that Labour's Alternative Economic Strategy (AES) – based on import controls, public subsidy of industry and foreign exchange restrictions – and the EEC were incompatible. And for so many the AES was the ark of the covenant. Nothing, certainly not the Common Market, must impede it.

And so the votes could have been weighed, not counted. The demand for a referendum was defeated by 5,830,000 to 1,072,000 and the NEC statement – a dreadful document – was carried by 6,213,000 to just 782,000. A motion, too, calling for withdrawal from the EEC was carried by 5,807,000 to 1,000,000 – far more than the required two thirds majority to go into the manifesto's Emergency Programme of Action 'well within the lifetime of the Labour government.'

The delegates cheered and cheered, as they did a week later with more justification at the Tory Party Conference.

We might have survived a general election fighting for withdrawal from the Common Market. But there was no way we could win one advocating unilateralism.

Support for disarmament, however, had grown throughout the Party and the unions. Benn himself joined Joan Ruddock, then CND's head, on the anti-nuclear rostrum. We went, indeed, to the 1981 Conference naked with a fully unilateralist policy from the NEC in its statement on *Nuclear Weapons and the Arms Race*. Ironically, when that was pushed through, Benn was away ill and Foot – faced with a split between the NEC and the Shadow Cabinet – wanted to defer a decision until talks with the European Socialist Parties and a visit to the Soviet Union had taken place.

The left just steamrollered over him. Whatever we tried to change, including ratification of the SALT II agreement, the result was always the same – 14–3 against Healey, Betty Boothroyd and me, with Foot abstaining. And so it went when Heffer and Kinnock moved and seconded that the dreadful NEC statement on defence should go to Conference.

The suicide note was signed off in a flourish. While Michael – who had been going to 'ban the bomb' demonstrations since the beginning of time – had abstained at the NEC, he pulled out all the stops for unilateralism at the Conference. 'Such proposals command all my sympathy and support . . . Do not let anybody tell me, as some attempt to do, that these are just the ravings of an old nuclear disarmer like myself. Nothing that I have seen persuades me that the CND campaign was wrong; indeed I think it was right.'

When he ended his parliamentary report with the words: 'I am a peace-monger, an inveterate, incurable peacemonger. That is why I can call for the support of this whole movement', Conference roared its approval.

And so, much to the disgust of the small handful of us, we went further along the unilateralist road. The only saving grace is that withdrawal from NATO bit the dust. In our next manifesto, we were being committed to the kitchen sink: no Polaris replacement of our Trident nuclear submarines, no neutron bombs nor US bases.

One of the themes of the resolution was taken up in a motion from Edinburgh North CLP on Civil Defence. The mover? Future Cabinet minister Alistair Darling, who condemned civil defence as a sham and called for support for Labour local authorities that declared nuclear-free zones!

Our front-bench defence team, meanwhile, were apoplectic with rage. Talk of mass resignation was in the air. Having been used so publicly as target practice, none was called in the debate. Brynmor John, our chief defence spokesman, stomped out of the hall at the left's 'swindle' that denied him a say. The rest of the team – future NATO General Secretary George Robertson, Arthur Davidson and Peter Snape – were on the brink, too, of quitting *en masse*.

The endorsement of the unilateral statement was carried on a vote of hands. Because there was no card vote, however, it did not get the recorded two-thirds majority which would have meant its automatic inclusion in the Party's manifesto.

Ironically, the vote to leave NATO also looked to have been carried by a show of hands. When the chair of this shambolic Conference, the leftie Alex Kitson, called a card vote on that, however, the left were fuming. It was overwhelmingly defeated by the union block votes. Like me, however, he had more important things to think about like control of the Labour Party. There was a lot to fight for.

FOURTEEN

Foot Won't Help

For some reason I'll never know, after all the fratricide in Brighton in 1981 the bookies still made Labour favourite to win the general election. I did not rush to the betting shop! Quite apart from suicidal policies, worse still we moderates still did not have a majority on the NEC even though the hard left had been pushed back. The balance, particularly given the shaky nature of Syd Tierney's and Sam McCluskie's support, lay with Foot and his close friends Kinnock and Joan Lestor. This sad fact of life only came home to us slowly on the right.

Immediately after the NEC election results, the right wing union barons – not least a jubilant Terry Duffy – were gunning for the left. Benn certainly was not his usual perky self, knowing full well he was first in our sights. At a private mid-week meeting of right wing union officials the plot thickened. The softer left, like Lestor, would be offered a deal – a free run at some of the NEC committees in exchange for removing Benn from the chair of Home Policy and Heffer at Organisation (the 'Org' as I less than fondly called it). Sam McCluskie, who had long cherished 'Org', was our candidate for the latter with me in reserve.

All this was self-delusion, wishful thinking, a mirage: we simply did not have a majority. Foot had control and firmly believed that it was in the interests of the Party to appease Benn and his supporters. After Conference Foot had every chance to put the skids under Benn and Heffer, but decided to let them keep their power base.

It was just more of the same. Ever since he had been elected, Foot had bent over backwards to come to terms with Benn. 'I am sure we can help each other and the Party,' Michael wrote before one of their many *tête a têtes* on 18 November, 1980. At this meeting, Benn set out what he wanted from Foot – reform in the PLP, a left/right balance in the Shadow Cabinet, a shift of power to the NEC and an electoral college. Not much of a shopping list at all!

Foot should have simply showed him the door. Instead, he expressed the hope that Benn – who coveted the Shadow Home Secretaryship – would be elected to the Shadow Cabinet. Is it any wonder then that Benn confided to his Diary: 'A very full and important day. I think I can have good working relations with Michael. I like him. We don't have to have those awful rows about incomes policy and I think it will be a creative relationship.' It certainly was – Benn kept on creating trouble.[1]

Later Foot fell from grace a little when he told Benn, very uncreatively, that he was not prepared to shift Merlyn Rees from Home and asked him to consider Environment. Benn said he would think about it but he had set his heart on the 'Home Office, or Leader of the House or some special policy appointment linking up with the NEC' – more delusions of grandeur!

When the Shadow Cabinet election results were announced in December, 1980, it was clear that Benn's wish for a balanced Shadow Cabinet had been fulfilled. Eight moderates and four left-wingers – Stan Orme, John Silkin, Albert Booth and Kinnock – had been elected. We on the right were delighted: neither Benn nor Heffer were in. Hattersley came top followed by Eric Varley and Gerald Kaufman. It was very balanced without him!

Benn made up the tail end, two votes behind Kinnock with Heffer a further 17 vote behind. It clearly showed the PLP had no faith in Benn. He commanded neither respect nor support.

Following the resignation of Bill Rodgers, however, Benn finally squeezed into the Shadow Cabinet at the end of January. In a sign of much worse to come, that very day he had a blazing row with Foot after attending a left wing caucus, something of which Michael naively disapproved. According to Benn's Diaries, Foot asked: 'You try to fix votes in advance, don't you?'. Benn replied: 'No, I try to reach a general agreement about things'. Michael responded: 'You're a bloody liar.' Benn, steamed up, returned to the left caucus where the barmies tried to cool him down.[2]

A few days later, realising that he had jeopardised his future, Benn shuffled back to Foot: 'Let's just forget last week completely,' he said, asking to be made the Shadow Spokesman for Regional Affairs instead. Foot, however, let him stew.

By March, in Benn's eyes, Foot had become the 'Leader of the right' having attacked Militant and named Bristol, with Liverpool and London, as one of its centres of influence. Benn later gave this as a reason for being driven to contest the Deputy Leadership. In reality he had decided this much earlier and enormous rows followed, leaving Michael white with anger. Foot made it clear he would oppose him and accused Benn at Shadow Cabinet of 'sabotaging policy'.

In June, Foot finally laid down the gauntlet in the row of all rows. Benn, defying a Shadow Cabinet decision to abstain on a defence vote, not only signed a Tribune Group amendment but also voted for it. 'It is a question of trust and I have been humiliated,' Foot snapped and then read out a statement attacking Benn and inviting him to stand against him as Leader. 'There was a lot of banging on the table by Shadow Cabinet people,' Benn observed 'and John Silkin looked at me like a cat about to spring on a mouse; the hatred there was unbelievable'[3]

The clash caused a great stir. Typically Skinner suggested to Benn that he should fight Foot. Benn for his part, seeing Foot attacking him on TV, concluded bitterly that 'he sounded like Ramsay MacDonald in his rambling days'. More trouble was only averted when Benn was forced to retreat into hospital by a nasty illness. We wished him a slow recovery.

Despite this constant turmoil, however, Michael simply did not learn. Indeed, the response to Foot's olive branch of support for the 1981 Shadow Cabinet elections was pure Benn: he made it clear that he would only go into the Shadow Cabinet as the upholder of Conference decisions and would not be bound by collective responsibility

Foot, caught off balance once again by the sheer cheek of it all, was forced to go on ITN to make it clear – to the country, if not to Benn – that there could not two kinds of Shadow Ministers. There had to be the same conditions for them all.

Benn, however, ploughed on regardless. Impertinently, he linked standing for the Shadow Cabinet with continuing to be Chairman of Home Policy on the NEC. And amazingly – this sado-masochistic two-step could only amaze – Foot took the point, letting it be known to the NEC that he was not seeking changes in the Committee chairmanships. He then arranged things so that Benn, Heffer and Lestor commanded a majority on Home Policy, Organisation and International. Foot simply would not risk a row with the left.

At the first NEC after Conference, however, the left just failed to steam-roller through a list of names agreed between Ron Hayward and Foot which would have kept complete control with the left. Despite Foot's fixing, we had some success with Organisation, adding Betty Boothroyd and David Williams – a moderate from COHSE – and heavily defeating Laurence Coates, the Young Socialist Militant supporter, who had replaced Tony Saunois on the NEC. The composition of the Committee was such, however, that if Foot wanted Heffer to remain as chairman, he would do so.

The committees then duly met on 9 November to appoint the chairs. With Foot holding sway, the results were a foregone conclusion, but we mods decided that a stand had to be taken. As I told my local *Sentinel* after the NEC elections:

> If nobody else is nominated against Mr Benn, then I shall accept the nomination to stand against him as Chairman. I think that Michael Foot is wrong to have supported Mr Benn for the Chairmanship of the Home Policy Committee. Tony Benn is an albatross around the neck of the Labour Party at the present time and could stop Labour from winning the next general election. I believe that those in the middle ground ought to continue and be counted against extremism. I would have preferred that Neil Kinnock would have chosen to stand against Tony Benn. But as it appears that no-one from the Tribune Group is prepared to take him on, I will do so myself even though the composition of the committee makes for certain defeat.[4]

My counting was as accurate as ever. Before going to Home Policy, I went to 'Org' where Heffer beat me by 13 votes to 7 for the chairmanship. At Home Policy, Benn beat me by 12 votes to 5. The dozen included Kinnock, Lestor and Doug Hoyle. My faithful four were Gerry Russell, Betty Boothroyd, Denis Healey and Eric Varley. And so, due to the intervention of Foot, the row within the left had been patched up, albeit temporarily.

'Mr Golding's was a forlorn challenge,' *The Times* remarked:

The margin of his defeat was increased by the absence of three trade union members, Mr Allen Hadden, Mr Sydney Tierney, and Mr Sam McCluskie. The result dismayed those in the party who had hoped that the more even balance achieved when the new National Executive was elected at the Annual Conference six weeks ago might be reflected in the committees. Their fears were at once confirmed when the organisation committee decided, at the instance of Mr Benn, to reject an appeal for an enquiry into the Trotskyist Militant Tendency, which is steadily growing in influence in the party . . .

. . . It is time to say that Mr Foot's continued attempts to appease the unappeasable and to placate and accommodate Mr Benn have brought him and the party into public ridicule, scorn and disrepute.[5]

After the results, all hell broke loose within the PLP, with most of the scorn rightly reserved for Michael. The Manifesto Group had, indeed, called for a further investigation into Militant as a step towards proscription and expulsions. Foot's support for Benn, however, now stymied all that.

The next day, the humiliation continued. Again, *The Times* was accurate:

The left wing of the Labour Party remained firmly in the saddle after four more elections yesterday. In sub-committees of the national executive committee, members of the so-called hard left, supporters of Mr Wedgwood Benn, secured two committee chairmanships, in each case by a single vote. Miss Joan Maynard was voted by seven votes to six into the chair of the youth committee, defeating Mr John Golding of the centre-right. It was Mr Golding's third failure in 24 hours . . .[6]

The left kept control of its power base and Foot kept not only Benn, but his acolytes too. Just a day later, he was to regret it. On 10 November, the first anniversary of Foot's election to the Leadership, Benn repaid his support in typical fashion – with a statement from the front bench regarding renationalisation of the oil industry without compensation that left Foot beside himself with anger. Shirley Williams, quoted in *The Times*, likened Michael's currying favour with the left as 'like patting a tiger on the head'.[7]

Shirley was right. It was an astonishing decision by Foot to let Benn wind up the Commons debate on energy. Most of the Shadow Cabinet was livid and Foot hit back, accusing Benn of being responsible for the advance of the SDP and giving him an ultimatum to abide by collective responsibility. Foot was outraged, too, by a vicious article in *London Labour Briefing*, titled *The Myth of Tolerance*, containing a hit list of Labour MPs who failed to vote for Benn as Deputy Leader. Benn, of course, simply sidestepped the Leader's demand that he repudiate it.

I summed it all up in my usually kindly way: 'If Mr Foot wishes to keep a mad dog, he must expect to be bitten'.

On Thursday, 12 November, 1981 Benn crawled back to Foot yet again, agreeing to make a statement to the PLP at 6 pm. When it came, it was hardly to Foot's liking.

'The question is: is Tony going to help us with the next election or not?' he told the PLP. 'My response to Tony's statement is that it has gone some way but not all the way, and I take it that he accepts what I have said and will abide by it. If he can't I hope that he will make that clear. I challenge Tony Benn to answer.'

Benn immediately shifted all the blame on to the Shadow Cabinet to the accompaniment of the usual cat calls which he, like Heffer, generally attracted from otherwise civilised beings.

Foot then asked Benn to meet him the following day to sort things out, only to be further upset when Benn – who was going to Bristol – tried to fob him off until the weekend. He then issued a statement completely denouncing Benn.

'Foot drops defiant Benn,' screamed the *Guardian*'s Saturday headline:

Michael Foot last night finally abandoned his attempts to keep Mr Tony Benn on the bridge of the Labour's parliamentary flagship. In a statement which amounted to a political keelhauling, he accused him of being both misleading and offensive during this week's row and said that he would be unable to vote for him in the Shadow Cabinet elections.

'I have done everything in my power to persuade him to accept the doctrine which all other present Labour Shadow Cabinet Ministers and most of their predecessors have been prepared to accept. I regret he still says no,' Foot said in his statement. 'Any deliberate effort to evade that requirement is destructive. It is not possible for me or many other members of the Labour Party to accept the view that people genuinely seek the election of a Labour govern-ment unless they are prepared to give practical effect to that view by their words, their actions and the acceptance of collective responsibilities.'

As Benn rightly concluded, that was the end of him – he never recovered. The irony was that, as he made clear in a long *Guardian* article, *Putting the Record Right*, it was my own probing of him at the NEC that persuaded Benn to conclude that re-nationalisation without compensation was, indeed, Party policy. It was poetic justice. For once he was right, but even his family and friends told him that he had blundered.

In consequence, in the Shadow Cabinet elections he gained just 66 votes. It was nowhere near enough (and Healey, magnanimous as ever, suggested he only got that because of sympathy over his health). Benn wrote: 'I have mixed feelings but I'm glad not to be in that Shadow Cabinet.' The feeling was mutual.

FIFTEEN

The Wild Wood

In 1981, the lack of a majority on the NEC for either left or right brought an even sharper edge to the battles for control of the Party, with prolonged struggles over expulsions and parliamentary selections.

During the inquest into the 1983 general election massacre, the Party's new General Secretary, Jim Mortimer, argued that we had spent too much time on internal discipline and too little on Party organisation. In one sense he was right, but yet in another completely wrong. Until the left had been stopped from disrupting the Party and driving out good members and MPs, we had no hope of getting enough electoral support to make it worthwhile organising.

With the left in control until then, the monthly meetings of the NEC had long been like Mole's travels through the Wild Wood where 'every hole . . . seemed to possess its face, coming and going rapidly, all fixing on him glances of malice and hatred: all hard-eyed and evil and sharp.' Callaghan, indeed, had generally described them as purgatory.

Indeed, the atmosphere on the NEC was unlike any committee I had served on before. I was used to rough exchanges but not to such an atmosphere of hate and hostility. With their power, the hard left bullied their way around. They sneered, they were sarcastic, they shouted. While the polite, well-mannered trade union officials Russell Tuck and Allan Hadden would merely take exception to their nastiness, even Jim Callaghan and Shirley Williams, the most experienced of politicians, were decidedly put off.

I pampered my own vicious streak and gave as good as I got. Rather than absent myself from committees to avoid the aggro, as others did, I attended assiduously and let the insults go over my head. One of the advantages of being small is that you don't have to duck. At these meetings Heffer aped the playground bully; Skinner ritually poured sarcasm on the right; Benn expressed synthetic righteous indignation; and Joan Lestor froze us with her 'holier than thou' looks. Both Audrey Wise, the 'Black Widow', and Joan Maynard, 'Stalin's Granny', sneered as if they were sentencing us to the guillotine. And while Frank Allaun uttered weasel words, Alex Kitson behaved as if he had been 'elected' to the Comintern and was going to take full advantage until he himself was purged. At one and the same time, they were both ludicrous and intimidating.

After Callaghan and Williams had retired hurt, reenforcements arrived. Healey was as rough and tough as any of them and Betty Boothroyd and later Gwyneth Dunwoody had all the courage in the world.

In the Labour Party, the NEC is tasked with managing the Party and upholding the constitution. With this sack of weasels, however, we had nothing but mayhem. They saw it as their devil-driven duty to undermine local parties by keeping trouble makers in. They played havoc with local councils by deifying, not driving out, those who defied the whip. Under the banner of 'tolerance', all the efforts of the National Agent, David Hughes, to bring some order to the madhouse were trashed by this intolerant lot.

Between November 1978 and January 1981, the NEC reversed so many recommendations for expulsion – and allowed so many appeals against withdrawal of the whip – that Labour's regions were playing hell. Why waste time conducting internal enquiries, when the NEC overturned them in such a politically prejudiced way?

One particularly outrageous example occurred on Benn's patch in Bristol. In 1979 seven new local councillors broke the whip, were duly warned and signed an undertaking promising good behaviour in the future. The following January, after argument, a budget strategy was agreed by the Labour Group. Bristol South East CLP, however – Benn's mob – did not like this. Even though both the Group and the local District Party had given support to a legal budget, at the May Council meeting, eight councillors rebelled and, in consequence, the whip was withdrawn. Quite rightly, they were turfed out of the Labour Group.[1]

They appealed and an enquiry was subsequently conducted by Walter Brown, the Assistant National Organiser, and two members of the Regional

Executive. After the familiar argument about implementing Tory cuts, breaking the law or not, Brown, as ever, sought to placate all sides. With the two regional members he upheld the appeals of the three first-time offenders and the one abstainer. As for the rest, it was recommended that they be re-admitted after just four months' suspension.

Walter's judgement smacked too much of fear of Benn. But Benn's mates on the 'Org' would not even accept this, went even further and upheld all the appeals. The right meanwhile knew that it would be pointless to challenge the decision at the full NEC. In any event, Michael Cocks – the Chief Whip and MP for Bristol South who loathed Benn – gave us the nod that they would be dealt with in other ways. Later Dawn Primarolo, then Benn's Bristol South East Constituency Secretary, wrote to complain over foot-dragging in restoring the rebels to their influential committees.!

It was a portent of bitter battles to come in Bristol that would do for Benn once and for all. But in these darkest hours, the NEC fell into such complete disrepute in its handling of discipline cases, that some moderate local parties rebelled, declined to implement its decisions and refused to accept trouble-makers back.

It would be too tedious to give a blow-by-blow account of these disputes. While occasionally an honest decision was given – as when a Mrs McCarty, a stalwart Labour lady, was allowed back into the Bootle party after having been hounded by the Trotskyites – more often than not they were politically biased. Occasionally those on the left tried to ease their consciences by reducing the sentences of good, honest, moderate people, pursued by the comrades, who should never have been punished in the first place.

One of the most outrageous cases surrounded the expulsion in 1980 of an activist in Oxford, Ted Heslin, who openly admitted membership of the Workers' Socialist League, a Trotskyist organisation fully signed up to the dictatorship of the proletariat. It also had a deeper political significance because the failure of the expulsion attempts so upset Shirley Williams that I believed it to be a contributory factor to her defection.

It was an open and shut expulsion, which the 'Org' endorsed, but which the full NEC referred back at the instigation of Joan Maynard. Those who voted for expulsion at the 'Org' had clearly been leant on with a vengeance by the left outside. The case dragged on for months, until the left upheld his appeal at the same meeting they refused to expel the members of the Social Democratic Alliance.

To its credit Oxford CLP, fed up to the back teeth of Trotskyite harassment and disruption, refused to reinstate the man and it was not until the spring of 1981 after a year of time-consuming guerrilla warfare that he was finally re-admitted. Heslin 'in', Williams 'out' did not seem a good swap to me.

Shirley went, but I stayed, not prepared to be bullied out of the Party to which I had belonged for 36 years. When, in October 1981, we finally achieved a 'hung' NEC, I decided to copy the left's tactics against them. In this I was guided skilfully by my brothers in the Swinton House Group, so-called after our meeting place, the ISTC headquarters on the Gray's Inn Road near King's Cross to where the St Ermin's Group had decamped.

While I could often not tell one left group from another, apart from Militant, John Spellar in particular was a fount of all knowledge. The brothers were able to tell me, in disciplinary cases and in selections, who deserved protection. They also gave me a hit list of the totalitarian left and, like one of Cromwell's Inspector Generals, I did my best to rid the Party of devils and heretics.

The battle over endorsement of parliamentary candidates was central in the struggle to save the Labour Party. Colleagues in trouble would buttonhole me in the tea room and ask for help. Following sad cries from the heart, I gave support to those from the soft left, like Robert Kilroy-Silk and Maureen Colhoun, as well as to the right.

To defend moderate candidates, we had to fend off, in particular, the left's demands to outlaw short-lists of one. We had to make sure that MPs knew that, despite the advice and wishes of the NEC, they were still within the rules. At the NEC in May, 1981, indeed, we secured the adoption of a list of eight candidates which included Betty Boothroyd who had offended the left by being selected on a short-list of one at West Bromwich West. Eric Clarke, Joan Maynard, Tony Saunois and Dennis Skinner voted against their endorsement while comrades Benn, Heffer and Huckfield abstained.

Later in the year, despite ASTMS objections – again over a short-list of one – we also endorsed Geoff Lofthouse MP as the candidate for Pontefract and Castleford. In September, 1982 the National Agent reported that, although the 'Org' had endorsed Roger Godsiff as the candidate for Birmingham Yardley, 'further information had since been received from the Regional Organiser'. I expected trouble, even though Roger – as ever – had kept strictly to the rules. After some debate, he was re-confirmed. Had Roger been standing for a safe Labour seat, though, I am sure the story would have been different!

Not that I supported every candidate beaten by the left. When Arthur Lewis alleged irregularities in the Newham North West selection, I just could not bring myself to give him support. We would, though, have fought for Eric Ogden – who was beaten at Liverpool – had he not departed to the SDP before we had a chance to do so. At his selection, Eric had been expected to win against Brian Sedgemore, but he withdrew at the last minute to go to Wigan (which Les Huckfield took with my help!) and in the confusion Bob Wareing, much to his surprise, beat him.

My main activity was trying, mostly unsuccessfully, to stop the selections of the left. One source of threat from the left was from Euro-MPs competing for a Westminster seat. When Richard Caborn won Sheffield Park, Eric Varley moved that the 'Org' should re-consider the validity of MEPs standing against sitting MPs. We were defeated.

While the voting remained mostly factional, in September 1982, the moderate group went different ways over the endorsement of Paul Boateng in Hemel Hempstead. After claims of irregularities, a motion to endorse him from Skinner was defeated by 15 votes to 7, with Heffer abstaining. Instead, the constituency was to receive a visit from the Chairman and National Agent. Thereafter Russell Tuck, who was himself active in Hemel, played the part of Blind Pew and delivered the 'black spot' by opposing his endorsement. This was defeated, however, by 9 votes to 16. While Foot voted with Russell, four moderates including Betty Boothroyd voted for Boateng, who would have been beaten had they not.

When the Militant Pat Wall was endorsed as the candidate for Bradford North, for me it was yet another huge setback. The row started after the deselection of sitting MP Ben Ford in 1981 and an enquiry, headed by myself and Alan Hadden was ordered after a string of complaints. My involvement caused some eyebrows to be raised – it was said that I had appeared on TV saying that Wall would be endorsed over my dead body.

That was false, but it was raised so often throughout that I came to believe it myself.

I put my heart and soul into this, as we should never put up Militant candidates for any election, let alone the general. The hearing in Bradford was very tense. Ford's charges in the main did not hold water and yet I had to do something to justify my reputation as the scourge of the left. I had a bad reputation to uphold. The task was made even tougher by the fact that Hadden, who chaired the enquiry, was scrupulously impartial.

My first job was to rattle the Militant witnesses. At the time I was so overjoyed at their bitter complaints that I spun the proceedings out so much that their witnesses tired and went home. This, of course, was a standard Militant tactic in ward, trade union branch and CLP meetings – but they did not like being on the receiving end.

The witnesses for either side were placed in different rooms and looked after by Llin. She describes the experience beautifully:

We arrived on a dreary Sunday morning in Bradford where the streets were deserted and the only place open was the building where the enquiry was to be held. Fortunately there were four rooms coming off the main hall where the enquiry was to be held, so that the goodies and the baddies could be kept separate from one another – essential to avoid bitter arguments and abuse. Firstly I put the few goodies in the nice comfortable room and then the baddies in an ugly, poorly lit room. My job was to look after the enquiry team and the goodies. This was made easier because I found a kitchen at the back from which I could carry drinks to the team and the goodies while they were waiting. I also found a cafe where I sent one of the goodies to bring back food for all of them.

The baddies, about 11 of them, were not so fortunate. I visited them, often apologising that they must wait for food and drink until they got out. Even though the enquiry seemed to be going very slowly, they must not go out, however, in case their evidence was needed. So concerned was I, that they got the impression I was on their side – rather than being the partial wife and agent of John Golding. I expressed my deep concern that there was no way I could get them a drink and real regret that there seemed to be nowhere near at hand that was open. I expressed my disgust that the enquiry team would not allow me to go through the main hall to the kitchen. Believing two of the judges were antagonistic, they smiled at me and appeared to trust me totally. I was only surprised that they didn't produce an application form for Militant there and then. The goodies' evidence was taken first, and they were allowed to leave, as the enquiry dragged on and on.

Even when finally the baddies were called, I persuaded them as they came out that it was vital to the cause for them to remain just in case they were recalled to give evidence again. The enquiry was spun out until after 6 o'clock in the evening when the cafe was shut. I had condemned them to a day shut up in a darkened room without food and drink without them asking once who I was. Knowing what they were doing to long-serving members in many CLPs, I felt that they deserved it!

Apart from all the dodges, I had received good advice from a Labour QC, who had studied the papers carefully and pinpointed sufficient breaches of procedure and rules to lead my impartial colleagues to join me in recommending against Wall's endorsement.

At the 'Org', the lefties, true to form, dismissed these as 'far too trivial to justify withholding endorsement'. Foot, defending Ford to the best of his ability, argued that they should not brush aside the report 'drawn up in good faith by NEC members appointed to enquire into the circumstances,' but he was deserted by Kinnock and Lestor and so it was decided to endorse Wall.

At the full NEC, however, Betty Boothroyd managed to get Wall's endorsement referred back by the narrowest of margins, with Foot and Judith Hart voting for us.[2]

Then for once we moderates had a rare stroke of luck. At the weekend before the 'Org' was to meet again, the *Sunday Times* dropped the bombshell that Wall had advocated the overturn of the state at a Socialist Workers Party meeting.[3] 'I was speaking out against violence, not in favour of it,' Wall protested, but the rallying cry for extra-parliamentary action upset Foot greatly.

I, of course, supported strongly as ever by Betty, tried to use this to dispose of the Militants in general, but we lost heavily by 5 votes to 13. We were also unsuccessful in putting the skids under Wall himself. A new selection conference was, indeed, held in Bradford, but I was barred from carrying out a further inquisition, and Wall won again.

Later, I tried to overturn this both at the 'Org' and the NEC, where on a recorded vote, we were defeated by 14 votes to 9. Again, Foot voted with us, but it was no use.

We were more successful in the long running saga of Brent East in preventing newt lover Ken Livingstone from being elected in 1983, but this saga belongs to another chapter.

The loss of control by the Bennite left in the autumn of 1981 gave us more power to our elbow. Even when the NEC was more evenly divided, however, there was a tendency to want to cut right wing Labour Group Leaders down to size. This was certainly true of Jack Smart, the attractive, able and intelligent, moderate leader of Wakefield, whose suspension of dissident councillors was lifted.

That the tide was turning, however, was shown by a typical left-right dispute of the time – a punch-up between Manchester City Council's Labour Group and the City Labour Party. The battleground was familiar: to cut council services in response the Tories' public spending squeeze – 'to do the Tories' job for them,' as the left would put it – or to resist cutbacks and square the circle with stinging rises in the rates.

In an escalating tit-for-tat, before the NEC intervened in September, 17 rebel councillors were expelled from the Labour Group. In response the City Party, chaired by Graham Stringer, now MP for Manchester Blackley, rejected some 30 sitting councillors as candidates for the 1982 elections. The Manchester air turned blue as the insults flew thick and fast. Stringer, in particular, objected to leading members of the City Party being characterized, variously, as as 'alien beings' or 'totalitarian'.

The enquiry report, in the event, was even-handed, calling for greater tolerance and an end to the not-very-civil war. At the NEC, however, typically the left attempted to have it both ways, with Skinner and Huckfield seeking to have the rebels re-admitted on their own terms and to uphold the ban on the moderates standing again. A year earlier, they would doubtlessly have won. But, with the NEC now hung, they were unsuccessful in wrecking the delicate ceasefire finally negotiated in Manchester and other places, like Coventry, where the Party had turned not on the Tories, but on itself.

A similar dispute in Southwark, however, was to have far-reaching consequences for the Party nationally in the run-up to the 1983 general election.

Again, budget rebels – 11 of them this time – had been suspended and a regional disciplinary enquiry ordered. Hardly surprisingly, the left wing London Labour Party came down heavily on the rebels' side, upholding the appeals and recommending their reinstatement. Meanwhile, the left in Southwark was also abusing its power in the Party to exclude long-serving councillors from the approved panel of candidates, thus effectively de-selecting them.

The *Guardian*'s Martin Linton summed up yet another tricky situation well in December after Foot backed my call for an NEC enquiry:

> The Labour Party face a daunting task in the inquiry into the affairs of the Southwark party which the Organisation Committee approved yesterday by '17 votes to 2 . . . There has been a running battle between the Labour group, dominated by the Right, and the borough's three Labour Parties, Bermondsey, Peckham and Dulwich, now all dominated by the left, since the bitter controversy over Southwark's new town hall three years ago. It culmi-nated in the withdrawal of the Whip from the eleven rebel left-wingers.
>
> The left took its revenge this year by dropping 12 leading councillors, including Mr John O'Grady, the Leader of the Council, and several committee chairmen, from the panel of candidates, thus depriving them of standing for reselection in next May's borough election. Mr (Peter) Tatchell took a prominent part in the process . . . The situation has been further confused by the defection of 14 Labour councillors to the Social Democrats, including two of the councillors dropped from the panel of candidates.[4]

It was yet another fine mess, which the left had dropped us in! A NEC peace mission led by Judith Hart inevitably failed and in February, 1982 the 'Org' ordered the reinstatement of the council leader and others on to the panel of candidates. The scene was set for the carnage, as we shall see in a later chapter, of the Bermondsey by-election.

In addition to battles between factions in local government, there were indi-vidual cases of importance – and none more nationally so than the row over Tariq Ali, the prominent commentator and conscience of all things Marxist.

Ali was known as a member of the International Marxist Group (IMG), who had stood against Syd Bidwell in Southall at the previous general election as a

Socialist Unity candidate, getting the grand total of 77 votes. Syd – an old revolutionary himself, with whom I travelled home many nights by car to my flat in Ealing – disliked him, always describing Ali as the 'rich playboy'.

Benn's view of Ali was very different: 'He's so civilised and charming,' he wrote. Ali had rung Benn to chat about a new socialist society and tell him that he was thinking of joining Labour before it came before the 'Org'. Later Ali also told Benn how he had told Foot at a party that he had left the IMG, but Michael had said we couldn't let him into the Party for the moment, as it would be difficult.

When the matter came before 'Org', the National Agent David Hughes suggested we interview Ali because he had nonetheless written in *Tribune* that he remained a Marxist. We needed, Hughes advised, to see if he accepted a parliamentary road to socialism and had broken his links with the revolutionary Fourth International.

Syd Tierney, however, was bitterly against Ali – being a strong supporter of the 'Society of Syds against Playboys' – and said he wouldn't believe a word Ali said. Others of us, too, were not as charmed as Benn by Comrade Ali. I moved and Healey seconded 'that Tariq Ali be not accepted into membership of the Labour Party'. Despite a rearguard action by Benn, we voted not to accept his application.[5]

An interview Ali gave to Peter Kellner in the *New Statesman*, indeed, could not have been clearer. The difference between his position and Benn's, he said, was that 'in the ultimate analysis, the state and its institutions cannot be reformed,' adding that it would be ultimately necessary 'to sweep the whole thing aside'!

As so often happened, however, due to the gaps in our rule book, taking a decision and implementing it against opposition were two very different things.

In this case the opposition came from the Hornsey CLP, which although told not to do so, admitted Ali in December nonetheless and in March, again in defiance, issued him with a membership card. The regional report into the meeting speaks volumes about the tactics of the left at the time:

> A motion was before the meeting to accept Tariq Ali into membership and instructing the constituency Party Secretary to issue him with a membership

card. This motion should not have been accepted. The chairmanship of recently elected Jeremy Corbyn, backed by newly elected Treasurer Pauline Ashridge, was the most extraordinary study of bias and manipulation of rules and custom that I have ever witnessed.'

Despite being told again that Tariq Ali should not be a member, on a recorded vote they decided to admit him by 39 votes to 21 . . . Max Morris said he would not admit Tariq Ali to meetings and the Membership Secretary refused to issue a card, but Pauline Ashridge then moved that the officers issue a card and this was carried.[6]

Jeremy, of course, is still beating the hard left drum, but now in Islington North, while faithful Max is still soldiering on in the loyalist cause in Hornsey.

By the April 'Org', when Healey and I proposed that Ali again be excluded from membership, he had written to Heffer saying that he really had left the IMG and now accepted the constitution of the Labour Party. Remarkably Skinner accepted his rejection, but recommended he be advised to reapply in a year's time. The moderates did not want him at any time, however, and that was the decision.

It was a case which was going to run and run and I would need to seek advice on how to play it from my brothers at the Swinton House meeting. We had one dangerous fanatic causing damage to our image with the electors and we just couldn't afford to take in another.

SIXTEEN

The Goodies Gang Up – Benn Cast Away

Attendance at secret meetings played a big part of my life in 1981 and 1982.

On the evening before the monthly gatherings of the NEC, I would go at 5 pm to a meeting of the brothers at Swinton House. These were efficiently organised thanks mainly to Roger Godsiff and John Spellar, who drew up the agenda, our host Sandy Feather and Bryan Stanley who normally took the chair. Usually, there were about 10 to 12 people present in all.

It was my job to give a report on what was happening on the NEC. Although we had a few successes on constitutional issues close to our hearts, I usually had to impart bad news. That it was Foot not the moderates who had control of the NEC, our failure to remove Benn and Heffer from their chairs, the legal difficulties in dealing with Militant, that we couldn't expect 'one member, one vote', Peter Tatchell, Tariq Ali . . . just recalling the succession of failures depresses me no end!

But for all our setbacks, the group was soon to claim the biggest scalp of all. Benn had inflicted this war on innocent bystanders. He and his barmies had done for so many decent folk in the Labour Party. Soon it was time, in true Sicilian style, to pay him a visit, return the compliment and do for him and his Leadership ambitions.

Before we delivered the horse's head, however, one of our most abject disappointments came with the replacement of the Party's General Secretary. Through the Group, Terry Duffy quickly established Alex Ferry – then the General Secretary of the Confederation of Shipbuilding and Engineering Unions – as the right wing candidate even though several of us on the NEC had never met him. But while Terry had no problem with we moderates, who owed him so much, he didn't manage to sell him to Foot who commanded the controlling votes.

Neither apparently could the left persuade Foot to support their favourite son, Bob Wright, a left wing member of the AUEW who was heavily involved in Benn's factions, nor Ronald Keating, a left winger at NUPE. Faced with two rival candidates, neither of whom he wanted, Michael did the obvious thing and found his own, Jim Mortimer, who would be acceptable to the left. Seeing the writing on the wall, Wright withdrew. For me the oddity at the time was that I knew all the candidates except for Ferry, for whom I whipped the moderates and voted myself. The selection in mid-December with Judith Hart in the chair was a formality, as the result had been well fixed by Foot. On the first ballot, Ferry was a vote ahead, but I didn't hold my breath. I knew that Mortimer would pick up the two maverick loose votes – and win by 15–14, he did. Foot had got his way for once.[1]

I was in two minds about having Jim as General Secretary. When I was Secretary of the Twickenham Constituency Labour Party, I had failed to persuade him to help in the 1964 London elections (in my eyes always a sin), knew of his connections with the left and CND (an even bigger sin) and of him as a kind, considerate man (the biggest sin of all, as it was a total disqualification for office in the Party at that time!).

At his interview, Jim followed Foot faithfully, calling for defence spending cuts, the removal of US bases and an exit from Europe. He also made, for me, some more appealing points, stressing full employment as top of his priorities and his strong trade union connections. I also knew him from my days as a minister to be a top-class conciliator with a reputation for integrity and intelligence. He had shone, too, when chairing the debate at Blackpool between Healey, Silkin and Benn. Best of all he was a good administrator.

Moderates hold varying views about Mortimer today. While some remember him for getting the finances under control and taking on Militant, others believe that his association with the left in London since he retired has revealed him in his true colours. Whatever judgement one makes, Mortimer, like Foot, was hopeless when it came to campaigning in the general election. How different things might have been had he accepted my offer to give him experience on the streets in 1964!

One thing is certain, at the time his appointment was a reverse for the mods and this defeat strengthened our efforts to get control of the NEC.

At the brothers' meeting in Swinton House, the most important item of the year was a report on the NEC elections. Immediately after Conference we would hand out thanks to all – mainly earned by Roger – bask in our own glory for a few minutes and then, at John Spellar's prodding, get cracking on preparations for the following year. An analysis would be made by Roger, union by union, so that 'the gains made this year were built upon in next year's elections.'

Drawing up a winning list was a long-drawn out business involving talking to key people in the unions. In January, 1982, even after much work, we still could not settle on our list. The good news at this time was that the National Association of Labour Clubs were likely to dump the dreadful Les Huckfield, who held the Socialist Society Section seat on the NEC, in favour of Foot acolyte, John Evans.

By April we knew, courtesy of my most reliable press contact Tony Bevins, whom the left-wing Labour Liaison '82 were going to support. Along with those we could never vote for, they included Sam McCluskie and Alex Kitson. So we automatically put them on our list and their election was ensured. Sam, of course, often voted with us; and while I preferred the friendly Alex of the dog track to the ruthless Kitson of the NEC, it was vital he was on because of deals big unions did with his, the TGWU.

The same was true of nominees of other big unions. We had no choice but to support the AUEW replacement for Gerry Russell, whoever he was. It could have been Mickey Mouse as far as we were concerned, although obviously it would be a bonus if he had the Terry Duffy stamp of approval.

Again from big unions, Neville Hough (GMWU), Russell Tuck (NUR) and Syd Tierney (USDAW) automatically went on the list. To these existing members from the big battalions, we added Alan Hadden (Boilermakers), Roy Evans (ISTC), David Williams (COHSE) and me (POEU).

That left two places to fill. We then had what Roger always described as 'a wide-ranging discussion' about who was to get them. Denis Howell had one – because we owed APEX a lot and Denis himself had been personally very supportive of the group. While the same could also be said of the

EETPU and its President Tom Breakell, whom we finally put on, it was this which caused much gnashing of teeth.

The EETPU, namely, was unpopular in many places not only because it supported extreme right policies, but because it recruited aggressively, too. Its highly intelligent leadership also had a nasty habit of treating lesser mortals with a biting scorn which would have qualified them for the 'Denis Healey School of Personal Relationships'. Given the importance of the EETPU on the right wing, however, we had to ask the brothers to swallow hard and do their best to sell Breakell.

Having disposed of the union places, we turned to the Women's Section and agreed to support three MPs – Betty Boothroyd, Gwyneth Dunwoody and Shirley Summerskill – but we were still scratching around until July to fill the slate. After Diane Hayter withdrew, we finally settled on Eileen Gallagher and Ann Davis.[2]

Eileen Gallagher was a first-class EETPU trade union official, similar in character to those two great fighters Betty Boothroyd and Gwyneth Dunwoody, but whom would again be extremely difficult to sell. With Anne Davis, a strong-minded, efficient member of the West Midlands Regional Executive, it would be easier. As Anne was little-known, it would be possible to get widespread union support for our dark horse if we could manage to keep it quiet from the left that we were supporting her.

We also felt confident that we would get Eric Varley re-elected as Treasurer and also went through the motions of agreeing to support to the Labour Solidarity list which had been drawn up for the Constituency Section. So we asked for backing wherever possible for Jack Ashley, Roy Hattersley, Gerald Kaufman, Neil Kinnock, Peter Shore, John Smith, Barry Jones and Giles Radice. It was a hopeless task. Only Kinnock was ever elected – but the effort was made and we in Newcastle-under-Lyme at least always did our duty – thanks to Llin.

Selecting candidates was one thing, but the numbers game was everything. So it was critical for us to keep track of the movement in membership numbers on which the unions, friendly or hostile, were affiliated to the Party. We were still smarting from the blow during Conference week in 1981 when the EETPU lopped £18,000 off its support for the Party, equivalent to 60,000 members and that crucial number of votes.

'Why should we go on pouring money into Walworth Road, for it to be used against us?' Frank Chapple, the EETPU's General Secretary, asked. The answer, Frank, was that it was simply playing into the hands of the left to cut the size of your affiliation and this was the message we sent out from Swinton House straight afterwards.

As well as at national level, we also tried to influence the local course of events. At each meeting reports were given from the union Political Officers Group, of which I was one – such as 'the on-going work being done in Birmingham and Bristol' to affiliate friendly union branches of the AUEW and POEU.

We also linked activity between unions to counter the growing influence of the 'Broad Left' in our power base. We took a great deal of interest in what was going on within the TUC itself, too, where Bryan Stanley's successful campaign to change the basis of union representation gave us great encouragement.[3]

We also received reports on the Labour Solidarity campaign within the CLPs, although I must confess that some were more supportive of the efforts of Hattersley and Shore than I was. My doubts were eventually borne out when the mods in the Constituency Section actually received fewer votes in the NEC elections of 1982 than the previous year!

We decided furthermore that we must try to get some influence at Labour women's gatherings, including the TUC Women's Conference. In this period, the barmy women were very much on the march. They made a terrible impression on the world at large – indeed, long afterwards trade union officials who had any experience of them refused to sponsor Labour women's conferences because they still carried the scars.

Later, in the Labour Party I was determined that whatever was done to give greater representation to women, it would not undermine the progress we moderates had made against the left. Later Benn quoted an Ann Pettifor as saying:

Women are excluded from power by men. There are fewer women MPs than there were in 1945. Women are trying to displace men – that is why there is resistance. They are kept out by the structures of the party, they are frustrated by men at the Labour Conference. The annual Women's Conference needs to choose its own standing orders, to elect its own executive, elect the women's section at the Annual Conference and to have a woman on every shortlist. There will be great resistance and we know John Golding is mobilising against it. The Women's Committee of the NEC has been taken over by a right-wing bloc, and this is a serious problem.[4]

She was right – there was no way I would agree to the loss of union control over the Women's Section on the NEC unless there were to be substantial changes elsewhere on the NEC which left it in moderate control.

Fixing Benn in Bristol

But now it is time to pay that visit to Bristol. One of the Swinton House Group's most important initiatives in 1982 was to do everything possible to ensure, following parliamentary boundary changes, that it was the Chief Whip Michael Cocks and not Benn who obtained the only safe Labour seat left in Bristol. Benn, indeed, had long realised that the changes might carve up his Bristol South East seat as his Diaries show:

> I heard tonight that the new electoral boundaries in Bristol will produce only four constituencies – North, East, South and West – and that means that I will have to fight either Mike Cocks for the Bristol South nomination or Arthur Palmer, who will probably go for Bristol East . . . I must confess I am very uncertain about it, but clearly one seat will be winnable; I think probably East and South will be Labour, and North and West, Tory. I'll have to mend some fences with the Bristol Labour leaders, otherwise there will be pressure to see I don't get it. I just won't worry about it.[5]

Far from not worrying, he set his cap at Bristol South. Cocks clearly had by far the strongest claim, but Benn had no scruples. We started with the clear advantage, however, that Benn – unlike Cocks – had palpably neglected his constituency and in the eyes of his strongest supporters to boot.

I was not surprised, therefore, to read in his Diaries that in February, 1981 Dawn Primarolo told him that he wasn't doing enough in the constituency. She thought he tended to appear like 'Lord Bountiful'. He would pop into ward meetings for a bit and listen to what members were saying. But he wasn't appearing at local events or much else. Benn adds that she was nice about it, but it was a serious criticism and he knew, with all the meetings he did around the country, that it rang true.[6]

Clearly, however, he did very little about it. In April, 1982, the chair of his constituency again told him that he was not active enough in Bristol. Press criticism was also having an effect. Benn said he felt a sort of fatalism about it:

> I no longer believe that in Bristol views are any different from those of people in London, though I used to think they were. Every time they turn on their TV sets and see me engaged in some controversy or other, they ask why they can't see me in Bristol. There is a sacrificial element about it and the price may well be my defeat.[7]

He had taken the attitude that, as the people were no different in Bristol from London, he may as well live in Holland Park. And so he spent little time mixing with the people in his constituency day-by-day. During holidays, he was found on the family property in Essex, not in Bristol, and at other times he just made fleeting visits – overnight stops in a hotel. In other words, to my mind he was effectively an absentee MP.

On top of all that, many more people would go into the new Bristol South constituency owing allegiance to Cocks than to Benn. Although Benn had die-hard supporters, many ordinary people thought he was unbalanced and the more they came into contact with him, the more they were convinced of it. Those fanatics who ran Benn's 'Leadership machine', too, were London-based and had no understanding of nor clout in the provinces. What was discussed at smart dinners in Hampstead or Notting Hill Gate, cut no ice out here.

The brothers, however, did not believe in leaving things to chance. John Spellar went into action and initiated an increase in EETPU affiliations to cover the new constituency. Roger Godsiff took his soundings and, in consequence, it was decided to send me to Bristol to teach people on the ground how to organise themselves effectively

I was sent to do this because of the work I had put in elsewhere, successfully affiliating POEU branches to help the union get sponsored MPs.

Unions could affiliate to any constituency where members lived, which meant some branches would join ten or more. Another message I learned to ram home was to find loyal Party members, establish what union branch they belonged to, get it to affiliate and send them as delegates to GMCs – just attending the meetings we needed them to.

So I went to Bristol on 23 November, 1981, bumping into Benn in the buffet car on the train on the way down. As he travelled first class and I second class, there was no danger that we would meet in our seats. It seems he always said goodbye to his beloved Levellers on the platform in London.

By 11 December, Dawn Primarolo had reported to Benn that I had been down to Bristol urging trade unions to affiliate to the local parties. 'This is, of course, in preparation for when Mike Cocks comes up against me for the new Bristol South constituency selection', Benn wrote.

On 15 December, he continued:

> Dawn Primarolo has sent me the notes made by a trade unionist on John Golding's visit to Bristol to address the local trade unions on 23 November. Golding apparently asked full-time officials to join GMCs; they needn't attend regularly, he said, but they could go to the annual general meetings and to the selection conferences and, as this matter was so confidential, it would be better if nothing was written down and all communication was by telephone.[8]

My efforts were given a great boost when *Tribune* published details of my visit. The report was written by Nigel Williamson and Chris Mullin – obviously very slow writers because it didn't appear until the following July – under the headline 'Secret plan to flood CLPs with union delegates. MPs plot against Bristol Party.'

> Tribune has a copy of an unofficial note of a private meeting held in Room 127 of the Draganora Hotel in Bristol on November 23 last year,' it went on. 'The meeting was apparently held on the initiative of John Golding and Roger Godsiff (Political Officer of the Association of Professional, Executive, Clerical and Computer Staff).
>
> According to the note, John Golding opened the meeting by saying that its purpose was 'to bring together trade unionists in the Bristol area willing to be

active in promoting the need to defeat the influence of the far left in local CLPs which in his opinion was driving moderate activists into the Social Democratic Party' . . . Golding 'expressed the need to protect Michael Cox's [sic] back against the far left who would be supporting Benn'.

The meeting, *Tribune* rightly noted, was attended by officials from APEX, POEU, the TGWU and the EETPU, but we were also told we could rely on support from officers of Engineering Section of the AUEW, from the GMWU and also the NGA. A loyal APEX official volunteered to act as co-ordinator. *Tribune* also noted that:

> [Golding] warned against committing anything to paper and suggested the telephone as a means of contact. Interference in the affairs of an MP's constituency by another Labour MP is considered a serious offence in the Parliamentary Labour Party.[9]

Tribune made repeated attempts to contact me, but I never answered their calls. I did, however, talk to *The Times*.

> Labour's hard left *Tribune* newspaper yesterday accused John Golding, a prominent member of the party national executive and MP for Newcastle-under-Lyme, of plotting against Mr Wedgwood Benn on his home ground of Bristol.
>
> Its report said that Mr Golding, assistant secretary of the Post Office Engineering Union, had visited Bristol last November 23, 'with a plan to flood Labour Party management committees in Bristol with right wing trade union delegates'.
>
> Mr Golding said last night that he had not had time to read the *Tribune* report, but he added: 'It is not a conspiracy, it is a determined effort to make certain that Mr Benn does not depose Mr Cocks, Labour's Chief Whip, who could be in competition with Mr Benn for a safe seat after boundary changes. I very much hope that moderates everywhere take away the message from Bristol that the only way to stop Mr Benn and his cohorts is to become delegates of constituency parties'.
>
> 'The message I took to Bristol was that there was no need for working

people to get involved in a theoretical wrangle. All they have to do is to become delegates to their constituency parties and go to crucial meetings to vote for traditional Labour supporters. In this way, they can stop Mr Benn and his friends from taking the Labour Party away from working people.'[10]

The general result of my visit was that the local unions knew precisely what to do if they wished to get rid of Benn. As well as publicising my efforts, *Tribune* also gave a helping hand to John Spellar, who had been as busy as I had. *Tribune* wrote:

> The attempt to destabilise the Labour Party in Bristol appears to be part of the nationwide campaign by right-wing trade union officials to flood constituency management committees.
>
> EETPU members all over the country have been receiving letters from the union's General Secretary, Frank Chapple, urging them to take part in a campaign to 'restore the Labour Party to being representative of ordinary voters'. Chapple's letter says that within the small bodies that control the Labour Party at local level . . . well organised extremists have managed to stage a takeover – a bit of a coup in fact. Over the years, ordinary working people have been replaced by new groups of left-wing extremists – mainly teachers, polytechnic lecturers and social workers.
>
> The EETPU is one of the few unions where nominations for constituency management committees can be made not only by branches, but by Head Office. Where branches have refused to accept the delegate nominated for them by head office – as for example in the case of the central London branch of the EETPU last year – they have been closed down and amalgamated.
>
> Whatever the object of the exercise, it has little to do with encouraging trade unionists to become active in the Labour Party. As the EETPU's Head of Research, John Spellar, told the *Financial Times*, EETPU delegates were not expected to 'continue to turn up month after month . . . two or three times a year will be enough'.[11]

Any help that we could get in putting our message across was very welcome. We just regretted that too few of our people would see it. The exercise, though, was a spectacular success. Benn was tempted to fight Robin Cook for the Livingstone seat in Scotland, but decided to stay in Bristol. And he knew for certain his time in Bristol was up when he saw a TV programme, *People and Power*, which revealed how well we had sewn up Bristol South.

The selection took place on Saturday 7 May, 1983, where Benn wrote of the audience:

> I could see a few friends, but there was a sea of trade-unionists who had been brought in under the Golding aegis and women in their early sixties from the Co-op Women's Guild. I swear many of them had never been to a political meeting before in their lives. I knew I was going to lose, so I was relaxed, made a speech, answered a few questions and left.[12]

He was right. Michael Cocks won, fought Bristol South at the general election and remained an MP. The next day Benn beat Ron Thomas in a selection at Bristol East, but lost at the general election.

SEVENTEEN

A Phoney Peace and a Real War in the Falklands

For many months after the 1981 Annual Conference, the Party was in even greater disarray than ever. Following Foot's failure to get a grip, his ratings in the opinion polls plummeted. At one stage MORI gave him a 63 per cent dissatisfaction rating, with only 17 per cent expressing satisfaction. And that was with the public – had it been taken in the PLP, it would have been worse!

The SDP had become more credible, winning by-elections at Warrington, Croydon and then Crosby with Shirley Williams and riding high in the polls. Indeed, at one stage they went into a clear lead over Labour, causing more and more MPs and members to desert. The electorate was not only totally put off by the civil war in the Party, they were upset because the wrong side was winning.

The seriousness of the crisis was debated almost immediately after the Conference, on 18 November, 1981, at a special PLP meeting held on the State of the Party. Benn was kicked from pillar to post. Jack Straw, then a man of the left who had voted for him in the second ballot, blamed him for Labour's collapse in the polls. MPs queued up for their pound of flesh. And Foot, too, declared himself a fully-paid up member of the 'sick and tired brigade'.

There is no doubt that, in the outside world, Benn was seen not only as dangerous, but also as potty. This view was confirmed when he repeated his claims that he was the true Deputy Leader because some who had voted for Healey had deserted to the SDP. The reaction was sheer incredulity: Healey wondered whether Benn might next assume some other role such as Pope or even Queen. Full of self-delusion, Benn – still hopeful of beating Michael

Cocks to a safe seat – was busy raising new armies and preparing new campaigns.

Then, in January, 1982 came yet another conference at the ASTMS' Country Club in Bishop's Stortford, a lull in the fighting, when a peace settlement was reached between the left and the right, which lasted all of a fortnight. The conference came about partly because TULV had been attacked by the left following my visit to Bristol. Not being a NEC committee chair, I was not there. But I knew that the unions' aim was to establish financial control and put an end to Benn's manoeuvres.

After the meeting a declaration of Labour Party-Trade Union Accord was published, urging sweet unity and co-operation between the various factions. 'The smiles on our faces denote that peace has at last broken out in the Labour Party,' Basnett declared to the press. 'We agreed unanimously to turn our backs on the miseries of the last two years,' Healey summed up.

Benn, however, was ominously silent. Indeed, the unfortunate thing was that – as Les Huckfield stated in a rare telling observation – 'very few, if any, of those attending the meeting, have been given any authority, guidelines or mandate by their organisations to settle or agree anything'.

This applied not only to Basnett but also to Benn, who claimed that his paper *Working for Unity* had led to the 'tacit understanding that we would fight the next general election under the existing Leadership of Foot and Healey with a manifesto based upon the 1981 Conference decisions, a moratorium on constitutional changes, and a halt to any purge of left individuals or groups.'

Not all of his friends, however, agreed to a complete ceasefire, Mullin, Banks and Meacher included. At one of Benn's get-togethers the following Sunday, there was a virtual rebellion among the disciples. Benn for once, however, dug in firmly against his motley collection of hawks. And, to be fair, his determination to focus on beating the Tories, rather than his own side, lasted some time – almost a fortnight.

Foot, meanwhile, was interpreting the spirit of Bishop's Stortford in the oddest of fashions in two articles in the *Observer*. In the second, the paper's political editor Adam Raphael summed up under the headline 'Foot lays the blame on Benn':

Mr Michael Foot blames Mr Tony Benn today for being directly responsible for the internal wrangling which is threatening, he says, to destroy the Labour Party's chances of returning to power at the next election. The Labour leader's article . . . threatens to rip apart the recently concluded peace of Bishop's Stortford which was meant to end the internal party feud. Mr Foot in his detailed attack against Mr Benn accuses him of perpetrating a monstrous perversion of the truth in claiming that the Callaghan government of which he himself was a member had betrayed the party.

It is a measure of the damage that has been to the Labour Party, says Mr Foot, that 'treacherous notions', such as accepting the inevitability of Labour's defeat at the next election were now being hinted at.[1]

Nonetheless at the January NEC, we endorsed the accord. Indeed, I seconded the motion put by Doug Hoyle, although I must admit I had not the slightest faith in it, nor felt that it would in any way restrict my activities. Neither apparently did Benn, because he had already been to County Hall to found his new, ill-fated organisation, Labour Liaison '82. Chaired by Norman Atkinson, it was yet another Benn vehicle designed to capture the Leadership.

The Falklands War

The phoney peace of Bishop's Stortford was overshadowed in 1982 by Mrs Thatcher's very real war in the Falklands. Indeed, the Argentinean dictator General Galtieri saved both Thatcher and, longer term, the Labour Party when the Argentinian troops formally surrendered on 15 June, 1982, having invaded the Falklands at the beginning of April.

Before the war, both Labour and the Alliance were neck and neck at 33 per cent in the polls, with the Tories on 31½ per cent; one month afterwards, the Tories had leapt ahead to 46½ per cent, while Labour with 27½ per cent had nosed in front of the Alliance's 24 per cent.

I do not intend to write of the war, save to show briefly how it heightened public consciousness of Labour's divisions. From the beginning the Labour Party was split and, as ever, Benn played a central part, coming out straight away against sending the British task force.

At the PLP immediately after the invasion, Foot urged that we must not oppose sending in British troops. British opinion would not have it and the Tories would have a field day. Besides, Britain had the UN Charter on its side and the moral right to use force. Benn's view was that the war was another Suez: wrong, unpopular and one that we were bound to lose. And at the NEC at the end of April – when Foot and Healey presented a sensible motion calling for discussions with the Secretary General of the United Nations – Benn and Judith Hart started a major bust-up by calling for a cease-fire and the withdrawal of the task force.

In my 'Diary of an MP' in the *Sentinel,* I summed my feelings up:

> I don't often speak on defence or international matters – or know much about them . . . Today, however, I oppose Tony Benn's motion – defeated 15 votes to 8 – which calls for the withdrawal of the task force. If [US General Alexander] Haig or the United Nations fail to get Argentina out of the Falkland Islands, then we are going to have to act. We cannot allow a fascist dictatorship to take democratic rights away from any of our people. Nevertheless, it is important to try to avoid having to land troops which is why the United Nations must be given a chance if Haig fails. No way, however, should the Labour Party undermine the morale of our troops or give any boost to the Argentinian right-wing bully-boys.

This view was shared by Heffer, who this time could express it openly because the Militant Young Socialist Laurence Coates also lined up against Benn. They both abstained, leaving the usual hardcore loonies to antagonise our working-class supporters even further.[2]

The heated debate continued at the PLP next day, where Healey reported on his visit to the UN. There George Robertson, Secretary of the moderate Manifesto Group, future Defence Secretary and head of NATO, attacked our own newspaper *Labour Weekly* for giving so much space to Benn and the anti-war lobby. In 1979, our policy was that we would not hand over the islands to the junta, and we confirmed it in 1980. The Party view was clear – Foot and Healey were the leaders of the Party and deserved our unanimous support. Benn refused, however, to bow.

Then on 30 April, the US peace terms were rejected by Argentina and the ageing battleship *General Belgrano* was torpedoed. At the NEC, Foot and

Healey were still nonetheless plugging the 'send the Task force, but don't use it' line, while Benn and Hart called for an immediate truce. Again Heffer supported Foot. Listen to ordinary people, he told Benn, knowing only too well that Benn was unlikely to meet any. A vote, however, was never taken. When Heffer got upset and started a row, the debate was cut short and Betty Boothroyd and Gwyneth Dunwoody moved a successful vote to block Benn's 'troops back' motion. On 19 May, Argentina dug itself further into trouble by rejecting the UN peace terms.

Meanwhile all the careful work of Foot and Healey was being undermined by the opponents of the war. On 5 May a motion for a truce hade been signed by 65 MPs, Labour and nationalists, and the following Sunday Benn spoke at an anti-war rally with Tam Dalyell and Donald Soper, amongst others. The day after Argentina dismissed the UN, 25 MPs met and decided to vote against the government, defying Foot, who announced that the Shadow Cabinet was going to abstain over the war. In the end, 33 MPs went into the lobby against the government. Foot, having told them that it would be a stab in the back if they did so, sacked Dalyell, John Tilley and Andrew Faulds – normally a strong critic of Benn – from the Labour frontbench. Benn, helpful as ever, declared that the Labour Leadership had failed the Party and the nation.

His idea of helping the nation was to march to Downing Street on 23 May, two days after the British invasion began, hand in a letter and to continue to divide the NEC until 14–15 June when the Argentinian troops surrendered. Even when people rejoiced at our victory, Benn persisted in attacking the tragic and unnecessary war. That, of course, just looked like sour grapes to those who rallied behind Thatcher because of her single-minded purpose. In a few short weeks she had enjoyed a massive jump in the opinion polls to nearly 50 per cent, established herself firmly and stopped the rise of the SDP. As they never recovered thereafter, it can be fairly said that the war – and Thatcher – had probably saved the Labour Party, too, despite all Benn's endeavours to destroy it.

Back to Labour's War

Having this unexpected help from Thatcher, we right wingers went to the 1982 Annual Conference at Blackpool with mixed feelings. Roger Godsiff, though as cautious as ever, thought that we could improve on our successes the year before and we knew that we would get support for Foot's 'softly, softly' opposition to Militant. Acceptable policies on defence, the Common Market or the economy, though, were a dead duck.

Benn meanwhile went in a despondent mood, fearing a backlash against the left. After his discharge from hospital, too, he had realised he was almost completely ostracised in the House of Commons, a huge drawback for anyone wishing to be elected in the electoral college. To that end, Benn had wound up his 'Rank and File Mobilising Committee' in favour of a vehicle with broader representation, including MPs, to further his ambitions. Tony Banks had been at the fore in urging Benn to contest the Leadership against Foot in 1982, but at an early meeting of the left that had been blocked by 'Gorgeous' George Galloway, of all people.[3]

Benn's new group – the 'Labour Liaison Committee 1982' or 'Labour Liason '82' – was, according to Vladimir Derer, to be 'low profile, should not adopt a tactic of confrontation and should seek to ensure that it is our opponents who are creating disunity'. It had a small steering group, including Galloway.[4] This new praetorian guard suffered immediate setbacks, however. Tribune refused to be involved and so also did the left wing Labour Co-ordinating Committee, anxious to avoid further disunity. Within CLPD, Derer also shared that view – although he, too, was on the '82 steering committee, he wanted to lie low until after the general election.

Merely to create one new group could not satisfy Benn's love of raising new armies. At the same time, too, he was also creating a new left wing caucus in the PLP, encouraged by the bitter split within Tribune when Kinnock and his allies abstained in the Deputy Leadership election. So back in October 1981, Benn brought together a group of people, which included not only the usual suspects, but also John Prescott, Clive Soley and John Tilley. This led to the formation of the Campaign Group of MPs, which first met on 25 November, 1981.

Although he was not a regular attender, Campaign did give Benn a new parliamentary base and he decided not to rejoin Tribune. Ironically, the Campaign lot then hijacked the *Tribune* weekly under the editorship of Chris Mullin and turned themselves into an 'editorial committee'. It was socialism, I suppose, in practice.

All these secret meetings and conspiracies had not gone unnoticed – they rarely do. The problem of Benn was raised repeatedly at a special meeting of the 'Org' in July, 1982 to discuss a string of disastrous by-election results. From Croydon North-West, Crosby, Glasgow Hillhead, Beaconsfield (where a young Tony Blair was the candidate), Mitcham & Morden and Coatbridge & Airdrie, the message from the electors was the same: if you can't agree, we're not voting for you. The internal feuding was bleeding us dry. On the doorsteps, Benn was cursed and candidates asked which side they were on. In Croydon, I had found Ken Livingstone's name constantly linked with Benn.

In a distinctive contribution to the 'Org' inquest, Tony Blair trailed New Labour by talking about the difficulty of translating Party policy – our Alternative Economic Strategy – into the practicality of people's everyday lives. Throughout his campaign, disunity was always a distraction. His general impression was that traditional Party supporters had withheld their vote until we made ourselves relevant to the problems they faced.

Most of discussion, however, centred on 'Old Benn' rather than 'New Labour', with Tom Clarke wanting him to declare public support for Foot. Skinner meanwhile was concerned that we weren't confronting criticisms of Benn on the doorsteps – imagine us trying to convince electors that Benn wasn't actually mad, he just said mad things! In any case, many of us really did believe that Benn had lost his marbles.

Though the left prepared hard for the 1982 Annual Conference, it had been much easier for their fixers, when they effectively controlled the NEC. Now, however, Foot could pretty much decide for himself what the NEC put to Conference. Nor could the left decide on the Conference Arrangements Committee, as it was still effectively controlled by the trade unions.

In 1982, CLPD sent out nine model resolutions to constituency parties covering subjects from the defence of Peter Tatchell and Tariq Ali to nationalization of Britain's biggest 25 companies and outlawing short-lists-of-one. Their main concern, however, was to defend Militant and either throw out the Party's report on Militant or else cynically prevent its implementation.

They also drew up a 'slate' that set out to replace Neil Kinnock and Joan Lestor with Norman Atkinson and Audrey Wise to try and get the NEC back on side. Comically, however, a set of minutes fell into Tony Bevins' hands at *The Times*, which reported in detail on their machinations.

As a result, some trade unions withdrew their support and Labour Liaison '82 collapsed. Although, it was later claimed that these minutes were false, the edginess of some of those named persuaded me that they were accurate enough. Of course, they were daft to have kept them in the first place, but we were definitely grateful for their stupidity, as the minutes make for fascinating and damning reading.

According to the notes, among the 24 allegedly attending the Labour Liaison '82 'slate' meeting were Benn, Meacher, Banks, Mullin and Derer of CLPD. For the constituency section of the NEC, they decided to support the usual suspects, including Benn and Heffer, for their slate of seven while persuading Militants like Ted Knight and Pat Wall not to stand. With ultimate cynicism Benn proposed, according to the notes, that Meacher stand as the eighth candidate. 'The runner up was important,' Benn is quoted allegedly as saying, 'in case Foot dies in the next year'. 'Activities' were also 'to be undertaken against the candidature of Kinnock and Lestor'.[5]

The pattern was repeated for the other sections. Among the women, after much disagreement, they opted for four, including Margaret Beckett, but could not settle on a final candidate with Clare Short and Patricia Hewitt among CLPD's suggestions. 'Leaflets', however, 'attacking Betty Boothroyd, Gwyneth Dunwoody, Shirley Summerskill and Dianne Hayter are to be distributed'.

This time the left paid closer attention to the unions, with attacks encouraged on the moderates – David Williams of COHSE, Roy Evans of the ISTC, Denis Howell of APEX and, naturally, myself. As one of the left's favourite journalists, Peter Hildrew of the *Guardian* wrote:

> A much fiercer contest is expected for the trade union seats on the Labour Party National Executive Committee at the Party Conference in Blackpool later this month. The left slate for this will include the new deputy general secretary of NUPE, Mr Tom Sawyer and Mr Terry Fields of the Fire Brigades Union.[6]

Laying into the Left at Conference

The 1982 Conference played a crucial part in Labour's 1983 election defeat by sowing the seeds of what Gerald Kaufman later called the 'longest suicide note in history'. Paradoxically, it was also crucial to the victory, finally, of we moderates over Benn.

At Conference, Geoff Bish's 'dream child' was vitally important – *Labour's Programme 1982*, the compendium of policies designed to form the basis of the general election manifesto. It had not had an easy birth. Progress on finalizing the NEC's draft was slow and the whole process unsatisfactory because none of us were well enough briefed to respond to the master plan for socialism being placed before us. We had no idea of the real cost of all these admirable proposals or the administrative difficulties involved in introducing them. Michael Cocks, the Chief Whip, and Peter Shore, the Shadow Chancellor, who raised such mundane matters were regarded by the left as agents of the Shadow Cabinet sent to stir discord and frustrate the will of the people.

The fight over the policies was not a straight left–right battle. There were areas where I, for example, led the fight against the moderates of the Shadow Cabinet because of my union involvement. I was strongly opposed to Shore's thoughts on incomes policy and, being a victim of my own propaganda, favoured hardline re-nationalisation and an extension of public ownership.

Once policies had been agreed on the NEC, they had to be discussed with the Shadow Cabinet through the Policy Co-ordinating Committee. The Shadow Cabinet, although having a majority of moderate members on it, was itself divided and the Leader, indeed, was of the left. Not that Michael acted as a great left wing leader on the NEC. There he was seen by the hard left, totally wrongly, as the creature of the right. More confused the situation could hardly be!

The truth is that, although we used our new strength to defeat the left, it was Foot again who called the tune. In May, when Frank Allaun and Joan Maynard for example tried to push through a draft foreword to the programme which Michael did not like, he left it to me and Gwyneth to stop this. In June, when the left challenged Foot's own draft, we moderates saved it with the support of Michael and his friends, Kinnock and Lestor.

Not that Benn didn't have some success. Union recognition in the armed forces crept in, as did repealing Michael Heseltine's housing legislation. There were some brighter moments, however, when in June we removed any reference to swamping the House of Lords.[7]

It would be very, very boring to give a blow-by-blow account of all the long arduous meetings – they are best covered under subject matter. It should be said, however, that huge chunks were approved by the NEC without votes being taken. The whole exercise was a disaster for Labour. At Conference, *Labour's Programme, 1982* was carried by 6,420,000 votes to just 224,000, considerably more than the two-thirds majority needed to make it the basis of the election manifesto. We would, therefore, head towards the election with the triple disasters of unilateral disarmament, withdrawal from the Common Market and our Alternative Economic Strategy.

The platform on defence again included cancellation of Trident and closing all nuclear bases.

When Healey tried in committee to get these removed, he was doomed to pathetic failure being defeated by 19 votes to 6. Only Gwyneth Dunwoody, Denis Healey, Gerry Russell, Shirley Summerskill, Eric Varley and I voted with the goodies.

One important consequence of this vote was that it brought home to me strongly that there was no way in which we could change defence policy before the general election. Even though Betty Boothroyd and Neville Hough had been missing, and Russell Tuck might be brought back into the fold, the multi-lateral cause was a dead duck. This pessimism was re-inforced when we were defeated again at the full NEC in June, when we picked up only one extra vote – Betty's. The most I could rely on was nine out of an NEC of 31! A real bricks-without-straw job, if ever there was one.

And if we could not win in the NEC, there was no chance of overturning it at Conference, where Foot came out as passionately as ever in support of unilateral disarmament. To great applause he declared:

> I say that the greatest task that this Labour movement of ours will ever have to undertake when we get the next Labour government, is to carry out our policy for securing nuclear disarmament in this country and throughout the world.

And unlike the year before, a front bench spokesman was called, as Foot now had a defence team that actually supported our insane policy. In the event, it was Denzil Davies who presented the line which was to fail so badly in the general election:

> One of the best safeguards against nuclear war is a reasonable level of conventional defences, and one of the charges against Margaret Thatcher is that by spending billions and billions on ever more lethal nuclear weapons she is in fact cutting our conventional forces and thereby increasing the danger of nuclear war. We must cancel Trident. We must also not allow cruise missiles in Britain.

Robin Cook also banged the drum again:

> I come to this rostrum to beg Conference, to ask Conference, to plead with Conference to vote for unilateral disarmament . . .Do not be afraid of unilateralism. Do not be afraid of the choice the British people will make if we give them a clear choice between the nuclear arms race under Thatcher and nuclear disarmament under Michael Foot.

Robin is a first-class racing tipster – I concluded, however, that he knew far more about horses than about people.

And so in 1982, Conference, whipped up to a frenzy by Foot, Lestor and Cook, also carried a disarmament proposal – by 3,433,000 votes to 3,401,000 – which, in addition to unilateral disarmament, closure of US bases, opposing arms sales to all fascist regimes, massive defence cuts and nationalisation of the arms industry, also included provisions for alternative jobs 'such as artificial limbs as devised by the Lucas Aerospace Shop Stewards Committee.'!

When the main motion on unilateralism was carried by 4,927,000 to 1,975,000 – more than two to one, thus making it manifesto material – there was jubilation in the hall. Even the Tories could not have been so excited at the certain defeat of the Labour Party at the next general election.

In one of those oddities, however, which Healey said he could never understand – so how could I – the motion on withdrawing from NATO was as ever massively defeated. There were no such redeeming features when we again discussed the Common Market. Then everything was negative.

With only three people – Healey, Betty and Shirley Summerskill – voting with me, even I had long given up trying to change this folly.

We international socialists had, it appeared, to leave the Common Market not only because we didn't like foreigners, but also because it was seen as a serious impediment to the introduction of the Alternative Economic Strategy. The AES indeed was the cornerstone for everything: from the wealth this would provide everything could be afforded, including massive wage settlements if the unions would only like to negotiate these freely with their employers.

The full panoply of our wish list – full employment, increased public spending, capital investment, welfare spending, industrial co-ops, import controls, a shorter working week, controls of rents, prices and bus fares, increased wages, pensions and social security and a redistribution, of course, of both wealth and power to working people – was, surprise, surprise, carried on a show of hands.[8]

One of the difficulties for Peter Shore in the AES was that it made no provision for an incomes policy, which neither the Party nor the unions would support.

Incidentally it was, however, the union opposition of Doug Hoyle, Clive Jenkins's pet parrot, that killed off the proposal to take the finance industry into public ownership. At the Home Policy Committee it had been decided by seven votes to five to take over the big four clearing banks but when this came to the full NEC, there was a different story to tell, as Hoyle and Foot watered it down to taking 'reserve powers' only. Jenkins was very good at looking after his own interests!

At Conference, the left were more successful on the floor, where CLPD's proposition to nationalise a quarter of the largest 100 companies was carried. They failed, however, in for them the key area of internal party democracy. They lost heavily on the question of the 'proscribed register' and another demand to outlaw short-lists of one in parliamentary selections.

The organisational blows to the left continued, too, with the announcement of the NEC election results, which were given just before a bomb scare that drove us on to the seafront to discuss them excitedly. The first results, in the constituencies, were very disappointing. Labour Solidarity's right wing candidates did very badly. Peter Shore, Roy Hattersley and Jack Ashley did the best, but failed to come anywhere near a winning margin. While

Kinnock managed to save his seat, the hard left made one gain, with Audrey Wise knocking Joan Lestor off because of Benn's 'list'.

Other results, however, were much better. John Evans thrashed Les Huckfield in the Socialist Societies, for one. And we were even more delighted to hear the results of Roger Godsiff's efforts, as Eric Varley hammered Meacher by a margin of three to one. There was even more good news to come. In the Women's Section, we finally defeated Stalin's Granny Joan Maynard as our dark horse Anne Davis swept in with votes from right and left. Betty, Gwyneth and Shirley Summerskill also romped home, along with Judith Hart, beating both Margaret Beckett and Renee Short.

We rejoiced generally, too, at the union results, despite the election of Tom Sawyer. His victory was hardly a surprise because Basnett had done the usual deal for NUPE with the other big unions. Doug Hoyle, however, was out and what really amazed us was that Tom Breakell had knocked off Eric Clarke of the Mineworkers. Although Tom was a very good man, it was impossible to believe that an electrician could have been elected![9]

This totally unexpected result sparked off one of those accidents of fate. Clarke went to the scrutineers to query the figures being sure, from the deals that had been done, that a mistake had been made in the count. Then he was allowed to examine the actual ballot papers and discovered that the reason was that the NUR had unexpectedly not cast their traditional vote for him.

During these checks, however, a further mistake was found. And when Dorothy Lovett, the chief scrutineer, announced the new results on the Wednesday, the atmosphere was electric. When she announced that Breakell now had 2,772,000 votes and Clarke 3,062,000 votes, there was wild applause. It looked as though Eric's bum would remain on his NEC seat. But the left clapped too soon. Dorothy appealed to the comrades to wait while she read the whole list.

The buzz of excitement was electric as she ran through the names. Denis Howell 3,221,000. And then the penny dropped. Although Clarke had beaten Breakell, he had not beaten Howell who would take the electrician's place. For us, it was as if Alan Shearer had limped off to be replaced by Michael Owen.

The left's mood turned grim. Clive Jenkins, ever one to grab a chance, then moved that the ballot should be re-conducted. Seconded by Arthur

Scargill, this was accepted by the chair, Judith Hart. Then the moderates' big guns were brought out – Terry Duffy, Roy Grantham, Bill Sirs and Bryan Stanley – and the demand for a re-ballot was defeated by 4,636,000 votes to 1,538,000. It would be nice to think that the arguments had swayed Conference – however, the truth is that the vote was fixed by Basnett, telling NUPE that if they voted for another ballot, he would withdraw support away from Sawyer. It was at this point that I gave him his first gold star ever for good behaviour.

It was not the only miraculous recovery in a bad week for policy, but a good week for the NEC. I was also to be cured of a strange annual virus. In Brighton, the year before, I had developed the most awful buzzing in my ears, which was very worrying, until it disappeared on returning home. Then in Blackpool, it returned and I began to panic. I complained bitterly to Llin about it, but having worked in hospitals she showed no sympathy. Then suddenly on the Thursday evening, in a bar, after a week of great anxiety, it got worse and worse.

I turned round suddenly and discovered the source of the strange hissing sound. It was coming not from within my overworked head but from young, left wing delegates. For two years they had carried on their hissing without my knowing it. Realising that it was a sign of hatred, rather than nature's warning of overwork, I started to revel in it. I only hoped that the hissing would be even greater the following year.

EIGHTEEN

Taking Control

There had been great excitement after the NEC election results were agreed at Conference. I was not so excited. I had seen so many false dawns so far and knew that, although we had increased the number of solid right wingers, we were by no means in a majority. Handling a group which included Ken Cure of the AUEW and Denis Howell, on the one hand, and Syd Tierney and Sam McCluskie on the other, was never going to be easy.

Additionally, I was very wary of Michael Foot. He had kept Benn in all his positions of power and influence the previous year – and goodness knows what he would do this time. At Conference he had told Benn he wanted him in the next Shadow Cabinet and I knew that Tierney would never give me a majority against Foot. McCluskie would also be loyal to Foot although I hoped, if only out of sheer spite, he would draw the line at supporting either Benn or Heffer.

Despite a move by Tierney, indeed, to change the system of electing the NEC's all important committees, it had been decided to stick with the usual method – deciding their composition at the first NEC following Conference and then leaving it to each Committee to elect a chairman from amongst its members, subject to later ratification by the full NEC.[1]

This was important. In reality, what it meant was that the ruling faction chose a chairman for each committee and then ensured that there were enough of their supporters to get that through on each committee the first time it met. Battle, therefore, would follow bloody battle.

This time, after so many years' hard labour, I could at last glimpse the prize. But we still needed to lay the ground meticulously. Nothing could be left to chance. So I went earnestly through my usual process of consultation with moderates who had been on the NEC for some time or who nobbled me in the House of Commons tea room. That settled pretty well who would be supported for what chairmanship.

Thankfully, this time the job was fairly painless. I knew what everyone wanted and gave it to them. As they all wanted different things, it was easy to get agreement. The only problem I might face was with Tierney, who was still uncertain about whether he would go along with everything I wanted.

On the Monday before that historic NEC, *The Times* set the scene, predicting:

> Mr Benn is already certain to lose the chairmanship of the powerful Home Policy Committee. The centre-right majority would on the following Wednesday ensure that it had at majority of at least three on the Home Policy Committee . . . John Golding 'an aggressive moderate' would be elected Chairman . . .
>
> Speculation that Mr Heffer, this year's party vice-chairman and therefore a member of key committees ex-officio, might stand down, seem wide of the mark. Mr Foot, whose allies will be discouraging the right from overplaying its hand, wants to sustain those who have sought to nurture party unity – Mr Heffer included.[2]

The *Guardian* also made great play of the 'Foot factor'. 'The Leader Mr Michael Foot is expected to use his influence on the Party's new right-orientated National Executive Committee to try to save the important committee chairmanship held by Mr Eric Heffer. But Mr Tony Benn's power base seems lost . . . Mr Foot and his immediate allies hold at best a delicate balance of power on an Executive which some now regard as 15–14 in favour of the right'.[3]

Short of political news for Monday's papers, journalists had rung round on the Sunday afternoon. Someone on our side had told them the moderate list; someone in the Heffer camp was passing on their hopes about Foot.

Whatever was said on the Sunday, in the event Foot did nothing to save anybody, although almost certainly he could have done. But *The Times* was completely wrong to believe that:

Michael Foot was powerless to prevent the overthrow of Jim Mortimer's proposals which would have given the majority on the main committees to a combination of the hard and soft left, with Mr Foot and the soft left holding the balance.[4]

For this reason, I was very apprehensive when on the day before the crucial NEC meeting which would decide, I was summoned to Foot's Office. There were no polite preliminaries – he regarded me as completely beyond the pale, particularly since the speech I had made on fixing to the Parliamentary Labour Party.

He asked me what I intended to do. Wondering whether he had already stitched up things with the General Secretary and others, as he had done the previous year, I replied simply that I was determined to secure changes.

I confirmed what he already knew from reading the papers and presumably from talking to Kinnock. I told him that we had asked Neil to be Chairman of Home Policy but he apparently was too busy and so I would take it. I would have preferred to be chairman of Organisation but Russell Tuck had seniority. Thankfully Sam McCluskie as Chairman of the Party was out of the running.

Foot was particularly interested to know whom we intended to run as chairman of International and was evidently relieved when I told him that it would be, as the papers had already reported, Alex Kitson – a left wing hard-line unilateralist. The truth is that Kitson's friends McCluskie and Tierney would have voted for no-one else, so we were forced to make a virtue out of necessity.

Foot then asked me if we were going to have a pre-meeting to settle our slate. My reply – that I hadn't arranged anything – was true but totally misleading, in other words a good political answer. For some time the trade union group on the NEC had rarely, if ever, had a meeting. I was left to fix everything on the telephone or by meeting people one by one, face to face. I would then work out a line I thought each member could go along with – the lowest common denominator approach – ring round and sell it.

In general, this worked a treat – after the trade unionists had agreed directly with me on the phone, they invariably delivered what they had promised. Now, however, we were in a somewhat different ball game. The new factor was the involvement of the research assistants, the special advisers of right wing front bench members of the NEC. In the tea room we called them the 'chocolate soldiers' because they had been financed by the Rowntree Trust before Ted Short introduced money for opposition parties.

The chocolate soldiers had an enthusiastic but simplistic view of conspiracy. You called a meeting, got agreement from like-minded colleagues and then bulldozed your right wing policies through. And so, full of excitement, they had arranged a meeting themselves before that crunch meeting of the NEC.

Unfortunately, they did not take the care that I was used to from seasoned operators like Roger Godsiff. I had been told that we were to meet at the Red Lion pub in Whitehall – far too close to home! – but when I got back from my encounter with Foot, I learned that the venue had changed for the worse. It was now fixed for Locketts restaurant, the favourite haunt of many journalists and politicians for wining and dining at the expense of those who buy newspapers!

My worst fears were justified when, on going in to the private room booked, we had to pass Foot himself sitting at the doorway waiting for someone!

The atmosphere inside was mixed. Denis Healey was looking distinctly uncomfortable – he always had an aversion to what he described as the 'trade union mafia'. Indeed, many years later he told me that he didn't know who was worse, the left wing fanatics or the union fixers. That we trade unionists were doing his dirty work for him seemed to have totally escaped him.

The hard right wingers, Betty Boothroyd, Denis Howell and Ken Cure, all looked pleased with themselves and had an air of anticipation. Others, more middle of the road such as Anne Davis, looked more apprehensive – wondering what was going to happen and whether they would fit in to such a conspiratorial gathering. Russell Tuck, as ever, was totally relaxed just wanting to get on with it.

The chocolate soldiers were all agog with excitement, making up as ever for their lack of status by much consulting of papers and each other. They were always good at looking busy and important. Unfortunately, when McCluskie saw them he exploded. 'Who the hell invited them?' he demanded. 'They invited themselves,' I replied truthfully. 'Well we don't want to see them again,' he said. 'Tell them they must not come.'

This later I did, much to their disgust – they never said nice things about me after that. Partly, this was out of spite because I had stopped them from playing with the big boys, but also because they never understood the complexity of the political make-up of the so-called Moderate Group on the NEC. Consequently, they always thought that more should have been achieved than was really possible.

The reality was that some members of the Moderate Group were ill at ease with their membership at all. I recalled how, at the beginning, McCluskie would not even attend meetings with Shirley Williams and other MPs. The truth, as well, was that he was always putting himself at risk in his union. His General Secretary was Jim Slater, a hard left supporter. His close friend, remember too, was Alex Kitson.

While McCluskie was happy dealing with me, he was uncomfortable talking in front of people he did not know or trust. Often, he would absent himself from meetings if he thought he could not deliver what the others wanted. Certainly he would have preferred not to have had supposedly clandestine meetings in the media's field headquarters. Against this background, bright ideas from busy babies, like the chocolate soldiers, could have really put the skids under carefully crafted alliances and convenient compromises.

For now, however, the meeting went on. It was naturally assumed that I would continue as convenor of the Moderate Group and this I did. I told them how the old guard had agreed to carve up the chairmanships – they had already read much of this in the papers anyway. Then we spent most of the time sorting out the changes that we needed to make to the committee memberships to ensure that we had sufficient votes to elect them.

I reported on my discussion with Foot and although there were murmerings when I revealed that Kitson was to take International, there was no confrontation.

As we went through each committee, deciding who to delete from the list of names proposed by the General Secretary and who to add, I made notes. I never had minutes taken – everything was either confined to my head or scribbled on my agenda. This was, indeed, a most chancy business as I was one of the world's worst at losing things. I once lost a whole union art exhibition on the Underground, but fortunately this time I managed to keep the crucial record safe by tucking it into the inside pocket of my shabby suit.

Next morning at the NEC, the atmosphere was intense. The waves of hatred and hostility towards me started even before I produced from my inside pocket what was by now a very scrubby piece of paper, the death warrant of the hopes, aspirations and ambitions of so many around that table. I thought at the time that I should have worn a wig and a black cap, as I announced the sentences of execution.

We started with the membership of the Home Policy Committee, Benn's power base. This first vote would determine whether, after years of blood, sweat and tears, we finally swept the left out of their positions of power – or whether we retreated, scarred and bloodied, to re-group once again. The vote would depend on personality, as well as politics. It would rely, crucially, on the tussle between woolly sentiment and hard-nosed reason in the mind of Michael Foot.

I suppose it was hardly surprising that the left looked so angry when, with my customary grin and speaking as slowly, flatly and – frankly– as roughly as I could manage, I moved the deletion of the names of Frank Allaun and Jo Richardson from names proposed for Home Policy and the substitution of the ultra-reliable Ken Cure and Gwyneth Dunwoody instead.

You could have cut the atmosphere with a scalpel, as the roll call took place. As each name was called out and they replied in a single word 'for' or 'against', I mentally added up the score. It started alphabetically and badly.

Allaun – against, 0–1; Benn – against, 0–2; Boothroyd – for 1–2, Laurence Coates – against 1–3, Ken Cure – for 2–3, Anne Davis- for 3–3, Gwyneth Dunwoody – for 4–3, John Evans- against 4–4, Roy Evans for 5–4, Foot – everyone held their breath, until he said 'abstain' when some on the left made what can only be politely described as 'disapproving noises' 5–4, Golding – for 6–4, Alan Hadden – for 7–4, Judith Hart – against 7–5, Healey – for 8–5, Heffer – against 8–6, Neville Hough – for 9–6, Denis Howell – for 10–6, Kinnock – against 10–7, Kitson – against 10–8, McCluskie, Chairman – abstain 10–8 (now it was the turn of our side to look upset, but this is what I had agreed with him as being for the best), Jo Richardson – against 10–9; Tom Sawyer – against 10–10, Dennis Skinner against 10–11 (I could sense the anxiety felt by many on our side, as the left inched in front), Shirley Summerskill – for 11–11, Syd Tierney – for 12–11 (that's it, I thought, thank goodness – now we have it!) Russell Tuck – for 13–11, Eric Varley – for 14–11, David Williams – for 15–11, Audrey Wise – against 15–12.

Syd Tierney's vote and the abstentions of Sam McCluskie and Michael Foot had seen us home!

Except for Benn, who had been expecting it for months, some on the left took the defeat very badly indeed. For some reason which still evades me, Kinnock was particularly upset and offered to come off the Home Policy Committee and give his seat to Jo Richardson. As I regarded her as a particularly dangerous leftie, I made sure the moderates defeated this proposal.

Then, by 20 votes to 6, it was resolved that the composition of the Home Policy Committee be approved. It gave a clear majority to the moderates to elect whoever they wished as chairman when the Committee next met.

We then turned to International. Here, with the sensitivities of Syd, Sam and Michael in mind, we made no move to increase the numbers of moderates. Kitson and the supporters of CND could have the day (the statement by Benn in his Diary for 27 October, 1982 that 'there was a clean sweep of the left on all the committees' is, therefore, strictly untrue). When I moved the replacement of our allies David Williams and Betty Boothroyd (a passionate multilateralist) by Anne Davis and Roy Evans, there was no opposition.

Then the truce ended and conflict broke out in earnest. The tension reached new heights, however, when we reached the Organisation Committee. This was the key body in the fight for the soul of the Party. It had been run for too long by Heffer under the tutelage of the Liverpool Trots. I, in the cleansing spirit of one of Cromwell's Inspector-Generals, moved and Healey seconded, the deletion of the hard left Audrey Wise and Laurence Coates and the substitution of Alan Hadden and Shirley Summerskill instead.

Far from Heffer having a more favourable result than Benn, however, as the press had predicted, for him it turned out worse.

The amendments were carried by 16 votes to 11, with Foot and McCluskie again abstaining. Not only had all those who had voted against Benn voted against Heffer, but John Evans did also. Indeed, when Evans responded 'yes' in support of my proposal, foaming at the mouth almost, Eric started to shout, bellow abuse and to bang the table.

As ever, the joke was on the clown from Merseyside, but never before in such satisfying circumstances. 'Eric Heffer blew up,' Benn recorded, "'You buggers are trying to break the party'". *The Times* also described the scene colourfully:

> As the purge continued some on the left reacted in fury. Mr Heffer, in a loud and angry outburst, told the moderates that they were doing the party much harm. Mr Neil Kinnock, a close associate of Mr Foot, intervened along similar lines.[5]

In the next vote, perhaps it was because of Kinnock – usually no fan of Eric – that the committee's composition was only approved this time by 16 votes to 9. It was, however, plenty. And, as for Heffer's shouting and bawling, as Benn noted: 'No one took the slightest notice.'

By now exultant, we moderates then took control of the Youth Committee. Given the unpopularity of the Militant-controlled Young Socialists, this should have been the easiest task of all, but it was not. Whenever an issue appeared clear, personalities had the nasty habit of muddying the waters.

While it had been decided that Denis Howell chair the Youth Committee, his parliamentary neighbour Tierney could not go along with this at any price. Being unable to get on with Denis at all, Syd withdrew from the committee before I moved and Ken Cure seconded the deletion of Allaun, Skinner and Wise in favour of Howell and Anne Davis instead.

At the roll call, Tierney joined with the left, including John Evans, to oppose. This meant we won by only 14 votes to 13, with 2 abstentions. Again, had Foot and McCluskie voted with the left, we would have lost.

This narrow result meant that we needed to keep Michael compliant. For this reason, when I heard that Foot wanted Judith Hart on the Finance and General Purposes Committee, which was not as all powerful in the Party as in many trade unions, I moved that she be added and did not object when Skinner moved Audrey Wise.

To get control of Press and Publicity, which certainly was on the agenda, we needed to remove no-one, but to make certain of a majority I moved that Alan Hadden, Neville Hough and Russell Tuck be added. This time, the left did not bother to oppose.

At this time we were still having trouble with groups of barmy women, so it was important, too, to get control of the Women's Committee. To achieve this, I moved the deletion of Benn and Skinner and the substitution of Ken Cure. Once again, Tierney voted with the left, so another key change was carried by a single vote, with Foot and McCluskie carrying on abstaining.

We allowed Heffer, however, to be added to the Staff Negotiations Committee, the most unpopular committee of all, before turning to another contentious area.

The TUC–Labour Party Liaison Committee was considered of high status and important in the formulation of policy. Tension swelled again when I moved, and Healey again seconded, the deletion of Benn and Hart in favour of Tierney and four hard right wingers, Betty Boothroyd, Neville Hough, Ken Cure and myself. This time, Tierney abstained with Foot and McCluskie, so we had a majority of 14 to 12.

The National Council of Labour and the National Joint Council, which had ceased to have any importance, were nodded through on the basis of Jim Mortimer's left-right compromise proposals.

Then came our one slip-up. When we came to the National Labour Women's Committee, Shirley Summerskill – who was not always predictable – decided suddenly to withdraw. Jo Richardson acted quickly and moved, with Benn seconding, that Audrey Wise be added. As our troops had not been alerted to this and given the appropriate marching orders, the left won by 15 votes to 6. It hurt me a lot. I just do not like to see fish come off the hook no matter how many I have caught previously, but I quickly recovered the situation by moving the deletion of Benn and the substitution of Ken Cure, Denis Howell and myself.[6]

We moderates were exhilarated and the left utterly demoralised, as we walked out of Walworth Road that day. What we had done that morning was to end the dominance of extreme left wing socialists in the Labour Party and bring about the fall of the Benn–Heffer axis, which would never carry credibility again. It was high time. They certainly had it coming. But it was a coup achieved by the skin of our teeth. The satisfaction at a job well done swelled with the next day's headlines. Ian Aitken, a strong supporter of the soft left, wrote (and I quote – deliberately, gloatingly – at length):

> Mr Tony Benn and his left-wing allies got their political come-uppance on Labour's National Executive Committee yesterday. The militant moderates, newly re-established in majority control, ruthlessly wiped them out of control on all of the party's key policy and organisation committees.
>
> No mercy was shown, although many left-wingers raised a whimper of complaint as the right-wing juggernaut rolled over them. They protested that the right-wing's insistence on swinging the balance their way was bound to polarise the party and store up more trouble in the future. Mr Foot, who studiously avoided participating in the procedure by abstaining in all the votes, acknowledged that some changes of personnel in the party's controlling committees were bound to take place. But he tried to draw the attention of NEC members to the fact that the crucial task for the party was winning the next election rather than winning its internal battles.
>
> Mr Foot's reward for this approach was a brutal condemnation from Mr Dennis Skinner, one of the left-wingers who lost his seat on a number of crucial committees.
>
> 'Michael hasn't got any guts left.' he told the committee. It was the most bitter of many angry interjections from left-wing members as they watched the majority work its way through each of the NEC's sub-committees removing left-wingers and adding right wingers to their membership by votes varying between 16–11 down to hairbreadths majorities like 14–13.[7]

I recall *The Times* with almost equal relish. 'The operation dismayed the left,' it reported, quoting one 'prominent left winger': 'When we had control we allowed the right some positions of power. They have left us without a crumb.' (I would have thought the chairmanship of the International Committee more than a crumb – or perhaps not) 'Another NEC member said: 'It was overkill. They went right over the top,' *The Times* added. 'But the changes were made without any protest from Mr Benn. According to one source, 'he took his punishment like a man'.[8]

The truth is, of course, that Benn knew that he was doomed, while Heffer, expecting to be saved, was shocked that his reprieve never arrived.

Having come so far, for me mercy was hardly high on my list, as Aitken observed in the *Guardian*:

However narrow the majority, the right did not fail in a single vote.[not true but almost]. The moving spirit throughout this procedure was Mr John Golding, a trade union member of the committee and a leading right-wing MP.

Time after time, Mr Golding moved the removal of Mr Benn, Dame Judith Hart, Mr Skinner, Mr Lawrence Coates of the Young Socialists, Mrs Audrey Wise and Mr Frank Allaun from the list of names recommended by the party's general secretary, Mr Jim Mortimer, for membership of one or other of the committees. With almost equal frequency he proposed the substitution of names like Dr Shirley Summerskill, Mr Ken Cure of the Engineering Workers, Mrs Gwyneth Dunwoody or Mr Alan Hadden.

Right wingers were in no mood to apologise for what they had done. They insisted that Mr Benn and his left-wing supporters had behaved with equal ruthlessness when they found themselves temporarily in control of the executive. It would have been weakness to fail to respond in similar fashion, once the Conference vote had re-established the right-wing majority on the executive.

There is little doubt that yesterday's events will deepen the trenches in which the two wings of the party glower against each other . . . Neither side seems ready to recognise the obvious truth of Mr Foot's appeal for unity on the brink of a general election campaign.

Aitken, whose father had been a Research Officer of the AEU, was very friendly with the soft left and spent much of his time talking to them in Annie's Bar in the House of Commons. The overall verdict of the *Guardian* – always anti-union block vote – in its editorial, therefore, was hardly surprising.

The message from the one section of the party [the constituencies] in which votes cast bear some relationship to the views of living, breathing, card carrying, conscious party members is clear. The constituencies want the Labour Party to be led by exactly the sort of people who were routed, booted or humiliated (according to the paper of your choice) by the new NEC.

Foot, it pointed out for good measure,

> will be forgiven a brief moment of pleasure at the humiliation of Brother
> Benn. He should be less than happy at the thought of Mr Benn being joined
> in exile by other assorted left-wingers. It is more than likely that yesterday's
> decision has helped to end the isolation in which Mr Benn has found himself
> since the race for the deputy leadership.

How wrong it turned out to be.

The Times viewed it very differently. In its editorial, it recalled that a year
earlier 'there was much speculation that this would be followed by sweeping
changes in the chairmanship of NEC committees . . . But in the mistaken
pursuit of party unity, it was decided to make none of these changes. So the
moderate wing gained only limited advantage from the altered composition
of the NEC itself, which gave it an uncertain majority . . . In this year's
elections the moderate wing secured a sure majority, and at yesterday's
meeting of the NEC they made full use of it'.

My summing up in 'Diary of an MP' in my local *Sentinel*, of course,
pulled no punches:

> The Labour Party NEC meeting was quite lively! Since I was elected (on
> to the NEC) in 1978, I have been among the minority who strongly
> supported Jim Callaghan's government. Ever since I was a kid I have
> supported Labour and have wanted more than anything to have Labour
> governments. This has been put at risk by the defection of the SDP whose
> members lacked the courage to stay and fight. And by the distrust of the
> extreme left among our Labour voters. Today I made certain that Tony
> Benn's influence was broken by removing him and his supporters from
> some key committees. Now we can get on with the job of persuading
> working people that Labour can repair the damage done to our country by
> the Tory government. We have to win the next general election to create
> jobs and to save the welfare state.

Some of the loyalists were bitter nonetheless that Tierney had, as they
thought, broken ranks but as ever I prevailed upon them to hold their peace.

I knew that Syd had only joined our group out of loyalty to the Leader – at that time Callaghan. If attacked and driven into a corner, he could almost certainly have joined Kinnock and John Evans in their voting.

That was the last thing we needed, particularly as after electing the members we still had to capture all the crucial committee chairmanships.

The first of those fabulous meetings took place on the morning of 10 November in Committee Room 20 at the House of Commons – the crucial Organisation Committee, Heffer's fiefdom. I ticked the loyalists off my list as they arrived one by one. Betty Boothroyd, punctual as ever, Ken Cure, Anne Davis, Gwyneth Dunwoody, our tower of strength, Roy Evans, Alan Hadden, Denis Healey, Neville Hough, Denis Howell, Shirley Summerskill, Russell Tuck, Syd Tierney and Eric Varley. Thirteen in all – unlucky for some, as they say at the bingo – and more than enough.

Audrey Wise and Laurence Coates came to witness the slaughter, too, even though they had been kicked off. Foot and McCluskie, as well, were there even though they were not going to vote. And then, waiting for the shooting to start, there were Benn, Heffer, Allaun, Kinnock, Richardson, Skinner and John Evans.

We also had the sort of audience attracted by public executions. Chief Whip Michael Cocks was there to rejoice in the come-uppance of the odious Heffer, who had given him so much aggravation.[9] Walworth Road staffers were there in force, realising that this was a major watershed in the history of the Party. You could have put the atmosphere through a wringer, when it came time and David Hughes, the committee secretary, asked for nominations. I nominated Russell Tuck and only heard someone else propose Heffer. The vote, however, was a foregone conclusion. Four for Heffer and 13 votes for Tuck. Now that was a slaughter and so Russell took the Chair. Frank Allaun paid a tribute to Heffer and Foot seconded.

In my own 'Diary of an MP', I was even more magnanimous:

Eric was bitterly upset and gave us the benefit of some strong advice. In time, however, he will see that it is all for the best. The extremists in his Liverpool constituency would never have let him implement the Conference decision against the Militant Tendency.[10]

We then trotted along to Committee Room 18 in the House for the removal of Benn from the chair of the Home Policy Committee. This time the atmosphere was far less tense than it had been in the morning. We trooped in to face a very depleted left, Benn, Evans, Heffer, Kinnock, Sawyer, Skinner, knowing that victory was certain. Loyalists were again out in force to watch the slaughter.[11]

Again, in my 'Diary of an MP', I wrote:

In the afternoon, up in room 18, I stood against Tony Benn as Chairman of the Home Policy Committee and won by 12 votes to 4. I can't claim that I was elated – I would have preferred that Neil Kinnock do the job. However, Neil refused on the grounds that he was 'too busy! Now I must get on with the job of preparing a plan for the next Labour government.'

It is important that the Party and the Shadow Cabinet agree with each other on the important items to be included in the manifesto. My inclination is to concentrate on jobs, housing, and saving the welfare state in the long campaign before the general election. The Home Policy Committee itself was placid – almost jovial. We need to prepare plans for reversing privatisation in detail – and this we decided to do.'

At the meeting, I presume John Evans voted for me this time against Benn. It was certainly the end of an era.

At the other committees we continued to do what we wanted. But the shock to the left was so great that they broke with tradition and challenged the votes at the subsequent NEC.

Both Kinnock and Judith Hart joined the hard left to challenge the election of Russell Tuck at Organisation and Anne Davis as chairman of the Women's Committee. They were roundly defeated by 15 votes to 10. When my election as chairman of Home Policy and Gwyneth Dunwoody's at Press and Publicity were challenged, while Hart still voted with the extremists, this time Kinnock abstained.[12]

We moderates came out of the NEC meeting feeling that at last things were truly going our way. Finally, we could hang our 'Under New Management' sign on the front door as we left.

NINETEEN

Under New Management

Following the fiasco of the clandestine Locketts restaurant meeting and the exclusion of the 'chocolate soldiers', moderate MPs on the NEC took more care organising meetings. We gathered first at Betty Boothroyd's homely flat near Victoria, but it was a little too far away from the Commons for the MPs to scurry back to vote (her later residence in Speaker's Court would have been far more convenient!). After trying Denis Howell's flat in Dolphin Square (very close to Heffer's), we eventually settled down at the flat of Betty's friend, Helen de Freitas, in Tufton Court – large, convenient for the Commons and extremely comfortable.

Unlike the crisp meetings with the brothers at Swinton House, these gatherings could drag on and on. Betty remembers how one evening, having started at 7.30 pm we were still going hammer and tongs just before the 10 o'clock vote. The mods wanted to stay and miss the vote – Howell took the very realistic view that we were going to be beaten by the Tories anyway, we always were, and so why bother – but I insisted on us going in case the left scrutinised the Division List, put two and two together and used our absence as a stick to beat us with.

We met the evening before every full NEC meeting. I had first to meet the brothers at Swinton House before going on to the gathering of MPs. They were very different affairs. With the brothers, all I had to do was take careful notes of what was expected of me. Although there were some tactical differences between John Spellar and Roger Godsiff and I, they were easily solved. In the chair, Bryan Stanley was ever masterful.

With the MPs, however, I had to bring cohesion not to well-disciplined machine men with a clear and shared sense of purpose, but to a group of

267

talented individuals with strong opinions on every subject under the sun. The whole group, indeed, agreed on very little other than not wanting the Labour Party to be run by Benn and Heffer.

Neither Healey nor Eric Varley attended these caucus meetings, although both went along with the right. On one occasion Healey remarked that he did not always agree with what I did, but I didn't ask him what in particular because I was happy so long as he voted with us. The reality was that sometimes I would have preferred to have voted a different way myself.

It was a very diverse and often unpredictable group. The most reliable were the hard-line, inflexible right wingers: Betty, Howell and Ken Cure. They would get impatient with me because I didn't move fast enough. Whenever I was cautious, however, it was for good reason. Neville Hough, the GMWU representative – a lovely man and a solid right winger – regularly brought requests from his boss Basnett, for instance, which I would always try to deliver. After doing his union duty, Neville would help me out on anything he could. Russell Tuck was extremely loyal, but would sup with the devil if it brought benefits. Others of the group did more than sup, sometimes they voted with him.

The Achilles heel of Shirley Summerskill – as right wing as they came – was Militant. She was fearful of the Trots in her constituency. Gwyneth Dunwoody was sound on virtually everything, but her greatest weakness was that she was pro-Peter Shore and passionately anti-Common Market. Alan Hadden and Anne Davis, both from the centre, were also anti-Market and wobbly on defence, as were two good union men, Roy Evans from the steelworkers and David Williams of COHSE. And as we have already seen, two of the others – Sam McCluskie and Syd Tierney – were both basically of the left, CND and anti-Market.

To keep this group together required a great deal of juggling, to say the least, as on most of the main policy issues they were split. Betty and Gwyneth went hammer and tongs over the Market. On defence, Alan Hadden supported CND, while Ken Cure was ready to bomb anyone who stepped out of line. There was not even agreement on economic policy: some backed Shore's secret push for an incomes policy (supported outside by Terry Duffy alone). Most of us from the unions ruled it out completely.

Militant was also a touchy subject. Betty, Denis, Ken and I were ready to hang them from the nearest lamp post. Others had important reservations. Shirley Summerskill always had to look over her shoulder at her local party, something that many MPs did. Anne Davis had idealistic qualms – 'we were all young once,' she said – and Syd Tierney would go no further than Foot was prepared to go and certainly not support a witch hunt. Despite the difficulties, however, fortunately we were able to deliver the vote to Foot for him to begin taking action, as we shall see a little later.

To try and reduce the tension at the meetings, I spent a lifetime on the phone establishing the sticking points of each of the group. On Sunday evenings, I would spend hours answering calls from Betty and Gwyneth – one close to Hattersley, the other to Shore, each complaining about the other and insisting on the incompatible. Undoubtedly, they were both prima donnas, but they were superb allies, too. Both had appeared on the stage and were real troupers on the NEC. Betty could freeze any leftie with her withering glare, later used to good effect as Speaker, while Gwyneth had got righteous indignation off to a fine art. With her well-practised snort she even made the very indignant Margaret Beckett look a novice.

Trying to manage this clash of egos left such a mark on me that I was dumbfounded as I watched Gwyneth, years later, so eloquently and rightly singing Betty's praises when moving the motion that she be Speaker. For a moment, I thought I had departed this life for a moderate whip's heaven.

We couldn't have changed the major policy platforms, anyway, but I did not even wish to try. I was still determined that the NEC did not adopt policies for the general election that conflicted with left wing Conference decisions. Having seen how Benn had so unfairly treated Callaghan over the 1979 manifesto, I set out to make sure Benn and his cohorts would get all the blame for our forthcoming defeat.

I was totally convinced that we could not possibly win. Weekend after weekend in my constituency, I had the reasons rubbed into me by people on the streets and in the working men's clubs. It was not only having Foot as the Leader (people just could not bring themselves to see him as Prime Minister), or daft policies or being fatally split. We simply didn't know how to pay for all the things we were promising, except by massive tax increases which people did not want to pay. There was too little time to change. The important thing was to hang the blame for our defeat firmly round Benn's neck. Then after the election we could do to the left what they did to Jim.

My hard right allies found this strategy as hard to bear as our legally enforced inactivity against Militant, so I had to steer them as far away from policy as possible. Both Betty and Gwyneth were agreed on the uselessness of the small NEC policy groups packed with members of the Hampstead set, so we reduced them substantially.

We were united, however, in our desire to contain the left and so we were more or less able to act as one over the likes of Tariq Ali and loony local parties, over which we did a good job.

Mind you, getting agreement at Tufton Court was one thing. Actually delivering the vote was another. I had to place myself at NEC meetings not only so that I could always catch the Chairman's eye, but also so that none of the mods could leave without passing me. I had constantly to keep a majority – or if that was not possible, to ensure that there was no quorum. I automatically scanned the room, counting all the time, working out whether I had a majority for coming items or not.

My mastery of this technique derived from the fact that my job while playing football in the school playground had been to know minute by minute how many were playing on each side, so we could disallow any goals scored if the other side had more on their team. As the numbers often exceeded 25 a side – and sides changed from day to day – this came to be one of the only useful skills I learned at school.

One of the problems was that there was often better attendance by the hard left than by members of our group. Missing votes could be vital. On one occasion, for example, in the 'Org' in 1983 in the absence of Russell Tuck, Heffer was elected by 4 votes to 3 to stand in as chair and we went on to suffer defeats over local government.[1]

While slip-ups occurred in committee they could, however, usually be rectified at the subsequent NEC. To that end, we increased the NEC quorum from 10 to 15 to make it impossible for the left ever to regain a working majority. If we mods had not got one, we only had to leave to stop decisions from being made until we had a majority again. This was later used by the hard left in our struggles over Militant! It was, however, a weapon to be sparingly used, so mostly I just had to carry on juggling.

Betty reminded me recently how, on one occasion, because some of our side had parliamentary questions, I had to let them leave one NEC meeting while I kept things going until they were able to honour a promise wrung from them and return. She particularly remembers seeing the penny drop suddenly with Skinner, who said: 'Oh, I see what is happening now.'

With the moderates in control and Jim Mortimer as General Secretary, one thing was not in question: the party's finances improved and we finally moved out of the red. Benn and Heffer's period of rule had been disastrous in terms of the administration of Head Office. Under Ron Hayward, it was totally hit and miss. For a party constantly preaching the virtues of planning, it was a disgrace. Nothing, neither finance nor staffing, was properly worked out in advance.[2]

One of our biggest jobs, too, was to bring some political sense to the groups within the Party. Whereever we looked we saw barmies or loonies. One new group was the nutty women who came to ruin the National Conference of Labour Women.

The central part of the struggle on the NEC, however, was the battle over the rights of sitting MPs, the endorsement of parliamentary candidates, local council discipline and the control of membership and expulsions.

One of the most important issues, by far, was re-allocating MPs after parliamentary boundary changes. The impact on MPs can be severely traumatic. It is bad enough that, at a stroke of the Boundary Commission's pen, a sitting MP can see his seat or majority disappear. This can be bearable if there is a Party machine doing its best to relocate MPs in winnable seats. If, however, the Party rulers are glad to have an opportunity to get rid of you to make way for left-wingers, the situation is doubly worse.

This was certainly the case back in June, 1981. When a paper on the effects of boundary changes and the procedure for selection of prospective parliamentary candidates was put to the 'Org', by a big majority it was agreed that existing MPs could effectively be removed on re-distribution of seats. Given the feeling against the PLP at the time, this sailed through the 1981 Conference.

Many of those sitting in the MPs block at Conference received this as a notice to quit. They were reprieved for the moment as Foot and Michael Cocks took legal action against the proposed boundary changes. When the case collapsed, however, Head Office set about implementing the 1981 decision and issued a letter to those constituencies whose boundaries were to change.

This caused consternation in the tea room and Betty, Gwyneth and I were left in no doubt about the anxiety. In consequence, we insisted there be a change. Fortunately, David Hughes was able to say, in all honesty, that the delay caused by the legal challenge made it impossible to implement the decision before the general election and, given the circumstances, we were authorised to lay the rules to one side.

We did so with alacrity, to the cheers of most of the PLP. Hughes then devised a system, which we adopted, whereby it would be possible for MPs and candidates where no major changes had taken place to hold on to their seats and avoid new selections. This was opposed only by the usual crowd, now joined by Tom Sawyer.[3]

A month later we extended this so that in large towns and elsewhere it was possible, even with substantial changes, for the MPs to avoid new selections.

This decision did lead to one local difficulty with Arthur Scargill on behalf of the NUM. If no selection was to be allowed in the new Sherwood constituency, the candidate for Newark would be endorsed for Sherwood. Scargill protested that with 11 pits in the constituency and two coking plants, the NUM ought to be able to nominate its candidate for this seat in which it had 13 branches and 20,000 members.

After a lot of to-ing and fro-ing, the 'Org' agreed that the case fell into a category whereby the new constituency could either select the existing MP or go to selection. After all this manoeuvring Willie Bach, a barrister, was kept as the candidate and he lost the seat by 658 votes in the general election – sunk by the large SDP vote.

In December, 1982, we received the results of the enquiry into the Newham North West selection at which Arthur Lewis was deselected Although the procedure had been accident prone and long drawn out, there was no reason to declare it invalid. So, sadly for the future world of sport, Benn's bag carrier Tony Banks was endorsed as the parliamentary candidate in a seat that not even he could lose.

While we were able to bring relief to a large number of MPs, we also provided some long-overdue protection to councillors in Manchester –

where the City Party remained a major thorn in our side – and across the country. In another victory for the moderates, sitting councillors could not be deselected by fiat, but would automatically be included on the endorsed panel of candidates.

It was time, too, for a reckoning finally with the troublemakers in Hornsey, who were still holding out for Tariq Ali and refusing to implement NEC decisions. So in November, 1982 we moderates decided to wield the big stick and disband the Hornsey party unless it fell into line. Warned legally not to do this precipitately, we did it strictly by the book. A Committee of Enquiry was set up, chaired by Heffer and including myself. We duly reported and, after a battle stretching back to the dawn of time, comrade Ali was finally expelled on 26 October, 1983.

Another key dispute concerned the Brent East and Brent South constituencies, which had been under six months' 'supervision' and investigated by Assistant National Agent Joyce Gould. By the time the general election was called, however, there were still so many disputes that Reg Freeson and Laurie Pavitt were imposed on Brent East and Brent South respectively. This kept 'Newtman' Ken Livingstone out, despite opposition from Benn. Not that this mattered. When Ken finally got to the House of Commons, he was like a newt out of water and was unable to make any impact or headway.

If only, however, we could have stopped Peter Tatchell from standing for Parliament in Bermondsey in the same way!

TWENTY

By-elections at Bermondsey and Darlington

As the Falklands factor saved Margaret Thatcher, so the Bermondsey by-election certainly helped to sink Michael Foot. It was one of two by-elections in the run-up to the 1983 general election, whose results were of crucial importance. In retrospect, the results at Bermondsey, which we lost, and Darlington, which we won, were both a disaster for the Labour Party. The first because it fatally undermined Foot's authority and the second because it persuaded him to stay.

The situation in Bermondsey was horrendous from start to finish. It arose from the decision of Bob Mellish, who had become Deputy Chairman of the London Dockland Development Corporation, to retire from parliament. Mellish was Roman Catholic, right wing and a machine politician. He had been chairman of the London Labour Party – before it turned to the left – and a Housing Minister and Chief Whip. Before the rise of the left he would have been succeeded by another good right-winger, almost certainly of his own choosing. As elsewhere, however, the Bermondsey party had been invaded by young, left wing extremists, one of whom was Peter Tatchell.

Tatchell, as the *Guardian* revealed in a sympathetic profile, was born in Australia and came to Britain as an objector against the Vietnam War. He became immersed in single issue groups such as CND, Troops Out and gay rights. He was once even beaten up in the Aeroflot office in London in a sit-in to protest at the Soviet invasion of Czechoslovakia.[1]

To win the Bermondsey nomination in a bitter fight, he had not only beaten the right wing candidate, but also a Militant nominee and Arthur Latham, the leftie who had replaced Bob Mellish as chairman of the

London Labour Party. In this, he had been helped by the NEC which had wrongly blocked affiliations by John Spellar's EETPU to the local party (although Foot supported my unsuccessful attempts to stop the NEC doing this).

In the normal course, Tatchell's endorsement would have been pushed through by the left with ease. In this case, however, Mellish – who was a shrewd operator – decided that it was not going to happen. He was bitterly upset that one of the ungodly left was to succeed him. That was not the main thing that motivated his crusade against Tatchell, however. As Chief Whip, Mellish had been very tolerant of opinion and not very ideological at all. No, his bitterness stemmed from the fact that Tatchell had been party to excluding some old-timers from standing as councillors again. These people had loyally supported Labour and Bob down the years and Mellish was not going to forget this.

He knew that at a general election Tatchell would be swept into the House of Commons. A by-election, however, would not be so certain, so Mellish threatened to create one. Foot knew, too, that the Social Democrats could well win in Bermondsey, which would really put the cat amongst the pigeons. For good measure, Mellish drew attention to an article in *London Labour Briefing*, where Tatchell called for extra-parliamentary action – a red rag to Michael.

> Surely more imaginative and defiant forms of protest are justified in response to the callous policies of this government? Indeed perhaps they are even necessary to motivate and inspire a large-scale popular opposition which can seriously challenge the authority and legitimacy of Tory policy. Such challenges, especially when combined with the industrial might of the trade union movement, are probably the only means by which this government will listen to the voice of the people and be deterred from its monetarist course. Debates and parliamentary divisions are fruitless cosmetic exercises given the Tories' present majority.

For Foot it was intolerable that anyone should attack the things that he held dear, revelled in and excelled at in this way. For Michael great rallies and debates in the House of Commons were at the heart of democracy and ought not to be dismissed so contemptuously as Sunday afternoon strolls. Why, indeed, did a man who thought these things want to get into parliament, anyway?

Mellish, having laid the fire, sat back and watched Jim Wellbeloved – an old colleague from the Whips Office but by now an SDP renegade – light the tinder. Though technically out of order, Wellbeloved asked Mrs Thatcher at Question Time to comment on the Tatchell statement. Foot took the bait and ran with it: 'the individual concerned is not an endorsed member of the Labour Party and as far as I am concerned never will be,' he retorted.

Mellish was delighted. Tatchell was now a dead duck. His goose had been well and truly cooked. As the news spread, there was a buzz of excitement in the lobbies and the tea room and consternation amongst the left. Those of us on the right could hardly believe what was happening. Some said Foot had got Tatchell mixed up with Tariq Ali, but that was black propaganda. At the PLP meeting, David Winnick supported Tatchell's selection. Foot agreed with Heffer that it was a matter for the NEC, but added: 'Let me underline that the issue of parliamentary democracy is at stake and if I had said nothing the SDP would have made the running.'

The endorsement of Tatchell came up at the 'Org' on 7 December, 1981, which for once I looked forward to. Foot spoke up and said he had seen Tatchell that morning to tell him he would be opposing his endorsement because of the offending article. Benn records in his Diaries Foot's reasons for opposing him:

They are not personal but a matter of political judgement. His candidature would be a disaster for the party. The NEC have to take account of this situation. The article he wrote in *London Labour Briefing* advocating anti-parliamentary action would be used by the SDP against the Labour Party in Bermondsey and elsewhere; it would be spread far and wide and is a gift for the social democrats. The article did not accord with our view of parliamentary democracy, and that is why I intervened in the House of Commons. I want to underline the fact that I could not have taken any other view. If he were to be endorsed, it would lead to a serious electoral disaster.

Knowing that Foot would have the support of his acolytes, Heffer as ever played for time, proposing another Committee of Enquiry. This was seconded by Frank Allaun, who supported Tatchell's stand against the Vietnam War and over homosexual rights.

I pointed out that Tatchell was totally unacceptable – even having pin-ups of Lenin in his flat. Lestor retorted she had pin-ups of Castro when she was young because she thought he was dishy. I thought in this case the attraction must be political not sexual, because not even Tatchell could regard Lenin as 'dishy'. I showed great restraint in not saying this, just in case I was wrong. There is no accounting for taste.

Skinner meanwhile, who could not abide Heffer's dodging and dithering, moved that Tatchell's selection be endorsed. I, of course, wanted to put the knife in there and then, too, and – backed by Healey – moved the exact opposite. The discussion that followed was chaotic. The hard left were bitter and the soft left supporters of Foot confused. Some thought Foot had made a mistake, but Kinnock to his credit argued that we were really deciding the direction of the Labour Party. Russell Tuck said we should endorse Michael not Tatchell. Someone, inevitably, said the fact that Tatchell was a homosexual made him less inclined to support him. Benn believed that Foot felt pressurised by the threat of yet more parliamentary defections to the SDP.

After the nastiness of the debate came the comic relief and at one stage there was total confusion about the decision that had been reached. What was not in doubt was that Tatchell's immediate endorsement was rejected – Skinner lost by the whacking margin of 14 to 5. Between Heffer's dithering and my knifing, however, there was a tie. Heffer then re-ran the vote and I nipped ahead by one vote. My rejection of Tatchell was then carried by 12 votes to 7, amid inevitable recriminations because of the muddle. I must say, however, that at that stage I was so unaccustomed to winning, that I couldn't keep a broad grin from my face.

Their decision caused a tremendous rumpus within the left. Tribune was again split asunder, as its chair Norman Buchan ruled out of order an attempt by the ultras to repudiate Foot. Reg Race, the spearhead of the Tribune hard left, stormed out of the meeting, shouting abuse at his colleagues over his shoulder. 'It is now going to be open warfare between the constituency parties and the Party Leadership. The Bermondsey party has been kicked in the teeth,' he told the press afterwards.

Walworth Road was certainly being inundated by massive support of Tatchell organised by left-controlled organisations. It was time for Foot's friends to fight back, as the *Guardian* reported:

> On a day when Mr Michael Foot's popularity rating in the public opinion polls dropped to a new low, a group of left-wing shadow ministers and senior Labour backbenchers rallied to his support. They produced a circular addressed to all constituency Labour parties backing Mr Foot's repudiation of Mr Peter Tatchell, the ultra-left candidate for Bermondsey. The circular, signed by Mr Neil Kinnock, Mr John Silkin, and Mr Stan Orme, as well as a number of backbenchers, is clearly intended as a response to Mr Tony Benn's move to rally a campaign against Mr Foot in the constituency parties.[2]

Fresh support had to be rallied again for Michael at the NEC on 16 December, 1981. At the beginning of the meeting, Frank Allaun asked that Tatchell be allowed to attend with some of his Bermondsey comrades. Although Foot supported the request, the Chairman, Judith Hart, ruled it out as it would create a dangerous precedent.

I had left the 'Org' with a broad grin, but that had since disappeared because Sam McCluskie, after having lectured us on loyalty, told me that he was changing sides because he thought Foot had taken leave of his senses. I was now full of apprehension.

At the NEC, Michael was unapologetic. In the face of attacks from Benn, Heffer and Skinner, he stoutly defended his actions. Far from caving in to pressure from the right, Foot said, his personal repudiation of Tatchell was entirely justified by the *London Labour Briefing* article, which amounted to a rallying cry for extra-parliamentary action. It was an issue the Party simply could not dodge, he said. Foot and we mods knew and cared, of course, that there was the small matter, too, of a by-election if Tatchell was endorsed where we would be devastatingly defeated!

So I crossed my fingers when Joan Lestor started to speak and was much relieved when she said it was a question of confidence in Foot. That surely meant her vote was going to be OK. So too was Kinnock's, who said that

Michael's action had not been thought out but: 'Tatchell is giving the Tories a cheap asset to use against us, and Michael has been goaded by the deputy leadership election, by Tony's response to his support for the Home Policy Chairmanship, by the Shadow Cabinet. There has been no loyalty from the left, and this is a loyalty vote in Michael, and we don't want it to be said of him that he copped out and was trampled on. I'm going to give critical support, and Tony may be thinking of giving the support that Trotsky speaks of. It's not bloody good enough. I'll speak of Tatchell to Conference, even if its my valedictory. What we have thrown away is victory at the next election, and the chance to get unilateralism, the alternative economic strategy, out of the Common Market, the education policy. We have demolished the Party's prospects by vanity, and we should support our people even when they are wrong.'

Heffer persisted in the doctrine that 'we have to do what is right' – by which I presumed he meant whatever Militant told him to do. This time he took the vote correctly, but from my point of view it was too close for comfort – 15 for Foot and 14 for Tatchell. The *Guardian* summed it up well: 'Neither Mr Foot nor his allies could have been in doubt that a defeat would have amounted to a vote of no confidence in his leadership. The fact that he survived by 15 votes to 14 provides him with a breathing space. But it could hardly be described as an overwhelming triumph, let alone a warm vote of confidence'.[3] I summed it up as 'a narrow squeak'.

Two days later, to the relief of many of us, Bob Mellish announced at a meeting of the PLP that he would remain in the Commons. And all might have gone well had it not been for the trouble over the local elections in Bermondsey. There, old-timers now stood against the official Labour candidates and Mellish supported them, so giving Benn a big stick to beat him with. And at the NEC in June, Benn duly raised the question of Bob's support for his 'old friends'.

The issue of Tatchell just would not go away and things turned far worse at the 'Org' in July, where I blundered badly. Then, we considered reports from the Regional Office, a letter from the constituency chair and motions from Benn and Heffer. Benn's, calling for the immediate endorsement of Tatchell, was roundly defeated – by 13 votes to 4. Heffer's, however, was a different kettle of fish, calling for more talks, a fresh selection process, precluding no-one – namely Tatchell – from standing.

All other things equal, we should have defeated this resolution by 9 votes to 8 but instead the minutes record it was carried unanimously. Whether we actually voted for it, I cannot remember. Certainly we did not vote against it. And the reason was that Foot had done a somersault. Because he disapproved of Mellish's actions – and had told him so – he supported Heffer's proposal to hold a fresh selection with no bar on Mr Extra-Parliamentary Action! So, while the left outside continued to organise for Tatchell, Mellish made life even more difficult by resigning and forcing a by-election.

This made the situation intolerably difficult. I knew that Tatchell, being a known homosexual as well as a wild leftie, could not possibly win any London seat at that time. At the Department of Employment, I had strongly defended a government grant to 'Gay Switchboard' in Luton and still bore the scars of the backlash. Since then, while canvassing in London, I had felt even greater hostility to the tolerant attitude of Ken Livingstone at the GLC. There was no way that the bigoted cockneys of Bermondsey would vote for Tatchell in a by-election and I said so with my usual brutal lack of sensitivity. For this reason, and because the election of an extreme left winger would do us even greater damage in the country as a whole, I did my best to ensure that Tatchell was excluded from the selection.

In November 1982, we considered a paper from David Hughes, the National Agent, on the situation in Southwark and Bermondsey after Mellish's resignation, which made it clear that the NEC could impose its own candidate. I seized the opportunity to move that, in the wider interest of the Party, Tatchell should not be permitted to stand. Benn, however, seconded by Kinnock, moved that CLP be allowed to proceed as already agreed by the NEC at Foot's *volte face* in July.

Then Denis Howell, who was not usually so soft, intervened with a compromise of sorts – that Party officers have talks with the CLP to convey the NEC's feelings about the selection of a candidate. Seeing my vote disappear, I withdrew my motion and the softy-softly approach was duly carried. Unfortunately, by the time we got to the full NEC, we learned that no decision would be taken. The skids had been well and truly put under the hardliners – of which I was the hardest.

The meeting with Bermondsey – involving Russell Tuck, Jim Mortimer and David Hughes – duly happened at the end of November. It was all amicable. Russell himself suggested the NEC's position that an open short-list should be adopted. The CLP, of course, was all in favour. It was a real blow but we had no alternative but to let things be for the time being (if only Denis Howell had played to the whistle!). And naturally Bermondsey Constituency Labour Party again selected Peter Tatchell!

When this came back to the 'Org' in January, 1983 (yes, this all-consuming affair had dragged on for well over a year now, until a general election was in the offing), I could not even get a seconder to my proposal to bar him again. 'To see John Golding in a minority of one was a straw in the wind that may be the end of that sort of right domination,' Benn commented, hopefully. The NEC duly waved Tatchell through – and it was all down to Michael, who had now even gone so far as to write to the man he previously so vehemently denounced, saying he would support him!

'The only reason', Foot said, without batting an eyelid, 'that I had opposed him a year ago was because it would have been a difficult time to have had a by-election.' Not surprisingly, I took a different view; 'I think the opinion poll which showed that Tatchell would win easily had a big influence,' I wrote at the time. 'However, I couldn't see what had changed since Michael Foot had first opposed him in the name of parliamentary democracy.' And I still can't.

It was not long, however, before I could say: 'I told you so', an exercise that on the NEC I was very practised at. I sat grinning at the 'Org' at the beginning of February, as the by-election swiftly descended into chaos. There were two huge rows before the campaign even began, leading to the cancellation of the opening press conference. Firstly, there was a massive bust-up with Tatchell over who the agent should be, the regional officer or his own man David Fryer. And secondly, all Tatchell's campaign leaflets were impounded by David Hughes, the national agent after he defied advice and had them printed at Militant's captive Cambridge Heath Press.

I, of course, was all for backing the National Agent. The Lefties produced amendments like rabbits from a hat but none had any chance, even though they required reading the Riot Act to the Bermondsey Party, because they did not back David's decisive actions. Following a 20-minute meeting with representatives of the NEC, Tatchell gave 'cast iron' assurances that he would now co-operate with them during the by-election.

The hassle, of course, hardly stopped. On the day before the by-election – Wednesday, 23 February, 1983 – the NEC held a seven-hour meeting and to get in we had to run the gauntlet not only of journalists – which I can't say I minded – but also of the Militants, including some holding the banner of the Bermondsey Labour Party. I presumed that they had got lost canvassing.

At the meeting, we expelled John O'Grady, the Independent Labour candidate, for standing against us – and then later five Militants. In between time, we carried a resolution asking the electors of Bermondsey to vote for Peter Tatchell. Some hope – on the eve of a by-election, we were hardly battling the SDP, but still going hammer and tongs at ourselves!

The following day the voters went to the polls. Fortunately, however, I had good reason for not going to Bermondsey again. I went canvassing there only once and on my way back could not decide which was worse, my reception on the doorstep or in the Committee Room. 'On Thursday I have the flu when I get up. However, I go to the Commons where I spend the day on the British Telecommunications Bill again,' I wrote in my 'Diary of an MP.'

> I return home early and go to bed feeling sorry for myself. I felt even sorrier when I was woken up in the middle of the night by the BBC asking if I would appear on the *Today* programme to talk about the 'Bermondsey massacre'. They had assumed I would be watching TV. In fact my caller had to tell me the result – Tatchell had got only 7,698 votes against 17,017 for Simon Hughes. We had lost a seat we had held for 60 years. At 7.30 am a car picks me up to take me to Broadcasting House. I say that the Bermondsey defeat was due almost entirely to the electors dislike of Peter Tatchell and the refusal of the Bermondsey Party to accept advice on the running of the election. Back in November I had warned the Organisation Committee of the Labour Party that Peter Tatchell would be crushed in a by-election.

I would have nothing to do with the proposition that this was a great victory for the SDP– Liberal Alliance and that they would replace Labour as the main opposition. The electors had followed Foot's original assessment of Tatchell and would have none of him. And they also reacted against Foot, whom they rightly accused of a climb-down.

In *The Times*, Heffer simply dismissed Bermondsey as a 'one off' with Labour divided and Mellish against us.

The truth is that apart from the first few days of the election campaign politics were almost totally submerged. Some of the newspapers behaved disgracefully and at the same time scurrilous leaflets were issued illegally. Lurid graffiti appeared on walls and a suggestive song was sung publicly by the 'Real Labour' candidate from the platform of a horse drawn cart.

Electors, he claimed, were not put off by Labour's policies or Foot but by the local Council and the Liberals' pavement politics. Cloud cuckoo Eric blamed the squabbles in the campaign (as if they had nothing to do with Tatchell), the expulsions and even a Tony Bevins article in *The Times* the previous day. Understandably, I found it rather hard to imagine that too many Bermondsey electors had Tony Bevins or *The Times* on their minds when they voted. They were not names normally bandied about in the pubs of Bermondsey.

In his Diaries, Benn typically drew a more personal conclusion: 'Poor old Peter Tatchell, who had been massacred by the press, only got 7,600 votes but he came out of it with considerable courage and dignity. I resolved there and then in that hotel room not to desert Bristol and that, when I go to Scotland on Saturday for a meeting, I will make a statement saying I couldn't accept nomination for Livingston.' Once again, this strengthened my conviction that every cloud has its silver lining. Had Benn taken the Livingston seat away from Robin Cook, as he intended, he would have been able to stand for the Leadership in 1983.

The Bermondsey by-election not only happily denied us the experience of Benn as Leader, however. It almost removed Michael Foot. Since his election, Foot had been continually under attack. His climb-down over Tatchell was just the latest blot on his copybook and sadly he never achieved popularity with the electorate. Immediately after his election Labour's lead had shot up, by 10 per cent, but still only 38 per cent thought he would make a good leader and as many thought he would not. Amongst Labour voters, only 58 per cent supported him. These ratings among the wider public compared very unfavourably with those of Thatcher (64 per cent),

Callaghan (57 per cent) and Wilson (75 per cent). Even Douglas-Home had achieved 42 per cent. Michael's election confirmed voters' conviction that the Party had swung further to the left. Two-thirds, indeed, believed Labour was 'left wing' and only 2 per cent thought it 'middle of the road'.

After the Bermondsey disaster, Terence Lancaster, the *Daily Mirror's* Political Editor, summed the mood up perfectly: 'Michael Foot's face said it all yesterday. To the TV cameras he spoke words of defiance, of carrying on, but his look was of a man of anguish – a politician in peril and a leader in near despair.' A poll that we commissioned ourselves showed that we were seen as old, decaying and out of touch. 'This could almost be a cruel description of how many former Foot supporters now view their 69-year-old leader', the *Mirror* continued.

In the days before TV, Foot could easily have become a major political figure like Disraeli, whom he – and I – admired so much. Under the glare of the cameras, however, he could not hack it. His image was just not right. They saw him as a badly dressed, old bumbling figure – the Worzel Gummidge tag stuck. The fact that, one year, I only just beat him for the *Guardian*'s worst-dressed MP award only serves to drive home the point.

One of the things that most upset the electors was his wearing of a donkey jacket at the Cenotaph on Remembrance Sunday. Michael could never understand why the public reacted so savagely – he seemed to have no inkling of how important the idea was to working class people that when you went to church you must wear your best suit and overcoat. When discussing the incident with Michael Cocks, he claimed that the Queen Mother had told him what a nice coat it was. 'What shall I do?' he asked. 'Put it in the dustbin,' came Cocks's brutally simple reply.

In the nineteenth century, Michael would have thrived. But he was too literary, too studied for this modern age. While Thatcher, Parkinson and Tebbit knew how to appeal to the worst in the working class, Foot had no idea how to appeal to their better instincts. Like Kinnock he was a superb orator at mass meetings, but useless in giving short sharp explanations which the general public would understand. Like so many on the left – Benn, Skinner and Kinnock included – Michael was a first-rate entertainer, but could not command widespread confidence.

It was against this background that after Bermondsey there was an immediate chorus for Foot to go, blown up by the newspapers but not originating from them. A MORI poll revealed that 58 per cent of the public thought that he should resign and only 32 per cent that he should stay. Foot himself did not want to go and it was bandied around even had he wished to, his wife Jill Craigie would not let him. He pointed out that he had been elected by the Party members and that he had a duty to them. When the papers reported that half the Shadow Cabinet wished him out, he said he was sure that couldn't be true: 'Not a single Shadow Cabinet minister has spoken to me in the sense described in *The Times*. Since they are all honourable men, I am sure they would have done so if they had felt that way.'

Benn, as usual, made matters worse by declaring that pledges of loyalty should be given by the members of the Shadow Cabinet to stop the whispering campaign – a proposal described by Kinnock 'as being as helpful as a rattlesnake in your bath'. In his Diaries, Benn records how a discussion had taken place in the Campaign Group the day before Bermondsey about the Leadership. Amid protestations of loyalty, what he didn't say was that of all the alternative names being bandied about, his wasn't among them.

As ever in these situations, the speculation in the tea room, the corridors and the lobbies of the House of Commons was intense. Having seen 11,000 votes disappear, Labour MPs made hurried calculations on the backs of envelopes. Few of them would have a job in three or four months time, if the Bermondsey result was repeated in a general election. Panic set in and he names of Healey, Shore and even Callaghan were all whispered behind hands held nervously in front of mouths. Some pressed the claims of two younger contenders, Hattersley and Kinnock. Some even wanted the 'dream ticket' of Healey and Kinnock.

Among the unions – desperate for a change of government – opinion was divided. While many union leaders thought Labour's position hopeless with Foot as Leader, they were reluctant to face him. They sat instead waiting for the Darlington by-election on 24 March, hoping against hope that Foot would then do the decent thing and resign.

Between them, Moss Evans and David Basnett discussed the situation and decided that it was so grave that a 'Council of War' should be held because Labour seemed unlikely to beat the Tories. 'There is need now for us to have a summit conference similar to that at Bishop's Stortford, to review the whole situation and put to rest completely these rumours about Michael Foot's leadership,' Evans told the journalist Paul Routledge, protesting the union's support and loyalty and rejecting a palace revolution that would install Healey and Kinnock. Frank Chapple of the EETPU also came out in support of Foot, whereas Terry Duffy was quite clear that he should go.

My view was simple: there was no chance of making any quick change. Any such suggestion would allow the Tories to use Benn as a bogey man with the electorate. The lefties would make Benn Prime Minister after the election, just as they made Ken Livingstone the Leader of the GLC, they would say. Even had we wanted change, the new election procedures would have made it impossible before a general election. More importantly there was no one to change to. There was no chance of replacing Foot with Healey. Although Denis was streets ahead with the electorate, the unions mistrusted and disliked him and the constituencies would not have him at any price. He had not even been able to get a majority in the PLP. Had he been shoehorned in as Leader in some mysterious way, there would have been civil war.

The manifesto, too, had in reality already been agreed and Denis disagreed with much of it. Although, following his NEC setback, Benn had forecast the previous autumn that there would be changes to our major policies, in fact this would have been impossible. Apart from the overwhelming Conference votes, if one took the Shadow Cabinet and the NEC together, there was a clear majority for the left wing policies on the bomb, the Common Market and our economic policy.

These considerations also ruled out Shore, who saw himself as Leader, and Hattersley. Neither, in any case, would have done a better job.

It has since been suggested that Foot saved himself by a fine, combative and brave performance on Brian Walden's influential *Weekend World* programme. That Sunday a MORI poll had given the Tories 39 per cent, the Alliance 34 per cent and Labour just 26 per cent of the national vote. In another poll at Darlington, the Alliance was one point in front of the Tories, with Labour a massive 13 per cent behind. Challenged, Foot the pacifist stood aggressively to his guns. Facing Walden, he stated that he was going to remain as leader even if Darlington was lost – the only way he would be removed was if his critics successfully put a candidate up against him. His firm stand impressed many.

In my view, he was saved because there just was no alternative. We simply could not find another Leader – and I certainly exclude Benn in this – who could credibly present our incredible policies at a general election. In short – and this was my unswerving view – we could not possibly win the general election.

With many others, I also thought we couldn't win the Darlington by-election due in March, either. The one bright spot was that there, unlike Bermondsey, we had an outstanding candidate in Ossie O'Brien. He was totally against Militant and made it publicly clear he wanted no help from them. Declaring support for Foot, he also made it clear that the by-election was about the massive rise in unemployment and not a vote of confidence in Michael.

Whether it was or wasn't, the support for Foot in the run-up was carefully orchestrated. Kinnock said he was proud to stand by such a man: 'I want him to be the leader of our country for I trust him with my children's lives. I trust him with the future of our people. I trust him with world responsibility.' Sam McCluskie, the Party Chairman, trumpeted that Foot was 'a man of honesty, integrity and honour who would lead Labour into the next general election'. Michael's wife Jill Craigie and even Benn joined in the act. In addition Jack Cunningham, put in to run the campaign, did a marvellous job.

The threatened closure of the Shildon Railway works, where 2,000 faced redundancy, helped us enormously and we won by a whisker, with a swing of 1.3 per cent towards us – remarkable after the belting in Bermondsey. Labour got 20,544 votes, the Tories 18,132 and the Alliance just 12,235 on an 80.1 per cent turnout. Coming a bad third was a real set back for the Alliance and the Liberals certainly felt that, after their great success at Bermondsey, the SDP had let them down.

In truth, in normal circumstances, in a region of towering unemployment, this would have been regarded as mediocre for Her Majesty's official Opposition. It was only a triumph given the wounds we had inflicted on ourselves. After the by-election, Healey well recognised the reality. 'We wouldn't win an election on a swing of less than 2 per cent,' he told the press. 'The real point is that this is the turning of the tide'. With Thatcher 13 per cent ahead of us in the polls and Labour barely a point in front of the Alliance, the last bit was an overstatement, to say the least.

The major consequence, indeed, of the Darlington by-election was that Foot stayed as Leader to fight the general election. While being pleased for Ossie O'Brien, some on the right would have preferred a defeat and Michael's departure, but that was now not to be. Certainly, talk of right wing conniving was never far away. In mid-April, the *Mail on Sunday* ran an article, recycling a 'plot' to dump Foot for Healey. Terry Duffy, Bill Sirs, Frank Chapple, Bill Whatley and Roy Grantham, it claimed:

> had decided to strong arm the right-wing majority on Labour's ruling National Executive into telling Mr Foot to stand down . . . their plan is showing some sign of success. Moves are now under way by some right wingers and moderates to get a discussion going at the next meeting of the Executive in 10 days on the performance of Mr Foot, 69, as Leader . . . it is being insisted from within the Executive that, despite Mr Foot's denials, a majority of his Shadow Cabinet now want him to make way for Mr Healey, his deputy . . . Neil Kinnock would be asked to be Deputy Leader.[4]

The snag with all this wishful thinking, as I have already made clear, was that there was still no right wing majority on the NEC. And the moderates included people who would never have supported Healey against Foot in a month of Sundays. The matter was not raised at the NEC and by 9 May, the general election had been declared.

Alternative speculation surrounded the possibility of a dignified exit for Michael and possibly leaping a generation to Kinnock, had Thatcher opted for an October election instead. My view was that it didn't matter anyway – with our policies we were doomed to lose the general election, whenever it took place.

TWENTY-ONE

The Longest Suicide Note

Benn had failed to get complete control of the manifesto, but it didn't make a scrap of difference whatsoever to the contents of our 1983 election platform – infamously described by Gerald Kaufman as 'the longest suicide note in history'.

When the moderates got control of the NEC in 1982, I was determined that the left would get the blame for the certain defeat in the coming general election, as we on the right had been blamed in 1979. And defeat was certain because left wing policies, the internal disputes and Foot's image made it impossible to win. Our stance on defence, in particular, was unpalatable to the electorate as a whole.

And it was no use thinking that things could be changed in the short run. The party as a whole, including key union leaders, supported the stance on our loony 'Alternative Economic Strategy', the Common Market and defence. On the so-called right-controlled NEC, there was a majority both for unilateralism and against the Market. Those of us on the hard, realistic right were in a small minority everywhere in the Party, in the Conference, on the NEC – everywhere, except among the electorate!

Immediately after I became chairman of the NEC's key Home Policy Committee, Geoff Bish – still the research secretary – proposed that a draft of our campaign document go to our next meeting and to the NEC before reaching Policy Co-ordinating Committee which linked the Shadow Cabinet and NEC. Sorry, Mr Bish, but there were new sheriffs in town. Gwyneth Dunwoody, looking like Margaret Rutherford in bovver boots, would have none of it. She looked at Bish as though he was a waiter who had short-changed her. I expected her at any minute to address him as 'young man' but instead she proposed, as the Tufton Court Group had agreed beforehand, that this time we do it differently. We didn't want Benn and the left to get at the document until it had been virtually cut and dried.

This was bumped through the NEC and in December a small drafting committee – Foot, Alex Kitson, Sam McCluskie and the Party's deputy chair and me – got down to work. The NEC itself would only see the document after it got to Policy Co-ordinating Committee and me again on Home Policy. Any difficulties, and we would have another meeting, which Foot would chair. We had turned everything on its head.

As ever, the following morning Tony Bevins in *The Times* got it spot on:

> Mr Michael Foot last night was given the power to dictate the terms of the Labour Party election manifesto. Mr Wedgwood Benn raised a faint protest that this system had not been followed for previous manifesto drafts . . . There was no doubt among Labour MPs last night that Mr Foot would take charge of the document from its inception.

When I presented the plan to the subsequent NEC, Benn tried to block it but lost. At the Home Policy Committee on 7 February, Benn and Frank Allaun got unanimous agreement that the campaign draft go to the NEC before the formal Clause V meetings with the Shadow Cabinet. But it was a hollow, meaningless victory. I presumed that they wanted to have their say before the document went to the Policy Co-ordinating Committee, but they hadn't actually asked for this, nor were they going to get it. They would get it only when the drafting by the Policy Co-ordinating Committee, which included members of the Shadow Cabinet, had sewn things up. By that time, what Benn & Co put forward on the NEC was largely irrelevant.

So far, too, we hadn't taken a blind bit of notice of the Shadow Chancellor Peter Shore in the preparation of our policies. Why should we? Although Foot had removed the abrasive Healey from the front-line confrontation with the trade unions and appointed Shore, his old left wing dining friend, as Shadow Chancellor instead, I and others had no great respect for his judgement or ability to get things done. To cite one example, in the Callaghan government I had experienced the frustration of sitting with councillors, union officials and employers, waiting for him to turn up to a meeting of the Liverpool Inner City Partnership after he had missed his train. And when he finally turned up, he had little to contribute, as he hadn't done his homework. As far as I was concerned, the train would travel without Peter once again. He had more say in the Liaison Committee, which brought together representatives of the Shadow Cabinet, the General Council of the TUC and the NEC of the Labour Party. It was here that Shore had the opportunity to win support because the TUC treated the Liaison Committee – run by Bish and David Lea under the watchful, cautious eye of Len Murray – as a place where they could talk directly to the Shadow Cabinet. For them, the front bench was far more important than the second XI from the NEC. The TUC put a lot of effort into its economic research and its briefing was far superior to the Labour Party's in every way. Its aspirations, however, were in tune with those of Benn and Foot, with targets to cut unemployment to 1 million within five years, implement trade and exchange controls and achieve an egalitarian taxation policy.

While Shore had no difficulty in accepting exchange controls, higher public spending and the unemployment target, he preferred to rely on devaluation rather than on import controls. And he so desperately wanted an incomes policy – which he tried hard, but unsuccessfully, to sell to the union leaders. Instead, our 'Lone Ranger' decided to go it alone and produced his own documents – 'The Alternative Budget' and 'Programme for Recovery' – including an incomes policy. He might as well have not wasted his time, the unions just would not accept it and the document was neutered.

NEC members, meanwhile, jumped up and down asking what Shore was up to. 'Who does this man think he is?', was the general tone. Foot defended his old dining chum, saying Shore's document was a contribution to the debate. So, as an afterthought, we decided NEC members should see it after all. Then we gave it a pat on the head, but decided not to publish it with the Party's imprimatur. In other words it was a dead duck. Not even his very own 'Tonto', Gwyneth Dunwoody, could help him.

Shore was more successful over industrial democracy, however, but the question of regionalism was fudged because of John Prescott's desire even then for elected regional government. At meetings of the Policy Co-ordinating Committee, too, Shore expressed serious reservations about the overall cost of our commitments.

Re-nationalisation was another important issue we thrashed out in the Liaison Committee. I had a particular interest in this as a well-paid official of the POEU because of the privatisation of British Telecom. Indeed on 9 February, 1983, I entered the *Guinness Book of Records* for a speech on the Telecommunications Bill. 'Mr Golding,' *The Times* wrote, 'who has effectively dominated the opposition attack on the privatisation legislation, began his speech at 11.30 on Tuesday morning and with lunch, dinner and rest breaks, completed it 19 hours later at 6.30 am yesterday.' As Llin commented to the newspapers: 'He does go on a bit.'

My union supported a policy of nationalisation without compensation, but this became untenable particularly after Benn ran into great trouble over it – with my help – in the autumn of 1981. Not only were moderates in the Shadow Cabinet against this hardline stance, but the NUR had acquired shares in railway hotels and was anxious not to lose its money. Following a special TUC conference and talks between Prescott and the NUR, a new formula was devised whereby shareholders would get back exactly what the government had received on privatisation. This formula of 'No speculative gain' subsequently went into the manifesto.

Long tortuous meetings were held in February over all our grand plans to save the nation, until on 16 February it was agreed that the timetable needed to be put back by a month, with a special NEC scheduled for 22 March and the joint NEC/Shadow Cabinet meeting two days later. For good measure, to help anyone unfortunate enough to read this document, a *Daily Mirror* journalist was asked to make our domestic policy readable. When at the March NEC meeting I moved and Foot seconded that we adopt the report, there were squeals from the left, but as we had fixed a press conference that afternoon for its launch we were determined to bulldoze it through.

After swatting some further manoeuvring by Skinner, the document was endorsed by 16 votes to 6 – well in time for the press conference.

Benn had one small success, as Julia Langdon wrote in the *Guardian* the next day: 'Executive members agreed to alter the 15,000 word campaign document . . . to include Benn's proposal that BP be brought fully into public ownership. Significantly [Julia liked words like 'significantly'] he won support from such right wingers as Mr Eric Varley and Mr John Golding.' At that time, I was still supporting nationalisation.

On other fronts, when Benn, as ever, went over the top, he was gunned down. He even lost an attempt to harden up our commitment against incomes policy, to include any wage restraint. I was going to hang him, sure, by going along with some of the barmiest policies he had got through the NEC and Conference. But it would be rope entirely of the mods' crafting.

At that fateful NEC, as we put the finishing touches to the suicide note, the longest debate was over our policy on angling of all things, a subject dear to my heart. The NEC agreed that the Party should help the country's 3.5 million anglers, possibly through grants to clubs that wanted to buy fishing waters. We included this under 'Animal Welfare' – which caused Alan Hadden, who believed passionately in welfare, to give Sam McCluskie and I some stick. He knew that we were both fervent supporters of other cruel sports, in addition to teasing political toads.

'At 12 o'clock on Tuesday, I go to the press conference launching 'Labour's Plan – the New Hope for Britain',' I wrote in my 'Diary of an MP':

> I sit between Denis Healey and Gwyneth Dunwoody. Michael Foot and Denis do most of the talking. I talk about unemployment, but the TV people are mostly concerned about Defence and the Common Market. I'm pleased with the document although a few errors have crept in. After the Press Conference I go with Jim Mortimer . . . for dinner to his house near Labour Party Headquarters. We watch unemployed youths trying to kill time in a Bermondsey street and find it very depressing.

The campaign document had a mixed reception at a meeting of the PLP the following month, where only about 30 MPs turned up. Meacher thought it to be a good document, which was damning enough in itself. Few, however, agreed with him. David Winnick expressed doubts about nuclear policy. George Robertson certainly wanted American bases to stay. Hugh Brown, MP for Glasgow Provan, was depressed by it all and Jack Straw thought there might be a credibility problem!

There certainly was one for Terry Duffy. At the AUEW conference in April, he warned that we would lose the election with unilateral disarmament and withdrawal from the Common Market. 'I am just as interested in peace as Mr Foot and I ought to be,' he said. 'I have been shot at more times than him. A bullet has even taken the chinstrap of my helmet. But to disarm in the way the Party insists is not the way to go about it.'

I added to my friends' general feeling of incredulity when at the April Home Policy Committee, I backed Benn, stating categorically from the chair that the campaign document was regarded by the NEC and Shadow Cabinet as the basis of the manifesto. There was no possibility that any other position would be adopted by the NEC. This should also apply to the Shadow Cabinet, since the document had been jointly endorsed by the NEC and the Shadow Cabinet. I then happily issued a press statement along these lines. On 27 April at the NEC, Benn thanked me for that!

While I was getting approving looks through the pall of pipe smoke from Benn, I got only black scowls from Roy Hattersley when, at around this time in the Commons chamber, he said he hoped we were going to fight in the formal 'Clause V' meeting for multilateralism and staying in the Common Market. Very briefly, I said no. Firstly we didn't have the votes – on unilateralism it was 23 votes to 19 in favour and as bad, if not worse, on the Common Market. Secondly, it would be mad to start a row at the beginning of the campaign. It was certain that we were going to lose the election so we had better make certain that no blame fell on the right. In any case, although I did not say this, Healey had stitched up a shoddy compromise on defence with Foot. What went into the manifesto on defence was, as Denis confirms in his autobiography, 'deliberately ambiguous'.

It was intended to accommodate both the unilateralists and the majority of the Shadow Cabinet, which thought it would be electorally disastrous to give our existing Polaris force up for nothing. What the manifesto finally said was that, though we favoured getting rid of Britain's nuclear weapons, we would seek a bilateral agreement with the Soviet Union to eliminate an equivalent number of Russian nuclear weapons at the same time. Foot and Healey agreed that, if asked what they would do if Russia refused such an agreement, they would just say that this would be a new situation to be considered if and when it arose.

On 6 May, 1983 we had a meeting of the Shadow Cabinet, union leaders and the NEC to discuss the election. Basnett said that defeat would be catastrophic for the movement. It would detach the unions from the Party. At this meeting Basnett suggested the election slogan: 'Caring makes economic sense'. Healey proffered 'Caring makes sense' or 'Who cares, wins'. Heffer suggested 'Labour is good for you'. The truth was, whatever their success for Guinness or the SAS, all our suggested slogans were dreadful.

At the NEC on the morning of 11 May, 1983, we prepared for the joint NEC/Shadow Cabinet Clause V meeting to be held at 2.30pm that afternoon. Whereas under Callaghan it had taken all day, this one lasted for under an hour. Sam McCluskie in the chair wanted a shorter version of our *War and Peace* length campaign document, but Bish said only a thousand words could be cut out and it wouldn't be worth it. I should have challenged, but didn't. Bish's view was that 'the campaign document was sufficient in itself; there was very little market for a 'popular version'.

Straight off, Benn moved that 'New Hope for Britain' be adopted as the manifesto, but Sam wouldn't accept motions. Opposition came quickly from Shore, who expressed the heretical view that manifestos were meant to win elections and the campaign document was a list of meaningless promises.

'Only one voice appears to have been raised in protest,' Ian Aitken wrote in the *Guardian* the next day:

> Mr Peter Shore, the Shadow Chancellor is reported to have delivered a vigorous speech in which he displayed his well-known Churchillian talents as an orator in an attempt to persuade his colleagues to look for votes in the electorate rather than brownie points with the Party. His protest is understood to have been slapped down in unusually vigorous terms by Mr Foot, who insisted that the only important question was the establishment of an effective unity on the Party's policy as a preliminary to fighting the Conservatives on the hustings.
>
> Mr Foot was supported by Mr John Golding, a trade union MP and NEC member who has become the most effective right wing member of the NEC .
> . . he is reported to have declared that Mr Shore's speech made Colonel Custer look like a candidate for the white feather.'

Indeed, I pointed out to Shore that the campaign document had already been a joint document between the NEC and the Shadow Cabinet.

> At least part of the argument remains unstated, however. The left wing, represented mainly by Mr Tony Benn, has been determined in recent months to

demonstrate its willingness to sink political differences in a bid for party unity. Behind this move is the conviction that the left is in danger of carrying the can for a Labour defeat in the general election. Right-wingers are equally determined to ensure that they will not be blamed if the party fails to achieve a majority on polling day, Mr Golding, above all, has no intention of letting Mr Benn and the left wing off by any right wing foolishness at this part of the campaign.

Aitken and the *Guardian* were quite right there.

As for the final adoption of the suicide note, the official minutes record the following: 'After full discussion the consensus of opinion was in favour of using the Campaign Document as the manifesto for the election, taking on board one or two minor textual amendments, including the inclusion of a statement on old age pensions within the emergency programme. It was also agreed that the Campaign Committee should consider the possibility of separate manifestos for Wales and Scotland.'

And so we charged into the Valley of Death, Labour's Light Brigade armed with a wish list as long as a Crimean death roll. 'It was a patchwork of painfully-made compromises, notably on incomes, nuclear weapons and the European community, and both left and right realised that to change a single stitch would involve unravelling the entire garment,' Julian Haviland commented for posterity in the indispensable compendium *The Times Book of the 1983 General Election*. 'The Labour manifesto offered an emergency programme to create jobs and give a new urgency to the struggle for peace and on these two items, in that order, Mr Foot was to concentrate most of his oratory to the end of the campaign and beyond.'

Llin, as my agent, says she loved this manifesto. If anyone rang asking for anything, she could find it. As she put it: 'Whatever they wanted, they could have.' Anyway, now we had our Socialist manifesto, we could now get on the best we could with losing the general election.

TWENTY-TWO

The 1983 General Election – Foot's Last Stand

We went into the general election with an unelectable Leader, in a state of chaos with a manifesto that might have swept us to victory in cloud-cuckoo land, but which was held in contempt in the Britain of 1983. We thought that things could only get better, but they got worse.

Organisationally, we were a shambles – but it was not for lack of good advice beforehand. In March, 1982, headquarters staff had prepared an excellent brief, highlighting 'new' election techniques being used by the Liberals – which have served them well right up to now – critically examining our own canvassing methods, our training, relations with the media and how to appeal to target groups. But no-one took a blind bit of notice – they were casting pearls before swine.

When the Campaign Committee for the election was created in October 1982, we put all the world, his wife and his donkey on it – although, come to think if it, Frank Allaun was kept off by Sam McCluskie's casting vote.[1] We did, however, add Judith Hart and Neil Kinnock on the grounds that we needed a few people on it who believed in the manifesto. If everyone had turned up – NEC members, Party officers, union leaders, the front bench – we would have needed to book the Albert Hall.

Far from welcoming experts, however, when pollster Bob Worcester of MORI was invited, the left demanded that he be excluded. There were interminable rows about who could present campaign papers and who should be circulated. From the start, it was divided and rudderless and just didn't work – much to the disgust of the unions, who pressed hard for tangible work, pleaded for decisions, but could not get them. On re-reading the 3½ pages of practical suggestions from a Special Conference with the unions at Woodstock, called on 6 and 7 May to inject some momentum, I re-live the feeling of despair that many of us felt at the time. The lefties really believed that we would sweep the country, if only we had party political broadcasts made by volunteers emphasising peace, a freeze on nuclear weapons and marching for jobs.

There were sensible contributions, but amid all the attrition, they seemed too few and far between. One, in the circumstances, I remember very well: 'Do national press conferences serve a useful purpose or do they enable a hostile press to set the agenda?' It was a question I would recall with a wry smile throughout the campaign.

When it came to the general election, the unions put in £2¼ million, plus help from the TULV Special Election Fund and an office in Walworth Road. Mobilising support among union members, however, was an uphill struggle. Despite all the effort, indeed, union support actually fell during the campaign – the more working people heard about our defence plans, the less likely they were to vote Labour, let alone help.

After the Woodstock Conference, far from dashing off to canvass, I travelled down south to fish on the Sunday for the House of Commons and Lords team in a charity match. While Roy Mason and I caught a netful, not a single Tory caught anything. How sad this Labour superiority could not continue into the polls!

The election clock was certainly ticking. I was in a TV studio the next day, 9 May, 1983, when Thatcher finally named the day. We were off. 'Just after 11.30 am Denis Healey tells me that there is to be a general election' I recorded events in my 'Diary of an MP'.

I go quickly back to the House of Commons where everyone has been looking for me. I discussed with Michael Foot how we would go about issuing our manifesto and the election for me is on! . . . Tuesday. In the morning, I go to the Campaign Committee in the Shadow Cabinet Room in the House of Commons. There is so much to arrange now that the election has arrived. In the afternoon, I go to the Parliamentary Labour Party meeting on the manifesto. It is a first class meeting – very good tempered. Wednesday. I go to Labour Party HQ early to discuss the manifesto. Then we have our last meeting of the National Executive Committee. At the NEC, I move that Reg

Freeson be the Labour candidate in Brent East and this is carried by 19 votes to 9! This will freeze Ken Livingstone, the Leader of the GLC, out and so there is bound to be a spot of bother . . . I go from the National Executive Committee to a meeting of Trade Unions for a Labour Victory at TUC HQ and then on to the House of Commons for our manifesto meeting.

It was all buzz. In Newcastle, it had been decided that it would be best all round if I stayed in London and Llin ran the constituency campaign. It was not only important not to be accused of leaving a sinking ship. In Newcastle, they also operated on the basis that elections were too important to allow candidates to muck them up. I always enjoyed canvassing, ever since I started in 1945, but when I do it for myself it can be very counter-productive.

In one election, I knocked at the door and asked the lady of the house whether she would vote Labour. 'Yes', she said, adding: 'You look like John Golding.' 'I am John Golding,' I answered, giving her the good news. 'No you are not,' she said sternly. 'Why do you say that?' I puzzled. 'Well,' she replied, looking me up and down with little enthusiasm, 'I've seen Mr Golding on TV and he is tall and good looking.'

On the Tuesday, therefore, instead of campaigning on the streets of Newcastle, I went to Walworth Road and the daily pattern began. At 7.15 am the staff had an editorial meeting for our briefing document, *Today*. I arrived well in time for the 7.45 am polling meeting with Bob Worcester, followed at 8.15 by the campaign meeting. At 8.45 we travelled to Transport House for the press conference. Then I waved Foot & Co off, as they dashed into the country to discover chaos in their speaking arrangements and create more chaos themselves by making up policy on the hoof. It would have been better if we had locked them in the basement of Walworth Road for the duration. At least that would have stopped Foot from speaking on platforms of Militant and all their tendency.

Virtually everything about the campaign was a disaster. Foot had many good qualities – as Leader he showed great concern for parliamentary democracy and great moral courage in helping individual MPs under pressure. Likewise, he did everything possible to keep the Labour Party together. While he lost the Social Democrats, he helped keep the majority of those of us on the right on side – a major achievement.

As the Leader in an election, however, he was a flop – a total disaster. In truth, Callaghan was a hard act to follow; he possessed so many of the qualities respected by the British working class and spoke in a way that most could understand. Many of the wider public simply could not follow the brilliance of Michael – they just didn't know what he was talking about. Worse still, he just didn't look the part. By the time we reached the election, there was nothing sadly he could do to repair the damage.

However hard he tried, the image of Worzel Gummidge stuck. He was not helped by an accident which left him struggling with a stick. That was not his fault. The donkey jacket at the Cenotaph, however, was self-inflicted and the memory stuck. He was hardly helped, too, by the constant murmuring against him in the PLP which was passed on to the political gossip gatherers in the Members' Lobby and Annie's Bar. This sniping came not only from the right; it also came from those who should have been propping him up.

The harsh reality, however, was that no replacement for Foot would have done better in the general election. No one could have changed the policy without a massive Party revolt, which by itself would have sunk us. We could not have withstood the charge, too, from the Tories and Liberals that any new Leader was merely a stopgap until after the election when Benn and the extreme left would take over. The fact that when Andrew McIntosh, a respected moderate, had led Labour to victory on the Greater London Council in 1981 he had been replaced by Newtman Ken Livingstone and Benn's bag carrier Tony Banks, would have been thrown at us again and again.

Thus, when Gerald Kaufman went privately to ask Foot to resign at the beginning of the campaign, he could have little hope of success or support. His request to Michael could only be regarded as one of the shortest suicide notes in history! There was just no alternative to Foot. While Healey began the campaign far more popular than Michael, the PLP and the unions would not have backed him against anyone else but Benn. Foot, meanwhile, had been a great friend of the unions while at the Department of Employment. Healey despised them and wasn't afraid to show it.

Some moderates did support Shore, but others of us thought of him as a damp squib. He also had the added disadvantage of being violently anti-Market and wanting to impose incomes policy on an extremely reluctant trade union movement. Hattersley and Kinnock, meanwhile, had not yet set out to persuade union leaders that we should skip a generation and so were not considered seriously as anything but deputies.

The reality was that we were stuck with Foot. And the only sensible thing in an election was to give him, and the policies he believed in, as much support as possible. Sadly, even this did not happen.

He was let down particularly on defence by Healey. Foot had never hidden the fact that he was an unreconstructed unilateral nuclear disarmer. He wore his CND badge with pride. As Leader, he was determined to fight the election on two issues – unemployment and nuclear disarmament – and he did so. He believed himself justified in this when right at the beginning he received the emotional, enthusiastic support of audiences at his meetings, who shared his idealism. While we were waiting for one of the first 8 am meetings, knowing what a sceptic I was, Michael told me that 'there were a thousand people at my meeting last night who gave enormous cheers to my statement on nuclear disarmament'. 'Yes Michael,' I replied, 'But have you thought of the tens of thousands outside who didn't go and think that you're barmy!'

One of those people was his Deputy, Denis. Healey was totally opposed to unilateralism and disliked our defeats on the issue intensely. To accommodate him, as we have seen, in key areas the manifesto was left ambiguous. Healey now claimed, however, that because 'unilateralism' was there in black and white, there was no chance of getting away with the shoddy compromise. My attitude was that if that were so, he should not have made it. The reality is that during the election, Healey departed from the script and did not hold the line, as he should have done.

This was certainly true when on the BBC's *Newsnight*, on being questioned by Heseltine and Owen, he muddied the waters by stating that for him the words 'carry through in the lifetime of the next parliament our non-nuclear defence policy' had a limited meaning. 'A policy of no first use of nuclear weapons was a non-nuclear policy, because it meant a conventional deterrent against a conventional attack,' he said.

The next day he qualified the manifesto even further in a radio phone-in, when he replied 'that seems sensible' to a caller who suggested that we keep Polaris if Russia refused reciprocal disarmament. This was immediately taken, of course, to mean that Britain's nuclear submarines would only be sacrificed if there were adequate concessions from the Russians. It was a position that Joan Ruddock, then chair of CND, understandably declared did not amount to a non-nuclear policy.

It certainly knocked Foot off course. On 24 May, after talking with Denis, in a delicately crafted speech in Birmingham Michael put his own gloss on the manifesto. Labour, he now said, would 'move towards' a non-nuclear defence policy and would 'move to' the removal of nuclear bases. As Julian Haviland of *The Times* commented, 'The commitment had become an aspiration'. But the next day on his old stomping ground in Cardiff, Jim Callaghan, summoning up all his former Prime Ministerial authority, stripped the wound bare. Polaris had at least 12 years effective life, Jim said, and should not be unilaterally thrown away.

Jim's intervention made the muddle even worse. At the 8 am meeting, we on the right were hit by doom and gloom when the left angrily reported the rumour that Jim intended to speak out that night. It was decided that someone should try to talk to him and, predictably, all eyes turned to me. I knew I hadn't a cat in hell's chance of persuading Jim to respond to any appeal from Walworth Road, but I could not dodge giving it a try. The conversation was short and to the point – he had already put out his statement and nothing could be done about it.

The truth is that he was frightened of losing his seat. I certainly understood the feeling. I had spent an hour one Sunday morning in the Wolstanton Working Men's Club in my constituency and been told by one sound man after another that they were not going to vote for me because of our defence policy. When I protested that I was a multilateralist fighting in a town where the chairman of the local CND was a leading Liberal, they replied: 'Yes, but Footie is for getting rid of our defence and he'd decide what happened in a Labour government, not you.'

Healey himself, wrongly and unfairly, put the biggest part of the blame for the muddle on Callaghan – skipping over the fact that he was the first to cause confusion and that Jim's rush of blood to the head came later on. It was the confusion between the Leader and Deputy Leader which caused most of the trouble, not Callaghan in semi-retirement trying to save his own skin. The defence policy lost us votes – but the shillying and shallying seemed to lose us even more.

The problem was made worse by the fact that one after another, those who had an eye on the succession to Michael got in on the act. Healey, the sheer cheek of it, expressed sympathy with Jim's speech, but said he would not go quite so far. John Silkin, Labour's Shadow Defence Secretary, told TV-am that he was absolutely committed to abandonment of all nuclear weapons within five years. Kinnock meanwhile stuck to the manifesto, declaring: 'The Labour Party has a non-nuclear defence policy and the Labour government will implement that policy.'

By the time they had all finished, however, none of us knew what a Labour government would do or wouldn't do. What a disastrous defence week it was.

And it blew what little chance we had of setting the pace. Before all the confusion on defence blew up in our faces, on 20 May, Bob Worcester had told the Campaign Committee: 'It is clear that the main issue which people think the politicians should be focusing on is unemployment (74 per cent)' . . . which puts it four times ahead of the other issues people most want to hear about during the campaign: disarmament/nuclear weapons (18 per cent) and inflation/prices (16 per cent).'

'The conundrum for Labour is that almost as many people (32 per cent) think that Labour would do a worse job than the Tories on unemployment, as think it would do a better job (39 per cent),' Bob continued. As the campaign went on, however, people's assessment of our ability to deal with unemployment got even worse – possibly because they were increasingly put off us by the slanging going on during the election.

Remarkably, however, Bob's advice was actually followed up, when we mapped out a campaign and finally, on 24 May – the day defence blew up – appealed to candidates not to deviate from it! For academic posterity, our 'road map to victory' at press conferences was going to be: 26 May, 'Caring makes sense'; 27 May, 'The Cost of Living'; 30 May, 'The economy'; 31 May, 'Caring makes sense' again; 1 June, 'Education'; 2 June, 'Law and order'; 3 June, 'The Environment'; 4 June, 'Housing under the Tories'.

We might as well have gone fishing instead. I still shudder at our performance at press conferences. Later, Michael Cocks reminded me of one particular highlight – a decision one morning that Denis Healey would explain everything on a blackboard, but then no-one remembered to take the chalk! I couldn't remember the incident myself, but then among the total chaos, it would have passed me by!

Indeed, the most surprising thing to me about about Julian Haviland's account afterwards in *The Times Guide to the 1983 general election* that he was complimentary about the press conferences. 'Labour were resourceful in finding and publishing private documents which, they claimed, revealed the government's real plans,' he wrote.

> They developed, and the Alliance took up, the theme of the 'secret manifesto' which they said the Tories' published manifesto, unspecific and reasonable in tone, was designed to conceal. Mr Healey, an uninhibited pugilist, cited leaked documents from the Think Tank and the Number 10 policy unit as evidence that Mrs Thatcher had lied about the trend of unemployment. Mr Neil Kinnock published a report by the National Economic Development Council in which he said ministers had suppressed the truth about the country's economic performance. An official discussion paper about co-operation between public and private medicine was produced as proof. Mr Foot said the Conservatives planned a serious attack on the National Health Service.
>
> There was indeed evidence from the polls that voters were anxious about Conservative attitudes towards the NHS. Although the grimmest constructions were put on ministers' most tentative notions, none of Labour's grenades seemed to breach the Tory defences. Sir Geoffrey Howe was able to maintain that there were no intentions that are not disclosed in the manifesto for raising taxes or cutting public expenditure.

My reaction to it all was quite different. Sitting there, I despaired as Peter Shore went on day after day telling the assembled journalists what was going to happen under a Conservative government. For me the issue was not what the Tories were or were not going to do, but what Labour would do. We had to do our best to establish the credibility of the Labour manifesto, and not spend all our time casting doubt on the the Tories and in consequence suffer harsh criticism from the electorate for mud slinging. On the doorsteps, the electors were asking questions which no one in London bothered to answer in simple, easily understood language: 'How are you going to afford it?' 'Can you get unemployment down, as you say you can?' 'Is Michael Foot up to the job?' 'How are we going to defend ourselves?'.

Of course, I didn't believe we could sell many of our policies, but at least we ought to try. We were bound to lose, but we didn't need to be beaten out of sight! Watching our front bench perform in front of the press was painful. It was clear that what mattered most was what appeared on the nine and ten o'clock news on the BBC and ITV. We needed pithy messages for the camera perched high up at the back of the hall, in the hope that working class people would be given reasons for voting Labour to repeat at work the following morning.

There was not much chance of that. Our spokesmen behaved as though they were in a college Senior Common Room. They showed off unmercifully, using their time to try and make a greater impression than the colleague who had spoken last, using obscure quotations from obscure articles in obscure journals. They fawned all over journalists from the posh papers that they read themselves and ignored the fact that, apart from the telly and radio, it was the tabloids where we wanted space. We needed to bring back the mass of the working class, not just the tiny minority of radical middle class broadsheet readers.

These clever, well-educated front benchers had no idea how to present our manifesto to the electorate. One day, after the press conference outside Transport House, a sympathetic radio man ran up to interview Michael. 'What three things will Labour do for the people if they win the election?', he asked kindly. 'Find everyone a job, make the world more secure and ensure that families have a better standard of living,' I whispered to myself, as Foot replied: 'You should read my article in *The Times* last . . .'. The reporter asked again and once more Michael referred him to *The Times*. As he wrapped up his cord, the reporter gave me such a look of pity.

It was no wonder that the TV producers got so little from the press conferences and sought instead footage of Michael, speaking with passion at mass meetings on the horrors of the bomb, where he was in his element.

One of the reasons that hardly anyone presented our policies, of course, was that apart from Foot, a handful of his followers and the Benn gang, no-one had any belief in our manifesto. Indeed, most were quite jealous of the Tory approach and wished that our manifesto was equally 'hidden'. Not only did Peter Shore, for instance, share Healey and Hattersley's dislike for our defence policy, but he was also disconcerted that our sums didn't add up and that we had no credible incomes policy. I didn't believe in the manifesto either, but as far as selling it was concerned, the left were right to be critical of the lack of conviction in the campaign.

So we spent our time picking the ball out of the net, instead, from own goals in the campaign. The Tories themselves were not perfectly disciplined. Francis Pym upset Thatcher by commenting on the drawbacks of a Tory landslide, and Denis Thatcher warned Margaret about being filmed nursing a sick animal: 'If you don't look out, we'll have a dead calf on our hands,' he quipped. But they were simply not in the same league when it came to making blunders.

Foot, for instance, was photographed at a protest against hunting. In these days of New Labour, nobody would have noticed, but then to associate with the barmy, woolly-hat brigade was to attract derision. It reinforced the public view that, in some way, Michael belonged with those who wanted to ruin the British way of life.

More important in the anti-British stakes were both Healey's and Kinnock's blunders on the Falklands, a subject we were doing our best, I thought, to avoid. Neil, without any consultation, accused Thatcher's Cabinet of sinking the *Belgrano* to prevent a peaceful settlement. Then Denis added to the stupid attack by saying that 'Thatcher gloried in slaughter'. Later Denis admitted that this was one of the greatest blunders of the campaign. It held people's attention for at least a vital three days.

To excuse himself, Healey blamed Jim Mortimer's inexperience for the chaos – for overloading the schedules of the Leader and Deputy Leader and driving them to a state of exhaustion, during which they were bound to make mistakes. This I think is a bit of old nonsense – they had both fought enough elections to have been quite capable of insisting on a programme they could cope with. Foot, indeed, coped very well and came out the other side in far better shape than many. The main stress Michael faced came from his constant belief of a threat to his authority. At one press conference he hardly commanded confidence, when he declared: 'I am the Leader and I am pressing the views that we will carry into operation under a Labour government.'

One the same tack, Mortimer's inexperience did cause us trouble when, on 26 May, trying to counter the damage Callaghan had done us on defence, he startled correspondents by stating that: 'At the Campaign Committee this morning we were all insistent that Michael Foot is the Leader of the Labour Party and speaks for the Party and we support the manifesto of the Party.'! With Foot looking uncomfortable, he kept on digging, by adding: 'The unanimous view of the Campaign Committee is that Michael Foot is the Leader of the Labour Party.' The press reports then made it clear that the meeting in question comprised Foot, Mortimer, Shore, Hattersley, Silkin, Sam McCluskie, David Basnett, Brynmor John, Jeff Rooker and me. In other words, what went round was that we had supported Michael in the absence of Healey!

In truth all that had happened at the campaign meeting was that, when Jim's maverick speech was being discussed, someone had shouted 'To hell with Callaghan, you are the Leader Michael' – a proposition in the circumstances that no-one could deny!

The campaign continued to go badly, as the opinion polls showed. Our private MORI poll on 21 May was damning enough. It showed that the electorate thought the Tories far better at keeping their promises, more likely to govern in the national interest, more likely to improve their standard of living and having the best team of people. And throughout the campaign, we failed to convince the vast majority of people that we could or would reduce unemployment to two million, let alone one. As the campaign went on, public cynicism about our claims just increased.

From the unions, Larry Whitty – one of Basnett's assistants at the time and a future Labour General Secretary during the Mandelsonian march to New Labour – was scathing about our central control and proposed a far more sensible schedule of morning campaign meetings to put us ahead of the game.[2]

By 30 May, however, as we entered the last week of the election, polls showed that defence was still the nuclear deterrent to voting Labour and that there had been a big increase – up 10 points to 59 per cent – in the number of people thinking we were making promises that the country couldn't afford. With Basnett and the unions urging us on, at our strategy meeting that day, therefore, we decided to emphasise our policies on jobs, the NHS, pensions and youth unemployment in terms that working people could understand. An 'Action Group' was formed – including the General Secretary, National Agent, aides of Foot and Healey, Hattersley, Whitty, Russell Tuck and myself. The daily press conference was switched to 12 noon.

Things had clearly become such a standing joke, however, that even when we were trying to put our house in order, the press saw more of a shambles. 'Foot Bites back!,' ran the *Daily Mirror* report of the revamp the next day. 'Labour name new action line up. Healey, Golding, Hattersley . . . I am still boss'. We just could not get away from the general lack of confidence in Michael's leadership.

Just the day before, indeed, in the *Mirror*, Michael had responded to yet more innuendo that he should resign. 'Absolute nonsense,' he said, giving the reporters their racy quotes. 'I have never run away from anything in my life.' Just for good measure, he added, too, that Labour was doing better than opinion polls suggested. Michael just didn't believe in the polls. This blind spot was made even more serious by the fact that he lived his life surrounded by fellow politicians and talented, urbane people in Hampstead. He hadn't a clue what was going on.

Worse was to come, when disaster hit yet again. Foot's position was undermined further by another article in the *Mirror* – the only newspaper friendly to us! – on 1 June, which picked up a statement that his wife, Jill Craigie, had been daft enough to make to a reporter on a local paper in Reading, of all places. 'Even if the Party wins, I shouldn't think he would stay on for long because it would be time to make way for a younger man,' Jill had said.

Her clarification later only made matters worse: 'I said when Michael has given most of his political career to opposing nuclear weapons, as he has done since they were invented, he is unlikely to renege on his principles. Towards the end of a man's life, in his old age, much like de Gaulle, people who have fought all their lives for a principle do not go back on them.' So now everyone was reminded of how old Foot was and we were back to big bad Benn lurking in the background, waiting to take over. All this and unilateralism too!

In the final days before the election, the newspapers took up with gusto the theme of the unions driving Foot out if he lost. By 4 June, the polls were showing that the Alliance was either just behind or a whisker in front of Labour. From now on the real interest was in the battle for second place and the Alliance threw everything into persuading Tories to vote Alliance. To ward them off, Thatcher 'suddenly' discovered that Labour wasn't so bad after all and 'would never die'. In response, David Steel commented rightly that Thatcher was trying to give Labour 'the kiss of life'.

Things were so bad we had to rely on the Lady in shining iron armour to come to our rescue. Not content to let the gloom stop there, on 6 June – just three days before the poll – Bob Worcester reported that we had now fallen even further behind on the small matters of keeping promises, raising standards of living, defending the national interest and having the best team! And we had lost heaps of ground on tackling unemployment and giving pensioners – a crucial segment of our vote – a better deal. The only thing we seemed ahead on was the amount of slanging we did.

One of my most vivid recollections of this disastrous election is that of Bob Worcester and I sitting repeatedly in the basement of Walworth Road before the 8 am meeting, crying on each other's shoulders about the way that the election was being fought without any regard to the realities of the outside world.

To rub it in, it was incidentally at one of these sessions that Bob brought to my attention another reality – a *Guardian* report that my union's conference had elected a left wing Executive, which had decided that I would be replaced on the Labour Party NEC. This came about ironically because the active members who voted for the Conference delegates at branch meetings had swung left, believing that the left would provide a better sword than the right to fight for the shorter working week under the next Thatcher government and a better shield against a new, privatised British Telecom. In the Broad Left group that won, Militant was influential and wanted my head on a platter. Thanks to the privatisation which I had fought more strongly than anyone else, they got it. However, I shrugged it off during the election in which there was still worse to come.

On 7 June, there was another bitter pill to digest: our private poll figures had the Tories on 44 per cent, us on 29 per cent and the Alliance on 25 per cent. The figures on the issues were devastating. We had small leads on unemployment and the NHS, but now trailed behind on education, as well as the economy, defence and Europe. We were behind the Tories in every aspect of campaigning – leaflets, adverts, direct mailing and canvassing – save their party political broadcasts. Later, I still found it hard to understand how we went in front on our TV broadcasts because on all MORI's measures – on recall, presentation and irritation – we were worse than the Tories.

Indeed, matters became so bad that I spent the weekend before the Thursday of polling day in Newcastle-under-Lyme. Joyce Gould, indeed, told me that one of her most vivid memories of the campaign was my telling her in a corridor that I would lose my seat if I did not get back to Newcastle, into the clubs and onto the streets. I did not want to lose my seat in parliament and have to return to the POEU, working full-time for a bunch of left wing loonies.

By the Monday, I was back again in London, where it was my turn to drop a small brick at the press conference with the Freudian slip that that we would be thinking things out 'in the years to come', when I should have said 'days'. This sad lapse didn't matter – I just couldn't compete with Foot or Kinnock.

On *Panorama*, Foot again modified the manifesto, talking of extra defence spending to strengthen our conventional forces. Kinnock meanwhile was provoked into a jibe about the Falklands – when a heckler shouted at Neil that at least Thatcher had guts, he responded: 'and it's a pity that others had to leave theirs on Goose Green to prove it.' Anyway, by now nothing really mattered. We were beyond help.

I returned to Newcastle for the eve-of-poll rally and on the following day my own skin was saved by Llin, my agent, and a marvellous bunch of helpers who produced a majority of 2,804 votes. They also worked for Gwyneth Dunwoody in Crewe and she scraped in by 290 votes. Others were not so lucky or so well-organised. More Labour seats tumbled and overall the Conservatives came in with 397, Labour 209, Liberal 17 and SDP 6. The only saving grace was that it was hardly the breakthrough the Alliance had been dreaming of.

At the Newcastle count, I listened as one after another our seats were lost. I must admit that when Benn's defeat came in – by 1,789 votes – we took issue with the BBC's assessment. We counted it as a Labour gain – just like the retirement of Frank Allaun and Les Huckfield before the election!

310

There were others, too, that I would not lament, including Joan Lestor, Alex Lyon and Bob Cryer. But there were colleagues I was bitterly sorry for – including Albert Booth, Arthur Davidson, Shirley Summerskill, Joe Dean, John Spellar, Ossie O'Brien, Frank White and Ken Woolmer.

Early on Friday morning, exhausted as always after an election, I took the train to join in the inquest and the inevitable search for a new Leader.

TWENTY-THREE

The Leadership Battle – Kinnock's Victory

Michael Foot could not have been disposed of more quickly, had he been suffering from a virulent, contagious disease. The very people who persuaded him to stand and defeat the electable Denis Healey were pressing for him to be buried, before he had time to recover from the deep wounds inflicted upon him by the electorate.

'Of course, I have to accept my responsibility in this matter,' Foot had said with great dignity straight after the defeat. Within two days, however, Basnett had already declared: 'We have got to start fighting the next general election now and for that we have got to have a Leader as soon as possible who will take us through that election.' Asked whether he thought Mr Foot would be leader this time next year, he said distinctly, 'no.'

Ken Cameron from the FBU, too, pronounced that on age grounds alone Foot should go quickly. On the Sunday following the election, grabbing the limelight as ever Clive Jenkins also announced that Michael – having refused the ASTMS nomination – was going and ASTMS would support Neil Kinnock. There was absolutely no need for this announcement – the closing date for nominations was not until 15 July. The UCW's moderate Executive had already decided to support Kinnock on the previous Friday, but privately without running screaming to the press. The left, however, simply would not allow Michael the decency of a proper period of grief.

On 11 June, the *Daily Telegraph* was among the first off the blocks with the runners: 'Mr Roy Hattersley, Mr Peter Shore and Mr Neil Kinnock are seen as the most plausible candidates, with Mr John Silkin and Mr Denis Healey classed as outsiders despite the latter's seniority in the party.'[1] And two days later, the *Mirror* had already written Michael's political obituary:

'If he had not become Labour Leader Michael Foot would have gone down as a great parliamentarian, the outstanding orator of his generation and the best-loved member of his Party . . . (not) one of the most spectacular political losers of all time,' the newspaper's political editor, Terry Lancaster, wrote in brutal fashion. Not only had we not yet shot Michael, but we hadn't yet had time to carry out the inquest on the cause of his execution. No matter, as ever in politics, his grave was being trampled well before it was occupied.[2]

From the start, Kinnock was a racing certainty. This is no judgement in hindsight. Travelling down to London on the train for the TV inquest the day after the election, I read that William Hill was offering 7/2 against Kinnock being the next Leader. There and then, in true Roger Godsiff style, I wrote out a list of unions and voting strengths on the back of an envelope. From what I already knew – or guessed – I quickly worked out that Kinnock would take the majority of this vote.

Then I consulted the list of Labour MPs, now more left wing than before, did a calculation for the PLP and decided that Kinnock could also win this vote. Having kicked Benn out of the frame – and knowing that there would be ballots this time in constituency parties – I was absolutely certain Neil would wipe the floor with anybody else who stood, including Hattersley. William Hill was offering the bet of the century.

So, on arriving at Euston I went straight to a Hill's betting shop and put £200 – by far the biggest bet I have ever had in my life – on Kinnock, before going to earn it at the BBC. There I chatted with John Cole, the energetic Ulsterman who was the Corporation's well-respected political editor and who told me that he thought Hattersley would win easily. In my usual tactless fashion, feeling euphoric about my bet, I explained the errors in his thinking.

I was so caustic about Hattersley's chances because, apart from the arithmetic, I knew that he hadn't a cat in hell's chance in a straight contest. I said that he was a no-hoper. Cole was surprised because Hattersley had done a lot of work in the PLP to advance his chances, since 1979 at least. He had spent time entertaining, listening to and cultivating MPs of all shades of opinion. His success in the PLP elections derived, indeed, from this spade-work as well as good performances at the dispatch box.

313

His weakness, however, was that he appeared to many outside the PLP as pompous, unfriendly and remote. His friends in the union movement were few and far between. True, he had captured Basnett and he was liked within the AUEW by Ken Cure and Gavin Laird. The General Secretary, Terry Duffy, with whom he was also on good terms, however, was more reluctant to support him. Within a week, indeed, of the contest being announced, Duffy was attacking both Hattersley and Kinnock for causing disunity within the Party.

Hattersley's support among union officials outside the GMB and AUEW was minimal – he just did not appeal as an individual to many moderate activists. Not even the right wing Electricians' leadership would support him and they eventually abstained in the final vote. And when Roy Grantham, the leader of APEX, was asked to tip the winner, he said he thought that Shore had the edge. Without Grantham's support and that of other moderate leaders, Hattersley had no chance. And the reality was that Roy did not have the support of the machine men, who had done so much work to turn the Party round. They felt they owed Hattersley nothing and had no obligation to deliver.

Part of the reason for this was that some of us were angry at his apparent jockeying for position with Healey. We were not alone in this. In November 1979 – according to Benn, at the time of the Leadership election that never was – Hattersley was telling Healey that, if he expected support, he had to take Benn on. He did this, Benn claimed, hoping that Denis would destroy himself, so leaving the door open for Hattersley himself to stand.

During the election campaign in 1983, as it became clearer and clearer that we were going to be annihilated, Hattersley was not, of course, alone among people seeming to care more for their position in the Leadership stakes than in taking the fight to the Tories. I vividly remember watching Denis looking over at Hattersley one morning at the Campaign Committee and saying: 'I enjoyed reading your election address, Roy,' to which Roy replied: 'I didn't know you had been in Sparkbrook, Denis'. Healey lifted his eyebrows, a weighty procedure, and replied: 'Oh, not that election, I'm talking about your article in *The Times*, campaigning for the Leadership of the Party.' While Roy had not actually written the piece, Denis clearly thought that he had inspired it.

As some of us plodded on towards the end of the campaign, stories came thick and fast about Roy's successfully persuading moderate union leaders to 'skip a generation'. Of course, at that time Basnett was only too willing to co-operate, still bearing a grudge against Healey's high-handed treatment of him when he was at the Treasury. Later, when he discovered that he had backed the wrong young buck, he changed his tune – but that is another story.

On 13 June, the same day it was burying Foot, the *Mirror* carried a clarion call to moderates, aimed at helping Hattersley.

> Now the party should look for someone younger, someone who could be in charge for as long as Sir Harold was. His first task will be to listen to the voters who deserted in their millions last week. It is no use having a party of the people which is deaf to them. The election of a new leader gives Labour chance yet another chance. It cannot have many left.

From the very start, however, Hattersley and his campaign manager John Smith lacked an enthusiastic team working within the unions – and not only because some of us were disenchanted and did not believe that he deserved the right's support.

In his autobiography, Healey blames Clive Jenkins for organising support for Kinnock almost as soon as the election results were known. I believe this, however, to be misleading. Kinnock was also at that time very attractive to the electors. When we went canvassing in Newcastle-under-Lyme – the centre of all things moderate! – electors spontaneously told us that Labour needed a younger leader like Kinnock. At that time, too, Labour voters liked what they saw of him on the box. Neil's fiery speeches at Conference had endeared him to those who thought and bluntly said that Footie was past it.

At Conference, he would ignore the time limit, capture his audience and captivate them with words and images. On the platform and on TV, he shone and that was crucial. After a very bad start on the NEC, too, he had not only abandoned support for Benn, Militant and the hard left but had become ultra-cautious. His ambition had taken him away from the idealism of the Alternative Economic Strategy. He was, as I dubbed him, now of the respectable left.

With Benn unable to stand, too, who were the self-appointed remnants of the true Bennite left to support? In fact, they were in chaos anyway. Bishop's Stortford and the 1982 Conference had knocked the stuffing out of them. Benn had also fled Tribune to his newly created Campaign Group. In his final days, he had busied himself trying to get the Greenham Women a Nobel Peace Prize and fighting the Speaker's election – but he had even given up on this after Ernie Ross commented that 'the others will say the loonies are playing silly buggers again.'

'[Michael Meacher and Frances Morrell] said we were defeated; we had no troops,' Benn wrote in his Diaries just before the election. 'I tried to cheer them up and said we were paying the price for victory; we have changed the policy of the Party completely in four years; we have wheeled democratic reforms into position; we are disliked because we have exposed and outflanked the others. Our real allies now are probably the trade union left.'[3]

These allies in the trade union left were to prove lacking, however, in the battle for the Leadership which followed Foot's decision to stand down.

Immediately after the election, on 12 June Chris Mullin held an inquest at his flat in Brixton. Grim photographs of the participants taken in the garden were reproduced in Benn's Diaries. They were the usual lot, who turned out on such occasions: Tom Sawyer, Jeremy Corbyn, Audrey Wise, Ann Pettifor, Francis Prideaux, Les Huckfield, Michael Meacher, Tony Banks, Mandy Moore, Frances Morrell, Reg Race, Jon Lansman, Jo Richardson, Stuart Holland, Alan Meale and Ken Livingstone. They all look as though the kiss of life – and one of Hattersley's fine dinners – would have done them the power of good.

Tribune meanwhile, edited by Mullin, had led the mourning for its leader now over the water. Smarting not only over Labour's defeat on the left wing programme it had championed, it was devastated by Benn's defeat in Bristol. Never again, it said, should Labour go into an election with leaders 'most of whom are so manifestly out of sympathy with the programme on which they are supposed to be campaigning'.

Benn said that there should be no personal recriminations and that they should look at the long-term changes needed to bring about a Labour victory next time on socialist policies. Mandy Moore – Tatchell's minder in

Bermondsey and a woman of obvious perspicacity – observed that, however they behaved, the right were certainly going to lay into them and they had better be ready for it. A lot of harsh words were also spoken about the incompetence of Walworth Road. Memories, however, were conveniently short – none of them appears to have remembered that they made the major appointments. Criticisms of the staff, of course, were intended to deflect the blame from the left, not increase it.

This meeting, one of the most bizarre in the history of plotting and scheming, quickly turned to the Leadership stakes. Benn had arrived early and Banks offered him his parliamentary seat so that he could stand for the Leadership. Benn rejected this as manipulative, but didn't think to point out that the seat was a Labour-won seat which Banks had no right to offer to anyone. Distracted by their fight for internal party democracy, they may have overlooked this small point about democracy as a whole.

Banks persisted with the idea of finding a seat for Benn. What he didn't explain, however, was the small matter of how he could resign, get Benn selected and ensure a successful by-election by 15 July – the last date for Leadership nominations. His unreality was compounded by the fact that if he couldn't have Benn, he wanted Skinner. Although Tom Sawyer and Jon Lansman were smart enough to recognise that Kinnock would win on the first ballot, others were so bitterly against Neil that they wanted to put up their own candidate.

Audrey Wise suggested what I dubbed 'the nightmare ticket' of Heffer and Meacher. There was little support for Heffer, however, so he was dropped. Jo Richardson declined and she along with Mullin supported Joan Maynard. Obviously appalled at the latest turn of conversation – because who in their right mind could contemplate 'Stalin's Granny' as the Leader of the Labour Party – Stuart Holland then backed Banks' suggestion that someone stand down for Benn, which he again said he could not contemplate. In the end, in desperation, the gathering decided to support Meacher for Leader, if he would stand, and Richardson for Deputy. The sane mind boggles at the thought!

Whether Heffer knew about this meeting, I do not know. On 15 June, however, he declared himself a candidate come what may: 'If you don't stand, you never get support. If you are always afraid of being defeated, you will do nothing', he said, claiming the support of more than the 11 MPs necessary to nominate him. That included four from Liverpool, including the Militant Terry Fields. His move was reported in the press as being welcomed by 'elements of the hard left, who had never forgiven Kinnock for refusing to back Benn for the Deputyship in 1981.'

Heffer refused to be drawn as to how he differed from Kinnock or which of the three possible candidates as Deputy he preferred – Meacher, Denzil Davies or Gerald Kaufman. The choice, however, was being made for him. Through Victor Schonfield, CLPD was already manoeuvring for its Heffer/Meacher 'also-ran ticket'.

When Benn's Campaign Group met on 22 June, therefore, Heffer had bounced himself into the fray as the hard left candidate. It was a very motley crew, which gathered at this meeting. Before the assembled comrades, backing Heffer, Jeremy Corbyn argued that Kinnock deliberately lost the Deputy Leadership for Benn in 1981 and that he had spent the general election preparing for the Leadership. Dave Nellist, meanwhile, also urged Meacher as Deputy and so that was that: Heffer and Meacher became the official left candidates. Wise had got her 'dream' and my 'nightmare' ticket.[4]

Heffer acted quickly to try and neutralise Kinnock's lead, writing to all the union general secretaries urging the 'widest democratic involvement of the membership' in the ballot. 'This is a Labour Party election, and whoever becomes the Leader and Deputy Leader, it must be decided by the membership of the Party and not by the television and the press,' he wrote. He was standing, he made it clear, on a commitment to Clause IV of the constitution, the extension of public ownership, unilateral disarmament and withdrawal from the EEC. Oh, and for good comradely measure, he supported a 'Socialist Europe'.

Alongside Kinnock, Hattersley and Heffer, the fourth leadership candidate was Peter Shore. He, too, had given the appearance of starting his campaigning during the general election by insisting on making ineffective press conference appearances, even though his message was clearly failing to get across. He constantly saw himself as Leadership material, which he clearly wasn't. If the Lone Ranger had some of the directness and political nous of his Tonto, Gwyneth Dunwoody, he may have gone places. But he completely lacked any such qualities.

Kinnock's campaign did not begin too well, with the *Mirror* clearly mobilising to throw political muck. 'Mr Kinnock, who is understood to be Mr Foot's chosen son for the succession, supports the Foot policies of unilateral disarmament and withdrawal from the Common Market. But this could harm him with some union chiefs who regard these policies as largely responsible for Labour's humiliating general election defeat,' the *Mirror*'s political editor Terence Lancaster wrote right at the start. 'He is also handicapped by his lack of ministerial experience. In contrast with Mr Hattersley and Mr Shore, his most prestigious administrative post so far has been as secretary of his university Labour club.'[5]

Far from making clear that Neil was his chosen son, Foot in fact remained publicly neutral – though the *Mirror* reported that Jill Craigie, his wife, had described Neil as a 'real Welsh wizard, a Lloyd-George-cum-Nye-Bevan figure'.

Barely had the starting whistle blown, though, and the *Mirror* was putting the boot in again. Neil, its political editor vouched, was:

> Michael Foot Mark II. He has less hair but more freckles. On policy however the two are as one. And it was on policy, not Mr Foot's personality, that Labour was primarily humiliated last week . . . So he would lead Labour with courage. I believe he would also lead it to another electoral disaster. Labour's task now is to find policies which will appeal to the computer programmers in the south east as well as the factory workers in the north-west . . . that does not mean abandoning socialism. It means finding something more realistic than unilateral disarmament and withdrawing from the Common Market.

The *Mirror*, reflecting the Hattersley strategy masterminded by John Smith, called for widest use of membership ballots. It paid dividends straight away as NUPE – which had surprised itself by voting for Healey in the Deputy Leadership contest – opted to hold a ballot of all its 600,000 members on the Leadership.

Neil fought back hard against the media campaign conducted against him. 'I do not think experience in the classic form has much to do with it,' he told the BBC. 'It has a lot to do with instinct, common sense, energy to do it, the desire to win, the ingredients of patriotism . . . that make the total preparedness, the equipment of being a leader of a movement or leader of a country.' Asked if it was not dangerous to be a 'gut politician', as he was sometimes described, Kinnock deftly replied that 'he responded to issues more with his head, than with his stomach'.

The media campaign cut little ice in the movement, however, and Neil's bandwagon quickly gained momentum. I meanwhile called on each of Kinnock and Hattersley to declare that they were ready to act as Deputy to the other. 'It is essential that both the respectable left and the moderate wing of the Party be represented in the Leadership team,' I told the press. 'The whole Labour movement ought to support the balanced ticket of Neil Kinnock and Roy Hattersley.'

There was good reason, knowing that Kinnock was a certainty, to try and forge an alliance between him and Hattersley. We moderates, namely, came to realise that not only was Hattersley likely to be beaten in the Leadership battle, but it was also possible that he might be defeated for the Deputyship, too. The thought of Benn's disciple Meacher becoming number two to Kinnock made us contain our dislike of Roy and do what we could to ensure his election. And we could only be sure he would get enough support if he tied himself to Kinnock's coat tails.

Roger Godsiff and I were duly despatched as 'black spots' by the moderates to tell Hattersley he could possibly not win and accept that, at best, he could expect to be Deputy Leader. In short, he could like the 'dream ticket' or lump it. Later, Hattersley took the opportunity to shoot both messengers but at the time his venom was mostly directed against me.

We were ushered into his home in Gayfere Street and the only other person present was Mary Goudie, now Lady Goudie and then secretary of the Labour Solidarity Campaign. After I explained with my usual bluntness why we were there, Roy started to explode (and recounted all that I had told John Cole!). He demanded to know if I would vote for him. I replied that would depend upon the votes at my very moderate constituency party, which was having the very ballot he had called for!

Refusing to believe he could be beaten, he demanded to know the figures. Roger, a much more polished performer than I, produced his tidy list from his pocket and began to go through it. Listing not only Kinnock's natural support, he also retailed also those who were going to vote for Neil, who could usually be relied upon by the moderates.

The scowl broadened darkly on Roy's face as the awful truth dawned on him. 'Do you mean to say that I am going to have to play second fiddle to a red-haired, Welsh windbag?' asked Roy. 'Yes,' I replied instantly, 'If you put it like that, you are going to have to pay second fiddle to a red-haired Welsh windbag!' He looked stunned, his eyes darting from one to the other of us, and asked: 'Do you know that I could be Deputy Editor of the *Observer* on £40,000 a year?'. I studiously refrained from asking him what colour hair the Editor had and we left.

Our visit bore fruit and a five-minute conversation followed between Hattersley and Kinnock, at which a bargain was struck. 'Labour leadership rivals Neil Kinnock and Roy Hattersley did a deal yesterday,' the *Mirror* reported. 'Each declared that he is ready to act as the other's deputy if he loses . . . Both of them made it clear that they are still determined to become Leader. But they have been persuaded by fellow MPs and trade unionists to stand as a team in the interests of party unity. This must be a blow to the hopes of the other two contenders, Peter Shore and Eric Heffer.'[6]

An immediate effect of the deal was that Kaufman pulled out of the contest for the Deputyship. His spot, however, was immediately occupied by the surprise decision of Gwyneth Dunwoody, then a Shadow Health Minister, to stand. Gwyneth was entering the lists, she said, 'not as a token candidate – a female among males – but as a member of a Party which has temporarily lost its way.' But she admitted one advantage of being a woman: 'You tend to say in fairly brusque terms what you think.' To be brusque, however, Gwyneth was never in it. Thanks to the Lone Ranger, it was Tonto herself who had lost her way.

Despite a few pathetic sideswipes directed at Kinnock by Shore over his lack of experience, the Leadership battle was really no contest. The whole campaign was very low key, as it was obvious to most people involved who was going to win. The real fight yet again was for the Deputy Leadership. At the outset, Kaufman and Denzil Davies were tipped as the main contenders, but they quickly gave way to the two real combatants, Hattersley and Meacher.

On the moderate side, we became increasingly bothered when Hattersley became embroiled in a tremendous row with Foot. Roy had persuaded the

Shadow Cabinet to recommend that 'one member, one vote' be applied, but Max Madden with a gang of Kinnock supporters prevented it from being taken at the PLP. Foot abstained and, according to his own account, Hattersley accused him of betrayal. Foot replied: 'I'll have the skin off your back'. 'You couldn't knock the skin off a rice pudding,' Roy retorted.

At the end of July, the *Observer* – Roy's true spiritual home – reported the unholy spat. 'Labour's dream ticket for the Party Leadership seemed to be disintegrating fast last night, with the supporters of Kinnock and Hattersley in a state of open warfare . . . Mr Hattersley's sharp exchanges with his leader have made him the object of scathing criticism on the left.' 'The question,' it reported one of Kinnock's advisers saying, 'is whether Hattersley could work with anyone other than Attila the Hun.[7]

The dispute led to a sharp change in the atmosphere of the campaign, with some on the left claiming Hattersley was in grave danger of losing out completely, with Meacher pipping him for the Deputyship. Though Roy denied it at a meeting near my own patch in Stoke-on-Trent, there was fevered speculation of a 'Shadow Cabinet strike', with leading moderates including Kaufman, Eric Varley and John Smith refusing to serve if Meacher came through. While Hattersley's camp turned its fire on Meacher, the left played 'Benn's jacket holder' up as the man for the unity ticket with Kinnock, while Hattersley offered nothing more than renewed conflict.

At this time, Benn also began to believe that Meacher would win what he could not – the Deputy Leadership of the Labour Party. 'On the Deputy Leadership, we were told that Meacher had about 200 CLPs, 33 MPs and three or four unions,' he recorded in his Diaries. 'Michael had spoken to Neil Kinnock about the possibility of running with him but Neil had been pretty non-committal. Michael Meacher looked good for the Deputy Leadership and Roy Hattersley's abuse of Michael Foot at the PLP meeting would be bound to help. NUPE are likely to nominate Kinnock and Meacher. Tom Sawyer said: 'Michael Meacher is a serious candidate, and we must make it clear he's not an *ad hoc* candidate for Tony. Some want Hattersley because they want him tied into the leadership.'[8]

Meacher's chances, however, were destroyed both because there was already too much of a head of steam behind the Kinnock–Hattersley ticket, and because he was so closely associated with Benn. Hattersley's bid for the

Leadership, meanwhile, was finally scuppered by the very ballots, for which he and Smith had pressed.

I saw this in Newcastle-under-Lyme, where in September 1983 my constituency party held a ballot for Leader and Deputy Leader in which 347 members voted. As in all constituencies which held an OMOV ballot, Kinnock came first – in Newcastle with 53 per cent, to Hattersley's 32.5 per cent, Shore's 9.2 per cent and Heffer's 5.1 per cent. For Deputy Leader, three choices were on the table, depending on whether Heffer/Shore, Hattersley or Kinnock were elected Leader. Kinnock just pipped Hattersley in the event of Heffer/Shore winning and won overwhelmingly in the case of Hattersley winning. In the event of Kinnock winning, Hattersley was the overwhelming choice for Deputy

The unions meanwhile did their level best to prevent the campaign from inflicting the same damage on the Party as had the Benn–Healey contest and it was kept away from the TUC following a motion I successfully moved on the NEC.

In the trade union ballots for leader, Kinnock won each of them. Of unions which did not have ballots, both the AUEW and the GMB voted for Hattersley, although Basnett tried to wriggle out of voting for Roy by asking him to withdraw. In the Deputy Leader election, Hattersley beat Meacher in ballots held in NUPE, the NUM and the POEU, despite support from the executive for the left wing candidate, but Meacher won in the ASTMS and the Seamen's Union.

There was a bitter battle once again in the TGWU, whose conference decided to nominate Kinnock but rejected Hattersley as Deputy. Its General Executive Committee, however, voted 19 to 17 to support Meacher but the General Secretary argued that this was not binding on the delegation, which subsequently decided by 27 votes to 18 to vote for Hattersley instead. Who said democracy didn't work!

And so on Sunday 2 October, 1983 the Party assembled in Brighton for the Annual Conference and the Leadership election, which was a foregone conclusion. Everyone knew that Kinnock would be Foot's successor, the question was by how much. The biggest surprise, indeed, to many was John Spellar's ultra-right-wing EETPU, which – after a big internal row – abstained.

In the event Kinnock won the Leadership battle easily, as did Hattersley in his bid to become second fiddle to his 'red-haired Welsh windbag'. Neil trounced everyone in the unions and constituencies. The closest Hattersley came was among the MP's section – but it was a measure of Kinnock's triumph that even there Hattersley only polled half Neil's vote. Overall, Kinnock commanded 71 per cent of the electoral college, to Hattersley's 19 per cent, Heffer's 6.3 per cent and Shore's even more derisory 3.1 per cent. Hattersley, too, slaughtered Meacher – by 67 per cent to 28 per cent.[9]

Compared with the carnage two years before, it was a pretty painless election – except for me down the line, as Hattersley never forgave me for delivering the black spot.

The 1983 Conference – The Inquest and More Blows for the Left

Hard on the heels of Benn's defeat at the general election, the slaughter of Heffer and Meacher gave the moderates an enormous fillip. Clearly, we were still upset by the scale of our election defeat and the inquest had hardly begun before we were in throes of another Leadership contest. But we were relieved that only the most fanatical of the ultra-left, like Arthur Scargill, would lay the blame at our door.

To my mind, my tactic of losing on the left's terms paid off. It was an election we were bound to lose and now the left could not blame the right. Indeed the only criticism I received was months later from *Tribune* which even the *Guardian*, rarely as kind to me as *The Times* or the tabloids were, poked fun at in a leading article: 'Cold comfort, comrades'. In the leader, a miner refuses to vote Labour. ''Tis that John Golding, the General Jaruzelski of the Labour Party. 'Tis his merciless witch-hunt of the honest lads and lasses of the Militant that I canna stand.' He might, he says, vote for Thatcher. 'Say what you like about her,' the pitman mutters, 'she's never said one word against Ted Grant the whole campaign.'

Almost predictably, indeed, only Scargill criticised the Labour manifesto for not being radical enough. Saying that another five years of Conservative policies could lead to social violence, he called for extra-parliamentary action by the trade unions, including political strikes against the government. Arthur's never learned!

For many who had once blindly supported the left, their conviction in the certain success of socialism had been badly shaken. It would never again be as easy for Benn and Heffer, or their ilk, to appear as prophets on the way to the promised land.

That would be underlined later during the 1983 Conference with the third key event of the week, after the election of the Leader and Deputy: an enormous vote against Militant. We made more progress in the NEC elections, too; there were the first signs of more realism in policy–making; and we fought off a further assault on the independence of the PLP.

At the conclusion of the annual ritual of the NEC elections, while there were substantial changes in people, the moderates came out with one net gain. Kinnock and Hattersley of course, replaced Foot and Healey. With my own union executive now captured by the left, I failed to get the NCU nomination, but was replaced instead by a good moderate, Tony Clarke of the UCW. Another casualty was Denis Howell, who fell because Tom Sawyer and Rodney Bickerstaffe of NUPE – with the involvement of the left fixer Alan Meale – had told the General Secretary of COHSE at breakfast that they would not vote for its moderate nominee Eric Ambler, unless COHSE backed the NUM's hard leftie Eric Clarke. Howell, whom COHSE had backed but now couldn't, was the sacrificial lamb.

From the left's point of view, however, the stitch-up misfired somewhat when Doug Hoyle beat not only Howell but Clarke, too. While some believed Clarke was the unluckiest man alive, I knew that he often brought trouble on himself by relying too much on Meale's advice. I saw a good example of this at Folkestone races one day, when Eric nearly went bankrupt as a result of following Alan's consistent run of losing tips.

An odd gain was Renee Short, who was elected on the 'moderate slate' this time, having been turfed off the NEC by the mods when she was on the 'left slate' in 1981! Equally oddly, Ann Clwyd swept in, having both Alan Meale and Roger Godsiff working for her.

Not that barmy thinking had disappeared entirely. The unions were still capable of helping the left to pass unrealisable motions at Conference. One of the more lurid flights of fancy was a motion that all spokespeople be fully signed up to socialist policies before speaking to the press – that would have disqualified two-thirds of the PLP! Conference, indeed, vented its spleen against the press with a rash of motions following the media's prejudice in the general election.

True, in the normal course, the media had a strong Tory bias. But these were extraordinary times and in the 1983 election it was our policies and the leader more than anything, stupid, that fuelled the onslaught. Conference blindly, nonetheless – with the support of the NEC – endorsed the manifesto on which we had been slaughtered. Crucially, there was no shift on defence. Foot's position, indeed, was that of a someone who believed that the electorate, if only they reflected, would eventually come to agree with him!

Foot's despairing stance (for me, at least!) showed he had learned little, if anything, from our election humiliation. His approach, indeed, had not much changed from the very first meeting of the new PLP in June after the polls. There Foot was given a huge ovation (the losers, of course, were not present). Michael 'hit out at the opinion polls and at a Conservative machine, more powerful and with fewer scruples than before', but insisted he was not looking for excuses. Labour had had to face 'similar odds' in the past and had overcome them through the 'sheer strength' of our case. With more time to put over its policies, he maintained, the Party would have won. He urged Labour to rebuild for the next election, saying that: 'If we cannot show enough political intelligence to unite we cannot hope to lead the country. That is one verdict we could hear on the doorsteps.'

Healey, meanwhile, while paying tribute to Foot for his 'energy, zest and friendliness' throughout the election, quoted Oscar Wilde's dictum: 'The play was a great success, it was the audience who were at fault'. He said quite rightly that we could not simply ignore the electorate; we had lost a quarter of our support during the election itself – remorse and repentance should be the order of the day.

Not that Benn was remorseful at all. He truly believed he had played no part in the defeat whatsoever. In July, addressing a Campaign Group meeting, he said that it was important that the left 'nip in the bud the myth that if only the Party hadn't changed its policy, if only it hadn't gone for the democratic changes, we would have romped home in the election, because it wasn't true.'

At the subsequent NEC in July, Healey pressed his case further, calling for a radical shake-up of the Party. 'Conference cannot make policy unless it is totally reorganised . . . The big unions are not in tune with their members . . . We must revert to a situation where the Shadow Cabinet provided Leadership to the Party, not the NEC.' After that meeting, again in my 'Diary of an MP', I wrote: 'The moderates had a good day. We are supposed to have an inquest on the general election, but I successfully move that we do this at a special meeting in September. Everyone is too exhausted to face another few hours.'

We eventually had our inquest at a special NEC meeting on 12 September just before Conference, as the Leadership election was entering the final straight. It certainly threw up some oddities – to anyone used to the slick, 24-hour news agenda campaigns of the 1990s, that is, but not to us who had to deal with the shambles that was HQ. During the election, staff had to leave Walworth Road by 9.55 pm come hell or high water, as one absurd example.[10]

Then Jim Mortimer, the General Secretary, made a very fair assessment. The role of TV was underestimated, the organisation certainly had defects, but disunity had been a major handicap. The SDP had harmed us, with a switch at the end of the campaign of 2-3 million votes. Our council house policy was unpopular, too, and defence had diverted us from other issues. Sawyer in turn blamed Callaghan for the row over Polaris, but acknowledged that, although the policy was supported by the activists, it had not got the confidence of the mass of the people. Was this, I wonder, his first step on the road to Damascus?

Foot, however, again pronounced that the manifesto was fine and we should stick with it. 'I stand by socialism,' he said, 'but it has to be put across more intelligently.' There was also a blazing row between Skinner and Healey of the good (bad), old-fashioned kind. Skinner attacked Callaghan and Shore for raising the question of the witch-hunt during the election. In his Diaries, Benn records the blunt defence given by the old pugilist: 'Denis Healey retorted that . . . Papandreou had expelled 500 Trotskyites from his Party in Greece two years before the election, and that Mitterrand had won because of his rearmament programme. Our slide began in 1981 with the Party split, with the image of extremism and the Labour Party rallies.'[11]

'New Labour' has since gained a reputation for the slickest – some would say 'too slick by half' – campaigning in British political history, with no expense spared in bringing in the advertising, marketing, TV and film-making professionals. In 1983, however, little effort was made to spice up and focus our efforts, forlorn as they might have been. Our campaigning was just dull, soulless and tired. An offer, for example, from 'Arts for Labour' to produce broadcasts was rejected and they were placed into the hands of a firm which never once attempted something imaginative.

During the inquest, Mori's Bob Worcester dealt at length with the opinion-polling we had, at least, done. We started behind the Tories on most issues, he repeated, and did progressively worse as the campaign went on. At the outset, we were in front on just five, but of those we ended ahead on just three. And even on these, the verdict was soul-destroying: our lead on jobs and pensions was slashed as time went on and the only issue we gained on was social services. We were making promises, the electorate believed, which we simply could not afford. Worst of all – horror upon horror – we ended up behind the Tories again, as we had in 1979, as the party which showed the 'most concern for people'. Our policy on Europe, which the left thought was a sure-fire vote-winner, went down like yet another lead balloon!

Taking the wider view, Bob put the unanswerable case that while policy should not be determined on the basis of polls, neither should it be fixed without knowing public opinion. You ignore it at your peril. 'Both Labour's strategy and much of its tactics were in place before taking public opinion into account,' Bob concluded. 'Research should have been used at least a year before to discover this significant image problem and concerted action taken . . . Research doesn't measure truth, it measures perception. For the public to perceive the Tories under Mrs Thatcher as the party with the greatest concern for the majority of the public is nonsense; yet that was the perception. To ignore this is foolish; to fail to know it is foolish ignorance.'

Others delivered scathing attacks based on a lifetime of political campaigning – notably Gwyneth Dunwoody and Denis Howell. And I drew heavily on their experience when I spoke for the NEC on the inquest at Conference, which, being in private session at the time naturally received great publicity!

I began by stating that the faults were with the national campaign and not in the local constituencies. I described how a week before polling day, when I travelled from London to Blackpool to visit the POEU Conference, Llin and Maureen Maddox, one of our stalwart footsoldiers in Newcastle-Under-Lyme, had got on the train at Crewe with the sole purpose of presenting me with a long scroll listing all the iniquities and mistakes of the Campaign Committee, before they got off at Preston to return to the fray.

On the journey, I was belted from pillar to post. I told Conference:

As I read the scroll I knew that our private polls were showing how badly our campaign was going. We had failed to convince the people that Labour would provide strong leadership, that we would defend Britain, that we would cure unemployment, that we could afford to pay for what we promised. Many council tenants firmly believed that Labour was unfair to those who wanted to buy their own houses. Above all, we failed to make our policies on youth unemployment, on the NHS and on pensions central to the campaign. We failed and our people are suffering in consequence.

Of course the main problem was in not getting our policies across; but we cannot dodge the fact that some of those policies were unpopular. If we had listened to the electors or taken the polls more seriously, we would have done better. We cannot afford any longer to fight elections on a 'like it or lump it' basis . . . We cannot blame the electors, nor can we lump all blame on the media. Of course in the general election the papers, except for the *Daily Mirror*, were unfair. But so they were in 1945, 1964, 1966 and 1974. Whatever we say about the papers, however, this election was won and lost on the box.

Whereas what appears in the newspapers is selective, to a great extent we ourselves determine how we are seen on TV. It is up to us how well we perform and how we come across to families in their own homes. In the general election we lost on TV because of ourselves, not because of any bogeys in the media. These were our 'own goals', our self-inflicted wounds, which they showed, not theirs. It was our disagreements on defence that appeared, not theirs.

It was our fault that we talked so much about the horrors of the bomb and so little about our plans for a strong, non-nuclear defence. It was we who neglected youth unemployment, the health service, pensions and other bread-

and-butter issues . . . We also failed to speak in simple terms to the electors. Thatcher, Tebbit and Parkinson spoke simply, appealing to the prejudices and fears of working people. Instead . . . too often we gave them jargon and incomprehensible gobbledegook.

Of course our people gave too little support to Michael Foot. No man could have kept so much dignity as things went wrong . . . Let us not find scapegoats; we were not robbed, we threw it away. It was a terrible campaign. Brother Chairman, the Campaign Committee was the nearest I have got to life among anarchists. I am talking about the professional politicians, not the staff. It was not the staff of Walworth Road that let us down; it was we in the Leadership.

Our election manifesto, approved by the NEC and the Shadow Cabinet alike, stuck strictly to Conference policy. Let me say to some critics, I believe that, had we not fought the general election on the policies of Conference, this week the Party would have been in tatters. But we did fight the general election on the policies of Conference. We did stay true.

I might have added under my breath 'and that's how we threw it away'.

Foot took responsibility for the defeat, but clearly he had not learned, especially on defence. In any case, Ron Todd of the TGWU would not countenance any change over our unilateral policy. He and the so-called Labour Disarmament Liaison Committee ensured that Labour remained frozen in the political wilderness.

Despite this fossilised approach, on many other issues at the 1983 Conference there was a disposition to think again – over public ownership and the causes of long-term unemployment, for example. And crucially it showed over the Common Market, as withdrawal ceased to be an item of faith and there was movement towards acceptance of Britain's membership of the EEC. While the option to withdraw remained (as a face-saver!), the emphasis now shifted to working with European socialists to promote a European policy on employment and social justice.

A few years later, sitting on the General Council of the TUC, I realised why it was that the trade union leaders had suddenly come to love Brussels. When Thatcher denied unions access to Whitehall, they went to Brussels instead and found that their arguments in defence of workers received a sympathetic hearing from – another of her pet hates – the practical officials in the European Commission. The unions had found a back door and tried to use the EEC as a counter-weight to Thatcher.

The Bennites, however, were not yet in full retreat. At this Conference, a long-rumbling constitutional battle came to a head, namely attempts by the left to subdue and subsume the PLP into the Party as a whole. This had, of course, been the reason for the drive for mandatory reselection. It had, however, also played out for years in a battle over who should control the so-called 'Short money' – given to help opposition parties in parliament formulate policy. As far back as 1979, the left on the NEC tried to grab any paid help – or special advisers, as they are now known – for the Party and therefore themselves. It was yet another argument between Benn and Callaghan, which just rumbled on and on. It was part and parcel, too, of Benn's attempts to curb the Leader's great powers of patronage. He wanted the Leader to be controlled more by the PLP and for the Party to control the PLP.

Discontent about Jim's exercise of patronage was by no means confined to the left. There were a fair few others in the PLP who were far from satisfied with their lot. Between 1974 and 1979, many bright young things were unhappy that others of us not so bright nor polished were made ministers, while they remained on the back benches because Callaghan followed the old ways and kept a balance. That simmering discontent, iron-ically, manifested itself in the summer of 1979 when both Benn and Heffer for the left and Philip Whitehead and John Horam from the right argued for more elections for front bench jobs!

The argument over reining in the PLP dragged on at Conference year after year. The NEC should have reported back in 1982 after we kicked the left's last attempts into the touch of 'remission' but, as I mentioned earlier, we sadly forgot to do so and Eric, very satisfyingly, had to apologise.

After the general election, instead of conducting a root-and-branch review of how we lost so badly, instead the 'Org' in July found itself debating again the touchstone issue – for the left, if not the electorate – of the 'PLP Standing Orders'. Refreshingly, Kinnock joined Foot strongly and at length defending the independence of the PLP. So long did Neil go on, indeed, that the chairman Russell Tuck felt obliged to intervene: 'Welsh oratory is very impressive,' Russell commented, 'But you did say 'Now my final point' three times, Neil, and I think we should vote.'

At the 1983 Conference, the left pushed again – calling for a commit-ment to implement Party policies to be added to the standing orders of the PLP. Furthermore, it wanted major parliamentary decisions to be taken at the weekly meetings of the PLP by recorded vote, which would be available for the Party to see. This was a world away from the private, sounding-off sessions we were used to, where votes were not taken, and I opposed the resolution for the NEC.

Our MPs have also been elected by the people. Our Party was created by Keir Hardie and others as a fierce, uncompromising advocate of parliamentary democracy. Since the beginning, the Parliamentary Labour Party, while having its role set down in the constitution, has kept its autonomy,

I laid down the gauntlet from the rostrum. What the left, of course, wanted to do was change the whole constitutional standing of a Member of Parliament, to turn Labour MPs into mere ciphers, no more than messen-gers of the great extra-parliamentary left fixers – who now, of course, included Benn.

I told the comrades:

I would not want it to be a condition of my being in parliament that I had at all times and on all occasions to implement the decisions of Annual Conference. My Constituency Labour Party would be appalled if they thought I was merely to be a delegate from Conference to Parliament.

I am not alone in not wanting to be bound by all Conference decisions . . . Our Denis has put it often that he does not want to have to be committed to Conference decisions because they are generally made by the right-wing block vote . . . I have even heard Eric Heffer utter similar doubts. They remember things like German re-armament and they are conscious that sometimes they do not agree with the Conference decisions. They sometimes think that their consciences tell them that the Conference decisions are wrong.

One of the big problems facing this proposition is what you do with people who break the standing orders by not speaking and voting for Conference policies? Do we discipline them? Expel them? If so, should we have done that to

Eric Heffer and Neil Kinnock because of their earlier attitude on devolution? Or when the NEC decided on a Falklands policy, should we have disciplined or expelled Tony Benn or Tam Dalyell for opposing this policy? . . . Let me make it clear to the left in the Party that it is their causes which will suffer most if we adopt this proposition.

But the biggest sufferer would be the Party itself. There is nothing the press and telly would like more than a weekly bust-up at the PLP with a list of names . . . If the recorded vote is to be used as an instrument in the – I almost said witch hunt – harassing of MPs at local level, that is the last thing we want in the next parliament.

And how daft to tell the Tories of our parliamentary tactics a week in advance. You might as well have the Tory Chief Whip sitting in the Parliamentary Labour Party . . . We would be better employed taking Labour's message to the people than spend hours wrangling amongst ourselves in the Palace of Westminster.

The left were duly beaten off again – but this was to be my last speech from the platform. I also learned during the week that I would not go into the Shadow Cabinet. I had upset Hattersley bitterly by riding roughshod over him when telling him bluntly that we were not going to fight to overturn left policies at the Clause V meeting before the election. I had magnified the sin by delivering the black spot and voting for Kinnock.

I remember Jack Cunningham stopping me on the front at Brighton looking very troubled and concerned. He told me that to get on the right wing list I had to go and bend my knee to Hattersley. Refraining carefully from the use of such words as 'big bag of lard', I told him that I would bend to no-one. Later Terry Duffy insisted that I go on the list, but naturally Hattersley ensured that his cronies were told privately not to vote for me.

When Hattersley and Kinnock met at breakfast to reach understandings and Neil proposed that I be supported for the Shadow Cabinet, Hattersley turned me down. In a matter of months, the left had me off the NEC and the right had stopped my promotion. Those that live by the sword . . . ! My only consolation was that Benn had suffered more – mostly at my hands.

At one point in his Diaries, Benn noted plaintively:

If I had not stood down from the Shadow Cabinet after 1979, had played a less active part in the campaign to change the policy and to bring about the democratic changes, and had not stood for the deputy leadership, and if I'd gone to find a safe seat this year, I would have been in the running now. I may even have won. But history didn't work out in that way, and the price paid for playing it differently has been enormous in personal terms.

I have lost successively my seat in the Shadow Cabinet, the deputy leadership of the Labour Party, the Chairmanship of the Home Policy Committee last October after Conference, and, this year, my seat in Parliament. Four major setbacks. But the reward is that the Party has, I think, been irreversibly shifted back towards socialism and is more democratic, and that is the most important thing of all.

This irreversible shift back to socialism is presumably what we know as New Labour and more democracy the 'one-member one-vote' ballots we on the right had urged all along!

The truth is that we were like a couple of bare-knuckle fighters, who had knocked each other to the canvas. The audience, having enjoyed the scrap, would now slope off, unmarked themselves, into the night to make their own way in the world.

Despite my personal setbacks, on returning from Conference, Llin wrote: 'Maureen [Maddox], John and I have returned from this Conference with a feeling of hope and unity for the future. There can be little doubt that this Conference was to be a watershed in the history of the Labour movement. It proved a Conference of great unity. The Conference of 1979 was one of great bitterness with much fist-waving, hissing and intimidation of delegates . . . this week while representing all shades of opinion, [they] showed a tolerance of the point of view of others that was heartening.'

And while the 1983 Conference, and its aftermath, were a great setback for me personally, I could still come away knowing that we had finally stopped the march of that most perfidious group of all, Militant.

TWENTY-FOUR

The Fall of Militant

Neil Kinnock's remarkable attack on Militant at the 1985 Party Conference is now seen by many as the turning point in the battle against the 'Tendency'. It was, however, the 1983 Conference which crippled Militant, taking away much of its strength and influence and discrediting it as a national force in the Labour Party. No longer would it be seen by a majority of activists as a legitimate voice of the left. If it was not a job well done, at least it was a job well worth doing, saving the Party from being taken over slowly and by design by a group of fanatical Trotskyites.

It was also as long and excruciating a battle as could be inflicted on poor souls like myself, to get action against the most dangerous left wing barmies of all, when the evidence all along was as plain as the nose on your face.

I have described earlier how I discovered the growing strength of Militant and how the NEC refused to deal with the problem. Not only Benn and Eric but Kinnock and Lestor, too, gave them support or succour against those on the right who wanted them outlawed.

To get the 'soft left' to realise that they, too, were under threat from Militant was not easy. Michael Foot, a true parliamentarian if ever there was one, was haunted by his own past from the days when he was a leading light in the fight by the Bevanites against Gaitskell for the soul of the Party. And, as we have seen, after the Underhill Enquiry, he had refused to allow publication of the Militant documents, which proved that the 'Tendency' was an organised conspiracy against the Party.

The argument over publication refused to go away. In the autumn of 1979, Neville Sanderson, the MP for Hayes and Harlington – who had been fighting a running battle with the left in his constituency – wrote to the

General Secretary asking for copies of the Underhill documents from Transport House. Based on the previous decision, Ron Hayward refused. When Sanderson wrote again, the issue was put to the NEC's Organisation Committee.

One of the barriers, however, to it being taken seriously was that few people took Neville Sanderson seriously. His outrageous remarks were a source of delight to a group often found in the tea room at ten in the morning. As he sat there in his barrister's suit, entertaining us with his la-de-da voice about the Trots in his constituency, he seemed like a character from P. G. Wodehouse. Nowadays he would hardly even be noticed – except that he was male, and well over 30 – but in the tea room of 1979, he stuck out like a sore thumb.

My job, as I conceived it, however, was to try to get the Militant documents released first to the NEC, and then demand that they go to everyone else. As I wrote in my 'Diary of an MP' at the time: 'Monday. Thinking of the people who keep on asking how I am enjoying my holiday, I leave Silverdale at 5 am to attend committee meetings of the Labour Party Executive! The main item is an argument about the document on the Militants – Marxists who believe in revolution rather than our democracy. They have joined the Labour Party to use it for their own ends. Reg Underhill, the former National Agent wrote a report on the Militant tactics which was locked up in Transport House. At the NEC Organisation Committee, Shirley Williams and I tried unsuccessfully to get the document released. We will certainly try again.'

We did and we failed. Again at the 'Org', under Heffer's chairmanship, we were denied sight of the papers. 'The Party is totally against witch hunts,' Heffer told the press. 'We believe that Trotskyist views cannot be beaten by disciplinary action but by superior arguments.' Under instructions from Liverpool, Heffer had no intention of giving in. He argued that the demands were all a press plot to divert Labour from attacking Tories. As for the documents themselves, they 'had reached the party in plain envelopes and without covering notes and were therefore suspect as authentic versions of Trotskyist activity,' he said.

After Shirley and I had came up empty-handed, Reg Underhill declared that he would he would publish the papers himself if the NEC failed to act.

In an interview with *The Times*, he reminded Heffer that it had taken four years for him and others to convince sceptics in the 1960s that the 'Keep Left' organisation of the time was under the wing of the Socialist Labour League (now the Workers' Revolutionary Party).[1]

He also took issue with Heffer's oft-repeated claim about the documents arriving anonymously. 'I have never made any such statement.' Reg said. 'The various documents came from disillusioned supporters of Militant; some had notes with names and addresses; others were handed to me personally, and some were given to other persons, with the request that they be passed to me. The disclosures in *The Times* of recent documents reinforces their authenticity . . . surely Mr Heffer and the NEC will take heed of what is told by fellow MPs of what is happening in their constituencies.'

At the same time, the *Mirror* also came out strongly for publication:

Mr Eric Heffer, a member of Labour's NEC, says a media campaign against Trotskyites . . . is designed to frighten Labour voters and help Mrs Thatcher . . . Not in the *Mirror* it isn't. This paper has consistently supported the election of democratic socialist governments. It still does. It is the Trotskyites who do not. Mr Ted Grant, leader of the their organisation, the Militant tendency, wrote to the editor of the *Mirror* this week: 'We stand for the ideas of Marx, Engels, Lenin and Trotsky . . .' Fine. That's up to him. But they are not what the Labour Party stands for. If they were, that would really help Mrs Thatcher. The truth is that the campaign is led by Lord Underhill, a party official for 45 years and its National Agent for seven of them. It is supported by most Labour MPs. They're worried because Militant has its own members, subscriptions, newspaper, policy, income and employees. On the face of it that breaks the Labour Party rules.

Mr Heffer even doubts whether all the evidence against Militant is authentic . . . But how can the ordinary Party member judge whether it's genuine or not when Mr Heffer and his colleagues refuse to publish it?[2]

At the NEC in January, 1980, however, the chairman refused to allowed discussion of correspondence and further documents from Underhill, referring them instead back to the 'Org'. The pressure from the press, however, was clearly having an effect on Foot. At the NEC meeting, he moved that the original decision in 1977 not to publish effectively be considered again.[3]

After a bitter debate, however, Foot was defeated by a narrow margin. At the subsequent long and sharp 'Org', an inquisition was comprehensively blocked by Benn – who was well aware of the true nature of the threat posed by Militant – but he did invite them to make available details of their organisation, membership and finance, just like other left groups. It was small comfort, but in those days it counted as progress.[4]

Then came the first signs of a conversion by Kinnock – clearly reflecting Foot's views and also possibly Clive Jenkins', who told Benn he wanted 'Militant out of the Party'. After Benn's motion, Neil successfully proposed setting up a sub-committee to 'read and review the documents which have come into the possession of Lord Underhill since the last enquiry.' Its effect, sadly, was marred somewhat by an amendment from the mini–Militant Tony Saunois, carried on Heffer's casting vote, which added an investigation into 'links between sections of the Labour Party, bankers, industrialists, the CIA and other enemies of the Labour movement'.[5]

Despite this daft amendment, Neil's move could have led to action against Militant, but it all went wrong again – and it is hard for me to know with certainty why. Maybe it was because Kinnock was trying to bend over backwards to appease Benn after press revelations in late February, 1980 of a soft left meeting which decided to curb Benn's activities.[6] Whatever the reason, at the subsequent NEC not only could I not get support to remove the offending Trot amendment, but a Benn/Heffer proposal was carried which abandoned Neil's enquiry even before it had started![7]

Underhill, of course, was absolutely right to call for action on his report and urge a crusade against Militant. I, for one, however, urged him to hold fire on publishing on his own until we had exhausted all channels within the Party. Once again, however, the blockheads continued to block publication by the NEC of the Militant documents, inviting Reg instead to publish his material off his own bat.

Foot, however, was coming under increasing pressure to act. The right wing Manifesto Group of MPs, then chaired by John Cartwright, had two meetings with him at this time over the issue and were single-minded in their determination to rid the party of Militant. But it was now not only the right who were complaining to Michael, so too were some of his old Aldermaston marching comrades. To many of them bullied by Militant thugs, the Tendency was not just a 'bunch of friendly neighbourhood Marxists'!

During the course of 1981, Foot was bitterly attacking Militant. At a special meeting of the PLP in November, indeed, he described them as a 'pestilential disease' – but frustratingly, he made it clear, he would not resort to surgery. And at the NEC, it was difficult even to make progress even after the gains at the 1981 Conference – this being blocked effectively by Kinnock.

Shortly after the Conference, for instance, the Manifesto Group asked the NEC to initiate an enquiry, which Benn rejected. A counter-proposal from me was defeated by seven votes to three. And, as *The Times* reported after-wards:

> The seven included three soft left supporters of Mr Foot who has always opposed any action against Militant while strongly criticising the group. The three were Mr Douglas Hoyle, Miss Joan Lestor and Mr Neil Kinnock. Mr Golding said afterwards: 'It is obvious that the soft left is terrified to act against Militant.'[8]

The red plague must have hit Hampstead hard in the following weeks, however, because after years of inaction, events moved apace. At the NEC in late November, I routinely challenged an 'Org' decision rejecting the re-instatement of a 'proscribed list', not expecting anything other than opposition. Then, surprisingly to say the least, Foot popped up to say that 'there was a case to look at some aspects of the Militant Tendency by the Organisation Committee but that he was against expulsions'. I could hardly believe that I might be hearing the first strains of the clarion call to arms.[9]

But this really was the turn of the tide. From then on, I became accus-tomed to withdrawing my motions, to second those moved by Foot, which would be carried while Heffer would be defeated. Winning took some getting used to, but I coped very well under the circumstances. Things went ahead at the December 'Org', although not quite as reported by Benn that:

'John Golding proposed that there should be an enquiry into Militant and Michael said he was against proscribed lists but he thought this action was necessary'.[10]

In fact, it was Foot who proposed that – and I quote this remarkable moment in full:

> This committee instructs the General Secretary and the National Agent to provide a report on the activities of the Militant Tendency and whether these conflict with Clause II[iii] of the Constitution of the Labour Party; to obtain from the organisers of Militant Tendency details of the scale of their operation within the Labour Party, its funding organisation, full-time staff and international connections; to obtain from all regional organisers of the Labour Party their assessment of these matters in their regions including such places as Bradford, Liverpool, Bermondsey and Swansea and on the state of the Party in their regions.

Michael still did not believe in witch hunts, but by this time he conceded that Militant's activities were more than 'a pestilential nuisance'. 'If we don't take action, I fear that there will be some members of the Party who will be encouraged to leave us, and that is a matter of great concern to me. It is necessary to take action now to stop any collapse of morale in the Party,' he told the NEC. For Michael, at the time it was crucial to take action because of the threat from the SDP.

Benn, of course, laid into Foot. 'I am not going to support the thought police,' he said. 'And I shall fight like a tiger to prevent expulsions and proscriptions.' But he got as good as he gave, however, as Joan Lestor tore into him. Benn had a lot to answer for, she said, because of his failure to repudiate the intolerance of the ultra-left.

The rise of the SDP had certainly concentrated the minds of the soft left. As the *Guardian* wrote:

> The truth is that Militant is extremely unpopular outside its own ranks of dedicated supporters. Its members are regarded as sectarian, monotonous and humourless, bogged down in the jargon and slogans of the left – to be tolerated only so long as they are relatively harmless.[11]

340

By now, however, they were far from harmless or unsuccessful. They had six parliamentary candidates, an increasing number of councillors, reliable support in 45 or more constituencies at Conference and because of them we were losing elections we should easily have won – such as the Euro-seat contested by Terry Harrison and a GLC seat by Ted Grant.

Certainly, too, Michael no longer regarded them as harmless and his motion was carried by 10 votes to 9. We were on our way, brothers. At least we thought so, until we were soon stopped in our tracks when Russell Tuck's proposition from the NUR – calling for organisations to submit details to see whether they met the criteria for Party membership – was defeated.

At the next NEC in December, 1981, therefore, I was apprehensive when Benn challenged Foot's enquiry again. My fears increased when after lengthy discussion, we mods failed to put the issue to a vote. I breathed more easily again, however, when the vote was finally taken. Benn's attempt to shield Militant was defeated by a thumping majority – 19 votes to 10, with Kinnock voting on the side of the angels.[12]

Militant reacted furiously to the decision, saying it would resist ferociously: 'The decision flies in the face of the express views of the rank and file of the Labour Party and trade union movement,' its 'Editorial Board' said in a statement to the press. 'Marxism has always been a part of the Labour Party, it will continue to remain so. The right wing's attempted purge and witch hunt will be defeated.'

Despite the resistance, Ron Hayward and David Hughes conducted their enquiry and reported to a meeting of the NEC on 23 June, 1982. Ron, ever one for recognising the big occasion, began by announcing that following concerns about leaks to the press, he had himself supervised the typing, copying and despatch of copies of the report to NEC members. While that seemed to us mods as a recipe for disaster, we still voted to proceed when the lefties tried unsuccessfully to delay things. Then there was a moment of true black comedy when Benn suddenly announced that he had seen someone on the roof placing television equipment to record what we were saying. I scoffed at this and upset them enormously. It was then solemnly resolved that the broadcaster responsible be asked to remove their equipment.

Then, the light relief over, we turned to the Hayward–Hughes report on Militant, which concluded that it was 'a well-organised caucus, centrally controlled . . . and with its own programme and policy for separate and distinctive propaganda'. After all his shilly-shallying and years of delay, Hayward had finally been forced to admit the blindingly obvious.

So far, so good. As ever, however, there was a snag. Nothing in this saga was ever straightforward. Patrick Seyd in his book *The Rise and Fall of the Left* put the difficulty in a nutshell: 'A problem for the report's authors was that any proposal to ban the group on the grounds that it contravened Clause II section [3] of the Party constitution would have led to demands for the expulsion of other groups which also had their own programme and distinctive propaganda.'

The problem of separating out many of the internal groups to which we belonged, Manifesto and Solidarity for example, from Militant was to plague us throughout the months to come. The solution, the report suggested, was to create 'a register of non-affiliated groups of members to be recognised and allowed to operate within the Party'. All such groups must apply to and be acceptable to the NEC. Certain principles would have to apply – all groups must be open, democratic and certainly not secret, operating their own discipline nor be associated with any international organisation not supported by the Labour Party or the Socialist International. The register would be updated annually and include details of the aims, officers, employees, membership and accounts of recognised groups. Any group infringing the rules would be given up to three months to comply – or, together with the individuals involved, be liable to disciplinary action under the Constitution and Rules of the Party.

Then, crucially, the Hayward–Hughes Report declared: 'If the NEC accepts the above recommendations, it is our opinion that the Militant Tendency as presently constituted would not be eligible to be included on the proposed register in the light of our findings.' Foot immediately moved to accept the report, saying we had a duty to protect the constitution, and I seconded him, declaring that we would never get the working class vote back if we didn't take action against Militant.

Predictably, both Heffer and Benn moved to reject the report. It became quite clear that we would win, however, when Joan Lestor declared that – although she had voted against having an enquiry – she supported having a register. Kinnock also spoke in favour, arguing that

Militant was an organisational menace. Benn in a long rambling speech – though not as long or rambling as Eric's amendment – asked: 'Are we to be told by Denis Healey, who doesn't even support Party policy and who is going to examine those who do, to decide who can stay in the Party?' 'I have been a member of the Labour Party for forty years and I shall die an unregistered socialist,' he added. 'I will not register and CLPs will not expel.'

Naturally all the rest of the hard left had wanted to get in on the act and, before Michael wound up, we had to suffer the tedium of Jo Richardson, Laurence Coates, Dennis Skinner and Eric Clarke all going through the motions by speaking against.

Replying to attacks that he was now doing to others what had been done to him, Foot pointed out that Militant was a party, a secret conspiracy with paid organisers, and the Bevanites were not. 'Tony,' he said, 'has raised a lot of red herrings which were absolutely laughable.'

After defeating Heffer and Benn, Foot's motion was carried by 16 to 10, with just Doug Hoyle abstaining.[13] In a rearguard action, the hard left tried unsuccessfully to put off the implementation of the decision. Again, though, they did manage – these exponents of open government – to prevent publication of the evidence.

It was, Benn recorded, 'a horrible meeting'. For him maybe, but not for me and the brothers. We were finally on our way.

The backlash from CLPD was bitter and fierce. I gave the 1982 prize for hypocrisy, though, to their allies on the Labour Co-ordinating Committee for their statement: 'Witch hunts, slates, expulsions and other attempts to manipulate the Party's electoral and policy making machinery for sectional gain should cease'. A bit rich, said some of us, having seen how the left had manipulated things to their own advantage year after year. At the pre-Conference meeting on 26 September, 1982 the NEC decided to opposed the left's planted amendments to defer a decision on a register for 12 months.

The Tribune Group, as ever, was split – as was CLPD – on whether they should follow Benn and refuse to comply with the NEC. Within CLPD, Frances Morrell, Reg Race and Chris Mullin took a hard line but they were beaten by 12 votes to 11 on their Executive, which agreed to accept the registration procedure. Despite the splits among their leaders, the left was nonetheless still able to mobilise a great deal of support. A Militant rally at Wembley, to which Benn and Les Huckfield sent messages of support, attracted 3,000 people. The majority of CLPs opposed the register and union conferences carried motions against expulsions and witch hunts.

Despite all their efforts, when the 1982 Conference debated Militant on the Monday afternoon, we were fairly confident of victory. Whether we could have won so easily, or at all, had we put the issue of expulsion of Militant members more explicitly is more questionable. Later, Militant made much of the fact that: 'nine out of ten CLPs voted against the register. In the case of a number of big trade unions whose block votes were vital to the acceptance of the register, their votes were cast contrary to clear policy decisions by their annual conferences or national executive committees. The votes of the TGWU, for instance, were cast against the clear rejection of the register by that union's executive. The votes of the GMWU, NUM, USDAW and the TGWU were cast against the clear rejection of bans, proscriptions, and any witch hunt at their annual conferences'. On this, Militant were right – this was a clear victory for 'fixing' rather than persuasion.

The Enquiry had found that *Militant* was not just a newspaper, but an organised faction with its own long-term programme, principles and policy, a substantial number of full-time organisers, and its own publishing house, Cambridge Heath Press. It had its own caucuses in several trade unions, owned the fund-raising company WIR Publications Ltd, which had raised hundreds of thousands of pounds, and had its own international network, too.

The evidence for these statements came from its own published documents, from minute books and records, from statements made by former and present Militant members and from the Labour Party Regional staff. It was, however, fundamental to the report that we distinguished between the inner circle and the wider circle of Militant sympathisers.

At Conference, Jim Mortimer opened the debate with a lengthy diatribe against the Militant conspiracy. 'We are not initiating a witch-hunt or a purge. We are upholding the rules and constitution,' he concluded. Later, in October, Militant challenged the NEC's arguments, but they did not bother to do so in the debate.

As we moved in for the kill, two of the St Ermin's Group stalwarts Roy Grantham and John Spellar moved the crucial Composite Motion 48, supported by the NEC, stating that:

> Conference re-affirms that the NEC has a duty to declare that organisations not in conformity with [the] Constitution are incompatible with membership of the Labour Party. Conference further believes that only by taking firm action can we reassure our voters of our commitment to democratic socialism and thus defeat the Tories at the next election.

'When and if Militant fails to comply we demand that the editorial board must go, that the paid sellers go, and that the Militant prospective candidates be removed,' Grantham told Conference, outlining the moderates' uncompromising bottom line.

'Militant have a perfectly legitimate right to organise a Trotskyist party in this country,' Spellar followed up from the rostrum. 'They have a perfectly legitimate right to put their views to the electorate of this country, and a right to get the derisory number of votes that such parties have always had. What they do not have a right to do is to live parasitically inside this democratic socialist Party. Parasites can live compatibly with some hosts, but some parasites kill the body they live in – and Militant is killing us with the electorate. In this discussion there will be talk of witch hunts, and there have been some witch hunts in this party over recent years – witch hunts of ordinary, decent party members, decent councillors, decent MPs.'

Then came the turn of Alan Sapper of the TUC Left Group to move Composite 49, appeasing Militant by opposing 'all bans, proscriptions, witch hunts and proscribed lists in the belief that continuing democratic debate must operate freely in the Labour Party . . . Conference therefore firmly rejects the proposal to maintain a 'register' from which some Party members would be debarred.'

'The same right wingers who are behind this witch hunt were in the same organisation that campaigned for Labour victory with Owen, with Williams, with Rodgers,' Sapper continued. 'They are still friends with these people. Hattersley said the other day that he would like to welcome them back. At the same time as he wants to expel socialists from the Party. The truth is this. He not only wants to bring them back, he wants to bring back their policies, the policies that lost us the last general election. They want to reverse the decision on reselection, on the election of the Leader, on unilateral nuclear disarmament. This is what it is all about comrades. This is not a constitutional issue; it is a political issue. They want to reverse all the gains we have made over the last two years. This is what these comrades are up to. They have lost the political argument, and now they seek by organisational means to keep their grip over the Party'.[14]

The debate, as ever, was rough and – for those who did not know how the union vote was already lined up – extremely tense. Delegate Ricky Ormonde from Cardiff South East was right up there with Spellar: 'Militant are dishonest. I would say to the men on the platform: take off the kid gloves, stop pussy-footing around and do what thousands of Labour supporters in the country are crying out for you to do.' Reg Underhill, who had fought courageously against Militant for years, asked simply from the rostrum: 'Why do Militant deny the truth?'

In truth, at this Conference they didn't. They skirted round the issues. For the left, Martin Flannery argued that Militant was an irrelevancy and a very small irrelevancy. Pat Wall, the Militant parliamentary candidate, trotted out the standard Militant line, arguing that the unions had no authority to vote for the NEC position.

Foot, winding up for the NEC, said that he had moved the motion on the NEC because of the weight of evidence. It was not a witch hunt, it was defending the constitution. With the union vote sorted, the St Ermin's motion was duly carried by 5,087,000 votes to 1,851,000 and the left defeated by an even bigger margin – 5,227,000 to 1,645,000.

The problem was that, while we won at Conference, we now hit stormier seas when Militant cut up rough on the legal front, as our rule book was deficient. Unfortunately, to say the least, it gave us no power to expel members of an organisation within the Labour Party. Militant gained legal advice that the register was unconstitutional and expulsions could be challenged in the courts. It continued to deny, of course, that it had any organisation but by now no-one believed them. Sadly, in November, we received legal advice of our own that we could not proceed against Militant, as we wanted – the rule book as it stood just did not permit it.

This was a terrible blow – not only to me, but also to those in the St Ermin's and the Tufton Court Groups. Instead of initiating a bloodbath at the next 'Org', as I would have ideally wished, at Foot's suggestion I moved that the General Secretary report to the next NEC meeting, recommending how we should proceed in the light of the legal advice. Heffer countered by proposing we meet with Militant instead, but was defeated by 12 votes to 5. Benn meanwhile moved not to proceed at all, but was defeated by 13 votes to 5. My proposal was carried by the same measure – and so we started again.

At the next NEC, we considered the new report from Jim Mortimer together with a letter from the Militant Editorial Board, dated 23 November, 1982. Mortimer, in introducing his report, referred to two basic points in the legal advice to the party: [i] that the NEC was obliged to act in accordance with the Rules and Constitution of the Party and [ii] that the NEC must observe 'natural justice' in any proposed disciplinary action against groups of Labour Party members.

Foot, however, generally supported Jim Mortimer's report. Although this knocked the stuffing out of us, we could only go as far as Foot and his friends would go. The winning of votes was everything, gestures nothing. My philosophy was that it was better to get something than nothing.

So we went through the report, paragraph by cautious paragraph. After making proposals for constitutional change, Mortimer concluded that, 'while many electors wanted action against Militant, many in the Party were opposed . . . It would play into the hands of the 'Militant Tendency' if by our action we now contributed to the switching of the debate to wider expulsions. The preferable course is to concentrate attention on the central organising group and then to win other sympathisers of 'Militant' by the strength of our arguments.'

This, of course, was totally incompatible with what APEX and the EETPU had expected from the passing of their motion. Grantham and Spellar wanted the heads not only of the Militant Board on platters, but also those of the paid sellers and Militant's parliamentary candidates.

As Mortimer's report pointed out, however, not only did we not have the names of sellers, but merely selling the newspaper was not a ground for expulsion. He recommended, therefore, deferring action. There was no way that we could vote for this and so, playing for time, we resolved that this paragraph and the accompanying recommendation be deleted

We were also in trouble over the question of the parliamentary candidates. Michael Crick in his book *The March of Militant* wrote:

Quite a few NEC right-wingers blamed John Golding for not taking more advantage of the majority they had on the NEC and felt strongly that bad planning on Golding's part allowed Militant to get away. Some regretted that they left it to Golding to co-ordinate their work and privately one or two later felt that they might be better off without him. If the right had been determined, there is little doubt that the parliamentary candidates could have been dropped. The NEC can choose to abandon any candidate it liked and can override the wishes of the constituency party concerned. The problem then would have been the reaction of local parties, and ultimately the NEC would have had to impose its own candidates upon the constituencies. As far as Militant was concerned, all the right could do was to follow the cautious lead of Jim Mortimer and Michael Foot.

This, however, was ill-informed nonsense. While it is true that my fellow hard-core right-wingers – Betty Boothroyd, Ken Cure and Denis Howell – were very discontented about the lack of progress we were making and would happily tell this to whoever would listen, the majority of our group were as cautious as Mortimer. It was not true that the rules provided for the candidates to be dropped. Oh, that they had contained such a provision! We could easily stop candidates from being endorsed, but once endorsed we could not remove them. Unfortunately, Michael Crick is the sort of barrack room lawyer who had plagued my life since I first took office in the Labour Party and unions – friendly, imaginative, inventive, ingenious and wrong.

The reality was that we had lost the battle over endorsement at the beginning of 1982. In February, 1982, when the candidature of Terry Fields arose, with Healey's help I tried to delay his endorsement until the Militant enquiry was finished, but we were beaten by 13 votes to 3.[15]

At the 'Org' on 8 March, I moved with Betty's support 'that consideration for endorsement as prospective parliamentary Labour candidates of self-confessed supporters of the Militant Tendency be deferred until after decisions have been taken on the enquiry report'. This time, we were beaten by 13 votes to 5.

By September, 1982, too, although I was still saying it was totally wrong for supporters of Lenin and Trotsky to be standing for Labour, it was clear we were going to have difficulty if any of their by now eight parliamentary candidates denied that they were part of the Militant 'inner circle'.

For good measure, Mortimer's report named the eight Militant candidates. Along with Fields, they were – Edward Harrison (Liverpool Edge Hill), Derek Hatton (Liverpool Wavertree), Tony Mulhearne (Liverpool Toxteth), Cathy Wilson (Isle of Wight), Dave Nellist (Coventry South East), Rob Finch (Brighton Kemptown) and Pat Wall (Bradford North). Jim was certainly 'edgy' on the whole subject of parliamentary candidates, however. After naming them, he wrote:

> If the suggested notice of motion on the 'Militant Tendency' is adopted, the named candidates should have the opportunity to reply to the allegations or claims made about them. They should be asked for their observations on the allegation or claim that they are associated with the 'Militant Tendency'. If the notice of motion on the 'Militant Tendency' is adopted by the NEC, the named candidates should be asked to give an undertaking that forthwith they will not promote the 'Militant Tendency'. Their replies should be considered fairly by the NEC.

As a stiffener, I secured the inclusion of past as well as present Militant members by 12 votes to 11 with Foot, Kinnock and John Evans voting against. Mortimer's recommendations on the candidates having been amended in the way I wanted, they were put to the vote and carried by 13 votes to 9, with Kinnock abstaining. This time Foot voted with us and Evans against.

The General Secretary's report was then endorsed by 15 to 8 (Judith Hart was missing), with a long preamble setting out the case against Militant and concluding: 'Accordingly, the National Executive Committee declares the 'Militant Tendency to be ineligible for affiliation to the Party.'

To satisfy the lawyers it was also decided that this motion should be placed on the agenda for either the December, 1982 or January, 1983 meeting of the NEC, that members of the editorial board of Militant should be informed and be given the opportunity to make representations to the NEC and that any appeal against a disciplinary decision of the NEC could be made to the Annual Conference of the Party. This, of course, was for the benefit of the judges, so we could show that 'due process' had been observed. The intention, of course, of us mods was to show them no mercy, just as they had made so many decent Labour members' lives a misery.

A game of legal cat and mouse followed. On 6 December, 1982, we considered a letter from *Militant*'s Editorial Board seeking conditions for a meeting with the NEC that month. They asked for copies of the resolutions, NEC papers and other documents. They also demanded a clear explanation of the 'claimed constitutional basis' of the disciplinary measures against Militant and, amongst other things, an assurance that the meeting would not discuss their expulsion from the Labour Party. For good measure too they added that 'if the NEC had proposed to the 1982 Conference that the Party should revive the old systems of bans and proscriptions, there is no doubt it would have been overwhelmingly defeated'. The NEC agreed to none of these demands, whereupon on 9 December Militant responded that they were coming 'under protest' but wanted details of specific allegations, evidence and opportunity to state their case They repeated that the NEC had no authority for expulsions and their warning that they might go to the courts.

On the 10 December, too, Mortimer received solicitors' letters on Militant's behalf, stating that they were indeed applying to the High Court for an order restraining the NEC, until such time as their clients had been given full particulars of the evidence. Another letter asked for the evidence and yet another for an adjournment of two days until after receipt of the evidence. At the NEC on 15 December, however, an attempt by Skinner to stop us going ahead was defeated by 17 votes to 11.

The atmosphere nonetheless was tense. As I recorded in my 'Diary of an MP':

At the NEC, we began on tenterhooks because Militant had applied for an injunction against us in the courts the day before and the result was not

350

known. It was about 11 am before the news came that the judge had thrown out Militant's claim. Although we did not know it at the time, it was a close-run thing. We had escaped, it appears, only because Militant did not ask in a reasonable time after the adoption of the Hayward-Hughes report and had failed to answer questions for three months.

At the NEC, legal advice was then given on how to conduct the business. After much further skirmishing from the left, with my support again Foot successfully moved that the procedure advised by the General Secretary be accepted. The left vote of 9 against included the hardy annuals like Benn and Heffer, of course, but this time they were joined by the newcomer among the left line-up, Tom Sawyer. Great buckets of whitewash have since been used on Tom – all I know is that then he did everything he could with the hard left to make it impossible for us to take action.

The *Militant* Editorial Board – Peter Taaffe, Ted Grant, Lynne Walsh, Clare Doyle and Keith Dickinson – then came in to address the NEC. Again, however, they did not seriously attempt to answer the charges that they were a separate organisation within the Labour Party and so against its Constitution. All they did was to threaten us with trouble if we took action. Had they threatened me with boredom, I might have trembled, but trouble is what we thrived on.

The drama mounted. At the chair's request, they then withdrew. After some discussion of their comments, the procedure was settled and *Militant*'s Editorial Board came back into the meeting. After the reading of a solicitors' letter, each of the Militants made comments and again withdrew.

The 'old firm' of Foot and Golding then moved and seconded a motion declaring the Militant Tendency ineligible for affiliation to the Party. In response, Heffer, Audrey Wise and Laurence Coates moved a very long amendment declaring that the NEC had no authority to act against Militant. Benn and Skinner, for their part, moved a very short one stating that no action should be taken. After the usual barney, our motion was carried and the two amendments were each lost by 18 to 9.

For me, it was certainly a morning to remember, but it was too early to start whistling yet. Into New Year, 1983 and Militant's solicitors warned us on 7 January not to take decisions at our meeting of the 'Org' three days hence. They challenged, too, the decision we had just taken in December. At the 'Org', while we beat off yet another motion urging no further action, following legal advice we were forced to defer consideration of Jim Mortimer's paper *Militant Tendency – The Next Step* until the full NEC. This was interpreted by the media as a sign that the moderates were weakening. But this was nonsense, as having talked to a majority of them, I knew that the will to act against Militant was as strong as ever.

The problem was that, as ever, Mortimer's paper was not as robust as it might have been. While it confirmed that the resolution carried in December made 'all members of the Militant Tendency ineligible for membership of the Labour Party', it wobbled on the way in which this should be implemented.

One option, he wrote, would be to proceed with the process of expulsion. This would involve individual notice of the charge and opportunity to reply, which 'should be considered fairly'. Expulsion, however, would meet with other difficulties. It would have to have a firm definition of 'membership' for starters. Secondly, the courts might ask to see the evidence. It was unlikely that any Militant would make the same mistake as it had when it applied to late for its injunction. The third and perhaps most important difficulty was that it exposed an inconsistency in Party practice over the eligibility of organisations to affiliate. Since 1973, the NEC could reject small, single-purpose organisations, yet no attempt had been made to declare the members of those groups ineligible for individual membership of the Party. In short, our custom and practice might have been shot to pieces in the courts.

The second option open was to request the dissolution of the 'Militant Tendency' as a party within the Labour Party. If this were adopted, and accepted by the Editorial Board, there would be no expulsions and 'Militant' would continue to exist as a weekly journal.

Having heard all this, following legal advice, Foot and I successfully moved procedures which would make it possible to expel Militants without being successfully challenged in the courts. I then moved, and Gwyneth Dunwoody seconded, a motion to take action against the Editorial Board. Benn, Richardson and Wise again tried to put off the action but were once again beaten – by 18 votes to 8.

The day of reckoning was near. Militant again tried their damnedest to stave off execution. Before the NEC on 12 February, the Editorial Board requested a deferral of the decision over their expulsion. Rejected, they issued a writ to declare 'that the NEC has acted unconstitutionally in declaring the Militant Tendency ineligible for affiliation to the party, and will try to stop the expulsion of the Editorial Board.'

When it came to the meeting, there was a real bust up between Benn and Sam McCluskie over a document from Benn, which had allegedly not been circulated. While I enjoyed Sam attacking Benn in a language that the Westminster schoolboy couldn't make head nor tail of, I quickly killed off this nonsense by moving the meeting on to the real meat. The General Secretary, I moved, should open the questioning of the Editorial Board, they should be allowed to make individual statements and then questions should then be allowed from NEC members. Denis Howell said it was monstrous to put questions and there were other comments from Foot and the Black Widow, but nobody on our side was really listening. We were waiting for the enemy.

Jim Mortimer put the questions and Peter Taaffe replied for them all to begin with. While accepting that they published the paper *Militant*, they denied that there was a Militant Tendency, challenged the 'secret evidence' and said that organisational measures against ideas would fail. One by one, the others joined in the protest. 'I have worked in the Party I am not a careerist. This is a show trial,' Lynne Walsh exclaimed, while Clare Doyle, Keith Dickinson and Ted Grant made comments to the effect that 'the rank and file are on our side – we will be back when the right have joined the SDP and the Tories'.

After nearly two hours of cross-examination, the five left defiantly. 'We intend to fight this decision throughout the length and breadth of the Labour movement,' Taaffe told the waiting media, warning of High Court writs to come. It was the last convulsions of a vampire impaled on the wooden stake. Of course, he knew the writing was finally on the wall. Inside, the obligatory attempt was again being made by Heffer and Richardson, strongly supported by Sawyer, to postpone a decision. Alex Kitson, however, railed passionately against delay: 'They deny there is an organisation, but one of them is a member of my family and I know there is an organisation,' he said.

The diehard eight, plus Tom Sawyer, voted with Militant but there were 19 votes to proceed. By the same margin, the meeting went on to agree to my motion, seconded by Neville Hough, that the five should 'be expelled forthwith'. Foot spoke out in favour of the expulsions and voted with us. 'We have taken a wise decision,' I told the press afterwards, with barely concealed elation. We had finally nailed Militant the most pernicious, evil and dangerous bunch of them all.

It was still not quite over, however. The intimidation, for one, barely ceased. On 3 March, 1983 Peter Taaffe had the gall to hold a Militant meeting in my constituency, Newcastle-under-Lyme. 'John Golding is one of a group of right wing Labour members whose policies have been tried and tested and failed,' he told the assembled comrades. 'He has been one of the main organisers of the right-wing of the NEC and he is behind the drive to expel Militant supporters . . . We will not go away and still regard ourselves as members of the Labour Party and we will be re-admitted'. His visit to Newcastle was part of a nationwide campaign, but he hasn't in fact yet come back. I suppose, though, that 20 years is a short time in politics.

The legal barrage also continued. We received threatening letters from the solicitors and writs, which meant that we had to defer further discussions on Militant. This included a proposal of mine to create a sub-committee to consider further action against Militant members. It was, however, not taken and so we went into the general election with Militant candidates. Right up to the summer, too, Heffer – fearful as ever of the comrades in Liverpool – fought an unsuccessful rearguard action to keep in the 'infamous five'.

And then we came to the Annual Conference in 1983, the ultimate appeal body against NEC decisions, or the last refuge of the desperate, depending on your point of view. Again, Taaffe spoke first. Again, he denied there was an organisation. 'Do not think that the expulsion of five people is the end of the matter. We will not go out and form a separate party or any nonsense like that,' he ranted. 'We still consider ourselves as members of the Party and we will fight to get back in. We will be rehabilitated into this Party when those who are demanding our expulsion are in the rogues' gallery with the Browns and other traitors to this movement,' he railed, to the comrades' applause.

'I would ask Jim Mortimer again,' Lynne Walsh shouted.

Why is it that we have never, never been allowed to see one piece of this evidence in order to reply to the charges that have been made? We have been attacked for going to the courts, but if we had not taken legal action it is absolutely clear that we would have been expelled forthwith . . . Remember that Denis Healey, John Golding and others boasted that hundreds of Militant supporters would be expelled from the Party immediately after last year's Conference.

However when we went to the NEC, we were confronted with what could only be described as a kangaroo court. No detailed charges, no evidence, no questions and no discussion were allowed in that meeting. In effect, comrades, we were allowed a few last words before the NEC executed a pre-determined sentence as far as the five were concerned.

Keith Dickinson spoke of his support for unilateralism. Clare Doyle defended Militant's finances. Ted Grant referred to the constitutional reforms: 'There is no way you will succeed with these expulsions. We will be back. We will be restored if not in one year, in two or three years. We will be back. At every trade union conference, at every ward, at every GMC, at every shop stewards committee meeting this question will come up and we will be back.'

Despite the applause, Mortimer took the speeches head on. He spelt out what was as plain as daylight about Militant, the organised conspiracy within the Labour Party. Conference had instructed the NEC to enforce the constitution and that is what they had done. Opportunities had been given to Militant to express their point of view but they did not reply within the three months. Only after Conference had approved the Hayward-Hughes report did they ask to discuss the matter with the NEC. They had the opportunity twice to appear before the NEC even though they were taking legal action. They were given the opportunity to appeal to Conference, although they had no defined right to do so.

'The distinctive nature of the Militant Tendency is that they are a Trotskyite entryist group,' Mortimer told delegates. 'We could not publish the evidence because of advice from lawyers that we should not do so because, with the legal threat posed by Militant, the matter could go before the courts.'

At the end of Mortimer's speech there was a ten minute break so that the all important union delegations could take decisions. Then five card votes were taken – one for each of them – which resulted in the expulsion of the entire *Militant* Editorial Board.

The smallest margin, for the record, was the expulsion of Ted Grant – by 4,972,000 votes to 1,790,000. In other words, Conference's endorsement was overwhelming.

Having seen the way the votes were stacked, the delegate for Tottenham moved that the rest of the debate on Militant and witch hunts be abandoned in favour of more important business, but the unions would have none of that. They wanted blood. After the usual attacks from the left, Jack Straw declared that carrying of pro-Militant motions would 'deal this Party a near mortal blow'.

Russell Tuck, who as Chairman of the 'Org' had done so much for this victory, made it clear that it would not be out of order to read Militant – only to sell it! John Maxton described graphically how badly Militant had behaved in his constituency during the general election.

'Nobody in this party is witch hunting,' he said. 'A witch hunt means one of two things. In its original sense it means hunting little old ladies for no reason except for their mildly offensive behaviour. In its modern sense it means persecuting people who have committed no offence, giving them no trial, no hearing and no ability to defend themselves. The Party has not done that to Militant. The Party has given Militant every opportunity to defend itself.'

Jack, Russell and John each spoke against a background of slow handclaps and barracking as they forced home the case against Militant. For all the shouting, however, the delegates knew the size of the vote meant that Militant was finished as a national force in the Labour Party. The days of Trotskyite bullying were numbered.

TWENTY-FIVE

The Fall of Benn

The 1983 Conference also marked the effective end of Benn's career as a politician of any influence within the Labour Party. Kinnock was determined that Benn would never again call the tune and he did not. Despite all the intrigue, all the manoeuvring, all the efforts – which, by his own account, left him so often physically exhausted, depressed and disenchanted – and despite all the changes to the Labour Party constitution to help achieve his ambitions, Benn had failed to become either Leader or, for that matter, Deputy Leader.

One by one, the left wing organisations which he used so effectively became disenchanted with him and fell apart, whilst the right adopted their tactics and organised effectively to take power and influence away from him. On the left, by the way, Benn's relations with the Communists were not as friendly as they were with Militant (the commies were very anti-Trot). He saw the old communists as very conservative and they viewed him as a crackpot. Eric Hobsbawm, for one, thought Benn had lost his marbles. His proposed oath of loyalty for Tribune Group candidates, of course, greatly upset the dwindling number of MPs on his side.

The history of the Labour Party is not just about factions – important though they were – it is also about personalities. And to understand this troubled period you need to realise not only the undoubted talents and charisma of Anthony Wedgwood Benn, but also his deep flaws and weaknesses. Without these fatal flaws, he would undoubtedly have been celebrated as one of the great leaders of the Labour Party, rather than remembered as someone who did so much damage to it.

One of these failings was an inability to get on with those around him who were, at the very least, his equals. On reading, for example, his own account of the Sunday evening dinners held by left wing ministers during the Callaghan government, it is clear that he was incapable of keeping up reasonable relationships with his peers. While they were doing their level best to keep the ship afloat, Benn was doing his best to sink it or at least disassociate himself from any responsibility.

He constantly makes disparaging remarks about his colleagues. He described Albert Booth, a most effective Secretary of State and shrewd thinker, for example, as a 'sort of clockwork teddy bear' and Foot variously as 'a dogsbody', 'a stuffed dummy who contributes nothing' or else 'entirely an establishment figure'. A document of Foot's is 'absolute, rootless liberal claptrap' and time after time he says he is 'completely finished with him'.

Of course this antipathy was hardly one-sided. In one bitter row as far back as October, 1977 Benn recorded that Foot blew his top and shouted 'face the real problems – you have got to help the lower paid.' He was red with anger'. The rows with Foot were endless partly because Benn would never face up to the real problems of the day, but more so because his accounts of the Callaghan government were inaccurate, to say the least.

It was not only Foot who found it difficult to deal in straight terms with Benn. Three other Labour leaders – Wilson, Callaghan and Kinnock – found him impossible to get on with. Indeed, Wilson even made reference to Benn's 'lunatic eyes' on TV – although, obviously thinking of m'learned friends, he quickly changed this to 'wide staring eyes'. It is obvious, too, that from 1968 Benn had an equally low opinion of Wilson.

Callaghan, whom some of us thought was far too tolerant to political opponents, also quickly got fed up with him. He just could not fathom why Benn did not use his influence for the good of the Party. Jim hated the way, too, that Benn deliberately used the NEC and Conference to undermine the Labour government. In 1977, for example, Benn refused to go along with Callaghan and Jack Jones to discuss ways in which we could avoid yet more own goals through a bad Conference.

Benn also records a nasty row over Europe in July, 1977. 'Jim, red-faced, pointed his finger at me. 'You are working against us'. Then in the following November, Benn's aide Meacher left a photocopy of a letter on a machine in the Commons which a Tory found and handed in to Callaghan's office. It summoned a meeting in Benn's office on the Direct Elections Bill of recalcitrant ministers. Jim, incensed, ordered Benn to cancel the meeting. During the Lib–Lab pact, Benn also made it extremely difficult for those, including union leaders, who were desperately trying to save the Labour government.

His relations with Kinnock were always edgy. As early as 1978, while commending one of Neil's speeches, Benn says it made him feel slightly uneasy. Then in early 1980 there was much reporting that the soft left – Hart, Kinnock, Renee Short and Doug Hoyle – were fed up with Benn and had decided to break away from the hard left and join up with the mods on the NEC. Despite Kinnock's 'constant and troubled denials', Benn said that he thought that there was something in the story, but wanted to remain friendly with Kinnock.

That friendliness certainly did not survive the events of April, 1981, when Benn bounced the soft left by announcing his candidature for the Deputy Leadership. Nor when Benn made life more and more difficult for Foot. In June 1983, Benn declared that he had no intention of supporting Kinnock for Leader. Kinnock in turn announced publicly that he didn't want Benn elected to any chairmanship, let alone to that of the Home Policy Committee. After the election, Neil's remarks about Benn were scathing.

Benn's ruthless disregard of the people around him meant that in the Cabinet, Shadow Cabinet and PLP he was detested. Benn, indeed, continually records this loathing in his Diaries. He rowed, time after time, with people in the tea room. Once, at the time of the SDP defections, he even got involved in a fracas with the ultra-respectable Leo Abse, MP for Pontypool, in the Division Lobby. Abse had just overheard Benn making one of his trademark snide remarks about the right: 'Well, the Labour Party is now led by two groups of people: those who want to leave the Party in order to fight it and those who want to stay in the Party in order to fight it.' Leo then told Benn plainly that he was destroying the Party. 'After more words,' Benn recorded,' everybody crowded round: the clerks in the Lobby heard every word of it and I came home feeling slightly distressed at the bitterness in the Parliamentary Party'.

Benn caused yet another row when in October, 1981 with a group of hard left MPs, he produced a draft joint statement to be issued by Tribune Group candidates for the Shadow Cabinet. This caused tremendous resentment and Norman Buchan told Benn it was Stalinism. This intellectual discussion, again in the Division Lobby, continued with Buchan shouting at Benn: 'Over 20 years, you've just been out for yourself. You are arrogant and you think Party policy belongs to you.' Equally rigorously, Benn replied: 'Oh, get stuffed.'

Other members proffered him advice more quietly. On one occasion, Alf Dubs and Jack Straw brought home to Benn how much support he had lost in the PLP as a result of his actions and Benn resolved to be more patient. Shortly afterwards in 1981, too, Robin Cook told him that he was becoming isolated with the far left and out of touch. Benn reflected, of course, that 'parliamentary opinion is getting out of touch with the Party, but I get on very well with Robin Cook and I like him. I listened carefully to what he said.'

He wasn't always as tolerant. In December 1980, sitting beside Benn in the House, Dale Campbell-Savours, the MP for Workington, told him that when he arrived in 1979, he was a Benn supporter. Since then, however, he had found him so dogmatic and bitter, that he no longer was. 'I did turn on him, because I had actually had enough,' Benn recalled his response. 'I don't see why all of these MPs should sit about in the Tea Room, read the newspapers and believe every word. I rather lectured him.'

The lecture obviously went in one ear and came out the other, because many months later Dale, together with fellow MPs David Clark and Derek Foster, had yet another go at him. Once again he reminded Benn of what a hated figure he had become, bringing the Party to the brink of disaster. What, Dale asked, was Benn going to do about it?

Dale's views were pretty typical of the PLP, from which Benn was almost totally alienated at this time. Benn's own Diaries show had bad it had all become. 'The PLP meeting at 5 was most unpleasant. There was a backlash against the Conference,' Benn wrote on one occasion. 'I stayed at home all day. I must admit that, just at the moment, I feel such an outcast from the PLP that it is hard to face going into the House. I don't go there unless I have to.' It is not surprising that by the end of 1982, too, on going to a party across the Thames, he was writing: 'There was a sense that County Hall was the bastion of liberty and socialism across the river from the House of Commons.'

Benn's isolation within the PLP can also be seen from his failure to get elected to the Shadow Cabinet, except as the runner-up in the event of a vacancy. In 1979 he refused to stand, saying he wanted the freedom of the backbenches. When in the following year, he stood and failed to get on by two votes, Terry Lancaster wrote in the *Mirror*: 'Last night his colleagues gave him that freedom again . . . in effect this was a vote of no confidence by the majority of Labour MPs in the man frequently tipped as a future Party leader.' The *Daily Mail*, too, quoted me as saying: 'This shows that the Parliamentary Labour Party has no faith in Benn. He cannot command respect or support.' And that situation continued. In 1981, he got only 66 votes; in 1982 he was beaten by 7 votes; and in 1983, of course, he wasn't even there to stand.

Is it any wonder that following the 1983 Conference Benn was writing: 'I am very depressed at the way I am slipping further and further into the political wilderness, and Caroline isn't very happy.' Benn went into the wilderness, however, because he lost the trust and respect of the bulk of people around him.

For a time his speeches were taken at face value. People were impressed by their verve and delivery and were persuaded by their content. And then the penny dropped. Benn's interpretations, to say the least, did not match the facts. Benn's attacks on the Callaghan government and the making of the 1979 manifesto had a big impact on people in the Party and the unions who heard them. The problem was that they just didn't ring true.

Even when this was demonstrated beyond doubt, Benn would never put the record straight. The myths he created continued. He mouthed the need for political virtue, yet behaved most disgracefully himself – to the point when many of us came to despise him for his hypocrisy. As John Morris once explained, to loud cheers in a PLP meeting, if a Conference decision went against Benn he would vow to fight again year after year; if someone else opposed a Conference decision, however, they were attacked by Benn as being against the Party. He would call on people to work for a united Party and then back policies he knew would be divisive.

Benn also called for more 'democracy', but opposed 'one member, one vote'. As Jon Akass of the *Sun* wrote at the time of the 1980 Conference, Benn believed that 'Democracy must end at the General Management Committee'. 'More people believe in flying saucers than attend constituency management committees . . . to regard these good people as grass–roots democrats, representing the millions who vote Labour, is as daft as regarding every saucer spotter as an astronomer.'

His public statements on reselection, too, were at variance with his urging of tolerance. The left's publication of a hit list of MPs who had not voted for Benn caused many more to question his sincerity. So too also did his refusal to allow the NEC to examine material on Militant, while he constantly campaigned for a Freedom of Information Act.

And while he was professing loyalty to his Bristol seat, he was already casting around for a safer berth. George Galloway had been asked to look for a new seat for him in Scotland. When in December, 1980, he suggested Livingston, Benn remarked: 'The sooner the invitation comes from one of the wards in the new Livingston constituency the better, and if I were adopted there before the selection conferences in Bristol I would be able to say that since I didn't want to cause any bitterness in Bristol, and since my seat had gone, the proper thing for me to do would be to move to another seat.'

It was never difficult for him to believe one thing and say another. At meetings he would call for industrial democracy but either fail to implement it – and Labour Party HQ is a case in point – or in private actually condemn it. In December, 1978 while discussing a steel closure, Eric Varley pointed out that the six elected steelworkers on the British Steel supported the boss Charles Villiers. Benn wrote: 'Of course, this is exactly what workers opposed to having representatives on company boards really fear – that they join the management intellectually and cease to represent their men. That is why, in my view, workers on the board are such a disaster.'

Those of us who came to expect these double standards could never take his sermons seriously. It was not only such cynicism which eventually drove more and more people against Benn. They also lost respect because of his crackpot ideas. It was as though he had sudden rushes of blood to the head and couldn't help himself.

He certainly had a great ability to upset people, too, by going out on a limb. In March 1981, for example, he said that the security forces were using Northern Ireland as a test-bed for Britain in the event of unemployment reaching four million. Benn's statements on Ireland, republicanism, the disestablishment of the Church of England, foreign nuclear bases, all touched raw nerves. It was not that he was necessarily wrong – the problem was that he generally went so far over the top that people, and ordinary working people particularly, thought he was barmy.

Gimmicks and gestures were a trade mark of Benn that upset many serious-minded Labour MPs. They remembered, for instance, his proposal to get the Queen to create a thousand peers as a way of dealing with the House of Lords. While we queued in the tea room to ask him to put our names down, John Silkin – the expert on such matters – described the idea as 'too clever by half, just an intellectual gimmick'.

Almost everything Benn said seemed to be for effect. Like Toad of Toad Hall, he always appeared to be chasing the latest fad. In Benn's case, however, it was not cars nor aeroplanes, but political ideas. As he got carried away with the latest book, he would suddenly forget Marx and be taken, for example, with the Levellers (who, I hasten to point out, would always have travelled second class) or Tawney.

Unfortunately, these being mere passing whims, he never came to a real understanding of the implications of any of them. His judgement, generally, was very shaky and never more so than when he commented – on reading a book on Attlee – that there was no real socialism in the 1945 Labour government. He also said of the Callaghan government that, in three and a half years, it had gone from being 'a Labour government with a socialist philosophy and a socialist programme' to being 'half way between having Tory policies and being anti-working class'.

The truth is that he constantly lacked judgement. After the Bristol riots, instead of closing ranks with his fellow Labour MPs and the government – who wanted an internal police enquiry, more resources for St Paul's and a Select Committee to take evidence – he urged instead that the groups who had caused the riot should be able to conduct their own enquiry into the police.

Once again, he found himself out of touch with ordinary people. In the situation which arose in Bristol, he was useless because he always seemed to be incapable of working out compromises which would carry different groups. As he could never unite the Party, because he wanted it Bennite and pure, so he could not reconcile different people in Bristol.

As Benn, for various reasons, neglected parliament from time to time, so he also neglected his constituency. He seemed to act in the mould of those old Tory members who had been gifted a seat and visited it from time to time as an act of benevolence. Reading Benn's Diaries, I was constantly compelled to compare my life as a constituency MP with his. My life at weekends and during parliamentary recesses was spent almost entirely in and around my constituency of Newcastle-under-Lyme. My time was spent constantly mixing with working class people and my social life revolved around the Party and local full-time union officials. Living in the constituency put many pressures on me, but it did mean that I was always aware of the mood of the Labour-voting public.

I say this because life was very different for Anthony Wedgwood Benn. And that difference came to have important political repercussions for Labour as the Party became, under his influence, farther and farther removed from the people.

For a start Benn did not live in Bristol. He lived in Notting Hill Gate and spent his holidays at the second family home at Stansgate in Essex. The people he mixed with were of the ruling class or the loony left. He spent Sunday evenings at dinners rather than working men's clubs. He spent a lot of time outside London, but this was always to address meetings of the faithful.

Outside this circle – the rulers, the loonies, the faithful – the folk he met were generally people in crisis. Between 1978 and 1983, the years covered by this book, he seemed little interested in Bristol. On several occasions, when he reports visiting Bristol by train, his excitement seems to have been more over what he had read or with whom he had travelled, rather than with the visit itself. And the visits often seemed to be brief. On one occasion, on 3 April, 1980, at the time of the riots, Benn was in the House at 9.30 am, went to Bristol for a press conference on the troubles and still got back in time for a tea party to celebrate his 55th birthday.

We see from the Diaries that Benn turns up for surgeries to give advice, attends important funerals and helps groups in trouble, often strikers or pickets. Many activities will certainly have been chopped out by the Diaries' editor but nevertheless the workload in Bristol appears very light. Indeed, as we have seen, he was attacked by his own party for doing too little in his constituency. Benn certainly did appear to be a prophet without honour in his own country. When he went to an NHS Day of Action, at British

Aerospace – the aircraft industry is a mainstay of Bristol's industry – the shop stewards wouldn't let him speak until after the official meeting was over. The steward who gave him a lift told him that the workers at Hawker Siddeley believed he was a Communist and against all defence for the country.

He appears to have done little campaigning for local elections and taken little interest in local council affairs or councillors in Bristol. While he was sickened, too, to find his local party to be in the worst state he remembered in all his 30 years, he decided not to get involved. In September 1979, when he went to see Dawn Primarolo, his CLP secretary, he found her under fire but he thought she would 'pull through'. And this at a time when he was the most powerful and influential man in the Party. In reality, while he supported Militant in constituencies across the country, his sense of responsibility for his own CLP appears to have been nil. While it was in debt, going broke and unable to mend the roof, he spends his time at marches and rallies which made enormous sums of money for CND, Militant and the like.

Benn recognised his unpopularity with the people of Bristol. But he did not see that it arose partly because he seemed to treat them with scant regard. He simply blamed the press for his unpopularity. He saw himself as hounded and persecuted merely because he was challenging the establishment. Journalists certainly did give him a rough time. But he mostly brought it on himself or else they reflected the thoughts of people who knew him, be it the right or 'allies' like Heffer, who would happily sit in Annie's Bar in the House and stick the knife into Benn.

Benn, of course, tried constantly to exploit the media himself. He was, after all, a superb PR man. That was his trade, selling himself to an admiring audience. But the TV and the press came to present a picture of him that varied from the one in his own mind's eye. It reflected the hatred and bitterness of those around him and focused so often on his stupidities. Of course they exaggerated and distorted, but they did not get it completely wrong.

Even his closest associates expressed concerns. His wife appears as a sound critic from time to time, not only of his speeches, but also his capacity for self-deception, for living in a dream world. In December 1981, for example, Caroline is even telling Benn that he is an embarrassment to the left. Frances Morrell, Benn's political adviser – whom he described as 'a difficult woman' – occasionally joined with Caroline to persuade him to behave. Like his wife, Morrell tried to tell Benn he was frightening people, but he would not take notice. For him the applause of his faithful was all. With these alone, he made contact – he was on their wavelength.

What he never understood was the difference between this small minority and the vast majority of non-political, non-activist, working class people. That for everyone to whom he brought 'hope', there were ten to whom he brought fear. It is not surprising – his contact with them appears to have been minimal.

If he had known them better, had lived in Bristol among them, and chatted with them as they went about their everyday lives, he would have had greater understanding. He would have understood their fears. For some the danger from Benn was his ideas, or at least the ideas he was borrowing from fanatics around him. He was detested because of them. But for others the great danger lay in the fact that with Benn in the driving seat, Labour was unelectable.

Typical of the ordinary person's view was at a presentation for an 84-year-old Party worker in Bristol, Herbert Rogers, who repaid him by saying: 'My advice to you, Tony, is to pipe down. People don't know what you're saying. They say you are a communist and a Marxist and they don't know what you're up to. What are you up to anyway?'

'What are you up to?' – that was the question that so many wanted to ask Benn. I never did. I was always sure that what motivated Benn was a belief that he was the Messiah and with his small group of disciples and his chosen people, he would create a heaven on earth.

The truth was however that many working class British people knew that what he was offering was, in fact, hell on earth. They would never vote Labour until he was removed. He was God's greatest gift to Thatcher and had to be stopped if the Labour Party was to survive. That is why our small group of trade union brothers, so totally opposed to the Tories and committed to Labour, rejoiced so greatly when we finally achieved his fall. Now, at least, we had a chance of winning an election.

EPILOGUE

Blackpool, Conference Week 1998

On the settee of this small flat, opposite the Imperial Hotel, scene of a few triumphs and many more setbacks in the 1970s and 1980s, lie – a well-chosen word – newspapers brought in by Llin. Their headlines are ominous. 'Defiant Blair tries to brush off left's poll triumphs'. There is a temptation for us oldies to say 'serves you right' to young spin doctors who have not yet learned that you don't take people for granted nor that being bright is no substitute for hard work in the fixing game. That, however, would be stupid – it is our hard work that would be thrown away by any big swing back to the left.

While I sit thinking of the olden days, Llin – who became Member of Parliament for Newcastle-under-Lyme in 1986 – goes to Conference and talks to many of the veterans and survivors of those battles. I know that she won't see Betty Boothroyd who, as Speaker, no longer comes (though living in the Speaker's House with its gilt decor must continually remind her of Blackpool's Winter Gardens). And while Roger Godsiff finds it hard to suffer the 'born-again Blairites', whose past he remembers only too well, John Spellar will not miss a minute.

In the Conference hall, those in the MPs' block no longer feel under threat as they did in the dark days. The vicious attacks, which created so much resentment, appear to be a thing of the past. Those from the traditional right look cynically on at the changes come over the left wing baddies from years gone by. Sitting in their New Labour clothes, as ministers or Lords, they tell us, indeed, that many of the things they once called for cannot be achieved at all. I am not certain that all those on the right welcome the sinners that repenteth. While they recognise that politics, including the Labour Party, needs born survivors, they are concerned that the political 'road to Damascus' has of late become more crowded than the M5 on a Friday afternoon.

Some of the main characters, of course, have passed away, including Reg Underhill, Ron Hayward and Joan Lestor. Eric Heffer died in 1991 having achieved further notoriety for marching off the stage during Kinnock's dramatic 1985 Bournemouth Conference speech against Militant. Others of the old left remain, however, more or less in their old unrestructured form – caught, indeed, as I am myself, in a time warp.

While Arthur Scargill has taken himself off into the wilderness, his friends remain lost in a Party they once controlled. Benn, after losing his parliamentary seat in 1983, still remained on the NEC but never recovered his influence. He was stopped by Kinnock from regaining the chair of Home Policy and became part of a depleted hard left clique lacking influence. Not even when he returned to the Commons as the MP for Chesterfield did he attract the support he once had. Indeed, when he stood for the Leadership against Neil Kinnock in 1988, he was humiliated. His spiralling descent continued when – after Party members were given the vote – he was removed from the NEC in 1993.

Dennis Skinner, save for one year, stayed on the NEC until the 1998 Conference when he failed to beat the government machine men in the Commons and be re-elected by his fellow MPs. While still having some success with his 'one-liners' in the Chamber on television, he must feel that the time has come to hang up his cloth cap. Once upon a time that image made a telling counterpoint against the lofty superiority of the Tory knights of the shires. Now, from the packed New Labour benches, it must seem archaic – amusing, but irrelevant to the present day.

Dennis should really join those of us in retirement who wonder why we were ever mad enough to be so involved. On going to by-elections these days, I am forced to receive instructions from 22-year-olds on how to canvass before being allowed to go out onto the streets. And reminders of your mortality are never far away. Last year when canvassing, I was answering a lady's question at the doorstep – 'How is Llin?' 'OK but working too hard' – when her husband came out, popped his head over her shoulder, looked me up and down and asked: 'Didn't you use to be Mr Golding?'

I did, indeed, use to be Mr Golding. So too did Conference used to be Conference. And the NEC was the NEC. But now all has changed. At Conference, only the anticipation and excitement of the Leader's speech remains. In other respects, Conference is totally different and far more under control than we ever had it. No longer are frantically cobbled-together composited propositions taken hour after hour through the week, so saving footwear from the old constant shuffle around union delegations.

There is no need now for Roger Godsiff – who overcame the opposition of Roy Hattersley to become the MP for Birmingham Sparkbrook & Small Heath – or John Spellar, who is now a Minister, to spend their time persuading those delegations to rally round the Leader. John, though, is very much in evidence, revelling in every victory for his old friends, including Dianne Hayter who has now gone onto the NEC. Spellar, indeed, is still to be seen leaning on lamp posts on the sea front urging the right on to even greater efforts to trample the left.

Policy is now formulated through a 'Forum' and is all cut and dried before arriving for final endorsement – rubber-stamping – at Conference. There is no need now for Barbara Castle's blackboard – except to remind her herself that pensions rises cost huge sums of money. New Labour has taken a tip from Old Barbara and delegates are no longer allowed to indulge their passion for spending other people's money with such alacrity. Some emergency motions are taken, but these are closely controlled.

For many of us this change in the character of Conference is welcome. And, as it took the Great Fire of London to rid us of the plague, so it has needed Peter Mandelson and his team to rid us of the pestilence that was this annual torture. The nature of the delegates has changed, too – and much for the better, from my point of view. They do not now come to boo, hiss and shout, nor attack the Leadership for selling out. They may not have the same energy, but give me these polite young things in suits any day to the leather jacketed yobbos of yesterday. For one thing, they do not lose us the votes of electors watching Conference on TV.

The change in voting procedures, too, has taken much of the tension from the Conference floor. Gone is the taking of votes on the Monday for the whole NEC and the nail-biting declaration on Tuesday. Now the

Constituency Section, which is barred to MPs these days, is conducted weeks before from among the whole membership.

The results at this 1998 Conference have given the government a majority on the NEC, but they are far from the overwhelming triumph they should have been. The result from Party members was abysmal. Four out of six of the left candidates were elected in what could so easily have been a clean sweep. The left was organised early in the constituencies and fixers for the Leadership were not only incompetent, but late. 'One member, one vote,' they found, does not necessarily provide protection for the virtuous, when candidates from the right are largely unknown.

Fortunately, new right wingers have been elected through fresh changes this year to the structure of the NEC, which brought in MPs, MEPs and local authority representatives. In this way Tony Blair has been saved too much humiliation – it could have been much worse. Had Skinner won in the parliamentary section, the fat would have been in the fire. To prevent this the Commons' whips ran a slate and worked hard to ensure that only the most reliable were elected. They were, but only just. That Skinner came within 25 votes of winning must be taken as a warning shot.

It may well be that, to keep the NEC safe and supportive, they will need to find their own Roger Godsiff for the Constituency Section, who would start immediately after Conference to build a machine to deliver the goods at the drop of a hat. This would mean circulating a slate of well-known candidates at a very early date.

Organisation is all-important. As we have seen, Roger Godsiff and John Spellar changed the history of the Labour Party dramatically in 1981 and 1982 by their spade-work in the NEC elections. Later, in 1984 and 1985, they continued to work wonders against all the odds in the trade union section in the NEC elections. Although out of the limelight, I could still work in the shadows and we used a new dodge of finding moderate candidates from normally left-voting unions! Roger also usually managed to get at least one left candidate to rat on his comrades and give us vital votes, with the promise of a few back in return which would make no difference at all. All this made sure that the far left were contained and could not call the tune again.

The importance of organisation, both on the NEC and at Conference, was highlighted by the difficulties faced by Kinnock in finishing off the purge of Militant that we had started. All was quiet until the 1985 Conference when Neil attacked the Liverpool Militants in dramatic fashion. Then a war of attrition took place in Liverpool – and elsewhere – which eventually led to the exclusion of virtually all Militants in the Party.

Tight organisation did not mean, however, that the right in these years became more powerful. Indeed, my successor as convenor of the Tufton Court Group on the NEC, Charlie Turnock of the NUR, had a very difficult time though he was much tougher disciplinarian than I had ever been. Like me, he never had enough right-wingers with him to make life comfortable and, on top of that, Kinnock created his own Tribunite majority, by detaching people from the hard left.

On the NEC, the right often felt neglected and slighted by Neil. They had protected him – now he was ignoring them. They felt particularly peeved that he placed obscure intellectuals, who had done little for us, in the House of Lords while failing to 'look after' those who had done so much for him and the Party.

Is it any wonder that to become a trendy leftie became so fashionable. Inside Parliament and on the NEC, Tribune became the group to join. It was rumoured, indeed, that even Tony Blair and Gordon Brown had become members. And so to the dismay of both the hard left and the right, the Party came to be governed once again – as Attlee said it should be – from the left of centre. While the politicians joined Tribune in droves, however, the Tribunites adopted the policies of the right. That is politics. The story of the Labour Party since Kinnock's election has been that of the abandonment of socialist policies and the traditional Labour image. As I expressed it to Skinner: 'We both lost, your socialism and my Labour' – although many would hasten to add that the British people triumphed in consequence.

After the 1983 general election, while Foot was still praising the manifesto, most sane people realised that sooner or later it would have to be ditched. Slowly a transformation was made, first by Kinnock, the accomplished innovator, then by the cautious John Smith and subsequently by the daring of Tony Blair.

The downright antagonism against the Common Market went quickly. As a bulwark against Thatcherism, Europe was invaluable. For that reason, I believe that Labour is now the party of the Common Market. Changes on defence were more difficult. While I was working for Neil in the Leader's Office, he once told me – pulling a face at the memory – that he would never abandon unilateralism because he had personally witnessed the horrified reaction at the constituency meeting to Nye Bevan's announcement that he had changed his position on 'the bomb'. In time, however, he did follow Bevan and change his tune.

So many of our old policies, beliefs and attitudes went out of the window. For me this was mostly for the best, though I was in the very small minority who regretted seeing the end of our commitment to public ownership and one of the many horrified to witness the start of the Party's detachment from the trade unions. For some of us, dinosaurs all, this transformation has been very sad. For through the unions, the Labour Party gave the working class a voice in politics, something that is becoming more vital as the educated and articulate take over. Union involvement is needed to protect the interests of those who cannot stand up for themselves, but also to give them a voice in politics. This is not always achieved through 'one member, one vote'.

My regrets notwithstanding, the argument for distancing ourselves from the unions – as for changing policy – was that sticking so closely to them made Labour unelectable. That was unanswerable, as far as I was concerned.

Regrettably, while having the courage to tackle many problems, Neil wasted his biggest asset – his personality. On his election, the posh papers spitefully, having backed the wrong horse in Hattersley, made jibes at Neil for not being an intellectual. Instead of thanking them for the compliment and reminding them that it took more charisma to become Leader of the Labour Party than to be the editor of a newspaper, he tried desperately to prove them wrong. He would have done so much better had he continued to be himself. My advice to him was always to address our own people 'speak to your Auntie' – on the basis that if we could persuade only a small extra part of the working class to vote for us we would win.

Sadly, he listened to 'intellectuals' like Patricia Hewitt instead. And that is one of the main reasons why we lost both the 1987 and 1992 elections and Neil never made it to Number 10 as Prime Minister.

Of course, he had a difficult fight against Thatcher. While she stuck to her line that Britain had recovered its self-respect under her, and very effectively reminded the electors of the horrors of the Winter of Discontent, in the 1987 election Kinnock and John Smith got into the same mess on tax that Foot and Healey got into on defence in 1983 – and the electorate punished them accordingly.

While we had not expected to win in 1987 anyway, we felt certain that we would do so in 1992 against John Major. It is hard to know why we lost. We were told on the doorstep that it was hard to trust a man, who would abandon so many of his principles. And this by the very people who had supported Neil in 1983 and asked for the very policy changes he made. After the event, we were told that the triumphalist rally held in Sheffield had made a disastrous impact on the electorate. At the time, I grumbled that Neil – having once again formed his view from Hampstead Hill – had foolishly focused on proportional representation in the last week of the campaign in an attempt to appeal to the Liberals. Had he just continued to talk about bread-and-butter issues, I believe, he would have won the election. But who really knows why?

One thing is certain. Thanks to the modernisers we won the 1997 election by a bigger majority than we could ever have dreamed. Whatever our doubts about New Labour, we cannot but applaud those who have made our Party professional and so successful.

To belong to and work for New Labour may not be as emotionally satisfying as it was with 'Old Labour'. But by winning the 1997 general election it has done far more for the working class than traditional right wing critics like Hattersley managed to do after 1979. And, if to win further elections and so stop the Tories, requires more change in the Labour Party to reflect the mood of electors, so be it. This may seem a high price to pay by some, but I believe it to be well worthwhile.

We veterans are bound to sit on park seats and remember the old days, some with more joy than others, and grumble about the policies of the New Labour government and the behaviour of the latter day chocolate soldiers. When we have got things off our chest, however, we old moderates need to get off our bottoms and go, as we always have, to the aid of the Party. All our history and personal experience tells us that we must ensure that Labour never falls again into the hands of the loony left. That much we owe to our people.

NOTES

Introduction

1. To avoid, hopefully, any frustration on the part of the reader, the following is a glossary of the names and abbreviations of trade unions which appear in this book.

    ACTT: Association of Cinematograph, Television and Allied Technicians.

    AEU: Amalgamated Engineering Union (became the AUEW in the 1970s).

    APEX: Association of Professional, Executive, Clerical and Computer Staff (became part of the GMB in 1989).

    ASLEF: Associated Society of Locomotive Engineers and Firemen.

    ASTMS: Association of Scientific, Technical and Managerial Staffs (joined the new MSF, the Manufacturing, Science and Finance union, in 1988).

    AUEW: Amalgamated Union of Engineering Workers.

    CATU: The Ceramic and Allied Trades Union.

    COHSE: Confederation of Health Service Employees.

    EETPU: Electrical, Electronic, Telecommunications and Plumbing Union.

    FBU: Fire Brigades Union.

    GMWU/GMB: General and Municipal Workers Union. Became strictly the General, Municipal, Boilermakers and Allied Trades Union (GMBATU: GMB for short) after merger with the Boilermakers in 1982. Known simply as GMB from 1987.

    ISTC: Iron and Steel Trades Confederation.

    NACODS: National Association of Colliery Overmen, Deputies and Shotfirers.

    NATSOPA: National Society of Operative Printers, Graphical and Media Personnel. Merged with SOGAT in 1982 to form SOGAT 82.

    NGA: National Graphical Association.

    NUBF: National Union of Blastfurnacemen. Joined the ISTC in 1985.

    NUM: National Union of Mineworkers.

    NUPE: National Union of Public Employees.

    NUR: National Union of Railwaymen.

    NUS: National Union of Seamen.

    POEU: Post Office Engineering Union (became the NCU, the National Communications Union, in 1985).

    SOGAT: Society of Graphical and Allied Trades.

    TASS: Technical, Administrative and Supervisory Section of the AUEW.

    TSSA: Transport and Salaried Staffs Association.

    TGWU/T&G: Transport and General Workers Union.

    UCATT: Union of Construction, Allied Trades and Technicians.

UCW: Union of Communication Workers (changed name from UPW in 1981).
UPW: Union of Postal Workers (changed to UCW in 1981).
USDAW: Union of Shop, Distributive and Allied Workers.

Chapter 1

1   Benn's Diaries: *Conflicts of Interest 1977–80*, 23 December, 1979, page 568.
2   Benn's Diaries: *Conflicts of Interest 1977–80*, 24 December, 1979, page 569.

Chapter 2

1   A detailed, if jaundiced, account of left wing tactics is to be found in the book 'Enemies of Democracy' by Paul McCormick, which tells the story of the left's ousting of Reg Prentice in Newham North East.
2   Benn's Diaries, *Conflicts of Interest 1977–80*, 29 September 1979.
3   Benn's Diaries, *The End of an Era 1980–90*, 21 March 1981.
4   With a general election looming, this was later endorsed, with amendments, by the full NEC by 13 votes to 10 on 24 January, 1979.

> . . . the NEC, following a meeting between the Home Policy and International Committees with the Chancellor of the Exchequer, continues to view with regret the government's decision to raise the Minimum Lending Rate by 2 1/2 per cent with its consequences of an increase in the mortgage rate, higher bank charges, deferment of investment profits and possible higher unemployment. We feel that the decision and the circumstances in which it was taken demonstrates a lack of effective democratic control over the Bank of England, the money market and the City in general. We consider that the government would be better engaged in adopting the alternative economic strategy passed by successive Labour Party Conferences.

5   A letter from Heffer on the relationship between Labour governments and the Party – together with a letter and a copy of the minute sent in 1976 by Benn to all ministers in the Department of Industry on the subject of the political role of Labour ministers, including those who are members of the NEC – was considered by the NEC's Organisation Committee on 4 December, 1978.
6   This group was to comprise of Benn, Heffer, Lestor, Maynard, Russell Tuck and myself, together with the National Agent and the General Secretary.

Chapter 3

1   The thinking behind this policy is well set out in Bernard Donoughue's *Prime Minister*.
2   Benn's Diaries, *Conflicts of Interest 1977–80*, 15 October 1978, p. 367. Here Benn also recounts a conversation with Foot about Callaghan possibly resigning over the issue.

3   Bernard Donoughue, *Prime Minister*, page 174.

> The country was 'virtually paralysed . . . The unofficial strike of road haulage drivers was made official,
> flying pickets were blocking the ports and there was shortage of food and medical supplies . . . Ministers
> considered sending tanks into the ICI medical headquarters to retrieve drugs and essential equipment. The
> strike of water workers had deprived many places in the north west of England of fresh water since the New
> Year. The sewage workers were threatening to join the water workers. The lorry drivers had turned down a
> 15 per cent offer and were demanding over 20 per cent. The railwaymen had called a national strike because
> they wanted a 10 per cent bonus on top of their 20 per cent wage demand. The nightly television pictures
> of violence and the brutal face of trade unionism were doing terrible damage to the Government and to the
> trade union movement itself. The pickets were ensuring a future victory for Mrs Thatcher.

4   See Donoughue again, pages 167 to 192.

Chapter 4

1   See *The Battle for the Labour Party* by David and Maurice Kogan.
2   The full motion, carried at the NEC on March, 1979, stated:

> That this National Executive believes that the Labour government deserves the confidence of the House of
> Commons in tonight's vote. The Labour movement, by its very nature, will always be impatient for radical
> reform and social change. We serve notice that as representatives of the Labour Party we will continue to press
> the case for the irreversible shift of wealth and power in favour of the working people of Britain, but we recognise
> that the Labour government has had to work against a background of world economic depression and no clear
> majority for most of its life in the House of Commons. In these circumstances, we believe that Labour has a
> record to be proud of in ensuring that the weakest in our society are protected from the worst effects of that
> recession, and in protecting jobs and industries which would have gone to the wall if left to crude market forces.

Chapter 5

1   Again for the record, the 13 Liberals, who voted against and thus helped usher in 18 years of
     Thatcherism, were: Alan Beith, Clement Freud, Jo Grimond, Emlyn Hooson, Geraint Howells,
     Russell Johnston, John Pardoe, David Penhaligon, Stephen Ross, Cyril Smith, David Steel, Jeremy
     Thorpe and Richard Wainwright. The 14th Liberal in the House at the time of the general election,
     David Alton, only won his seat in a by-election in Liverpool on 29 March, 1979, and took his place
     in the Commons on 1 April, two days before the election started.
2   Apart from Heffer, this meeting was also attended by Callaghan, Foot, Benn, Frank Allaun, Barbara
     Castle, Bryan Stanley and others from the NEC and Len Murray, David Basnett, Geoffrey Drain,
     Alan Fisher, Hugh Scanlon and Moss Evans from the TUC
3   Frank Allaun, Norman Atkinson, Benn, Tom Bradley, Alan Hadden, Heffer, Joan Lestor, Joan
     Maynard, Gerry Russell and Russell Tuck represented the NEC; Foot, Healey, Roy Mason, Bruce
     Millan, Peter Shore, Shirley Williams, and Eric Varley represented the Cabinet, while Ron Hayward,
     Geoff Bish and David Lipsey were Joint Secretaries.

4   Benn launched a savage attack on the manifesto process at the 1980 Annual Conference. As well as in this chapter, however, his failure to get his way at the time is well recounted in his own Diaries – see *Conflicts of Interest 1977–80*, pages 480–487.

5   *Daily Telegraph*, 12 June, 1979: 'Would our British system allow real socialism . . . how will Labour get sufficient support to carry out its socialist objectives and so create a genuine democratic classless society with real equality of opportunity and with egalitarianism as the perspective; and having done so, how will it be able to carry through that change without the opponents . . . resorting to undemocratic means to prevent it?'.

6   *Morning Star,* 21 June, 1979.

Chapter 6

1   At the December 1979 NEC, Callaghan moved an amendment against Huckfield which opposed the misuse of employer power, the Tory attack on union organisation and supported new car models to save Leyland, but left the issue of re-instatement to the investigation being carried out by AUEW Executive. Heffer, however, moved yet another amendment, hoping for Red Robbo's reinstatement. It was carried by 10 votes to 9 and the substantive motion by 11 votes to 9 votes.

2   This was amended at the subsequent NEC on 28 September, 1979 to include 'without prejudice to the right of the Special Committee of inquiry to examine all the items.'

3   The full composition of this working party was: Bryan Stanley, (Chairman), John Cartwright, MP, Eric Heffer, MP, Ian Mikardo, MP, Sydney Irving MP, George Park, MP, Joan Richardson, MP, Moss Evans (TGWU) Terry Duffy (AUEW) W.Alston (NULO) B.Kissen (Labour Parliamentary Association), D.Wise (Co-op), Ray Apps [Brighton Kemptown, movers of the 1977 Conference proposition] and Reg Underhill, National Agent (Secretary) .

4   Benn's Diaries, *Conflicts of Interest 1977–80*, 2 October 1979, page 545.

5   In desperation, they first decided to seek legal advice from an ex-whip Lord Terry Boston. But in December faced with the hard fact that they were not going to be able to find a lawyer sufficiently depraved to get them out of the mess, it was decided that Benn, Joan Maynard, Tony Saunois, Dennis Skinner, I and the officers discuss the matters with the lawyers. How I had come to take Russell Tuck's position as the statutory moderate, I cannot recall – perhaps it was when he was away sick. At the 11 February Organisation Committee, the Secretary reported that he had arranged a meeting with Queen's Counsel to be held on 13 February, 1980. During the discussion, it was mentioned that as well as obtaining advice on the Court action there should be a tidying up of the wording of the rules. It was also agreed to minute that it was the wish of this committee that an amendment to bring the Constitution in line be put to Conference and that the Committee was carrying out Conference's decision. In other words it was all the fault of the Conference and the left wing fixers and not the idiots on the NEC. Unfortunately I had to send in an apology for the meeting with Counsel, thus depriving Heffer, Benn and Maynard of the sight of my triumphant grin again as Conrad Dehn QC confirmed that the Conference rule change was faulty.

6   The full extent of this claptrap was as follows:

> The NEC has expressed concern at the number of cases of disciplinary action being taken by Labour Groups against Group members: All of us are aware of the vicious cuts in finance to local authorities imposed by the Tory government. We know that you face the dilemma of either putting up the rates by an exorbitant amount

or cutting vital services to the people who you were elected to serve. The alternative, if groups do neither, is seeing their Authority go bankrupt and facing the consequences of that situation.

The NEC is giving urgent consideration to the problems posed for Labour Groups. We must avoid getting into a situation where our elected local authority members are attacking each other over this issue and feel that the only remedy is to take disciplinary action against members of the Group.

During these difficult times, Labour Groups and their county and district Parties must meet together to discuss the policy to be pursued and the decisions to be taken. Each must support the other and greater tolerance and understanding on both sides must be exercised, if we are to avoid the Party getting itself in difficulties in a situation created by the Tory government.

We are strongly of the opinion that all Labour Groups should permit maximum flexibility. Groups must consult and reach agreement, for disciplinary measures are no substitute for a lasting settlement of this difficult problem.

7   At the NEC Organisation Committee on 5 September, 1980.

Chapter 7

1   Peter Simmonds, *Sunday Telegraph*, 29 June, 1980.
2   Yet another meeting of the PLP was held on the morning of 31 October, 1979 to consider what the NEC had done. After a row about whether the votes should be recorded, Fred Willey, the PLP chair, moved a motion which was carried by 133 to 61 that the PLP must be represented; Norman Buchan's motion opposing this, which had been drafted by Benn, was defeated by 137 to 50.

There could be no doubt about the depth of feeling against the NEC by the overwhelming majority at that meeting. The left tried to retrieve the situation by pointing out that 70 MPs 'did not bother to turn up', but they knew that this was a flawed argument. Apart from those with illness or other commitments, others were keeping their heads down because of left wing pressure in their constituencies.

The bitterness within the PLP was also expressed on 27 November, 1979 directly at a joint meeting of the NEC and Shadow Cabinet, with Lena Jeger in the Chair, by Fred Willey. He requested stronger representation, as did Callaghan and Peter Shore. Healey, as ever, used the occasion for abuse rather than persuasion, highlighting the problem of extremism. After belting them up hill and down dale, in typical Denis fashion, he asked the NEC to be wise and comradely! David Owen, meanwhile, highlighted the main issue as the manifesto.

All these pleas fell on deaf ears. The following day, Jim asked that the NEC defer a decision and hold an urgent meeting between the officers of the Labour Party, the officers of the Parliamentary Committee and those of the Campaign for a Labour Victory, in order to try to reach agreement. But the left would have none of this and in successive votes we were routed.

3   Basnett wrote several letters as Chair of Trades Unions for a Labour Victory (TULV) to influence the composition, but to no avail. The union leaders were particularly unhappy that the NEC had broken the agreed formula of five from each side plus Callaghan, by adding the NEC's vice-chair and Treasurer. They wanted Alex Kitson to withdraw and for the Treasurer to have no vote. If the NEC agreed to this, TULV would accept the Commission and recommend the PLP to do likewise.

4   A ludicrous attempt by Heffer and Saunois to replace him by Les Huckfield was easily defeated at the February NEC.

5   The commission initially comprised of Frank Allaun, Norman Atkinson, Benn, Eric Heffer, Joan Lestor, Jo Richardson, David Basnett, Terry Duffy (replacing John Boyd), Moss Evans, Clive

Jenkins, Bill Keys, Jim Callaghan and Michael Foot.

Three Working Panels were created: Organisation and Membership (Chair, Moss Evans), Finance (Clive Jenkins) and Political Education (Benn). The Chairmen of the main Commission were Michael Foot, David Basnett and Eric Heffer.

6   At the first session, it did, however, reach agreement on party finance – the individual minimum subscription would rise to £5!

7   Benn later revealed that Jenkins and Keys then turned on him and accused him of wrecking the arrangement they had that the electoral college and the manifesto would be part of a compromise on reselection.

8   Benn, Joan Maynard, Jo Richardson, Dennis Skinner and Tony Saunois attended a meeting to discuss the Commission's decisions on the 17 June, 1980. CLPD was clear that it wanted the unions and not the PLP to get 50 per cent in the electoral college and they did not want the college to ratify a manifesto drawn up by the NEC.

9   *Sunday Telegraph*, 29 June, 1980.

10 'We must make a fresh start', argued Clive.

> We have come to the end of the road . . . .you had a piece of paper put on your chair yesterday explaining the accounts. Pay no attention to it. It is defensive and self-serving and it will not do at all. The accounts give you a yellowing snapshot from the past . . . The truth now is that the Party has no reserves, an inadequate income, is moving into very serious high-interest debt, not just for this year but for the next five years . . .

The other things asked for by Clive were agreed by Conference – although what the NEC then did with them is another story.

11 Benn's Diaries, *The End of An Era 1980–90,* 11 June, 1980.

12 Composite 44 moved by Chris Ballard of Mid Oxon CLP included:

> Conference opposes all nuclear, germ, and chemical weapons, especially the proposed importation from America of Cruise missiles and up-dated Polaris technology. Conference calls for a commitment in the Labour Party manifesto to unilateral nuclear disarmament and for proposals to be made for producing alternative, socially useful products using the existing skills and materials in the arms industry without loss of jobs and for the planned transfer of resources to the poorer countries of the world.

Bill Keys of Sogat moved Composite 45 which included:

> Conference, whilst acknowledging that the safety of all people would best be served by multilateral mutual disarmament in the nuclear and conventional fields, demands that the new Labour Party manifesto- and any interim manifesto- must include a firm commitment opposing British participation in any defence policy based on the use or threatened use of nuclear weapons; a pledge to close down all nuclear bases, British or American, on British soil or in British waters, and a firm commitment to disbanding the defence sales organisation and reorganising arms industries to produce alternative products of social value.

13 NEC, May, 1982

14 The manifesto stated: 'We will retain the freedom to determine our own budgetary policy and to control our own currency. A Labour government will retain the power to impose controls on capital movements and will continue to resist any upward harmonisation of VAT or any reduction in the existing range of zero-rated VAT items in Britain. A Labour government would

not join an Economic and Monetary Union.' The manifesto also argued for a reduction in the level of Britain's contribution to the Community budget and a strengthening of the power of the British parliament.

15 At the 1979 Conference, Callaghan stated in his Leader's speech: 'As far as I am concerned it [the EEC] will continue to be hampered by its wasteful and costly agricultural policy, as well as by its institutional arrangements. I said before, and I say again now, that if Britain cannot get a satisfactory new financial settlement then we should announce, this government should announce, that we will put a net financial ceiling on our contributions. but having said that, do not throw the baby out with the bath water: Europe shares many problems; our trade unionists know this, they see it every day in their international contacts. many of the same problems they share with us – steel, textiles, the micro-economic revolution with its effect on jobs, all examples of issues that we will not solve by ourselves but would be better solved by co-operation.'

16 NEC, 28 January, 1981.

17 *The Sentinel*, 28 May, 1981.

Chapter 9

1 The vote was: Option 1: 6,283,000, Option 2: 434,000, Option 3: 11,000, Option 4: 431,000, Option 5: 6,000.

Chapter 10

1 Benn's Diaries, *Conflicts of Interest*, 19 December, 1979, page 566

2 See Ivor Crewe and Anthony King, *SDP: The Birth, Life and Death of the Social Democratic Party*

3 *Daily Mail*, 3 June 1980.

4 Joint Statement, 8 June, 1980.

5 *Sunday Express*, 4 February, 1980

6 *Daily Star*, 8 and 9 June, 1980

7 *The Times*, 11 August, 1980.

8 The letter signed by Roger Fox, Stephen Haseler and Douglas Eden declared that the SDA wanted him to win the election but added that: 'A Labour victory would threaten to place the extreme left wing in charge of the Party . . . In order to reassure Labour voters and allow us to vote Labour without a heavy heart, we suggest that you now declare that you will not appoint to your Government any MP who has associated himself or herself with totalitarian organisations and has not since repudiated it.' (*Guardian*, 9 April, 1979)

9 By 13 votes to 10.

10 The SDA leadership stated that a 'statement of aims was drafted reflecting the SDA's new and more positive approach . . . (it) was an expanding national federation of individuals and local political organisations, preparing for the future. They also announced details of its national organisation; the names of its regional secretaries and official representatives in different parts of the country and the results of a special poll analysis it had commissioned, indicating the likely consequences for Labour of the left forcing the centre to break away.' 'The SDA has its roots in the Labour Party where it began as rallying point for Labour moderates against left-wing extremism. SDA has led the fight

against the left for five years and will oppose official Labour candidates who support extremist policies.'

11 The SDA's comprehensive list of the leading left targets also included Frank Allaun, Norman Atkinson, Judith Hart, Joan Maynard, Jo Richardson, James Lamond, Sean Hughes, Stanley Thorne, Martin Flannery, Stan Newens, Ian Mikardo, Ernie Roberts, Stuart Holland, Maurice Silverman, William Wilson, Russell Kerr, Ernie Ross, Bob Cryer, Jeff Rooker and David Winnick. The damning evidence against the SDA – a leaflet, membership form and its intention to field candidates against the Labour Party – was laid out in all its glory at the subsequent meeting of the NEC's Organisation Committee on 7 July, 1980.

12 NEC Organisation Committee in September, 1980.

13 Seconded by Bradley, at the Organisation Committee in September, Shirley moved: 'That the National Executive Committee will remove from the Party any person who stands as a prospective Party candidate or publicly supports a candidate opposed to the official Labour Party candidate during an election campaign, or publicly opposes the official Labour Party candidate during an election campaign.' It was defeated by Benn & Co by six votes to four. The other resolution, proposed by tiny Trot, Tony Saunois, and seconded by Heffer: 'That the National Executive Committee should forthwith ask all the persons named recently by the Social Democratic Alliance as opponents of the Labour candidates at the general election or earlier to answer within a month whether or not they intend to go forward; and that those who do not deny this intention should be removed from the Party.' – was carried by nine votes to four. While Williams' motion was in line with the rules, however, the left's immediate witch hunt was totally unconstitutional!

14 The motion, seconded by Charles Kelly, read: 'That in the light of the decision of the Social Democratic Alliance to maintain a political organisation in the country with its own separate and distinct programme, principles and policy and to promote candidates for local and the next general election in opposition to the Labour Party, the National Executive is left with no alternative but to declare the Social Democratic Alliance to be, within the terms of Section [3] of Clause II of the Constitution of the Labour Party, an organisation ineligible for affiliation to the Party, and membership of this organisation is therefore incompatible with membership of the Labour Party.'

15 This time Neil Kinnock proposed that the words' 'such expulsion to stand until such time as the Party accepts the individual back into membership' be added: 'I accepted them knowing that they had no value other than to make it possible for him to say that it was a different proposition from the one the left had vetoed in September. This time it was carried by 6 votes in favour and none against.

16 I moved: 'That the NEC finds incompatible with membership of the Labour Party membership of political organisations having their own programme, principles and policy for distinctive and separate propaganda, and finds that the Social Democratic Alliance and the Militant Tendency both appear to have separate organisations as defined in Clause 2 of the Labour Party constitution'. Apart from NEC Organisation members, Party officers present as witnesses were: Bill Alston, Paul Carmody, Ron Hayward, Joyce Gould, Min Birdsey and David Hughes.

17 In his Diaries, *The end of an Era 1980–90*, p.43, Benn gives a flavour of the poison within the PLP. On 29 October, 1980, after contradicting Jim Wellbeloved's prediction of a split, he writes: 'All of a sudden the atmosphere turned nasty and Jim Wellbeloved rounded on me. Well I can tell you that these four issues at Conference – the Common Market, unilateralism, the House of Lords and nationalization by statutory instrument- will not be acceptable, we won't have it, we won't have it.'

18 Donald Macintyre, 23 February, 1981, in *The Times* reported that: 'The dominant right-wing faction in the leadership of the Amalgamated Union of Engineering Workers has secured a comfortable majority in the union's Labour Party and TUC delegations for the first time in recent years.'

19 The *Sentinel*, 12 March, 1981

Chapter 11

1   In his autobiography, Denis Healey reports that in 1979 the AUEW delegation meeting was a shambles. A key delegate was absent through a heart attack and someone attended who was only a visitor at the hotel waiting for a friend!

2   Donald Macintyre, *The Times*, 23 February, 1981: 'What has helped to swing the delegations to the right is a change of rule that allows them to be elected by divisional committees after branch nomination. The previous system of election by branch ballot has tended to help the left'.

3   See the *Guardian*, 18 February, 1981, report by Ian Aitken.

4   As ever, we assumed that Terry had leaked it. In truth Charles Rae had already reported in the *Standard* on 6 February, 1981 that 'Duffy leads fight-back by the Mods. Other union leaders to meet secretly next Tuesday'.

5   At the following meeting, in April we recommended Tom Breakell (EETPU), Roy Evans (ISTC) and David Williams (COHSE) be added.

6   Of this early period, Godsiff himself has written: 'In 1981 we made no deals. What had to be done was to line up the 'moderate unions' to support the recommended slate of moderates. This was the first time that it happened and proved that the composition of the NEC could be changed by co-ordinated organisation. To get the widest support from moderate unions we made sure that as many as possible union nominees were on 'our slate' and we emphasised the need for the unions to vote, as far as possible, for the whole slate but particularly for our most 'marginal' candidates.'

Chapter 12

1   Mullin's motion read: 'that this local party/branch calls on Tony Benn to accept nomination for the Deputy Leadership to implement the socialist programme agreed at Conference to restore full employment, to achieve nuclear disarmament, to expand the public services and to carry through Party policy.'

2   Benn Diaries, *The End of an Era 1980–90*, 21 March, 1981.

3   The programme was 1. Reselection of MPs, 2. Maintain NEC structure as it was 3. Control of the manifesto, 4. Electoral college to elect leader, 5. PLP to follow Party policy.

4   The holding of ballots was not without its problems however – even apart from the great expense of doing so. There were serious issues to be resolved of who should be given the vote – was there not a reasonable objection to Conservatives, SDPers and Communists being given a vote in a Labour Party Leadership election?. Apart from the ethical considerations, Bryan Stanley and I were uncertain about whether Tories and SDPers would vote to foist Benn on us as some defecting MPs had voted for Michael Foot. In the event we decided to restrict the ballot in the POEU to levypayers, still not all of whom were Labour supporters, but received legal advice that if we were going to hold a ballot this must include all of the members. This we eventually did through our branches, the result being an easy victory for Denis Healey despite the substantial work put in by the left. Other ballots were held in NUPE, NUM, COHSE and NATSOPA.

5   The delegation included left wingers Walt Greendale of the TGWU, Ken Gill of TASS/AUEW, Bill Maddocks of the National Union of Dyers, Bleachers and Textile Workers, Doug Grieve of the Tobacco Workers' Union and Ray Buckton and Johnnie Walker of ASLEF.

6   Benn's Diaries, 24 June, 1980.

7   Others present, Benn records, included Roy Hughes (Tribune), David Young, Frank Hooley, Peter Archer, Arthur Davidson, John Grant and David Stottard.

8   Benn wrote in his Diaries, *The End of An Era 1980–90*, 23 September, 1980, p.151. 'Went to the National Executive, where the barracking of Healey in Birmingham was raised. Alex Kitson said it was atrocious, and he proposed we pass a motion condemning the conduct of those responsible. Michael Foot said it was right to condemn it. John Golding supported condemnation, but said there had been co-ordinated barracking and he wanted a an inquiry by the Organisation Sub-committee – and he wanted a report from the Midlands Region and the stewards. He believed we must expel from the Party those who did this sort of thing. Dennis Healey argued that, since we financed these rallies, it just encouraged anti-Labour reaction and we should seriously consider whether it was worth having the rallies at all. Tony Saunois said, 'We must discourage the shouting. But, when John Golding addressed the YS, they heard him in complete silence. At my suggestion Jo Richardson said: 'We should add condemnation of the media handling of the campaign'. Betty Boothroyd didn't want the press matter added. I said, well I'm all for condemning, but who did it? We all know who did it. We all know it was the SWP, the WRP, the anarchists, the H-Blocks people- they heckled me for six minutes last year at a meeting. It was not orchestrated by people in the Party. As to the role of the media, I don't want to press it in this resolution if people don't want to do it, but I've been described as Oswald Mosley in the *Mirror* and as Hitler in the *Daily Express*, and nobody condemned that; and I have never made anything of it because I always thought Harold Wilson made a great mistake to complain about smears.' It was obvious from this that even Benn could see that bully boy tactics could rebound on him.

9   On 17 March, 1980. Others on the platform were Paul Foot (Socialist Workers), Hilary Wainwright, Tariq Ali, Audrey Wise and Stuart Holland.

10 Benn's Diaries, *The End of an Era 1980–90*, 25 September, 1981, p.153.

11 Benn's Diaries, *The End of an Era 1980–90*, 26 September, 1981, p.153.

12 Adam Raphael and Robert Taylor in the *Observer*, 27 September, 1981.

13 Following the TGWU conference, a very unsatisfactory consultation exercise initiated by the Finance and General Purposes Committee took place in which only 900 of the 7,800 branches took part. While Healey came out as the winner- by an aggregate regional vote of 885,990 to 845,614 taking 7 out of 10 of the unions' regions and 52.2 per cent of the branches which voted – the left refused to accept the result arguing that either Benn or Silkin had won in the largest regions. As the General Executive had not been involved in the decision to hold the ballot, too, they behaved as though it had never taken place. In time this produced a right-wing reaction from the general membership but in the meantime the fixers on the General Executive carried on regardless and voted to recommend to the union delegation that they vote for Benn (Benn 22, Denis Healey, 14, Silkin 4).

14 Surprisingly, NATSOPA, NGA, FBU and the Musician's Union all voted for Healey as well as the AUEW, Foundry workers, Footwear workers, GMWU, USDAW, EETPU, TSSA, UCW, NUR, COHSE, APEX, ISTC, POEU, NACODS, Blastfurnacemen and the ISTC, Labour clubs and Poale Zion and a number of smaller unions.

    Benn was supported by the Bakers, Scottish Carpet Workers, ACCT, UCATT, Dyers, AUEW (Construction), AUEW (TASS), Furniture workers, SOGAT, Lithographic Artists, ASLEF, Metal Mechanics, NUM, ASTMS, Sheetmetal Workers, NATKE, Tobacco Workers, Social Workers, Students, SEA, SHA, Royal Arsenal Co-op.

15 The first ballot results were: Healey 45.369 per cent; Benn 36.627 per cent; and Silkin 18.004 per cent. Healey's vote was made up of 24.696 out of 40 per cent from the unions, 15.306 from 30 per cent from the PLP and only 5.367 of the 30 per cent for the CLPs.

16 Julia Langdon, reported in the *Guardian* at the time: 'Mr Denis Healey's camp claimed they won extra last-minute votes from Silkin supporters such as Mr Frank Field and Dr Oonagh McDonald because of the intimidatory tactics of Mr Benn's supporters.' These were not the only ones to switch right across Don Concannon, Reg Freeson also voted Healey. Those abstaining, according to the *Guardian*, also included Stan Orme, Martin O'Neill, Guy Barnett, Andrew Bennett, Sheila Wright, Eric Deakins, Allen McKay, Jeff Rooker, Joe Ashton, Laurie Pavitt, Tom Pendry, Ted Garrett, John McWilliam, Harry Cowans, Norman Buchan, Russell Kerr and Arthur Davidson. In the second ballot, Benn again overwhelmingly won the constituencies – by 507 to just 119 for Healey

17 The correspondence between Godsiff's predictions and the actual results was remarkable. His notes read Evans 3,537,000 (versus 3,564,000); Williams 3,462, 000 (3,433,000); Howell 3,218,000 (3,258,000); Boothroyd 3,740,000 (3,793,000) Breakell 2,670,000 (2,374,000); Dunwoody 3,593,000 (3,725,000); Hayter 3,318,000 not enough.

He was a mite too cautious, however, on the Treasurship: he calculated that Varley would get 3,521,000 and Atkinson 3,454,000 – and the result was 3,839,000 to 3,252,000.

Chapter 13

1 Sadly my joy could not be totally uncontained. The re-admission of the three-year rule was qualified so it could be waived if the NEC thought that something was of 'immediate importance' – a big 'coach and horses' hole. Joan Maynard did, however, fail to deliver the CLPD objective that 30 resolutions could waive the rule – a gap of double-decker proportions!

2 Benn's Diaries, *Conflicts of Interest 1977–80*, p 521 of the NEC meeting on 16 July, 1979.

3 Benn's Diaries, *Conflicts of Interest 1977–80*, p 533, 10 September, 1979.

4 Interestingly, however, Castle thought that Clause V – governing the manifesto meeting – should be revitalised by electing PLP representatives to draft the manifesto.

5 Benn's Diaries, *Conflicts of Interest 1977–80*, p 533, 10 September, 1979.

6 Callaghan grumbled that this was only a strategic withdrawal because there were similar propositions from constituencies. But he clearly underestimated its importance. If carried, an NEC proposition could be implemented immediately – others would have to wait a year. Later, CLPD blamed Kinnock for their not getting control of the manifesto in 1979 and only re-consideration in 1980. Jon Lansman described it as a 'significant crime'.

Chapter 14

1 Benn's Diaries, *The End of an Era 1980–90*, 18 November, 1980, page 50.

2 Benn's Diaries, *The End of an Era 1980–90*, 27 January, 1981, page 76.

3 Benn's Diaries *The End of an Era 1980–90*, 3 June, 1981, page 135.

4 The *Sentinel*, 6 October, 1981.

5 *The Times*,10 November 1981.

6 *The Times*, 11 November, 1981. The Article continued:

> In the women's committee, Miss Jo Richardson beat Mrs Gwyneth Dunwoody by the same margin. Mrs Dunwoody was one of five moderates who displaced left wingers when the new NEC was elected at Brighton

six weeks ago . . . Miss Joan Lestor was unanimously re-elected to the chair of the international committee. Mrs Dunwoody was again nominated to oppose her, by . . . .. Miss Betty Boothroyd, but could not find a seconder. Mrs Dunwoody's inexperience in party in-fighting undid her: she was allowed under the rules to second her own nomination, but did not know it. Miss Lestor was certain to win in any event. She counts as a member of the soft left, having failed to vote for Mr Benn in the election for the deputy leadership. The fourth contest produced a tie. The hard left Mr Frank Allaun and the moderate, Mr Alan Hadden, twice polled eight votes apiece for the chairmanship of the press and publicity committee. The full NEC will have to resolve that.

In the event, at the subsequent NEC, Alex Kitson got the Chairmanship of the Finance and General Purposes committee by 16 votes in favour to 2 votes against and Frank Allaun, Press and Publicity, by 11 votes to 8 votes.

7 Tony Bevins, *The Times*, 11 November, 1981.

Chapter 15

1 In his Diaries, Benn himself wrote: 'I went to Bristol for a dramatic meeting of the council's Labour Group . . . The atmosphere was horrible. But the eight were impressive: they just read their statement and left it at that. However it did reveal the conflict between those who use socialism as a ladder into the municipal corridors of power, versus those who regard socialism as a campaign. What the expelled councillors now have to do is use the council chamber to expose what is happening, to launch a tremendous attack against the Tories and ignore the Labour Leadership entirely'.

2 The voting was 15 to 13.

3 Michael Jones, *Sunday Times*, 7 March, 1981.

4 *Guardian* 10.12.81.

5 Organisation Committee 9 December, 1981 – the vote was 11 to 6 against Tariq Ali.

6 Report by George Page, Secretary of the Greater London Regional Council, of a meeting held on the 24 March, 1982.

Chapter 16

1 The selection took place on Tuesday 15 December, 1981 at Transport House. Others shortlisted were Dick Clements, Bryan Davies, Joyce Gould and David Hughes. On the first ballot Alex Ferry got 14 votes, Jim Mortimer 13, Joyce Gould 1 and Dick Clements 1. I didn't hold my breath – I knew that Mortimer would pick up both of the maverick votes and win by one, which he duly did.

2 For this recollection and many others of the meetings at Swinton House, I have relied on the meticulous notes kept by Roger Godsiff. This one, settling the women's slate, was of 27 July, 1982.

3 At the 1981 TUC, Bryan Stanley secured automatic seats on the General Council for all unions with at least 100,000 members. That not only gave the POEU and therefore Bryan a seat as of right, but it also cut the influence of the left and the top union barons whose bartering decided who would be on. While the left tried vainly to change this back, we focused on organising elections among the smallest unions to maximise our influence there.

4 Benn's Diaries, *The End of an Era 1980–90*, 2 February, 1983, page 268.

5 Benn's Diaries, *The End of an Era 1980–90*, 11 November 1980, page 47.

6   Benn's Diaries, *The End of an Era 1980–90*, 28 February, 1981, page 99.
7   Benn's Diaries, *The End of an Era 1980–90*, 2 April, 1982, page 203.
8   Benn's Diaries, *The End of an Era 1980–90*, 11 December, 1981, page 182 and 15 December, 1981, page 183.
9   *Tribune*, July, 1982.
10   *The Times*, July, 1982.
11   *Tribune*, July, 1982.
12   Benn's Diaries, *End of an Era 1980–90*, 7 May, 1983, page 285.

Chapter 17

1   The *Observer*, 17 January, 1982.
2   At the NEC on 28 April, 1982, Benn, Judith Hart, Dennis Skinner, Frank Allaun, Eric Clarke, Joan Maynard, Jo Richardson and Les Huckfield supported bringing British troops back from the Falklands.
3   Meeting of the left, 22 November, 1981 at County Hall, London.
4   The steering group comprised Jon Lansman, Vladimir Derer, Norman Atkinson, George Galloway, Audrey Wise, Bob Wright and Walter Greendale. See CLPD's 1981 annual report.
5   The Labour Liaison '82 slate comprised: CLP section – Benn, Allaun, Richardson, Heffer, Skinner, Atkinson and Wise; Women's Section – Beckett, Maynard, Barbara Schwitzer, (TASS) and Hart ('Socialist Organiser and CLPD were strongly opposed to Hart, but John Lansman observed that she would be re-elected as chairman anyway and Tony Benn concurred with the comment that despite other matters she had taken a good line on the Falklands', the notes read); Socialist Societies: Les Huckfield ('believes he will lose'); Trades Unions – Eric Clarke (NUM), Doug Hoyle (ASTMS), Alex Kitson (TGWU), Charles Kelly (UCATT), Terry O'Neil (President of the Bakers Union), Albert Powell (President of SOGAT), Tom Sawyer (NUPE) and Sam McCluskie (Seamen).
6   *Guardian*, 16 August, 1982.
7   NEC on the 16 June, 1982. In his Diaries, Benn says that Michael Foot moved that 'Swamping the House of Lords' be removed, but the actual minutes record that Benn himself moved that the lines be retained and was defeated 8 votes to 9 (four lefties were missing and three of our gang). Again, the account in the Diaries is at odds with reality.
8   A Militant proposal calling for 'immediate action to bring into public ownership the banks, insurance companies, finance houses and the 22 major monopolies' under workers' control was, however, heavily defeated.
9   Those announced to have been elected were: Breakell, Cure, Evans, Golding, Hadden, Hough, Kitson, McCluskie, Sawyer, Tierney, Tuck, Williams.. Tom Breakell received 3,657,000 votes, while Eric Clarke got just 2,296,000. Sid Weighell of the NUR which failed to cast its vote for Clarke of the NUM, fell out with his Executive and resigned as General Secretary over the issue.

Chapter 18

1   Before Conference, Tierney had unsuccessfully tried to get the NEC to agree 'that all Chairmen of the Standing committees ie Staff Negotiations, Party Organisation, Home Policy, International,

Press and Publicity, Youth, Women and Finance be appointed at the first meeting of the newly elected National Executive Committee.'

2   Philip Webster, *The Times*, 25 October, 1982. He continued: 'But it was learnt yesterday, there will also be an attempt on Wednesday to vote Mr Benn off the powerful TUC-Labour Party Liaison Committee, which is made up of representatives of the TUC general council, the NEC and the Shadow Cabinet. Mr Benn's name is among the NEC members suggested for the committee on a list drawn up by Mr James Mortimer, the party's general secretary, but that is open to amendment and some NEC members believe that Mr Benn should be removed to help restore the party's credibility . . . . . . to lose the home policy chairmanship and his place on the liaison committee would be a severe blow for Mr Benn.' Webster revealed that 'Frank Allaun would lose his chairmanship to Gwyneth Dunwoody . . . . Eric Heffer was expected to lose his chairmanship to Russell Tuck. With the purge of the Militant Tendency imminent, this is a key chairmanship and Mr Heffer might have difficulties. He opposes the Leadership's approach to Militant and also has a strong Militant presence in his constituency city, Liverpool.'

3   Michael White, the *Guardian*, 25 October, 1982. After noting that the trade unions and the parliamentary right are generally expected to depose Benn he noted that 'there is talk that if the right wants a clean sweep 'it would put in Alan Hadden to Finance, Alex Kitson to International, Gwyneth Dunwoody to Press and Publicity and Russell Tuck into Organisation.

4   Philip Webster, *The Times*, 25 October, 1982.

5   Philip Webster, *The Times*, 28 October, 1982.

6   It was pointed out, however, that the NEC had first to agree to an increase in the number of representatives on the National Labour Womens Committee, before my motion could be put. This was carried by 15 votes to 12 as was the motion to change the composition. This time Syd Tierney came back into the fold.

7   Ian Aitken, the *Guardian*, 28 October, 1982.

8   *The Times*, 28 October, 1982. The paper also looked forward to action on Militant, but warned rightly that the battle was far from over. 'None of this guarantees that Labour has now put its house in order. A party peddling extreme policies does not automatically become attractive once it comes under the control of moderate politicians,' the editorial sounded.

'There is even more need for caution when it is appreciated that these latest decisions seem to have been made despite, rather than because of, Mr Foot. But the firmness with which the moderates have now acted at least encourages the hope that they may move on to correct some of the worst excesses in policy-making over the past three years.'

9   Among those present among the Labour staff were: Bill Alston representing agents, Bert Twigg, Bryan Davies, Jim Mortimer, Walter Brown, Joyce Gould, Max Madden, Roger Robinson and David Hughes, the Secretary of the Organisation Committee.

10   *The Sentinel*, 19 November, 1982.

11   Members attending this meeting from the Tufton Court Group were Betty Boothroyd, Ken Cure, Anne Davis, Gwyneth Dunwoody, Roy Evans, Alan Hadden, Denis Healey, Shirley Summerskill, Russell Tuck, Eric Varley and me. Sam McCluskie was there to relish the occasion but not to vote. The only officials present were Jim Mortimer, David Hughes, Joyce Gould, David Lea and Geoff Bish, the Secretary.

12   I was confirmed by 15 votes to 9 and Gwyneth by 14 votes to 9. Denis Howell was challenged as the Chairman of the Youth Committee by Allaun and Skinner but this was defeated by 16 votes to 9 with Judith Hart voting with the extremists. She abstained on the challenge to Alan Hadden who was confirmed by 17 votes to 8.

Chapter 19

1   Organisation Committee 25 July, 1983.
2   Because of the chaos, Basnett had decided that the Commission of Enquiry break with all tradition and examine the administration of the Party. The chaos, however, was more than they could deal with and so a Joint Enquiry of NEC members, senior officers, staff unions and outside advisers was created with Gavin Strang MP as Chairman. Its report went to the NEC in June 1982, asking for a Director of Finance, and expecting much from Jim Mortimer in creating a new administration structure.
3   The opponents were: Frank Allaun, Tony Benn, Laurence Coates, Eric Heffer, Jo Richardson, Tom Sawyer, Dennis Skinner and Audrey Wise.

Chapter 20

1   Article on Tatchell by Martin Linton, the *Guardian*, 8 December 1981.
2   Quoted by Ian Aitken in the *Guardian*, 11 December, 1981, and see Benn's Diaries: *The End of an Era 1980–90*, 16 December, 1981, pages 183–185.
3   *Guardian*, 17 December, 1981.
4   *Mail on Sunday*, 17 April 1982

Chapter 22

1   NEC of 27 October, 1982.
2   'At present the Campaign committee is supposed to do six different jobs in 25 minutes at 8 in the morning,' Whitty wrote in a detailed memo. '1. Define overall strategy of the campaign (not really done, certainly not at the Saturday meeting). 2. Prepare day's press conference. 3. Arrange schedule of future press conferences (haphazard). 4. Receive reports of and redirect polling effort (done in detail, but not followed up). 5. Receive reports on press and publicity and direct/redirect Party political broadcast and other planned publicity (not dealt with because few present have read the papers by then). 6. Receive and assess reports of organisational effectiveness (not done). Consequence: failing on PR.' He proposed a new, more sensible schedule to put us ahead of the game: '1. 7.00 Today programme 7.45 Campaign Meeting 8.40 Leave for press conference 9.00 Press conference 10.00 Assessment of polling, press and regional reports 11.00 Strategy Group. 2. The Campaign Committee meeting should be confined to (i) adjustment to day's press conference (ii) organisation of next day's press conference (iii) absolutely vital matters to which response is urgent – referred from Strategy Group. 3. The Strategy Group should consist of General Secretary, 3 members of the NEC (suggest John Golding + other chairmen), National Agent/Joyce Gould, Press Officer and member of Leader and Deputy Leader's Staff. This should cover overall strategy and key PR aspects.'

Chapter 23

1   Nicholas Comfort in the *Daily Telegraph*, 11 June, 1983.

2   *Daily Mirror*, 13 June, 1983. Terry Lancaster's piece continued in colourful, blood-spattered fashion: 'Party rebel, Aldermaston marcher, his post-war oratory ranked with Churchill, Ian Macleod, and at his best with his idol Nye Bevan. But in his private life he was shy, a man of infinite charm, often very funny and more interested in literature than in contemporary politics. Even his oratory has suffered. Once he would have been capable of leading a great crusade against the horrors of Thatcherism, but his speeches were well below his peak this time. And his manifesto was cluttered with his beliefs – unilateral disarmament and leaving the Common Market. The voters rejected these and so they rejected Michael Foot.'

'It was a presidential campaign fought by two gladiators. One of them had to die. And Mr Foot, stripped naked by a brilliant Tory campaign, was effectively killed off by Mrs Thatcher. The June sun shone yesterday for Mrs Thatcher. For Mr Foot after a long and brilliant career, all was over and it was darkness at noon!'

3   Benn's Diaries, *The End of an Era 1980–90*, 27 March, 1983, p.279.

4   Among the Campaign Group at the meeting were: Benn, Bob Clay, Martin Flannery, Dennis Skinner, Brian Sedgemore, Frank Cook, Dave Nellist, Mark Fisher, Willy McKelvey, Stuart Holland, Joan Maynard, Jo Richardson, Kevin Barron, Ron Brown, Jeremy Corbyn, Harry Cohen and Michael Meacher.

5   *Daily Mirror*, 13 June 1983.

6   *Daily Mirror*, June, 1983.

7   The *Observer* 24 July, 1983.

8   Benn's Diaries, *The End of an Era 1980–90*, 24 July, 1983, p.307.

9   The full figures in the Leadership election were:
Kinnock – 29.04 per cent (unions); 27.45 per cent (CLPs); 14.79 per cent (MPs); Total 71.27 per cent.
Hattersley – 10.88 per cent (unions); 0.58 per cent (CLPs); 7.83 per cent (MPs); total 19.29 per cent.
Heffer – 0.05 per cent (unions); 1.96 per cent (CLPs); 4.29 per cent (MPs); total 6.30 per cent.
Shore – 0.03 per cent (unions); 0.00 per cent (CLPs); 3.10 per cent (MPs); total 3.14 per cent.

10 We were indebted for this to Labour Party head office staffer Roger Robinson, who presented one of the most entertaining, critical but perceptive papers on the election at the NEC meeting. I refer to a number of his observations in the following part of the text.

11 Benn's Diaries, *The End of an Era 1980–90*, 12 September, 1983, p.316.

Chapter 24

1   *The Times*, 18 January, 1980.

2   *Daily Mirror*, 18 January, 1980.

3   NEC meeting 23 January, 1980. Foot moved the reference back of the decision to re-endorse the special report endorsed itself by the 1977 Annual Conference not to circulate the Militant documents to the NEC. It was defeated by 14 votes to 12.

4   Organisation Committee meeting, 11 February 1980. Benn prevailed by 8 votes 2. In this respect, a previous entry in Benn's Diaries of 18 December, 1979 is worth recalling, when *The Sunday Times* upset Tony Saunois with a report over an alleged £180,000 fund held by Militant. 'I told him (Saunois) that – witch-hunting apart– the Party was entitled to know about the finances of organisations inside it . . . I said people thought Militant was a piggy-back organisation, riding on the back of the Party and building up its own organisation – which is true.'

5   The sub-committee consisted of Heffer, Benn, Foot, Lena Jeger, Tom Bradley and David Hughes.

6   *Sunday Times*, 24 February, 1980 headlined 'Benn toppled by left-wing revolt' – about a soft left meeting which angered the left caucuses outside parliament.

7   NEC meeting, 27 February, 1980.

8   *The Times*, 10 November, 1981.

9   NEC meeting on 25 November 1981

10 Benn's Diaries, *The End of an Era 1980–90*, 9 December, 1981, p.180.

11 Martin Linton in the *Guardian*, 10 December, 1981.

12 NEC meeting, 16 December, 1981.

13 Those supporting Benn were: Allaun, Benn, Clarke, Coates, Heffer, Huckfield, Lestor, Maynard, Richardson and Skinner. Those against were Boothroyd, Dunwoody, Roy Evans, Foot, Golding, Hadden, Hart, Healey, Hough, Hoyle, Kinnock, Kitson, McCluskie, Gerry Russell, Summerskill, Syd Tierney, Russell Tuck, Eric Varley and David Williams. In his Diaries, Benn records: 'If Judith Hart and Alex Kitson had been there to vote, it would have gone the other way.' Not for the first time, his Diaries are mistaken.

14 After Sapper's contribution, Ray Whyte and Mildred Gordon also moved a resolution which opposed the Militant Tendency report. This was overwhelmingly defeated by 1,213,000 to 5,680,000.

15 At the NEC on 24 February, 1982 we again opposed, but I later withdrew the motion. I suppose this was at Foot's request.

SELECT BIBLIOGRAPHY

Tony Benn (Ed. Ruth Winstone):
- *Conflicts of Interest: Diaries 1977–80*, Hutchinson (1990)
- *The End of an Era: Diaries 1980–90*, Hutchinson (1992)
- *Against the Tide: Diaries 1973–76*, Hutchinson (1989)
- *Office without Power: Diaries 1968–72* (1988)
- *Out of the Wilderness: Diaries 1963–67*, Hutchinson (1987)
- *Years of Hope: Diaries 1940–62*, Hutchinson (1994)

James Callaghan, *Time and Chance*, William Collins (1987)

Bernard Donoughue, *Prime Minister: The Conduct of Policy under Harold Wilson and James Callaghan*, Jonathan Cape (1987)

Ivor Crewe and Anthony King, *SDP: The Birth, Life and Death of the Social Democratic Party*, Oxford University Press (1995)

Michael Crick, *Militant*, Faber & Faber (1984)

Michael Crick, *The March of Militant*, Faber & Faber (1986)

Denis Healey, *The Time of My Life*, Michael Joseph (1989)

David & Maurice Kogan, *The Battle for the Labour Party*, Kogan Page (1982)

Paul McCormick, *Enemies of Democracy*, Temple Smith (1979)

Andy McSmith, *Faces of Labour: The Inside Story*, Verso (1996)

Lewis Minkin, *The Contentious Alliance: Trade Unions and the Labour Party*, Edinburgh University Press (1991)

Kenneth O. Morgan, *Callaghan: A Life*, Oxford University Press (1997)

Greg Rosen (Ed), *Dictionary of Labour Biography*, Politico's Publishing (2001)

Patrick Seyd, *The Rise and Fall of the Labour Left*, Macmillan Education (1987)

The Times Guide to the House of Commons 1979, Times Books (1979)

The Times Guide to the House of Commons 1983, Times Books (1983)

Martin Westlake, *Kinnock: the Biography*, Little, Brown (2001)

Harold Wilson, *Final Term: The Labour Government 1974–76*, Weidenfeld & Nicolson/Michael Joseph (1979)

Guardian Obituary of John Golding

John Golding, the former Labour minister and MP for Newcastle-under-Lyme, who has died aged 67, was a tireless soldier of Labour's trade union right-wing. He possessed a natural political nous, authority and energy that bellied his short, but stout stature. For him or against him – he was the best friend you could have, or the worst enemy, if you found yourself on the wrong side – his sharp, impish sense of humour would always liven up the room.

He and his wife Llin, Newcastle-under Lyme's current MP, made a formidable political team instinctively "old Labour" in their support for the working class, pensioners, the unemployed and the rights of ordinary people to be represented by trades unions.

In more than 40 years of active politics, including 17 years as an MP, Golding would admit he made more enemies than friends. Often, as when he led the Labour moderates' fight against Militant in the late 1970s and early 1980s, the blood feud would come down to politics, pure and simple. Golding was uncompromising in his hostility towards dreamers and schemers on the left, including Tony Benn and Eric Heffer, whom he believed offered nothing for everyday folk.

At that time, when organising the trade union-led fightback for "common sense", he was justifiably known as the most influential man in the Labour movement. A master of every political trick in the book, he was bloody-minded enough to copy the left's tactics and use them to the moderates' advantage. In the Commons tea-room, MPs under threat but innocent in the finer arts of the rough-house – such as Robert Kilroy Silk– would frequently ask Golding how to get themselves organised.

"I'm fed up of this f'…in' idiot. I'm going," Eric Heffer once shouted at a home policy meeting of Labour's national executive, after Golding stalled another left quick-fix by giving the meeting a two-hour long insight into ordinary, working-class views on every subject under the sun. Alas, in a scene worthy of Basil Fawlty, Eric walked straight into one broom cupboard, then another, before slamming his papers down and shouting "Oh f… it, I'm stopping after all."

"And these were people who thought they could run the country," Golding remarked in the political memoirs he was near completing before suddenly failing ill at Christmas. The memoirs, strongly encouraged by Llin, are a testament to the trade union brothers – many from the West Midlands, including John Spellar, now a defence minister, and Roger Godsiff, MP for Birmingham Sparkbrook – who carried the torch during Labour's darkest hours before Militant was finally routed and the party began its tortuous climb back to respectability under Nell Kinnock, John Smith and Tony Blair.

Occasionally, the hostility to Golding was purely personal. It often fell to John to step where others feared to tread. In 1983, during Labour's leadership election – in the wake of a disastrous general election defeat and the resignation of Michael Foot as party leader – union tacticians calculated that Roy Hattersley simply did not command enough votes to defeat Kinnock. Hattersley would have to bite his ambition and be content with the deputy leadership instead.

"Do you mean to say that I am going to have to play second fiddle to a red-haired Welsh windbag," Hattersley exclaimed, when Golding was deputed to deliver the black spot. "Yes, if you put it like that, you are going to have to play second fiddle to a red-haired, Welsh windbag," came the uncompromising reply. Hattersley's undying enmity cost Golding a place in the Shadow Cabinet. If he was bitter at the time, the scars never showed. In politics, his attitude was that you win some, and you lose some. "I got Benn, then they got me," he said after losing to the left the position he always kept as political officer in the Post Office Engineering Union (POEU). That victory over Benn – the recapture of Labour's feuding NEC in 1982 after "five years hard labour", as he put it – was undoubtedly the high point of this strand of Golding's career. Using the moderate and soft left's narrow majority on the NEC, as Foot abstained, he ruthlessly removed Benn and his acolytes from all their positions of power.

To many, with Golding playing a key role in determining the 1983 manifesto, it remained a mystery why Labour fought the election on what became known as "the longest suicide note in history". The answer, if Golding was asked, was straightforward: he had already decided that because of all the feuding, Foot as leader and the Falklands to boot, Labour had already lost the election. He was cunning enough to allow the left enough policy rope to hang themselves, so the Bennites could never again blame the right as they had done after Jim Callaghan's defeat in 1979.

While the annals of Labour history will undoubtedly record Golding as one of the right's best ever "fixers", a label he took pride, in there was much more that that to his political career. Well-versed at an early age in politics and philosophy, he reserved a healthy disregard for ideologists with their heads in the clouds.

He went to Chester Grammar School before studying, eventually, at Keele University and the London School of Economics. He had begun his working life in the Civil Service in London as an "office boy" at 16, as he described it, then as a clerical officer at the Ministry of National Insurance and it was as a researcher with the Post Office Engineering Union that he returned to Newcastle to stand in a 1969 byelection.

It was then, too, that Golding first met his future wife, Llin, a hospital radiographer, Labour activist and the daughter of a former Labour MP, who was given the task of driving the young candidate during the election campaign. Both were already married, with separate families of their own, but 11 years later they were to tie the knot together a second time round.

After winning the Newcastle by-election, Golding quickly joined the Wilson government, first as parliamentary private secretary to Eric Varley, then minister for technology, then as a whip. As minister for employment from 1976, he was intensely proud of Labour's efforts to cushion the blows of unemployment and short-time working, despite the best efforts of the left to undermine the Callaghan government in the party and the unions.

To a born street-fighter, after 1979 (an election tainted by the tragic death of his eldest son), opposition under Margaret Thatcher came as second nature. Golding still holds the record for the longest-ever Commons speech – 11 hours and 15 minutes speaking to one small amendment – which successfully delayed the privatisation of British Telecom until after the 1983 election. It was a tactic, as one of the outstanding parliamentarians of his day, that he would use repeatedly to great effect. These days rules have changed, so Golding's record is unlikely to be broken, but delay was then often the only effective tactic against a massive government majority.

Golding was certainly not, though, one of those pompous MPs who enjoy the sound of their own voice. Indeed, he showed an almost childlike pride in his award by the *Guardian* in the 1980s as the Commons' worst-dressed MP.

In 1986, aged 55, Golding gave up the Newcastle seat after becoming general secretary of the newly-merged National Communications Union, following another vicious battle with the left. There, he had to summon all his negotiating skills in deft handling of strikes and disputes with British Telecom at the height of Thatcher's onslaught against the unions. To the end, he remained active in local politics, both in support of Llin and Newcastle's Labour borough council.

Politics aside, Golding's great passions were fishing, horse-racing and, latterly, Spanish. Weekend after weekend, he would throw himself waist deep into the rivers of mid-Wales or well-stocked lakes of Hampshire, with the Spanish ambassador often in tow. A fair cook, his family freezer was stocked to the brim with freshly-caught salmon and trout. Asked, too, how come the pot was always full of game, he said it was because of a case he was assisting at an employment tribunal. "The chap's good with traps," he would say, "I'm being paid in rabbits instead."

Just before his death, John took a new mischievous delight at running rings yet again around civil servants in his new appointment to a Ministry of Agriculture advisory panel on the plight of British fresh-water fishing. If the Sir Humphreys of this world thought they could "fix" any committee they liked, they got their lines snagged with Golding. They would always be caught out by the master-fixer himself.

Golding is survived by Llin and his second son, Simon.

John Golding, politician and trade union leader, born 9 March, 1931; died 20 January, 1999.

By Paul Farrelly, the *Guardian*, 22 January, 1999. © Paul Farrelly and the *Guardian*.

INDEX